SOUL BY SOUL

SOUL BY SOUL

LIFE INSIDE THE
ANTEBELLUM SLAVE MARKET

WALTER JOHNSON

HARVARD UNIVERSITY PRESS
CAMBRIDGE, MASSACHUSETTS
LONDON, ENGLAND 1999

Library of Congress Cataloging-in-Publication Data

Johnson, Walter, 1967–
Soul by soul : life inside the antebellum slave market / Walter Johnson.
p. cm.
Includes bibliographical references and index.
ISBN 0-674-82148-3 (alk. paper)
1. Slaves—Louisiana—New Orleans—Social conditions—19th century. 2. Slave
trade—Louisiana—New Orleans—History—19th century.
3. Afro-Americans—Louisiana—New Orleans—Social conditions—19th century.
4. Slaveholders—Louisiana—New Orleans—History—19th century. 5. New Orleans
(La.)—Race relations. 6. New Orleans (La.)—Social conditions—19th century. I. Title.
F379.N59 N4 1999
976.3'3500496—dc21   99-046696

For Grazia

CONTENTS

Illustrations follow page 116

"The being of slavery, its soul and its body, lives and moves in the chattel principle, the property principle, the bill of sale principle: the cart-whip, starvation, and nakedness are its inevitable consequences."

JAMES W. C. PENNINGTON,
The Fugitive Blacksmith

A PERSON WITH A PRICE

NINETEENTH-CENTURY New Orleans was, by the breathless account of its boosters, on the verge of becoming one of antebellum America's leading cities, a city to be compared to New York, Philadelphia, Baltimore, and Charleston. What had once been an imperial outpost, passed back and forth between European powers in faraway trades was, by the early nineteenth century, a city poised on the brink of commercial greatness. Along the city's waterfront, ships from Europe and around the coast, steamers from the Mississippi River valley, and thousands of flatboats were packed so tightly that one could walk deck to deck from one end of the city to the other. Stevedores and draymen, white and black, traced out tiny connections in the world economy, unloading and loading, moving goods that had been paper-traded miles away and weeks before: crates of clothes, shoes, and buttons; guns, tobacco, and textiles; china, books, and French wine; cattle, hogs, corn, and whiskey. Salesmen and sailors shouted warnings and instructions in a half dozen languages. Overhung by the odor of batter-fried fish and pipe smoke, the hopes of the lower South's leading city were reefed across the broad frontage where the Mississippi met the Atlantic: thousands of bales of cotton and barrels of sugar, stacked and flagged with the colors of the commission merchants responsible for their sale.[1] And though the city never managed to outrun the underachievement that accounted for the shrill edge of the boosters' accounts, New Orleans was throughout the antebellum period unsurpassed in one respect. Not far from the levee was North America's largest slave market.

In the same way that contemporary tourists concentrate on a few sights in their visits to "see" a given city, antebellum travelers and curiosity-seekers converged on the slave market when they went south to Louisiana in search of slavery. Rather than making their way out of the city to the sugar plantations that covered the broad alluvial plain at the outlet of the Mississippi, or traveling upriver to the cotton plantations strung along the banks from Baton Rouge to Memphis, they began in the neighborhood where today Chartres Street meets broad, boulevarded Esplanade—a few short blocks from the levee, past the cathedral and the gin houses and sailor's tenements that served the nearby docks. After the 1840s there was also a slave market further uptown, amidst the shooting galleries, cock pits, barbershops, and boot-sellers of the city's central business district. Both of these markets were really clusters of competing firms, each of which, in turn, maintained its own yard for keeping slaves—"slave pens" in the parlance of the trade—and frontage for displaying them.[2] Between September and May—the months that bounded the trading season—the streets in front of the pens were lined with slaves dressed in blue suits and calico dresses. Sometimes the slaves paced back and forth, sometimes they stood atop a small footstand, visible over a crush of fascinated onlookers. As many as a hundred slaves might occupy a single block, overseen by a few slave traders whose business was advertised by the painted signs hanging overhead: "T. Hart, Slaves," "Charles Lamarque and Co., Negroes." Here the traveling observers and writers found what they were looking for: a part of slavery that could be used to understand the whole of the institution. Slavery reduced to the simplicity of a pure form: a person with a price.[3]

The walls surrounding the pens were so high—fifteen or twenty feet—that one New Orleans slave dealer thought they could keep out the wind.[4] Inside those walls the air must have been thick with over-crowding, smoke and shit and lye, the smells of fifty or a hundred people forced to live in a space the size of a home lot. And the sounds that came over the walls from the street outside must have been muted and mixed—horses' hooves striking the stone-paved street, cart wheels and streetcars, fragments of conversation, laughter, shouting. Along the in-side walls were privies, kitchens, dressing rooms, and jails. The jails were sometimes as many as three stories high and built of brick.[5] They looked like the slave quarters that can be seen today in the yards of many New Orleans houses: steep-backed, one room deep, and fronted with railed galleries. In the nineteenth-century slave pens, however, those galleries were lined with barred windows and doors that locked from the outside. Behind the doors were simple rooms with bare pine floors and plain plastered walls; measuring ten or twelve feet across, they were intended for multiple occupancy. On the ground floor of one of the jails or across the yard were offices and a showroom. The traders' offices were probably the type of spaces where nobody sat down—places for drinking, pacing, signing, and counting. The real business took place in the showrooms, which were large enough for a hundred slaves to be arrayed around their walls, questioned, and examined. These rooms had finished floors and painted walls, a fireplace, a few chairs, and doors all around— a door from the offices where the traders did their counting and signing, a door from the street where the buyers gathered before the pens opened, and a door from the yard where the slaves waited to be sold.[6]

What follows is the story of these showrooms. It is a story of back and forth glances and estimations, of hushed conspiracies and loud boasts, of power, fear, and desire, of mistrust and dissimulation, of human beings broken down into parts and recomposed as commodities, of futures promised, purchased, and resisted. It is, in no small measure, the story of antebellum slavery.

The bargains sealed in the New Orleans slave pens were centuries in the making, late additions to a four-hundred-year history by which the trade in African and African-descended people transformed the New World. By the end of the fifteenth century, Portuguese merchants and soldiers had dotted four thousand miles of the west coast of Africa with outposts, where they traded for slaves to export to sugar- and wine-producing islands off the coast. The Portuguese were shortly followed to Africa by the other imperial powers of Europe: the Spanish in the sixteenth century, the Dutch, Danes, French, and English in the seventeenth. Beginning in the 1650s, when sugar planted on Barbados and in Brazil began to grow into huge profits for colonial planters and metropolitan shippers, the African trade was a central concern of Europe's colonial powers, each of which attempted to control it through exclusive licensing and colonial customs.

The word for the economic theory behind the trade has come down to us scrubbed clean by usage: mercantilism. Colonial staples, shipped from abroad and finished at home, would yield metropolitan profits, which would be shared with the monopoly-granting state. And colonial markets would consume domestic manufactures, profits again duties and taxed into state revenue. In practice this meant that well-connected investors could form themselves into syndicates like the Royal African Company and the Dutch West India Company and receive monopoly license from their governments to pursue trade in other parts of the world—license to make war on non-Christian kings and to snatch or purchase their subjects along the shores of a distant continent, license to have their slave-trade monopolies protected by governmental decree and their African-coast slave factories defended in European wars. Though punctuated by imperial conflict and political regulation, the trade's four centuries were, by and large, charted along the demand curves for colonial staples: tobacco, indigo, rice, cotton, coffee, and especially sugar. There was direct trade among the colonies and between the colonies and Europe, but much of the Atlantic trade was triangular: slaves from Africa; sugar from the West Indies and Brazil; money and manufactures from Europe. People were traded along the bottom of the triangle; profits would stick at the top.[7]

In the four centuries of that triangular trade, ten to eleven million people—fifty or sixty thousand a year in the peak decades between 1700 and 1850—were packed beneath slave ship decks and sent to the New World. Indeed, up to the year 1820, five times as many Africans traveled across the Atlantic as did Europeans.[8] And those numbers do not include the dead—the five percent of the human cargo who died in crossings that took three weeks, the quarter who died in crossings that took three months.[9] Behind the numbers lie the horrors of the Middle Passage: chained slaves forced to dance themselves into shape on the decks; the closed holds, where men and women were separated from one another and chained into the space of a coffin; the stifling heat and untreated illness, the suicides and slave revolts, the dead thrown overboard as the ships passed on.[10]

The United States Constitution, ratified in 1789, contained a provision that led to a ban on the importation of African slaves after 1808. Closing the trade was favorable to both opponents of slavery and a portion of slaveholders, mostly Virginians, who feared that the contin-

ued importation of slaves would dilute the social power that their own slaves supported. Because the enslaved population of North America had been self-reproducing for at least fifty years by the time the Constitution was ratified, the closing of the Atlantic slave trade did not mean that North American slavery would wither away through the high mortality and low birth rates that characterized slavery elsewhere in the New World. It meant, instead, that any expansion of slavery into the western states would take the shape of a forcible relocation of American-born slaves. In the seven decades between the Constitution and the Civil War, approximately one million enslaved people were relocated from the upper South to the lower South according to the dictates of the slaveholders' economy, two thirds of these through a pattern of commerce that soon became institutionalized as the domestic slave trade.[11]

In its earliest years the domestic slave trade was probably not recognizable as such. By the end of the eighteenth century slave coffles were a common enough sight on the roads connecting the declining Chesapeake—its soil exhausted by a century of tobacco planting—to the expanding regions of post-Revolutionary slavery, the Carolinas to the south and Kentucky and Tennessee to the west. But in these years the trade was a practice without a name or a center, a series of speculations made along the roads linking the small towns of the rural South into an attenuated political economy of slavery. As the coffles traveled south, slaves were sold at dusty crossings and roadhouses through an informal rural network of traders and chance encounters that continued to characterize much of the trade throughout its massive nineteenth-century expansion.[12]

At the end of the eighteenth century, the slave trade began to follow the international demand curve for cotton. Although slaves continued to cultivate the tobacco, rice, and indigo that funded the first expansion of American slavery, the invention of the cotton gin in 1793, the purchase of Louisiana in 1803, and the subjugation of southern Indians, finalized along the Trail of Tears in 1838, opened new regions of the South to cultivation and slavery. Slaveholders called it a "kingdom" for cotton, and they populated the new states of the emerging Southwest—Alabama, Mississippi, and Louisiana—with slaves brought from the East: 155,000 in the 1820s; 288,000 in the 1830s; 189,000 in the 1840s; 250,000 in the 1850s. As many as two thirds of these one million

or so people were carried south by slave traders, whose daily business resolved the diverging fortunes of the declining upper South and the expanding lower South into mutual benefit.[13]

Throughout the antebellum period the slave trade continued to follow the course of the world cotton economy. The boom years of the 1830s were followed by depression in the 1840s and then another decade of massive volume in the 1850s. Indeed, the price of slaves tracked the price of cotton to such a degree that it was a commonplace in the years after 1840 that the price of slaves could be determined by multiplying the price of cotton by ten thousand (seven cents per pound for cotton yielding seven hundred dollars per slave). Only in the 1850s did slave prices seem to cut loose from cotton prices in a cycle of speculation that made entry into the slaveholding class prohibitively expensive. Tensions increased in an already class-divided society, and a premonitory wave of anxiety swept across the slaveholding South.[14]

Between 1820 and 1860 the slave trade—urban and rural—accounted for a significant portion of the South's economy. It has been estimated that in slave-exporting regions of the antebellum South the proceeds from the sale of slaves was equivalent in value to fifteen percent of the region's staple crop economy. As those people passed through the trade, representing something close to half a billion dollars in property, they spread wealth wherever they went. Much of the capital that funded the traders' speculations had been borrowed from banks and had to be repaid with interest, and all of it had to be moved through commission-taking factorage houses and bills of exchange back and forth between the eastern seaboard and the emerging Southwest. And the slaves in whose bodies that money congealed as it moved south had to be trans-ported, housed, clothed, fed, and cared for during the one to three months it took to sell them. Some of them were insured in transit, some few others covered by life insurance. Their sales had to be notarized and their sellers taxed. Those hundreds of thousands of people were revenue to the cities and states where they were sold, and profits in the pockets of landlords, provisioners, physicians, and insurance agents long before they were sold. The most recent estimate of the size of this ancillary economy is 13.5 percent of the price per person—tens of millions of dollars over the course of the antebellum period.[15]

Along with the two thirds of a million people moved through the interstate trade, there were twice as many who were sold locally. Sales

from neighbor to neighbor, state-supervised probate and debt sales, or brokered sales within a single state do not show up in the statistics that have been used to measure the extent and magnitude of the slave trade. And yet state-supervised and local sales were as much a feature of the antebellum economy as interstate slave trading. Noting the frequency with which the civil courts sought solutions to slaveholders' legal problems in the valuation and liquidation of enslaved people, one historian has referred to the state as South Carolina's "largest slave auctioneering firm." Taken together, there were over two million slaves sold in interstate, local, and state-ordered sales during the antebellum period.

In the four decades before the Civil War, the tiny capillaries of trade that distinguished the early years gave way to a new pattern of trade. Although much of the trade remained rural and the majority of the traders itinerant, the tributaries of trade were increasingly gathered into a pattern of trade between large urban centers. This new intercity commerce was dominated by well-organized permanent firms, as opposed to the one-time speculations and itinerant trade that constituted the continuing rural trade. Slaves were gathered in Baltimore, Washington, Richmond, Norfolk, Nashville, and St. Louis and sent south, either overland in chains, by sailing ships around the coast, or by steamboats down the Mississippi. These slaves were sold in the urban markets of Charleston, Savannah, Mobile, Natchez, and especially New Orleans. Contrary to the popular image, most of these slaves were not sold quickly at large public auctions but in extended private bargains made in the slave pens maintained by slave dealers.[17]

Thousands of slaves from all over the South passed through the New Orleans slave pens every year in the antebellum period, their purchase and sale linking the city to both the larger southern economy and the regional economy of the lower South. Slave buyers from Texas, Arkansas, and Mississippi, as well as Louisiana, looked to the city for people to tend their fields and harvest their crops. Those whose slave-based agricultural ventures proved successful made their way back to the pens, this time looking for skilled artisans and domestic slaves who represented the high end of the slave market and could be found only in large urban centers like New Orleans. What the New Orleans slave pens sold to these slaveholders was not just field hands and household help but their own stake in the commercial and social aspirations of the expanding Southwest, aspirations that were embodied in thousands of black men, women, and children every season: the slaves out of whom the antebellum South was built.)

As slaveholders bound the South together with a criss-crossed pattern of trade and regional interdependence, as they made their way through market cycles and depressions and expanded the boundaries of the slaveholding South to the point of Civil War, they charted their progress by buying and selling slaves. Thus the history of the slave trade has often been represented graphically as an outline of prices and the volume of trade—rising into spiky peaks through the 1830s and then plunging into sharp decline, only to rise again in the 1850s. Or it has been represented cartographically as a series of migrating dots on a map—a black bulge being gradually forced southwestward. The shapes on the graphs and the maps are chastening: they trace the time-and-space history of one of the largest forced migrations in world history.

And yet the time-and-space outline of that trade does not fully describe it. Indeed, it could be said that the daily process by which two million people were bought and sold over the course of the antebellum period has been hidden from historical view by the very aggregations that have been used to represent it. Building upon what we have learned about the extent and importance of the slave trade in the political economy of slavery, we must now consider the roads, rivers, and show-rooms where broad trends and abstract totalities thickened into human shape. (To the epochal history of the slave market must be added the daily stories of the slave pens, the history of sales made and unmade in the contingent bargaining of trader, buyer, and slave.)

This project takes the form of a thrice-told tale: the story of a single moment—a slave sale—told from three different perspectives. Following from a tradition of work in African American history stretching back at least to W. E. B. Du Bois's *Black Reconstruction*, this book began with the idea that the history of any struggle, no matter how one-sided its initial appearance, is incomplete until told from the perspectives of all of those whose agency shaped the outcome.[8] The systemic brutality apparent from the perspective of the demographic map needs to be punctuated by the episodes of resistance that occurred on dusty roads; the counting up and parsing out of sales must be complicated with an account of the intricate bargaining that preceded the final deal; the central symbol of a property regime that treated people as possessions must be fleshed out with the power, desire, and dissimulation that gave it daily shape. Rather than charting a map of foreordained conclusions, I have tried to understand a slave sale from the contingent perspective of each of its participants—to assess their asymmetric information, expectations, and power, to search out their mutual misunderstandings and calculated misrepresentations, to investigate what each had at stake and how each tried to shape the outcome.

Much of this account relies on the nineteenth-century narratives of former slaves, the best-known of the six thousand published slave narratives that document every era of American slavery.[19] These are the survivors' stories, written and published in the North by those who had escaped or been freed from slavery. Printed in runs numbering in the thousands, advertised in the pages of antislavery newspapers, and sold at antislavery meetings, the nineteenth-century narratives were the stock-in-trade of abolitionism. Most of them probably ended up on the drawing room shelves of northern opponents of slavery, where they served as reminders of their owners' political commitments, or at least of their shared appreciation of the best intentions of the emerging northern middle class.[20]

The antislavery history of these narratives has made some historians wary of using them as sources for writing the history of slavery. In proslavery responses to the narratives, which were taken up by early historians of slavery like Ulrich B. Phillips, the narratives were treated as politically interested fabrications and were dismissed according to one of the most durable paradoxes of white supremacy—the idea that those who are closest to an experience of oppression (in this case, former slaves) are its least credible witnesses.[21] Recently, however, historians have followed the path of scholars like W. E. B. Du Bois, Herbert Aptheker, and John Hope Franklin, away from the "master narrative of American History" and into the slave narratives. These pioneering efforts have been bolstered by the careful scholarship of John Blassingame, Joseph Logsdon, Sue Eakin, and others, who have authenticated some of the more controversial narratives piece by piece. Locating telling details and matching them to other sources, they have retrieved the narratives from the race-tinged skepticism that dismissed them as fabrication.

But taking slave narratives for transparent accounts of reality can be as misleading as dismissing them entirely. The narratives, like all histories, were shaped by the conditions of their own production—the conditions of both southern slavery and organized antislavery. The narratives are by definition incomplete accounts. They are the stories of the escapees and survivors of an institution that gave up very few of either. The vast majority of the millions of people enslaved over the course of the history of New World slavery died as they had lived—in bondage. As the former slave William Wells Brown saw it, those who could tell the true story of slavery would never have the chance to do so: "slavery has never been represented, slavery never can be represented," he wrote.[22] Moreover, as a genre the narratives are dominated by the skilled and sometimes literate men who were disproportionately represented among the escapees, and this demographic fact skews their representation of slavery; the nineteenth-century narratives often elide or ignore the experiences of unskilled men and of women.

The narratives' account of slavery was equally shaped by the historical conditions of antislavery. Unconnected and sometimes unlettered, ex-slave narrators depended upon white northern abolitionists for their access to editors and publishers, their daily livings as orators, and whatever hope they had of freeing family members who remained in the South. White abolitionists, in turn, forced their own version of antislavery upon those who tried to tell their stories of slavery. "Give us the facts," Frederick Douglass was told, "we will take care of the philosophy." The impact of organized antislavery on the narratives must be considered in any effort to use them to write the history of slavery. As accounts which led up to a known ending—the escape of an individual slave—the narratives rarely enlarge upon the daily life, joys, and travails of enslaved communities. As stories of saved souls, they sometimes ignore the sufferings of enslaved bodies. As vehicles for supplying a moralistic bourgeois audience with the ideal slaves they demanded, the narratives often gloss over the anger, dissimulation, sexuality, and occasional brutality of real slaves' daily lives. As entrants into a rhetorical field dominated by white supremacy, they sometimes reproduce the prejudices of their readers.[23]

Though they require careful reading, the nineteenth-century narratives remain our best source for the history of enslaved people in the slave trade.[24] In what follows I have used three strategies to accomplish the dual task of reading the history of the many in the stories of the few and separating the experience of slavery from the ideology of antislavery. First, I have read the narratives in tandem with sources produced by slaveholders and visitors to the South. Many of the most mundane as well as some of the more incredible aspects of the narrators' accounts—from descriptions of where slaves slept along the road and what they ate in the pens, to the revelations that some buyers bought slaves as subjects for medical experiments and some slaves shaped their own sales—are supported by other sources. By reading these sources in juxtaposition, I have been able to use them to authenticate as well as interrogate one another.

Second, I have read the narratives for traces of the experience of slavery antecedent to the ideology of antislavery, for the "facts" provided by Frederick Douglass without which William Lloyd Garrison could not have fashioned his "philosophy."[26] The descriptions of events in the narratives often include telling details which could not be fully contained by the purposes of antislavery editors and amanuenses. Visual descriptions of other slaves, for example, can be read as evidence of the way strangers evaluated one another in the coffles and slave pens. Likewise, the biographies of other slaves, often presented as a scene-setting aside to the narrator's central struggle, can be read as evidence of a history of communal life and collective resistance among slaves in the trade which was largely excised from the narrators' printed accounts.

Third, I have read the narratives for symbolic truths that stretch beyond the facticity of specific events. Some incidents appear so often that it seems certain they are stock figures drawn from the reading of other narratives rather than from experience. These include the idea that illiterate slaves holding books for the first time would put them next to their ears to hear them talk, or that an escapee seeing a steamboat or train for the first time would run away, thinking it was the devil. But these stock figures have a truth of their own to tell: they gesture at the way the world looked to people whose access to information and technology was limited by their owners and the threat of violence. I have taken the same approach to the disquieting stories of slaves who mutilated themselves to avoid the trade or women who killed their children to spare them from slavery. Whether or not every one of these stories was true (and we know some were), collectively they tell a truth about people forced by their slavery into a doubled relation with their bodies and their children.[27]

In addition to the slave narratives, I have relied heavily on the docket records of approximately two hundred cases of disputed slave sales that came before the Louisiana Supreme Court in the nineteenth century. Louisiana, like other southern states, had detailed commercial laws regulating the sale of slaves.[28] In Louisiana, these laws were called redhibition laws, and they regulated the terms of warranty—what a buyer was explicitly or implicitly guaranteed by a seller—and the terms under which a sale of animals or slaves might be rescinded. Under these laws, slave buyers who felt that the people they purchased had "vices" of body or character could sue the seller for the return of the price they had paid. To sustain their cause, they had to prove both that the slave had been affected at the time of sale and that they had themselves behaved in the market as a "prudent" buyer would have, though they nevertheless might have missed the "defect" at the time of sale. These records, mixed in with the records of thousands of cases dealing with every aspect of slavery and law in antebellum Louisiana, were discovered in a courthouse basement in the 1980s and have only recently become available to readers at the University of New Orleans.[29] Ranging in length from a few tattered lines to hundreds of pages with attached exhibits, the docket records include the verbatim transcriptions of cases later decided by the Louisiana Supreme Court. Captured in the neat script of a law clerk are conversations a century and a half old: visitors describing the physical space of the pens and the bargains they saw made there; slave traders discussing their finances and explaining the daily practice of their business; slave buyers talking about their aspirations, anxieties, and the strategies they used to select their slaves.

Highly formalized and recorded amidst heated debate at a distance of time and space from the events they describe, the court records are no easier to read than the slave narratives. The testimony given by witnesses in these cases, though sworn, cannot be taken as a truthful account of what "really" happened in the pens. Indeed, I have generally read the docket records as if they contain only lies. And yet lies, especially sworn lies given in support of high-stakes legal action, must be believable in order to be worth telling: these lies describe the circumstances of a specific sale in the terms of a shared account of what was *likely* to happen in the slave market. A few stock stories supported much of the testimony: the story of dishonest trader and the duped buyer; or the story of the canny buyer who used the favorable terms of buyer-protecting laws to take advantage of an unwitting seller; or the simple story of the inscrutable slave and the honest mistake. These stories about slaveholders were underwritten and intertwined with stories about slaves: the buyer's story of the incorrigibly malign character who seemed sound in the market; the trader's story of a good slave driven to transgression or infirmity by a bad buyer; or the stories told by buyers and sellers alike of invisible ailments or slaves shamming an infirmity to undermine their own sale.[30] In these strategic appropriations of stock characters and in the conflicting and overlapping formulas with which lawyers and litigants framed their cases, I have sought slaveholders' commonsense opinion of the limits of what was possible in the slave pens.[31]

Letters written by slaveholders make up the third major body of sources for this project. In the overwhelmingly rural and increasingly mobile antebellum South, the substance of social relations was often epistolary. Many communities, families, and friendships had their primary existence in the form of letters mailed back and forth by their constitutive members—people who were rarely in the same place and who knew one another mostly through their letters. These letters, then, can be read as remote performances of the self, self-consciously produced representations that antebellum slaveholders offered to one another as versions of themselves.[32] Such letters are doubly revealing, for not only do they memorialize a single performance of the self but they reveal the terms which made that performance intelligible, the cultural register of the roles upon which their authors drew as they sat down to write. The letters thus recapitulate accounts of slaveholding selves that were likely to surface in other circumstances—conversation, gossip, fantasy, folklore, and so on. The letters are full of striving sons, masterful patriarchs, anxious brides, and dutiful wives, all of the recognizable social identities available to antebellum whites as they tried to make themselves make sense to someone else. And they are full of talk about slaves—slaves described, desired, bought, and brought home. The fact that slaveholders included so much about the slave market in their letters (much more, for instance, than they did about the duels that have figured so prominently in historians' accounts) is absolutely central to one of the arguments of this book: that slaveholders often represented themselves to one another by reference to their slaves.

Finally, I have relied on the chillingly economical descriptions of slave sales generated by the trade itself: the notarized Acts of Sale by which a sale was given legal standing, and the traders' slave record books, price lists, and advertisements.[33] These lists of names, ages, prices, and body parts have been used by many historians to chart the price history and demography of the slave trade. The sources produced by the traders have often been taken to be the most reliable accounts of the slave trade—free of the confused purposes and strategic (mis)representations of the narratives, court cases, and correspondence; but to me they seem less useful in constructing a historian's overview than in reconstructing a historical point of view. Indeed, they are the most apparitional of the sources I have used. They represent the world as a slave trader's dream: slaves without frail or resistant bodies; sales sealed without manipulation, coercion, or opposition; history without contingency. Like the maps and graphs they have been used to create, the traders' records treat a contested process as if it were a foreordained conclusion.

Historians have generally followed the traders in defining the boundaries of the slave trade around the commercial record it produced—a sale in the upper South to a slave trader as a beginning and a sale to a slaveholder in the lower South as an end. This definition of the slave trade, however, cannot withstand the centrifugal pressure of the competing perspectives presented by the narratives, the court records, and the letters. The slave trade did not begin or end in the same place for traders, buyers, and slaves. For slaves, the slave trade was often much more than a financial exchange bounded in space and time. A slave traders' short-term speculation might have been a slave's lifelong fear; a one-time economic miscalculation or a fit of pique on the part of an owner might lead to a life-changing sale for a slave. For buyers, too, the slave market was a place they thought about and talked about long before they entered the confines of the pens and long after they left with a slave. Comparing the sources produced by those on different sides of the bargain makes it clear that "a slave sale" was not a single thing which one could view from three different sides and sum into a whole—the way one might walk all the way around a physical object, measure every face, and then create a three-dimensional diagram. Rather, like a web of unforeseen connections, the morphology of a sale depended upon the point of departure. Time ran differently depending upon where you started the clock.

This history, then, is not organized around "change over time" in the traditional sense. It does not begin at one time (say 1820) and progress toward another (say 1860), providing an overview of the history of the slave trade in between. Still less does it offer a theory or a formal definition of the institution of slavery. Instead, it begins with the efforts of various historical actors—traders, buyers, or slaves—to imagine, assimilate, respond to, or resist the slave trade, with the desires and fears that gave the trade its daily shape. The scope and scale of the chapters shifts according to the efforts of the participants to understand and control the history in which they were joined. In some of the chapters the slaves have names and stories, in some they are slaveholders' fantasies, stripped bodies, or recorded prices. In some the traders have motives and strategies, in some they are ghosts stalking the daily life of the slave community or scapegoats for proslavery southerners' anxieties about the human selling and family separating that pervaded their "domestic" institution. In some the buyers imagine the slave market as a vehicle of self-amplification, a place where they could remake themselves in the image of the slaves they bought; in others they strip, question, and discipline the enslaved people through whom their imagined identities became material.

Maintaining these separate perspectives on the trade throughout the book, especially in accounts of the relentless objectification to which slaves in the market were subjected, can make tough reading. But it was out of the clash of conflicting perspectives that the history of the slave trade was daily made. As they went to the slave market, for example, potential buyers might have been self-consciously playing a part in the historical project of making manifest the expansionary destiny of the antebellum regime, or they might have made their slave-market choices with an eye toward crop calendars and cycles of commercial speculation, or they might have simply imagined their presence in the market as part of their own biography—the stages of a slaveholding life cycle marked out in purchased slaves. Slaves, on the other hand, might have framed the trade in terms of the sinfulness of slaveholders and their own providential hopes for salvation through suffering, or they might have seen their own sale as part of the larger demographic transformation of the slave communities of both the upper and lower South, or they might have imagined the trade in personal terms—the waiting to be sold which suffused every moment of the present with the fear of an unknown future, the heart-rending pain of losing loved ones to the traders, loss and survival in the shadow of the slave market. These various ways of imagining history—providential, political, economic, communal, biographical, and so on—were layered and intertwined through the daily process of the slave trade.[34] Many slaves trades, many versions of what was happening, met and were contested in every slave sale.

This book begins along the separate paths taken by slaveholders and slaves to the showrooms and leads up to the moment of sale in the market. The early chapters explore the radically incommensurable views taken by slaves and slaveholders of the relation of the slave trade to the broader system of slavery and follow this philosophical difference through the practical contests that defined the history of the slave trade: the efforts of slaveholders to coax or coerce their resistant slaves into the trade, the strategies the traders used to get their slaves to market, the slaves' efforts to make common cause with their fellow slaves and to resist the traders. The subsequent chapters of the book treat the contested bargains made by traders, buyers, and slaves in the showrooms and auction houses. In the slave market, the central tension of antebellum slavery was daily played out as slaveholders invested their money and their hopes in people whom they could never fully commodify. Even as the traders packaged their slaves by "feeding them up," oiling their bodies, and dressing them in new clothes, they were forced to rely on the slaves to sell themselves, to act as they had been advertised to be. Likewise, even as slave buyers stripped the slaves naked, probed their bodies, and asked them questions, they depended on the slaves to give them answers that would help them look beyond the traders' arts. The stakes were high, for their identities as masters and mistresses, planters and paternalists, hosts and hostesses, slave breakers and sexual predators were all lived through the bodies of people who could be bought and sold in the market. And so the questions the buyers asked and the examinations they made were also answers, accounts of their own origins and intentions.

During their time in the trade, the slaves had come to know and trust one another, and in the market they could share their observations of the slaveholders and collectively (and sometimes violently) resist them. Even those who did not revolt found ways to resist the trade. In the way they answered questions, characterized their skills, and carried their bodies—in the way they performed their commodification—slaves could use the information unwittingly provided them by the traders' preparations and the buyers' examinations to select the best among the poisoned outcomes promised them by the trade. Sometimes, at very great risk, they shaped their own sales.

Every one of the two million human-selling transactions which outlined the history of the antebellum South provided a way into its deepest secrets: into the aspirations of southern slaveholders and the fears of southern slaves; into the depth of the slaveholders' daily dependence on their slaves, despite claims of lofty independence; into the dreams of resistance that often lurked within the hearts of slaves; into the terrible density of the interchange between masters and slaves, whose bodies and souls were daily fused into common futures in the slave market. Running through each sale as well was the seeming paradox of a "paternalist" society which registered its historical progress through the number of people who were bought and sold in the market; the interplay of racism, patriarchy, and commodification in the system of slavery and the slave market; the attenuated hopes and survival strategies of slave communities living under the constant threat of dissolution; the repeated cycle of social death and rebirth which snatched people from their own lives only to transport and eject them into a marketplace where they were reanimated as pieces of living property; the strategies of individual and collective resistance used by slaves to shape and escape the fate plotted for them by the political economy of slavery; and the emotional volatility and frustrated brutality of slaveholders, whose fantasies could be made material only in the frail and resistant bodies of their slaves.

The history of the antebellum South is the history of two million slave sales. But to that history, to the history of the outcomes, must be added the daily history of the slave pens. The point in emphasizing the everyday life of the trade is not to diminish the chilling effect of that broad arrow on the map. It is rather to search out the shape of historical change in its moment of immediate expression and to explore the contingency of a history that was being pulled apart at the seams even as it unfolded over time and space. The quantitative dimensions of this history—the number of slaves traded over the course of the antebellum period, the amount of time they spent in the trade relative to time spent in the fields, their dollar value in comparison to the rest of the southern economy—are less important to my argument than the window into slavery provided by the moment of sale. In the slave pens, the yet-un-made history of antebellum slavery could be daily viewed in the freeze-framed detail of a single transaction on its leading edge—a trader, a buyer, and a slave making a bargain that would change the life of each. This, then, is a book not only about Louisiana, or the slave market in New Orleans, or the domestic slave trade as a whole, although it is all those things. This is the story of the making of the antebellum South.

CHAPTER ONE

THE CHATTEL PRINCIPLE

Long after he had escaped from slavery and settled in Canada, William Johnson's memory stuck on one thing his owner used to say: "Master," he recalled, "used to say that if we didn't suit him he would put us in his pocket quick—meaning that he would sell us."[1] That threat, with its imagery of outsized power and bodily dematerialization, suffused the daily life of the enslaved. Like other pieces of property, slaves spent most of their time outside the market, held to a standard of value but rarely priced. They lived as parents and children, as cotton pickers, card players, and preachers, as adversaries, friends, and lovers. But though they were seldom priced, slaves' values always hung over their heads. J. W. C. Pennington, another fugitive, called this the "chattel principle": any slave's identity might be disrupted as easily as a price could be set and a piece of paper passed from one hand to another.[2] Of the two thirds of a million interstate sales made by the traders in the decades before the Civil War, twenty-five percent involved the destruction of a first marriage and fifty percent destroyed a nuclear family —many of these separating children under the age of thirteen from their parents. Nearly all of them involved the dissolution of a previously existing community.[3] And those are only the interstate sales.

As revealing as they are, these statistics mask complicated stories. Signing a bill of sale was easy enough; selling a slave was often more difficult. Many slaves used every resource they had to avoid being sold into the slave trade. Families and friends helped some slaves escape the slave trade entirely and gave others a chance to negotiate the terms of their sale into the trade. Whether they were sold for speculation, debt, or punishment, many slaves refused to go quietly. They disrupted their sales in both philosophy and practice. In philosophy by refusing to accept their owners' account of what was happening, by treating events that slaveholders described in the language of economic necessity or disciplinary exigency as human tragedy or personal betrayal. In practice by running away or otherwise resisting their sale, forcing their owners to create public knowledge of the violent underpinnings of their power. However they resisted, hundreds of thousands ended up in the slave trade. These were the "many thousands gone" memorialized in the stories and songs out of which antebellum slaves built a systemic critique of the institution under which they lived. In these rituals of remembrance, the disparate experiences of two million human tragedies were built into the ideology of the "chattel principle."

LIVING PROPERTY

From an early age slaves' bodies were shaped to their slavery. Their growth was tracked against their value; outside the market as well as inside it, they were taught to see themselves as commodities. When he was ten, Peter Bruner heard his master refuse an offer of eight hundred dollars (he remembered the amount years later), saying "that I was just growing into money, that I would soon be worth a thousand dollars." Before he reached adulthood John Brown had learned that the size of his feet indicated to a slaveholder that he "would be strong and stout some day," but that his worn-down appearance—bones sticking "up almost through my skin" and hair "burnt to a brown red from exposure to the sun"—nevertheless made it unlikely that he would "fetch a price." Likewise, by the time she was fourteen, Elizabeth Keckley had repeatedly been told that even though she had grown "strong and healthy," and "notwithstanding that I knit socks and attended to various kinds of work . . . that I would never be worth my salt." Years later the pungency of the memory of those words seemed to surprise Keckley herself. "It may seem strange that I should place such emphasis upon words thoughtlessly, idly spoken," she wrote in her autobiography.[4] Condensed in the memory of a phrase turned about her adolescent body, Elizabeth Keckley re-encountered the commodification of her childhood.

Through care and discipline, slaves' bodies were physically incorporated with their owners' standards of measure. Henry Clay Bruce nostalgically remembered his youth as an easy time when "slave children had nothing to do but eat, play, and grow, and physically speaking attain a good size and height." But, Bruce also remembered, the daily routine he enjoyed was charted along a different axis by an owner interested in his growth: "a tall, well-proportioned slave man or woman, in case of a sale, would always command the highest price paid." As John Brown remembered it, the daily incorporation of his youthful body with his enslavement was a matter of coercion as much as care. Brown's mistress "used to call us children up to the big house every morning and give us a dose of garlic and rue to keep us 'wholesome,' as she said and make us 'grow likely for the market.'" Having staked a right to her slaves that stretched into the fibers of their form, she would turn them out to run laps around a tree in the yard, lashing them to make them "nimbler," forcibly animating their bodies with the spirit she imagined buyers would desire.[5]

Brown's memory makes another thing clear: the process by which a child was made into a slave was often quite brutal. As an adolescent, Henry was adjudged "right awkward" and beaten by his mistress, who thought his arms too long and hands too aimless for work in her dining room. Ten-year-old Moses Grandy was flogged "naked with a severe whip" because he "could not learn his [master's] way of hilling corn." Thirteen-year-old Celestine was beaten until her back was marked and her clothes stained with blood because she could not find her way around the kitchen. Twelve-year-old Monday was whipped by his mistress because his lupus made his nose run on the dinner napkins.[6] Just as the bodies of slaveholding children were bent to the carefully choreographed performances of the master class—in their table manners, posture and carriage, gender-appropriate deportment, and so on—motion by disciplined motion, the bodies of slave children were forcibly shaped to their slavery.[7]

From an early age, enslaved children learned to view their own bodies through two different lenses, one belonging to their masters, the other belonging to themselves. As Henry Clay Bruce put it about a youthful trip to the woods that ended in a narrow escape from a charging boar: "It was a close call. But we kept that little fun mum, for if Jack Perkinson had learned of his narrow escape from the loss of two or three Negro boys worth five or six hundred dollars each, he would have given us a severe whipping."[8] Whether by care or coercion (or by their peculiar combination in the nuzzling violence that characterized slaveholding "paternalism"), enslaved children were taught to experience their bodies twice at once, to move through the world as both child and slave, person and property.

Just as the chattel principle was worked into the bodies of enslaved people, it was also present in their families and communities. As Thomas Johnson remembered it, one after another his childhood friends were "missed from the company." Hearing that the man who took them away was a "Georgia trader," Johnson and his friends would run and hide whenever they saw "a white man looking over the fence as we were playing." The threat of sale, Johnson later remembered, infused his friendships with fear.[9] Thomas Jones remembered that the trade was present in his most intimate relations from the time he was very young: "my dear parents . . . talked about our coming misery, and they lifted up their voices and wept aloud as they spoke of us being torn from them and sold off to the dreaded slave trader." The account Jones made of his later attachments was similarly interpolated with the dread of sale: "I had a constant dread that Mrs. Moore would be in want of money and sell my dear wife. We constantly dreaded a final separation. Our affection for each other was very strong and this made us always apprehensive of a cruel parting." Likewise Lewis Hayden: "Intelligent colored people of my circle of acquaintance as a general thing *felt no security whatever for their family ties.* Some, it is true, who belonged to rich families felt some security; but those of us who looked deeper and knew how many were not rich that seemed so, and saw how fast the money slipped away, were always miserable. The trader was all around, the slave pens at hand, and we did not know what time any of us might be in it."[10] Under the chattel principle, every advance into enslaved society—every reliance on another, every child, friend, or lover, every social relation—held within it the threat of its own dissolution.

Slaveholders used that threat to govern their slaves. As slaveholder Thomas Maskell proudly put it to a man who had sold him some family slaves: "I govern them the same way your late brother did, without the whip by stating to them that I should sell them if they do not conduct themselves as I wish."[11] No matter how benign Maskell thought his own rule, it is hard to imagine that his slaves were not living in terror of making a mistake. Henry Clay Bruce remembered the nominally nonviolent power of men like Maskell from the other side: "Slaves usually got scared when it became clear that Negro-Trader [John] White was in the community. The owners used White's name as a threat to scare the slaves when they had violated some rule." "If a man did anything out of the way he was in more danger of being sold than being whipped," George Johnson likewise remembered.[12] Like a disease that attacks the body through its own immune system, slaveholders used the enslaved families and communities that usually insulated slaves from racism and brutality as an instrument of coercion, to discipline their slaves.[13] Among slaveholders, this peculiar mixture of ostensible moderation and outright threat was called paternalism.

As well as threatening social death—the permanent disappearance of a person as a playmate, parent, child, friend, or lover—the slave trade was understood by slaves as threatening literal death. After years of answering questions at antislavery meetings, Lewis Clarke explained slaves' fear of the slave trade to an imagined interlocutor: "Why do slaves dread so bad to go to the South—to Mississippi or Louisiana? Because they know slaves are driven very hard there, and worked to death in a few years." Or as Jacob Stroyer put it, "Louisiana was considered by the slaves a place of slaughter, so those who were going there did not expect to see their friends again." The fear of being sold south, wrote the Reverend Josiah Henson, the man whose life was thought to be the basis for Harriet Beecher Stowe's fictional Uncle Tom, filled the slaves of the upper South with "perpetual dread."[14]

"Perpetual dread," "always apprehensive," "the trader was all around," "the pens at hand"—the terms in which ex-slaves remembered the trade collapse the distinction between the immediate and the distant. Fear of Louisiana was a constant in Virginia, future sale was always a present threat. For slaves, especially those in the exporting states of the upper South, time and space were bent around the ever-present threat of sale to a slave trader.[15] Hundreds of thousands of times in the history of the antebellum South was this sinuous description of the relation of time, space, and slavery ratified in experience. It is, however, only in contrast to the carefully delimited accounts of the trade offered by their owners that the ideological importance of the slaves' version of the chattel principle can be fully understood.

SLAVEHOLDERS' STORIES

Among slaveholders, the slave market existed in a different place and time. Far from being ever-present in cities like New Orleans, the slave market was a quarantined space, legally bounded by high walls to "prevent them from being seen from the street" and banned from many neighborhoods throughout the antebellum period. The state of Louisiana outlawed the trade entirely during the period of panic that followed Nat Turner's 1831 rebellion, and the city of New Orleans (like cities across the South) taxed it at the same high rate as pawn shops, cock pits, and race tracks.[16] Like the business they conducted, slave traders were marginalized, through rhetoric more than regulation: "Southern Shylock," "Southern Yankee," and "Negro Jockey" they were called, the sorts of insults that marked them as figurative outcasts from slaveholding society. When Daniel Hundley sat down to write the description of slave traders that would be included in his proslavery account, *Social Relations in Our Southern States* (1860), he described the slave traders as a caste apart and assumed that they would be readily identifiable to even the most casual observer. In his description, slave traders looked almost as different from other southern whites as slaves did. "The miserly Negro Trader," Hundley assured his readers, "is outwardly a coarse, ill-bred person, provincial in speech and manners, with a cross-looking phiz, a whiskey tinctured nose, cold hard-looking eyes, a dirty tobacco-stained mouth, and shabby dress." You knew them when you saw them.[17]

Hundley's description of the traders' business represents a summary statement of a half century of white southern efforts to riddle out the implications that this thriving trade in people had for their "domestic" institution. He began by noting that the slave trader "is not troubled evidently with conscience, for although he habitually separates parent from child, brother from sister, and husband from wife, he is yet one of the jolliest dogs alive." But, Hundley continued, the trader's "greatest wickedness" was not his "cruelty to the African." It was the dishonesty and the avarice with which he threatened to poison social relations among white people: "nearly nine tenths of the slaves he buys and sells are vicious ones sold for crimes or misdemeanors, or otherwise diseased ones sold because of their worthlessness as property. These he purchases for about one half what healthy and honest slaves would cost him; but he sells them as both honest and healthy." Slave traders, according to slaveholders like Hundley, were family separators in a land of organic social relations, sharp dealers in a society of "honorable men," merchants of disease and disorder in an otherwise healthy social body. In the figure of the slave trader were condensed the anxieties of slaveholding society in the age of capitalist transformation: paternalism overthrown by commodification, honor corrupted by interest, and dominance infected with disorder.[18]

By embodying the economy in people in the stigmatized figure of the trader, Hundley was doing what countless southern laws and slaveholding commonplaces attempted to do: maintain an artificial and ideological separation of "slavery" from "the market." Never mind that it was "ordinary" slaveholders who decided to sell all of those diseased and disorderly slaves to the traders in the first place, never mind that the majority of family-separating sales occurred at the behest of upper-South slaveholders rather than lower-South slave traders, never mind that antebellum slaveholders went to the pens to buy and sell these uprooted people by the thousands: for Hundley, the traders' contaminating presence served as a measure of general cleanliness, an easily isolated element of an otherwise sound system, acknowledged only to be explained away.[19] Isolating the slave market as a place and limiting their definition of slave trading to a full-time profession allowed "ordinary" slaveholders like Daniel Hundley to insulate themselves from responsibility for the family separations, sharp dealing, and uncertainty that characterized their "domestic" institution. Scapegoating the traders was a good way to defend the rest of slavery.

But just as their money seeped through the southern economy and their prepackaged fantasies suffused the dreams of slave buyers, the traders' practice could not be contained by the bricks and mortar that bounded the pens. The entire economy of the antebellum South was constructed upon the idea that the bodies of enslaved people had a measurable monetary value, whether they were ever actually sold or not. Slaves were regularly used as collateral in credit transactions; indeed, rather than giving an IOU when they borrowed money, many slaveholders simply wrote out a bill of sale for a slave who would actually be transferred only if they failed to pay their debt. The value attached to unsold slaves was much more useful to antebellum business-men than that attached to land, for slaves were portable and the slave traders promised ready cash. In antebellum East Feliciana Parish, Lou-isiana, slaves accounted for eighty percent of the security offered in recorded mortgages. Similarly, slaves were used as collateral by pur-chasers of shares in Louisiana's investment banks. And slaves, even when they were not sold, were valued when estates were divided; coheirs could not be sure of their shares until the people owned by the deceased were translated into prices. Everyday all over the antebellum South, slaveholders' relations to one another—their promises, obliga-tions, and settlements—were backed by the idea of a market in slaves, the idea that people had a value that could be abstracted from their bodies and cashed in when the occasion arose.[20]

More than that, the daily business of slaveholding was measured in the terms of a slave market that existed only in slaveholders' heads—a market that made the value of their slaves seem to dance before their eyes, jumping and shifting, even as, day after day, the slaves did the same work they always had, tilling fields, nursing children, waiting tables. Slave buyers tracked rhythms, cycles, and tendencies in "the market" as they tried to decide when and where to buy slaves. Likewise, they consulted agricultural manuals that included rising slave values among the attributes of a good crop. Louisiana planter William Welhan duti-fully made a list of his slaves by age and value in 1856 and kept a running subtotal of their worth; in a document dated 1858 he broke that list down by age and sex and counted out the cash value he had in each of the market categories—$850 for males from 15 to 45 years, of whom he had twenty-nine, for example, totaled out to $24,650 in prime-age male property. Slaveholders like Welhan could track their fortunes in *Affleck's Planter's Annual Record*, which provided a convenient table by which slaves' annual increase in value could be tracked in the same set of tables as their daily cotton production, and a page at the back where the "planter" could fill in the value of his slave force, and calculate the "interest on the same at ten percent." Indeed, slaves' market value—"advantage, worth, quality"—was often cited as the best guar-antee that their owners would treat them well; paternalism itself, it turns out, was sometimes best measured in cash.[21]

The daily interchange between "slavery" and "the market" was so dense as to make the boundary between them indistinguishable; though bounded in place, in practice the slave market suffused the antebellum South. Slave traders held collateral on much of the economy and ideology of the slaveholding South: commercial instruments, daily business practice, common figures of speech, all of these depended on the slave market to make them make sense. References to the cash value of slaves signaled more than a simple awareness that any slave could be sold in the market: they were a central way of underwriting, understanding, and justifying antebellum social relations. In the slave pens the traders bought and sold the people whose notional value underwrote much of the business done in the slaveholding economy.

What "ordinary" slaveholders like Hundley believed distinguished them from slave traders, however, was that they could usually come up with a noncommercial reason for selling a slave. That is not to say that they were not capricious or greedy, for they often were. It is rather to say that "ordinary" slaveholders generally supplied public reckonings of what they did, reasoned explanations—accidents, opportunities, practicalities, necessities—that made clear why at one moment they decided to sell a slave whom they would otherwise have wanted to keep. The accounts slaveholders gave of their actions emphasized the specific events that led to an individual sale over the everpresence of the market in slaves and the inexorability of the chattel principle—they were circumstantial rather than structural. And they traced an imaginary line of self-justification between "slavery," where slaves were sold only by happenstance, and the "market," where every slave was always for sale.

There were probably almost as many reasons given to justify the selling of slaves in the slaveholding South as there were slaves sold. Josiah Henson, like many others, was sold because his master died and the estate needed to be divided equally among the heirs. Two men known by Isaac Williams were sold because they had run away after receiving a brutal beating; likewise, one of the men with whom Christopher Nichols had run away was sold out of the jail where he was taken upon his capture. Hunter was sold because he did not work hard enough for his owner, and John Brown was sold because his master was building a new house and found himself in need of some ready cash to pay for the work. William was sold to pay for the support of his owner's three illegitimate children. Moses Grandy was sold because his master defaulted upon a mortgage that Grandy had not even known existed.

Lucy Delany was sold because her mistress thought she was getting too proud and putting on "white airs"; Celestine was sold by her elderly mistress because the woman's son liked "to play and fool about her." J. W. C. Pennington's mother was sold because she had been raped by her master's son and her mistress found out about it. Henry Crawthorn was sold because his master was a "sporting character" and could not pay his bills. Mrs. Harry Brant was gambled away to a slave trader aboard a steamboat. A man known by Frederick Douglass was sold because he was tricked by his owner into saying that he was not happy with his treatment.[22] The list could go on and on: slaveholders always had some reason for selling a slave—an estate to divide, a debt to pay, a transgression to punish, a threat to abate. What they rarely had when they sold a slave, it seems from the accounts they gave of themselves, was any direct responsibility for their own actions.

Take Maryland slaveholder T. D. Jones's effort to explain why he had sold Eliza, for example. The occasion for his explanation was a letter from Eliza in which she asked that the slaveholder sell her daughter Janine to Louisiana so that mother and daughter could be closer to one another. While Eliza's daughter was not allowed to respond to her mother's letter, Jones reported that he had told her of it and "she seemed glad to hear from you & her countenance lighted up with smile at the names of Aunt Liza and Tillie Ann (as she calls you and her sister.) But she says she does not want to go away from her master." Jones justified his refusal to reunite Eliza's family with a paternalist homily: the bond between master and slave was so strong that not even the love of a (slave) mother for her child could justify its dissolution. And Jones went on to explain his attachment to Eliza's daughter by comparing the little girl to her mother: "I would be reluctant to part with her. She is petted as you used to be. She is a watchful little spy as you used to be; she has a good disposition, is neither cross, nor mischievous: she is useful for her services in the house, for going on errands, and for nursing & I should miss her very much." Still, Jones's description of the little girl to whom he was so attached sounds a lot like an advertisement directed at a potential buyer in the lower South—perhaps to the flagrantly wealthy Butler family of Louisiana who now owned Eliza and through whom she corresponded with Jones—and he promised to consider Eliza's request.

Jones's comparison of mother and daughter quickly led him into an exculpating account of why he had sold Eliza in the first place. He must have realized the twisted logic at the heart of his paternalist apologetic: if the attachment of master and slave was so sacred as to render it indivisible, and if it was Janine's similarity to Eliza that made her indispensable, what was Eliza doing in Louisiana in the first place? The master, Jones answered—and he was gaining energy now, baring the teeth behind the credulous homily with which he had started the letter—could not control the slave's disposition: "I think you will acknowledge that I was to you a kind & forbearing master & that you were an ungrateful servant & I think you feel assured if you had conducted yourself faithfully, no offer would have tempted me to part with you." As Jones put it, a mutuality that defied valuation characterized the relation of master to slave; Eliza had been traded away because she herself had dissolved those ties. That was paternalism, too, and he rubbed it in: "Your tender & affectionate services to your afflicted mistress created in me an attachment for you that nothing but your ingratitude & faithlessness could have broken."

But the memory of his own righteousness took Jones back to the time before he had sold Eliza, and along that path he found another of his old reasons for selling her. "Situated as I was after the death of my dear beloved and still lamented wife, the only alternative presented to me was to quit housekeeping or part with you—a painful one."[23] Jones was grasping: either it was Eliza's fault or it was the "only alternative"—betrayed mutuality or exigent necessity—that had led him to sell Eliza. But whatever it was, it was *not his fault*. Jones closed the letter with his sense of his own righteousness intact. There is no evidence that he ever acted on Eliza's request.

At the heart of the slave market, then, there was a contradiction and a contest. The contradiction was this: the abstract value that underwrote the southern economy could only be made material in human shape—frail, sentient, and resistant. And thus the contradiction was daily played out in a contest over meaning. Were slave sales, as so many slaveholders insisted, the unfortunate results of untimely deaths, unavoidable debts, unforeseeable circumstances, and understandable punishments, or were they, as so many slaves felt, the natural, inevitable, and predictable result of a system that treated people as property? Was a slave sale an untimely rupture of the generally benign character of the relation between master and slave or hard evidence of the hidden structure of that relation, a part of slavery that revealed the malign character of the whole? In the contest over defining what it was that was happening, slaveholders had every advantage their considerable resources could support—state power, a monopoly on violence, and a well-developed propaganda network that stretched from church pulpits to planter-class periodicals like *DeBow's Review*—to enforce their ideologically situated account as a transparent truth. And yet slaves were not without resources of their own: a developed underground that provided intelligence about coming sales and supported efforts to resist or escape the trade, knowledge of slaveholders' incentives and ideology that they could appropriate to subversive purposes, and, ultimately, an alternative account of what was going on—a systemic critique of slavery—which through their practical resistance they forced into the public record of the antebellum South.

FIRST SALE

That slaves were able to pass on so much information about the reasons their owners gave for selling them points to an important fact(many slaveholders were forced to consider their slaves a party to their own sale.)Some very few slaves ran away into the slave trade to escape brutal masters or tragic lives, and some very few others were able to gain their freedom by purchasing themselves. But for the vast majority of slaves, sale had a fearful character, and they did whatever they could to avoid it. Indeed, many slave sales had to be negotiated twice through—once with the buyer and once with the merchandise. Although very few slaves escaped a threatened sale, many resisted and in the process forced their owners into creating knowledge of the structural accountability that was often hidden behind well-turned public accountings and ritual avowals of circumstantial necessity.

Certainly, those whose owners died knew that their futures might be settled with a sale, and many accounts of passage into the slave trade begin with the dispersion of a slaveholder's estate.[24] Others, however, obtained knowledge of their sale from more mysterious sources. "At length the report was started that I was to be sold for Louisiana," remembered Lewis Clarke. "It was rumored that I was sold," likewise remembered Williamson Pease. Or, as Harriet Newby wrote to her husband: "Dear husband you know not the trouble I see; the last two years has been a trouble dream to me. It is said master is in want of money. If so, I know not what time he may sell me."[25] "The report was started," "it was rumored," "it is said": behind the source-protecting passive voice was hidden a network of informers that stretched into the parlors and offices of slaveholders who sometimes seem to have thought themselves impervious to the judgment of others and inaudible to the people who serviced their tables and stocked their shelves. Isaac Mason's information that he was going to be sold came from his master's son. Charles Peyton Lucas, a blacksmith, found out from his sister that the stranger who had watched him at work during the day had dined with his owner in the evening. "I won't take less than fifteen hundred dollars," she had overheard their owner say at the dinner table; "he is a first-rate blacksmith."[26] As much as slaveholders liked to think that their affairs were their own business, they could not stop their property from listening in on their conversations or gossiping with their associates or neighbors.

When they found out they were going to be sold, some slaves ran away. Lewis Clarke ran away as soon as he heard the "report" that he was going to be sold to Louisiana. Like Clarke, many of the escaped slaves whom William Still met at the northern outlet of the Underground Railroad dated their decision to run away to the time when they heard they were to be sold for debt or punishment. "The slave auction block," Still wrote, "indirectly proved to be in some respects a very active agent in promoting travel on the U.G.R.R." So, too, for those whom Benjamin Drew met in the free communities of Canada in the 1850s. Among them was Charles Peyton Lucas, who took flight after he found out from his sister he was to be sold. Another ex-slave interviewed by Drew was Benjamin West, who described his decision to run away in the following terms: "My master died and I heard that I was to be sold, which would separate me from my family, and knowing no law which would protect me I came away."[27] Facing both social death and literal death in the killing fields of the lower South, these men had nothing left to lose; isolation, hunger, exposure, tracking dogs, and the threats of violent capture and sadistic punishment that their owners generally used to keep them from slipping out from under their own prices could no longer provoke enough fear to keep these men from running away.

Most of those who ran away, perhaps seventy-five percent, were men. As historian Deborah Gray White has argued, shared childcare and an early age of first pregnancy made it more difficult for women to take on such risks than men. White also points out that men were more likely to face solitary sale than women. Particularly in the years before 1850, when men were being exported from the upper South in far greater numbers than women, it was men who were most likely to find themselves in a situation where they had nothing to lose by running away.[28]

But even those who were unable or unwilling to accept the privation and uncertainty of running for freedom could use flight to avoid sale. Moses Grandy remembered Billy Grandy, his childhood owner, as a hard-drinking man who often sold his people to pay for his entertainment. Though Grandy's mother could not hope to carry eight children to freedom, she was for some time able to keep them from getting sold. "I remember well," Grandy later wrote, "my mother often hid us in the woods to prevent master selling us." During that time the Grandy family lived on wild berries they found in the woods and potatoes and raw corn that could only have come from slaves who remained behind or lived nearby. Word that the slaveholding Grandy had relented came from the same quarter: "After a time, the master would send word to her to come in, promising her he would not sell us."[29] By enlisting the support of other slaves in the neighborhood and withholding her labor and that of her children, Grandy's mother repeatedly postponed their sale.

Edward Hicks used flight to renegotiate the terms of his own sale. Soon after he was sold to a Luneburg County, Virginia, slave trader, Hicks ran away. Lost and hungry after four days in the woods, he told his story to "an old colored man" he met on the road, and the man fed him and pointed the way back to Luneburg. When he returned, Hicks saw "some of my friends and brothers there," who told him that he had been advertised as a runaway, gave him some food, and advised him "to go to an old house where the cotton was kept and there to stay until the advertisement was over." Hicks was still hiding there when the slave trader gave up and set off for New Orleans without him. By the spring, when the trader returned to Luneburg for another season of slave buying, Hicks remembered, "there was a white man in Luneburg who wanted to buy me," and the trader, as was common practice, sold the chance of Hicks's capture "in the woods." Hicks concluded the story of his sale with a sentence that balanced the deal made by the slaveholders with that made by the slave: "It was settled at eight hundred dollars: then he sent out some of his boys to tell me, and in a few days I went to him."[30] The connection between Hicks and the man who eventually bought the chance of his capture is obscure: Hicks may have promised to come in before the bill of sale was finalized or he might have seized an unexpected chance to stay in Luneburg when it was presented him. What is clear is that he had plenty of help from neighboring slaves in escaping, hiding, and deciding when to come out. With the help of the very community from which he was to be separated by the trade, Hicks stayed away until he was satisfied with the terms of his own sale.

Behind other bills of sale were similar stories. In January 1853 Louisiana planter Augustus Walker bought 153 slaves from Joseph Hernandez of St. Augustine, Florida. The slaves were to be transported to Louisiana and put to work on Walker's Orleans Parish sugar plantation. After meeting with Hernandez once himself and sending his agent twice more, Walker thought he had finally worked out the details of the trade and sent a third man to Florida to take possession of the slaves. But, as difficult as it might have been to work out the legalities of the transaction, executing its terms proved even harder. In April Walker received word that his agent had been unable to take possession of the people the planter had purchased. "On the Negroes being informed they were to go to New Orleans and that we had come for them they demurred very generally," the agent began, "and when the time fixed for their moving came they declined going to New Orleans." That first night "about forty" of the slaves ran away; and by the time the agent wrote, more than 120 of the original 153 had disappeared. The sheriff had been notified, but Walker's agent closed by asking his employer to travel to Florida to solve things for himself. He added this to underline the seriousness of his request: "it is an act of revolt on the part of the Negroes and I fear we have not seen the worst of it."[31] The agent first estimated the situation as a negotiation gone bad—upon learning the terms, the slaves demurred and declined—but his conclusion made it sound more like an open war.

If the very communities threatened by the trade could resist sale, so too could slaves invoke their own value in an effort to preserve their communities. This is most obvious in the case of those who tried to save themselves from the trade by threatening self destruction. Ex-slaves from Missouri and Virginia told nineteenth-century interviewers of men and women who, threatened with sale to a slave trader, cut off their hands and fingers or took their own lives. Lewis Clarke, in answer to a question commonly asked on the antislavery lecture circuit, remembered "a slave mother who took her child into the cellar and killed it. She did it to prevent being separated from her child." "Other instances," he added, "I have frequently heard of."[32] The horror of these stories has caused many to doubt their veracity; running away, with all of the bodily danger and emotional isolation it entailed, is a type of resistance that is easier to assimilate. And, indeed, the value of answers to questions asked repeatedly by middle-class white antislavery interlocutors—whose own obsessions seem so economically condensed into the image of slavery escaped at the price of infanticide—might be understood as either literal or symbolic truth.[33] These events may have happened with the frequency Clarke suggested, or these stories may have been emblematic of feelings that were too contradictory or choices that were too difficult to explain without a concrete exemplar. What is clear, however, is that these stories had the same currency among slaveholders that they did among abolitionists.

In 1849 Joseph Copes, a physician who was in the process of moving from rural Mississippi to New Orleans, made a contract to send some of the people he owned to be hired out in Baton Rouge. Among those slated to go was a man named Ednoull; among those to be left behind was Ednoull's wife, Sally. But before the Mississippi River had subsided enough from its spring high to allow the slaves' passage, Copes's agent, William Arick, who was shipping the slaves, asked his employer to rethink his plans: "Your plan of taking Ednoull from Sally is a bad one," the agent warned. In a letter he wrote ten days later he explained why he thought so. "Ednoull tells me," he wrote, "that you and Mary Ann said when he and Sally married that they should never be parted and says that if I send him from her it will not do you or anybody else any good—meaning I suppose that he will kill himself." Ednoull was almost certainly risking a brutal beating by standing firm, but he made sure that the agent (and thus Copes) knew that they could do nothing worse to him than what they had already threatened. He would take his own life—and, he made explicit, destroy the value he embodied—if he were separated from his wife. When the appointed time came, Ednoull remained behind as the other slaves departed. "He openly said that he would kill himself if I sent him," explained Arick.[34]

Ednoull's victory was temporary, for six months later he was in Baton Rouge. In December 1849 Copes received a letter from his stepson

G. B. Davis, which urged him to reunite Ednoull and Sally in precisely the same terms that Ednoull had outlined to Arick, the agent: Ednoull had been promised that his marriage would be respected and threatened that he would not be valuable to anyone if it was not. Although Copes still controlled the slaves in 1849, the younger man was to take up ownership when he reached his majority. It is not known whether his stepson's urging led Copes to make good his promise, or indeed whether the young man made it good himself when he had the chance. What is clear, however, is that Ednoull had recognized that his threat was one his owner could not ignore, and that he was continuing to protest his treatment and to threaten his own destruction—and that of the value he embodied.[35]

(Slaves like Ednoull had one other tool at their disposal as they tried to resist a threatened sale: the terms of their enslavement. Ednoull's statement to the agent was a threat to his owner but it was also a reminder of a broken promise. By reminding Copes that the slaveholder had promised to respect his marriage, by recounting his history with Copes in the grammar of promise and obligation, Ednoull had changed the field of meanings that his removal had for his master. What had been for his master a detail of business was reframed by Ednoull as matter of the man's honor. Moses Grandy desperately invoked similar terms when he saw a slave trader carrying his wife away: "'For God's sake have you bought my wife?' He said he had; when I asked him what she had done, he said she had done nothing, but that her master wanted money."[36] Grandy, like Ednoull, had been betrayed, and he invoked the paternalist mutuality of the broken promise: if she had not behaved badly, the slaveholder should not have sold her. Charles Ball's mother pleaded in similar terms after she had been sold to a slave trader. Rather than following the trader, she ran after the local man who had bought the young Ball and took the child in her arms. "She then," Ball remembered, "still holding me in her arms, walked along the road beside the horse as he moved slowly, and earnestly and imploringly besought my master to buy her and the rest of the children, and not permit them to be carried away by the Negro buyers."[37] Ball's mother gave her son's new master a promise of paternalism: he could distinguish himself from the slave traders by buying and saving the family. Like Ednoull, like Grandy, like so many thousands of others throughout the history of the antebellum South, Ball's mother wept in vain.

Occasionally, however, when chided by their slaves or others, slave-holders did act in concert with the better selves of their paternalist rhetoric. William Green's mother convinced her owner ("she having nursed him when a child") to sell her son in the neighborhood rather than to a slave trader. Both Henry Clay Bruce and Moses Grandy recalled slaveholders' tearful wives and children interceding on the behalf of women and children who had been sold to traders. And when the Louisiana widow Jane Crisswell tried to sell her slaves at public auction, she was led by the "tears and promises" of a woman who feared separation from her children to cancel the auction and make the best of it with her slaves.[38] Tears and promises, feelings of betrayal, and pledges of mutuality—on occasion slaves could work the paternalist rhetoric of their owners into a successful critique of slaveholding practice. It should go without saying that slaves' invocations of their owners' paternalist promises were often strategic: they implied no internalization of slave-holder paternalism.[39] Barely escaping separation and sale by relying upon a slaveholder's attenuated sense of obligation was no more likely to inure slaves to their situation than receiving a beating would have.

These strategies emerged from the existing relations between slaves and slaveholders and were shaped by those relations. All of the forego-ing successful invocations of paternalist mutuality involved the separa-tion of a mother from her child. Most of the slaveholding intercessors were themselves women. The "paternalism" evident in these cases was the result of appeals made in a language that appears to have been unique to enslaved women and that was most effectively directed at slaveholding ones. This is not to say that slaveholding women were less invested in slavery than their fathers, sons, and husbands. Far from it: occasionally interceding on the behalf of the people they owned was one of the ways in which they performed their roles as slaveholding ladies.[40] The formalized gender roles that slaveholders prescribed for both themselves and their slaves, however, provided enslaved mothers with avenues of resistance that were not available to other slaves. The very social roles that made it difficult for enslaved women to escape sale through flight could be invoked against a threatened sale.

As a few of these stories suggest, the best that many slaves could hope for was the chance to find themselves a buyer who lived nearby. In order to preserve enslaved families, slave sellers occasionally allowed favored slaves to sell themselves rather than being put up at public auctions.

Thomas Clemson, for example, allowed Daphny—alone among the many slaves on the plantation he was liquidating—to find a buyer for her family before the public sale. Daphny, he noted by way of explanation for this particular favor, had been a gift from his father-in-law, John C. Calhoun, and had served the family faithfully. Mrs. Henry Brant pushed her owner into a similar favor by making "such a fuss" when he tried to use her to settle a gambling debt to a slave trader that "the people told him 'twas a shame to let me go to the trader—that I was too good a girl for that, having taken care of him in sickness—that I ought to have the chance to find someone to buy me."[41]

Others made desperate attempts to sell themselves from the slave pen. James Phillips wrote to his wife from Richmond, where he was awaiting shipment to the lower South, "Do pray, try and get Brant and Mr. Byers and Mr. Weaver to send or come on to buy me, and if they will only buy me back, I will be a faithful man to them so long as I live . . . Feel for me now or never."[42] By showing the named men the letter, as James Phillips urged her to do, Mary Phillips was promising them a lifetime of grateful good behavior and reminding them that the consequences of inaction were eternal: feel for me now or never.

It is not known whether James Phillips escaped sale to the lower South, but the vast majority of stories like his ended with a sale. For every story of successful struggles against the trade there were many, many more that ended like this: "Howdy and goodbye, for I never expect to see you again. Try to do the best you can, and if you have a good master behave properly to him, and try to think about your master in Heaven. If I had known you were going to be sold I would have been better satisfied, but I am very much distressed now at being separated from you. Remember me and I will think of you. Write to me after you are settled. Your wife Fatima."[43]

FINAL TERMS

Slaveholders, much of the literature on the antebellum South reminds us, were decorous people: they did not like scenes, at least not those choreographed by someone else.[44] Nor was it in their interest to have to negotiate with the people they sold as well as with those to whom they were selling. To protect their own impoverished accounts of a

slave sale from being publicly confuted and to prevent their commercial bargains from being undermined by their objects, many sellers resorted to ingratiation, deceit, and coercion—techniques often publicly identified with the unsavory character of the slave trader. No matter the language they used to describe their slave selling, no matter the reasons they gave, slaveholders knew from experience that their slaves went to sale unwillingly. Especially when faced with sale to a slave trader, slaves were liable to take flight, break down, or attempt an embarrassing public accounting of historical and mutual obligations. Never more so than when they tried to anticipate and outmaneuver their slaves' resistance to sale did slaveholders reveal the vast distance between their cover stories and the brutal underpinnings of their business. The few slaves who resisted sale shaped the market practice of many masters, forcing slaveholders to create public knowledge of their complicity with the traders by trying to anticipate their slaves' resistance.

Some attempted to palliate their slave selling with paternalist solicitude. "The Negroes will probably be somewhat distressed at being sold," Lewis Stirling advised his son, who was to oversee the sale of a group of the family's slaves, "and you must do what you can to reconcile them, tell them (which is the fact) that I owed Mr. Lyon and had no other way of paying."[45] A narrative of economic necessity protected Stirling from having to take responsibility for his own actions. But it was up to his slaves to be reconciled, to accept that commerce was a "fact" and their attachments illusory, that paying a debt was a necessity and preserving their community a luxury. If the slaves did not reconcile themselves to his account of events, Stirling's solicitude might be undermined by their distress. He might have to watch them cry, or catch them running, or beat them until they capitulated to his version of reality. By that time their sale would have taken on a very different meaning from the one with which he carefully prepared his son. Stirling had struck a self-saving bargain with his creditor, but the meaning—if not the execution—of that bargain remained to be negotiated with his slaves.

Other slaveholders were not willing to take the chance of making a second bargain, and they took steps to insure that they did not have to explain their business to their slaves. When Williamson Peace heard a rumor that he had been sold, his owner denied it. "There cannot be so

much smoke without some fire," Peace insisted, "everybody has got it that you have sold me." Still Peace's owner tried to convince him that things were another way: "he swore that it was a lie: that they were just trying to get me to run away." Peace later recalled that "[I] made up my mind to leave on the first opportunity" anyway, so he chose to go along with his master's ploy. He thought—rightly it turned out—that being sold in New Orleans offered him a better chance to escape than did remaining in Arkansas.[46]

Along with outright lies, some slaveholders used surprise to avoid negotiating with the slaves they were selling. As Thomas Clemson put it about the estate liquidation from which he spared only Daphny: "My object is to get the most I can for the property . . . I care but little to whom and how the[y] are sold, whether together or separated . . . the affair should be kept as secret as possible on account of the Negroes."[47] Though Clemson did not care himself, he realized the slaves would care how they were sold, and so he tried to take them by surprise. Charity Bowery's mistress made the same calculation when she sent Bowery on an errand while a trader came around to buy Bowery's twelve-year-old son Richard: "she didn't want to be troubled with our cries," Bowery remembered. Elizabeth Keckley recalled a similar story. Little Joe, the son of her owner's cook, was dressed in his best clothes one day and taken away. "When her son started for Petersburg in the wagon, the truth began to dawn upon her mind, and she pleaded piteously that her boy should not be taken from her, but master quieted her by falsely telling her he was simply going to town with the wagon, and would be back in the morning." Eliza, a woman Solomon Northup met in a Washington, D.C., slave pen, had been brought there by her owner (who was also her lover) "under the pretense that the time had come when her free papers were to be executed, in fulfillment of her master's promise."[48] None of these lies lasted long; at the end of each there was recognition and the slave trade. Neither mothers nor their children posed any great risk of running off to avoid a sale, but these slaveholders apparently cared about keeping their business free of the feelings of the people they sold. Whether it was the scene itself or the influence that open expressions of loss and betrayal might have on other slaves, their own family members, or even themselves, some slaveholders sidestepped the moment of truth with a lie. By so doing they assured themselves a smooth transaction but conceded that their economy could be sustained only at the cost of its pretense of humanity.

As a way of keeping slave selling free of the influence of the enslaved, mendacity shaded easily into coercion. While young Sella Martin was playing in his owner's yard, his mother was quietly called down to the privacy of the stable, where she was handcuffed and told that if she cried out she would be beaten. When Martin nevertheless saw her being carried away and tried to speak to the trader, the young boy's master drove him out into the yard. There, he saw his sister being led away by another man, who was "cuffing her to make her keep silent." Over the objections of his owner's wife and young son (who was his playmate), Martin himself was soon led away by still another trader.

James Smith remembered that slave traders planned to ambush his friend Zip when he was in the barn putting up a horse. Thomas Johnson was likewise trapped by traders who invited him to a house under the pretense of hospitality. William Troy did not see any pretense at all when he came across a slave sale that was being negotiated near Loretto, Virginia: "I heard the boy hollowing in the swamp; from hearing the shrieks I made towards the boy, when I went there, I found him [the owner] in the act of catching the boy to have him sold."[49] Back of every slave seller's strategy was the threat of violence: if he could not talk his slaves into the trade with unctuous apologies or trick them into it with secrets and lies, he could track them down, shackle their limbs, and forcibly carry them away. No longer, however, could he claim to be selling as a disappointed paternalist or helpless debtor: as one Virginia woman said of the slaveholder who had sold her daughters, "he was a mean dirty slave trader."[50]

For the slave economy to work smoothly, slaveholders had continually to consider the reactions of their unwilling underwriters. However they described their reasons for selling slaves, they had to consider the slaves' perspective to make sure they would have a body to go with the bill of sale. Their pre-emptive explanations, lies, and violence betray their awareness of the feelings of the people they sold. The threat of resistance thus forced a rupture in the tidy transcript of commercial necessity and moralizing self-justification by creating public knowledge of "ordinary" slaveholders' complicity in the world the slave traders made—a world in which hundreds of thousands of slave sales, many of them breaking marriages, most of them dividing families, all of them destroying communities, underwrote the history of the antebellum South.

MANY THOUSANDS GONE

The history of the slave trade is as much the story of those left behind as it is the story of those carried away. It is the story of separated lovers and broken families, of widows, widowers, and orphans left in the wake of the trade, only, perhaps, to be sold themselves at a later date.[51] Some of those whose friends or relatives were carried away by the traders had the comfort of information that came across the filaments of connection which spanned the enslaved South. Ann Garrison, who had been a slave in Maryland, told an interviewer in 1841 that her son, sold to a south-bound trader, was able to send a farewell from Baltimore via a friend who lived there. Those who could write sometimes sent word themselves. Kidnapped and carried to New Orleans by Hope H. Slatter in 1837, John Wesley Dunn tried to send word to his family through the Methodist Church seven years later. Charles Brown's grandmother, who was "jerked up and carried to New Orleans" without any warning, managed to write "a good while later that she would get free and come back and free her children." Others who could not write sent word by their owners. The letter Eliza sent to her Maryland master trying to convince him to allow her reunion with her daughter Janine (the one to which he responded with the litany of baleful excuses) was only half of the Louisiana woman's effort to reconstitute, if only for a moment, her broken family. Eliza also dictated a letter to her own mother, who lived in another part of Louisiana. Eliza's mother responded with a letter, dictated to her mistress, which reported that the older woman was in good health and provided directions that Eliza might use to come visit.[52] Though it is not known whether Eliza ever saw either her mother or her daughter, by writing she was reconstituting in greeting and remembrance a matrilineal family that had been sundered by the trade.

Because many of the traders followed the same routes year after year, the trade itself afforded some slaves the opportunity to get news of family and friends back home. In his narrative, William Wells Brown, who was hired to a slave trader, recounted two occasions when he had met men he had previously known in St. Louis along the trader's Mississippi River route—one in Natchez and one chained into a coffle aboard a boat bound for New Orleans.[53] As he traveled back and forth, Brown could articulate connections between those who had been separated by the trade. Perhaps such a link enabled James Smith to write this of a woman he had seen sold to a trader: "We heard sometime afterwards that a kind master had bought her, and that she was doing well."[54] Somehow Smith had managed to get a comforting piece of news about a woman who had been carried thousands of miles away.

The stories that came back along these links had a didactic import that outstretched their degree of certainty. Of the grandmother who had managed to send a promise to get herself free and return to purchase her family, Charles Brown later said, "She got free herself, as I have heard, but 'twas when she got too old to do any more work." What came back to Brown was a moral as well as a remembrance: a politically pointed story of the cruelty of slaveholders who would free their slaves only when the cost of supporting them in their old age outstripped their utility. In his own narrative, Lewis Clarke recounted the brutal story of a child taken from his mother along the way South and used by a slave trader to pay a bar bill. "This was the news that came back to us and it was never disputed." And it was Clarke who reported that as well as knowing people who had injured themselves to avoid the trade, he had "frequently heard" of them.[55] Clarke was careful to distinguish between what he had himself seen and what he had heard from others. He carefully marked a line between his own experience and the experiences of others which, through tellings and retellings that carried them ever further from their origins, had been transformed into an indigenous antislavery ideology.

Through talking about those who had been taken away by the trade, slaves used remembrance to speak larger truths about slavery. Whether they bespoke the cautious optimism of purchase by a good master, the studied pessimism of freedom granted too late to be enjoyed, or the bitter pathos of self-mutilation and infanticide, these stories bound tellers and listeners into a common account of what slavery was and what was wrong with it. They served as a part of slavery that illuminated the character of the whole, a set of common memories that could be continually animated through retelling and around which practical opposition to enslavement could coalesce.

Nowhere was this process more apparent than in the songs slaves sang about the trade. Traveling through Maryland, an antebellum traveler named John Dixon Long heard slaves singing the following song as they worked in the fields:

> William Rino sold Henry Silvers
> Hilo! Hilo!
> Sold him to de Georgy trader;
> Hilo! Hilo!
> His wife she cried, and children bawled,
> Hilo! Hilo!
> Sold him to de Georgy trader;
> Hilo! Hilo![56]

That song passed on an account of slavery—an answer to the question "What is slavery?"—that put the slaves' vulnerability to the trade at its center. In the song, as in the social history of the slave trade in the upper South up to the 1850s, the emblematic slave was male, and those left behind to mourn and remember him were women and children.[57] Moreover, the combination of the specificity and fill-in-the-blank anonymity of the names William Rino and Henry Silvers mediated between the personal loss felt by the bereaved and a common vulnerability to the trade which stretched beyond the realm of personal experience—an "imagined community" of enslaved people built out of the ritualization in song of the shared everyday experience of life under the chattel principle.[58] Through singing these songs, slaves translated the tragically isolating personal experience of the trade into a shared antislavery ideology.

Likewise the following transcription of "The Coffle Song" included by Sella Martin in his 1867 *Narrative*:

> Oh! fare ye well, my bonny love,
> I'm gwine away to leave you,
> A long farewell for ever love,
> Don't let our parting grieve you.
> (Chorus) Oh! fare ye well my bonny, &c.
> The way is long before me, love,
> And all my love's behind me;
> You'll seek me down by the old gum-tree,
> But none of you will find me.

I'll think of you in the cotton fields;
I'll pray for you when resting;
I'll look for you in every gang,
Like the bird that's lost her nesting.
I'll send you my love by the whoop-o'-will;
The dove shall bring my sorrow;
I leave you a drop of my heart's own blood,
For I won't be back tomorrow.
And when we're moldering in the clay,
All those will weep who love us;
But it won't be long till my Jesus come,
He sees and reigns above us.[59]

Alongside the material geography of the slave trade—the old gum tree left behind in the upper South, the cotton fields toward which the trade carried so many slaves in the lower South—this song set the imagined geography of the chattel principle. The slave trade was ever present and its effects forevermore; in every gang might be the one left behind, in every bird a message. In the drop of a heart's blood and the tears of the bereft were connections that stretched beyond the time-and-space of the coffle and the pen. And again, this song mediates between the everyday lived experience of any single slave within the trade, between the loneliness of personal loss and mourning, and the recognition of the commonality of every slave's situation—it transmutes individual experience into a common antislavery ideology.[60] The end of one slave's story thus became the beginning of another's: when they met the traders, slaves had already been prepared for struggle by the memory of the many who had gone before them.

CHAPTER TWO

BETWEEN THE PRICES

To MISSISSIPPI RIVER slave trader John White, slavery looked like this: a list of names, numbers, and outcomes double-entered in the meticulous *Slave Record* he kept during his two decades of selling Missouri slaves in and around the New Orleans market.

Cynthia Branham, 23, $515.00 — Sold to McRae through Coffman, $687.75

Isabel Evans, 17, $600.00 — Sold to Mr. Herne, cash $750.00

Eliza McAfee, 16, $725.00 — Sold to Richard McCall, *Returned*

McGwine Wilson, 30, $600.00 — Sold to Thos. Pugh, Lafourche Parish, account to 1st Decr. next, $1000.00

William Robards, 25, $750.00 — Sold to C. H. Harriss, N. Orleans, $875.00

Charlotte Robards, 21, $650.00 — Sold to Richard Jordan, cash $915.00

Laura Robards, 16, $700.00 — Sold to Dr. L. D. Couden, cash $400 dft. 30 days $315

Isabel Robards, 14, $575.00 — Sold to Col. Hale, cash $750.00

Frances Robards, 12, $650.00 — Sold to Mr. Cv. Krell, dft. cashed $584.00

Jane Young, 19, $649.75 — Sold by R. A. Layton in Mississippi, $750.00

Emilyee Carroll, 14, $500.00 — Sold to Mr. Brand, Donaldsonville, notes $1000.00

Joe Fields, 22, $715.00 — Sold to Etienne Landry, Lafourche, cash $800.00

Lydia Howard, 20, $575.00	Died in Texas
Jane Chipley, 20, $500.00	Sold in Texas by R. A. Layton, $700.00
Matilda Selby, 9, $400.00	Sold to Mr. Covington, St. Louis, $425.00
Brooks Selby, 19, $750.00	Left at Home—Crazy
Fred McAfee, 22, $800.00	Sold to Pepidal, Donaldsonville, $1200.00
George Adams, 15, $675.00	Sold to E. R. Patterson, Howard Cty., $750.00
Howard Barnett, 25, $750.00	Ranaway. Sold out of Jail, $540.00
Harriet Barnett, 17, $550.00	Sold to Davenport and Jones, Lafourche, $900.00
Jack Barnett, 20, $750.00	Sold to Madame Burke, Lafourche, sugar $1200.00
Martha Peacher, 25, $500.00	Sold to A. Hodges, N. Orleans, $825.00[1]

White was an unmistakably powerful man. He had the ability to make his version of slavery a reality; he could and did turn thousands of people into prices during his time as a trader. And yet, when White tallied his achievement, the record he left was incomplete; even White knew that there was more to the story than that. There was, indeed, more than he may have ever suspected.

Though slave traders were treated in slaveholding law and literature as an easily identifiable subset of the slaveholding population, the people who sold other people for a living had any number of actual jobs: interstate traders, local dealers, brokers, and salaried employees. Some made lifelong careers of the trade, while others traded slaves as a temporary occupation on the way to a better future. Some became rich and bought a measure of social respectability, their wealth washed clean through its very profusion. Others struggled from trading season to trading season, plying the dusty roads and rural markets of the antebellum South in search of a break that never came. For some, slave trading was a family business; for others, it was a one-time speculation; for still others, slave trading was a way to make a little extra money on the side of another job. As diverse as they were, slave traders shared a common social life in the pens, and a common approach to slaves: they were speculators.

The traders did the dirty work of redistribution in the slaveholders' economy, moving slaves between owners who no longer wanted them and those who did, making a living in the space between the prices they paid and those they received. To minimize the amount of information they had to gather, and to maximize their profits, they packed their slaves into categories of comparison and distributed them according to demand: they treated people like things. In its daily practice, however, the traders' business was personal estimation. Their profits depended on isolating the ill and containing the unruly, on keeping their slaves from forming dangerous alliances or threatening attachments in the coffles or pens—on recognizing and regulating the humanity of the people they bought and sold.

Slaves entered the trade alone and anonymous. Most had been separated from their families and communities, from those they had known and those who knew them. Under the ever-watchful eyes of the traders, slaves recreated their social identities through telling their stories and participating in shared cultural forms—they built a community within the interstices of the slave trade. There was nothing automatic or necessarily idealistic about this process. Like any community under severe stress, the community of slaves in the trade was shot through with exploitation, suspicion, and resentment. But for many slaves, the connections they made in the coffles and pens allowed them to establish networks of support that could sustain them through the trade. For some few others, these connections grew into conspiracy. Hidden by the neat rows of figures listed down either side of a trader's account book is a history of back-and-forth estimations, crass manipulations, hazy connections, and occasional revolts—the daily history of the slave trade between the prices.

SELLING PEOPLE AS A PROFESSION

The dealers' names were everywhere in antebellum New Orleans: Freeman, Wilson, Kendig; White, Rutherford, Botts, and Beard. The walls of the city were patched over with their posted bills, the newspapers punctuated by their graphic advertisements, and the coffee shops and saloons overhung with loose and speculative talk about their business. The interstate traders were the best known: Franklin and Armfield of Virginia, the Woolfolk and Slatter families of Maryland, the Hagans of South Carolina.[2] The large traders kept depots at both ends of the trade; Franklin and Armfield, for example, kept pens in Alexandria, Virginia, Natchez, Mississippi, and New Orleans and owned boats (one named the *Isaac Franklin*) for shipping slaves in between. These firms had employees—some salaried, some paid on commission—at both ends of

47

the trade, and through these employees they spread their buying and selling widely. Franklin and Armfield bought slaves all over Virginia before consolidating them in Alexandria for shipment south. John White sold the slaves he shipped south from Missouri through a network of agents that stretched from Texas to Alabama. Yearly, each of the large interstate firms transported and sold hundreds of people, and their annual accounts were reckoned in hundreds of thousands of dollars.[3]

Smaller interstate firms followed the same basic pattern—one partner selling slaves in the lower South while the other continued to buy and ship slaves from the upper—while minimizing their capital commitment by boarding and selling their slaves in the depots of larger traders and local brokers.[4] Many of the smaller firms created a small-town version of the interstate trade between urban centers. The Taylor family of Faquier County, Virginia, for example, had a permanent depot in Clinton, Louisiana. The largest number of interstate slave traders, however, were itinerant and independent men who bought slaves on their own account and traveled through the lower South selling as they went. Like Samuel Browning, who followed the 1848–49 trading season from Alabama (Bluff Port) to Louisiana (Milliken's Bend) to Mississippi (Blackhawk then Greenwood then Yazoo City) and back to Louisiana, they tracked hope and information from town to town in search of a sale. Though, individually, they dealt in smaller numbers of people than the leading traders—a year's business might be reckoned in the dozens rather than the hundreds—these traders accounted for a large proportion of the interstate business.[5] Taken together, the interstate traders, large and small, urban and itinerant, accounted for as many as two thirds of a million forced migrations in the decades before the Civil War, half of those involving the separation of an enslaved family.[6]

Most interstate traders spent the summer buying slaves. Wherever slaves were sold in the upper South—whether at court house estate sales, private sales on a slaveholder's land, or even in another trader's yard—interstate traders were there to buy them. The people they purchased were gathered in upper South slave pens and jails, where they sometimes waited as long as two months before being shipped south. Still others were purchased along the way as the traders began to transport their slaves during the autumn. William Cotton, who owned a slave depot during the early 1830s, spent his summers in Kentucky buying slaves. Similarly, John Hagan's yearly routine began in Charleston with slave buying during June and July; he continued in Virginia and then was back in Charleston in September, still buying, before traveling to New Orleans in October. John White's 1844–45 trading season ran from the day before Christmas, when he opened his books in New Orleans, to June 19, when he paid for his return passage to St. Louis. Over ninety percent of the slaves imported to New Orleans were sold in the six months between November and April.[7]

(The seasonality of the slave trade was tied to the cycles of the larger agricultural economy. In the upper South, exportation had to wait until after harvest, because hands were needed in the summer and fall to tend the crops; in the lower South, buying was delayed until after harvest because that was when buyers had money available to pay for slaves.) The rhythm of the trade marks its centrality to the economy of slavery; the historic role of the slave trade in binding the diverging fortunes of the upper and lower South into mutual interest was yearly recapitulated in the seasonal cycle of interregional trade. In New Orleans, at least, there was an even deeper seasonality to trade of all kinds. Less of everything was done there in the summertime, when the stifling heat turned the air pestilent and those who could afford to do so left town to avoid malaria.[8]

After the traders had gathered their slaves, they started them south. The traders' coffles, lined out along rural roads or packed onto the decks of ships, were part of the landscape of the antebellum South, especially in the late summer and early fall. In September 1843, the English traveler G. W. Featherstonhaugh came across a slave coffle in the woods near the New River in Virginia, which he described this way:

It was a camp of Negro slave drivers, just packing up to start; they had about three hundred slaves with them who had bivouacked the previous night *in chains* in the woods . . . they had a caravan of nine waggons and single-horse carriages, for the purpose of conducting the white people, and any of the blacks that should fall lame, to which they were now putting the horses to pursue their march. The female slaves were, some of them, sitting on logs of wood, whilst others were standing, and a great many little black children were warming themselves at the fires of the bivouac. In front of them all, and prepared for the march, stood, in double files, about two hundred male slaves, *manacled and chained to each other.*[9]

Featherstonhaugh's shock and dismay (he recorded that he had "never seen so revolting a sight before") is mixed with the fascination of a slow-motion description—tired huddles of people waking to the chill of an early autumn morning. He wrote as if there, by the roadside, he was really seeing slavery for the first time. Joseph Ingraham likewise recalled watching groups of a hundred or so slaves disembarking from a steamboat near Natchez and starting their way into the city "in a long straggling line, or sometimes in double files, in well-ordered procession." Like those who traveled on foot, slaves shipped through the trade seemed remarkable to onlookers—real-life manifestations of an aspect of slavery they had heard about but not seen. When Samuel Page discovered that a trader with about twenty slaves was aboard the schooner *Orleans*, for example, he immediately went to look at them. As he later explained, he did so out of "curiosity": "he had never been in the South and he had never seen a drove of Negroes for sale."[10]

The duration of the journey south depended upon the route and means of transport. The inland journey could take as long as seven or eight weeks on foot, with the slaves covering about twenty miles a day; shipboard around the coast from Norfolk to New Orleans the trip required only about three weeks; and down the Mississippi from St. Louis, it might only take a few days by the 1850s.[11] Some interstate traders traveled south with the slaves they sold; some hired employees to make the journey; and some simply wrote out a bill of lading and shipped the slaves as they would any other commodity.[12] Though their business was centered in large urban markets like New Orleans, the large interstate traders made occasional journeys to outlying markets—Donaldsonville or Cheneyville or Alexandria in Louisiana—where they sold slaves.[13]

In the urban markets, the interstate traders competed for business with local traders who purchased local slaves as they came on the market and gathered them for interested buyers to examine and compare. The daily routine of one of these men was described by a former business partner in the following terms: "Kendig is in the Negro trade; has seen him bidding on Negroes; sees him often in Negro traders' yards; saw him there again this morning." Bernard Kendig, the man of whom he spoke, bought three quarters of his slaves from Louisiana residents, the bulk of them in the city of New Orleans. His buying was done in the neighborhood around his own slave yard, in the yards of competing traders and at estate sales and public auctions held in the hotels near the slave market. Kendig bought and sold on his own account, closing out more than a quarter of his speculations within ten days, almost two thirds of the rest within a month.[14] Because he traded in a single market, his overhead costs—housing, feeding, and caring for the slaves he sold—were low, and so were his prices.

Large traders—whether local like Kendig or interstate like John Hagan of South Carolina—superintended slave yards in New Orleans. The City Treasurer's Census of Merchants listed nineteen such yards in 1854. These yards provided room and board for out-of-town traders and their slaves for a fixed daily cost (around twenty-five cents per day per person) and a cut (usually two and a half percent) of the business done in the pens.[15] Many of the slaves in these men's yards were being sold by the traders on behalf of people who would not have considered themselves professional slave traders. Interested sellers often contracted to have their slaves sold out of the pens, and interested buyers often contacted brokers to help them find slaves. When they were recorded by a notary public, these transactions bore only the name of the legal titleholders, seller and buyer, not the broker. It is a crucial omission, and one that has led historians to underestimate the extent of the business done in the pens. John Farmer to Francis Fisk, Louis Shelton to Mary Ann Cornish, Daniel Twogood to David Winn, César Martin to Joaquin Brabo, Antonio Costa to Mrs. Bonhomme Cohn: none of these sales were recorded as if a slave trader was involved, and thus they have been passed over by those who have tried to tabulate the traders' share of the broader market in slaves by counting out the numbers of traders' names on registered Acts of Sale. And yet it became apparent in the trials that emerged from these sales that every one of them had been arranged by a man described in court as a slave dealer or broker—Samuel Hite, Thomas Foster, Robert Wright, Réné Salain, Louis Caretta.[16] What appear on the surface of the commercial record to have been sales between neighbors or acquaintances often turn out to have been professionally brokered sales.

In fact, it sometimes must have seemed as if slave traders were everywhere in antebellum New Orleans. Charles Prince, whose occupation was "buying and selling Negroes and apprehending runaway slaves," for example, had no office but was "every morning" and "most of the day on the Levee." Similarly, during the selling season Samuel

Hite boarded in the slave yard owned by New Orleans trader Theophilus Freeman, but he spent his days making connections on the street, pitching the slaves in Freeman's yard to prospective buyers and sending a messenger to the pens to retrieve the slaves when negotiation reached the point of inspection. Hite, however, was more than a middleman for Freeman, for he apparently controlled his own information-gathering network of brokers. It was, for example, D. W. Bowles who initiated one of the sales Hite eventually sealed on the street. Bowles, who described himself as a "hotel keeper, bar keeper, and restaurant keeper who has also acted as a Broker in slaves, and has traded in slaves for his own account," had run into an old friend, discovered the man was in town to sell a slave, and steered him to Hite. For Bowles's trouble, Hite paid him five dollars. Later that night, after Hite had made the sale and pocketed the commission, another broker, Michael Glasgow, confronted Bowles at the bar of the St. Charles Hotel, demanding "why the hell he had not brought the Negro to him," and adding that "he would have given twenty-five dollars Brokerage." Bowles later maintained that he had not known that Glasgow was a slave trader until that moment. He had known the man only as a bar keeper at the Planter's Hotel, where Glasgow had been employed by none other than Samuel Hite.[17]

The tenor of Glasgow's remarks to Bowles suggests that the erstwhile bartender might have been making a play to control the slave-selling network of which he had once been a part. But even if the specific character of the business relation between Hite and Glasgow is unclear (indeed, it was at issue in the courtroom in which Bowles told his story), its geography is revealing. Bowles's testimony outlines a pyramidal network of information gathering and slave selling that stretched from the slave pens through the city's hotels and barrooms—a network in which every bartender was a potential broker and every broker tried to control every bartender. The lively traffic in information and influence that joined the slave traders to the hotels and bars where travelers and traders gathered and discussed their business suggests that the practice of trading slaves far outreached the cluster of pens publicly identified as "the slave market."

The commercial identities of the traders were sometimes equally difficult to define. Traders, brokers, and employees all had different stakes in a sale and different liability if a deal went bad. In practice, however, the differences were sometimes hard to divine. The legal form

of brokerage could allow traders who had been legally bankrupted to stay in business. Trader George Ann Botts, for example, did business as a broker in the name of a free woman of color, Ann Maria Barclay. As one witness to a transaction involving the couple remembered it, "Mr. Botts filled up the checks and Miss Barclay signed them." Legally, Botts was her agent; in actuality, he was her lover. Before that, he had been her owner. Similarly, Bernard Kendig did business in the name of a widow named Matilda Bushy, because, as one witness remembered, he had been bankrupted and "could not do business in his own name." When Bushy became insolvent, Kendig went on doing business in another woman's name.[18]

More common, and perhaps more confusing to slave buyers, was the traders' practice of selling slaves for one another, acting as brokers for men who were in theory their competitors. The account books of traders like John White are full of notations of commissions paid to traders who aided him in the sale of his slaves. Adding to the confusion was the fact that much of the daily work in the pens—feeding the slaves, overseeing their preparation for sale, and sealing the bargains that were notarized above the traders' names—was done by employees who had no financial interest in the people their employers sold. As one of these men put it about his employer: "if all his Negroes had died, I would have received the same compensation as if they had lived." Dissatisfied buyers who brought suits under the state's buyer-protecting redhibition law sometimes had a hard time finding a defendant to sue, as apparent partnerships dissolved into a chorus of conflicting descriptions of ill-defined commercial relationships.[19]

As mystifying as they may have been to uninformed buyers, the seemingly cozy commercial relations between the traders were sometimes shot through with deception. Trader Theophilus Freeman claimed that another trader had taken him for almost six hundred dollars by asking Freeman to front for him in the sale of a man who was a known runaway. Freeman claimed that he had been tricked into signing his own name to the bill of sale and left in legal jeopardy when both the slave and the other trader disappeared—the trader "with the money in his pocket." William Cotton found himself out more than the price of one slave when he discovered that a man whom he had employed to buy slaves for him in Kentucky had instead passed himself off as a trader in his own right, all the while spending Cotton's money

on fancy clothes, cheap liquor, and bad bets. Some speculators may never have known they were being taken. Two sets of books document John White's 1858 slave-selling season: one book records all of the business White did in 1858; the other, which records some of the sales found in the first book (along with many others not found in White's own accounts), is apparently the record book of someone who had a partial stake in White's 1858 speculation as well as in several other slave-trading ventures. While the second book matches the first in its accounting of the prices paid by White for slaves—the money spent by the firm—it is inconsistent in its accounting of the prices White received for slaves in Louisiana. Most of the prices in the two books match, but when the books do not match, the difference—ranging from twenty-five to three hundred dollars per sale—is almost always in the favor of the book kept by John White. White, it seems, was cooking the books he showed to his partner and skimming an extra share of the sales he made in Louisiana.[20]

In addition to the interstate traders, the local traders, the landlords, the brokers, and the employees, there were auctioneers who made a living selling slaves. State business, such as succession and debt sales, made up the bulk of the auctioneers' work and accounted for most of the slaves they sold. But the auctioneers also sold slaves for the "ordinary" slaveholders so carefully distinguished from the traders by Daniel Hundley, and, in exceptional circumstances, for slave dealers who could not sell their slaves in the pens. In effect, these men were licensed brokers for slaves and other sorts of property. In Louisiana their numbers were limited by state law, and they received a standard commission on the property they sold, one percent for state business and the standard two and a half percent for private business. Their offices—where, in the style of the traders' pens, slaves were available for inspection before a sale—were just south of the uptown slave market. Their auctions, held every Saturday, drew large crowds of onlookers. Beneath the rotundas of the city's luxury hotels, slaves were publicly exposed, cried, and sold along with all manner of other goods—furniture, cotton, livestock, and so on.[21]

The large trading firms were often family businesses, passed from one generation to another, and their principals were men of means: they lived in large houses, attended fine dinner parties, and held public offices.[22] There was apparently little stigma attached to the trade for

those who were successful at it (Daniel Hundley's claims notwithstanding). At one point John Hagan was planning a New Orleans suburb that would bear his name; John White was known by one of the honorifics common to the antebellum ruling class, Colonel White; Joseph A. Beard, New Orleans' most prominent auctioneer, was known as Major Beard. Some of these men—Isaac Franklin, for instance—had worked their way to prominence through the trade. The son of a Tennessee long hunter, Franklin parlayed the trade into six Louisiana plantations and six hundred slaves of his own. (On the land of one of his plantations, called then as now Angola, the state of Louisiana later built a prison.) J. W. Boazman's success story was more modest. A one-time slave-pen employee, Boazman eventually got together enough money to trade on his own account. The gains others made out of the trade were more fleeting. Theophilus Freeman, who owned a New Orleans pen in the 1840s, ended his life on the run from the law, having been accused of stealing slaves and defrauding his creditors.[23]

Trying to make their way upwards through the trade, many of the smaller interstate traders spent long periods away from home, sleeping out, traveling over muddy roads, or in close quarters on ships. Interstate trading was associated with young and single men—"until they find wives" was the way that one woman characterized the duration of the traders' careers. Or, as recently married Harriet Jarratt wrote to her slave trader husband, "I am afraid Dear Husband that you and Carson will keep up Negro trading as long as you can get a Negro to trade, and when you can't buy through the Country you will carry off al you can pirade at home, but one good thing Mr. Carson has no wife to leave behind when he is gone." Jarratt's response was to rework his wife's critique of his immediate failings as a husband into evidence of his deeper virtue: "The Negroes at home I never will take from you unless you wish it. So long as you are pleased with them I will try to be and when you wish them sold I will sell them . . . I have no disposition to continue Negro trading and hope to engage in something else by which I can accumulate a little and remain with my family." In closing, Jarratt underlined his incongruous paternalism with the phrase "*Howdy to the Negroes.*"

Jarratt, by his account, did not like trading slaves; he did it only by necessity. He was, instead, a good man working for the good of his small family. Perhaps realizing that his wife had been hoping for more than an earnest promise not to sell the family's slaves to Alabama (unless, of course, she wanted him to), Jarratt emphasized husbandly patriarchy over slaveholding paternalism in the next letter he wrote his wife. The letter began with a description of a trader Jarratt had met on the road. The other trader had been married only ten days before he left home with his slaves and, after months on the road, he still had fifty to sell. Jarratt protested that he had only eighteen left to sell, commended his wife to have sympathy for the other man's wife rather than feeling sorry for herself, and then communicated to her what must have been the substance of his conversation with the other trader: "we are both toiling for our wives and their little ones or with the hope of children."[24]

During the selling season the traders lived with one another. In New Orleans both interstate and local traders boarded at the houses of other traders, sold one another's slaves, served as witnesses for one another's sales, and executors for one another's wills. The company the traders kept was almost exclusively male, as were many of the spaces in which they entertained themselves. The traders usually took their meals in the pens, grouped around a single table, and socialized with one another, some spending their evenings, as ex-slave John Brown remembered of Theophilus Freeman and Thomas McCargo, going to saloons and gambling. The transactions that John White recorded in his day book began each morning in the pens, where he prepared his slaves for sale, settled accounts with other traders, and sold slaves. During the day White ventured out of the pens for "marketing" and to purchase the supplies that he used to prepare his slaves for sale. And at the end of most days there is a notation for "whisky" or "brandy and oisters" or "oister dinner with Mitchell."[25]

Some of the traders established close emotional ties. Before Michael Glasgow disappeared with Theophilus Freeman's money, there was, according to one trader, "great intimacy existing between Glasgow and Samuel Hite." The same phrase was used to describe the relations between William Cotton and Thomas Coot before business between them soured: they were "on terms of great intimacy," one witness remembered. Cotton paid for Coot's clothes and the house where they lived together, and when they were apart, Cotton signed his letters to Coot "your friend until death." When it became clear that Coot had spent the trader's money on liquor and gambling, Cotton apparently tried to salvage a relationship that was both personal and professional.

As a witness heard it, he told Coot, "I will give you a thousand dollars, and do you come and spend your days with me, and when I die you shall have what I have got."[26] Cotton wanted to put an end to his personal problems by purchasing his companion—truly a slave trader's solution.

The traders' letters to one another are full of phrases like "the traders tell me" or "the traders say," and if the recountings that follow are any indication, in the time they spent together the men in the slave trade talked mostly about business.[27] There was plenty to talk about: bank loans had to be repaid and the interstate money market considered; the prices of sugar and cotton had to be tracked; debts had to be collected and overhead costs reckoned. The records left behind by the traders are full of predictions, obligations, collections, and daily accounts. They were experts at imagining the economy: interest rates, crop yields, and slave sales interacted in their heads, suggesting the revealed principles of a wider market whose mysterious workings they tried to map and predict. More than anything, the records of traders, like those of John White, are filled with prices given and gained for slaves in the market.

SEEING DOUBLE

A trader had to be able to imagine two sales at once when he looked at a slave: the highest price he was willing to pay for a slave, and the lowest price he was willing to take in an eventual sale. Between these two prices lay his livelihood. That sort of double vision was easy enough for the traders who bought and sold in a single market, where information was maximal, risks were minimal, and profits could be sliced out of narrow margins and quick turnover. But other traders had to think a slave all the way through the market, to see themselves as a buyer in Richmond in March and a seller in New Orleans in May. There were various commercial arrangements designed to narrow the speculative distance between the first sale and the second. The most common was brokerage—matching a buyer to a seller without assuming a direct risk by buying the slave. Another way around the problem was to seal the second sale first by buying according to an order—sometimes a list—from a specific buyer.[28] Interstate traders, however, generally solved the problem by forming firms, going to slave sales, and writing letters to their partners about what they saw. To slave trader William Powell in Mississippi from his partner in Virginia: "In compliance with your request I have been making inquiries in regard to the prices of Negroes in this section and have attended some sales lately." To trader William Finney in Virginia from his partner in Alabama: "There are men selling here for any price almost, tho things is perfectly flat in New Orleans." Again to Finney from Alabama, this time one year later: "The quotations you sent from Richmond are too strong for this market, they leave but little room for profits."[29]

To limit the amount of information they had to send back and forth, the traders packed people into price categories according to gender, age, height, weight, and skin color.[30] Presiding over these matrices of physical comparison and price were the type of categories listed on a circular distributed by the Richmond firm Dickinson and Hill in 1860 (and preserved in the papers of slave trader William Finney): "Extra men, No. 1 Men; Second Rate or Ordinary Men; Extra Girls, No. 1 Girls, Second rate or Ordinary Girls." By claiming to represent a totality of human attributes without referring directly to any of them, the traders' tables fixed people in a system of comparison which was located solely in the slave market. The traders used these made-up market categories to compare physically different people to one another. "I saw fellows sold at Salisbury for 350 dollars, all others in proportion," wrote slave trader Tyre Glen to his partner. The phrase "in proportion" also appears in a letter received by slave trader William Crowe: "Likely tall field fellows young & lively is bringing Heare from $1025 to $1050, likely tall field girls no one has been selling Heare from $800 & I think from what the traders tell me women & Children, Boys & Girls & Middle Aged Men sell fully in proportion." The price circular sent around by Dickinson and Hill made a similar comparison of categories: "Our market is still dull, but very few No. 1 Negroes offering, 2nd & 3rd rate hard to sell . . . If you have any No. 1 Negroes on hand we would advise sending them in as they are wanted now."[31] In the traders' tables, human beings were fully fungible: any slave, anywhere, could be compared to any other, anywhere else. That was commodification: the distant and different translated into money value and resolved into a single scale of relative prices, prices that could be used to make even the most counter-intuitive comparisons—between the body of an old man and a little girl, for example, or between the muscular arm of a field hand and the sharp eye of a seamstress, or, as many nineteenth-century critics of slavery noted, between a human being and a mule.[32]

Through their commodity categories the traders could envision, track, communicate, and respond to subtle shifts in demand that occurred hundreds of miles from the places they did their buying. But the traders' categories kept hanging them up: what did a No. 1 man look like? what exactly made a woman "likely"? To introduce a greater degree of precision to their categories, the traders used examples: "say such as Shaxwalter"; "that is as likely as Aaron Shafer, Nelson Hatton, or Nathan Williams"; "Girls like Edmony & Margaret"; "Fully $100 better Girl than Margaret."[33] To get their point across the traders used names that summoned up individual slaves whom they had both known and conversed with as well as sold: they referred to a human history hidden behind the numbers they recorded in their account books. Good business required the traders to recognize the individuality of the people they hoped to turn into prices.

Indeed, the traders' speculations on the humanness of their slaves began even before the slaves entered the trade. Jacob Stroyer remembered that the Louisiana trader who bought his sisters made an immediate reckoning of his risks as he decided whether or not to allow the slaves he bought to see their families for a last time. Only "those who did not show any unwillingness to go" were allowed this slender privilege, Stroyer remembered. Those who seemed unwilling went to jail for safekeeping until they were carried south.[34] The traders knew that for the slaves this time meant the chance to gather belongings and say goodbye, and they rationed it as an inducement to insure a smooth passage into the trade. To the same end, the traders made promises to the slaves about future benefits if they did not resist the trade. Henry Bibb remembered the small-time speculators who bought him in Kentucky unctuously promising not to chain him or sell him to a New Orleans trader if he would go quietly and cooperate when they tried to sell him. Likewise, the Georgia trader who bought Isaac Williams, George Strawden, and Henry Banks in Virginia assured them that Georgia was not as bad as they had heard and promised that he would try to find them "as good places" as he could if they would "go without any trouble."[35] This was slave-trader paternalism, a disciplinary speculation on the feelings of the people they bought. The traders forcibly took possession of the time, hopes, and attachments of their slaves and gradually tried to trade them back as obligations.

As they lined their slaves up for the trip to market, the traders gave their estimations of their slaves' character a material shape. When Tyre Glen started south for the 1834 selling season, behind him were thirty slaves: "about sixteen fellows, seven boys, the balance women and girls, except one child . . . twelve fellows in the chain." Sometime between the time he bought the slaves and the time he started south, Glen had decided that the twelve men he chained posed a greater threat than the four he did not. Faced with groups of people they hardly knew, overland traders like Glen began by segregating them by sex. Bound two-by-two along a long length of chain, the men came first; behind them, unbound by chains, the women would follow. As John Brown described it, the slave coffle in which he traveled south was "a gang of Negroes, some of whom were handcuffed two and two and fastened to a long chain running between the two ranks. There were also a good number of women and children, but none of these were chained." Charles Ball likewise remembered that the men in his coffle were chained while the women were bound with ropes. Women, the traders believed, were less likely to run away than men.[36]

Sella Martin described a slave coffle as his mother had described it to him: "A long row of men chained two-and-two together, called the 'coffle,' and numbering about thirty persons, was the first to march forth . . . then came the quiet slaves—that is, those who were tame in spirit and degraded; then came the unmarried women, or those without children; after these came the children who were able to walk; and following them came mothers with their infants and young children in their arms."[37] The coffle Martin described was a series of identities arranged along the chain for easy supervision: those who seemed resistant followed by those who did not; those who had no attachments followed by those who were judged unlikely to leave family members or dependents behind to run away. The coffles were a reverse image of the commodity categories by which the traders selected their slaves—speculations on the very human attachments it was the traders' business to destroy.

By estimating and appropriating the emotions of the people they bought, the traders were cutting costs—saving on jail fees, boarding expenses, and perhaps even the price of manacles and links in a chain. They were using their slaves' humanity to protect their investment in human property. But as well as protecting their investments, the traders were protecting their lives. On the way to market, the traders were vastly outnumbered. Three to five men would oversee coffles that sometimes ran upwards of a hundred slaves; two traders' agents would find themselves aboard a flatboat with "twenty-six grown Negro men"; thirteen sailors and three overseers would be on board a ship that carried 135 slaves. To keep their slaves from plotting revolt, trying to escape, or even from getting to know one another, many traders forbade conversation among their slaves. Even the most innocuous word among the slaves in Charles Ball's coffle drew an angry response from the trader.[38]

The traders' worries increased as darkness fell. Many traders spent long nights sleeping in remote areas or aboard an ocean-going vessel, surrounded by their slaves. To protect themselves from their property, shipboard traders locked the slaves in the hold overnight. Similarly, those who took their slaves overland often made them sleep in their chains.[39] Other traders kept an even closer watch. One of the duties of William Cotton's hired assistant, Thomas Coot, was to "sleep in the same room with the slaves in order that none of them might run away." So, too, for Alexander Hagan, who slept in an open house with a group of slaves when he was a salaried employee of his slave trader brother, John Hagan.[40]

Distance reduced the risks for those who traveled south with the slaves. The farther slaves went in the trade, the more difficult it became for them to return to their homes or escape to freedom. A Kentucky slave trader recalled that the practice along the Ohio River was to keep the slaves "chained together two by two until we got to the mouth of the Ohio River, when they were unchained." Beyond the point where the Ohio flowed into the Mississippi there was slavery on both sides of the boat, and the slaves could be safely set to exercising on the deck. The man who carried Charles Ball south from Maryland kept his slaves chained all the way to South Carolina, where he told them, as Ball remembered it, to "give up all hope of returning to the places of our nativity, as it would be impossible for us to pass through the states of North Carolina and Virginia without being taken up and sent back." Soon after entering South Carolina, the coffle's chain was removed (at a cost, Ball remembered, of two dollars) and sold (for seven dollars). Tyre Glen, who hired an assistant "with the privilege of dismissing him at any time," made a similar estimate of the decreasing likelihood that his slaves would be able to escape. Glen's plan was to keep the assistant as far south as Columbus, Georgia, where he would sell some of his slaves, and then continue westward to Montgomery, Alabama, without the man's help.[41] For the traders, the trip south was broken into a series of speculations about its effect upon the slaves—estimations that balanced the cost in time and money of close supervision and tight discipline against the daily attenuation of the slaves' hopes as they were driven ever further from home.

As well as protecting themselves from attack, the traders had to protect their property from devaluation, which, from the traders' perspective, meant avoiding pregnancies and sexually transmitted disease. Henry Bibb and John Brown both remembered that men and women in the pens were separated for the night, and a visitor to a Richmond slave market described the jail as "a long, two-story brick house, the lower part fitted up for men and the second story for women."[42] Whatever contact there was between men and women in the pens was supposed to be limited to the daylight hours, at meals, on breaks between shifts against the wall, and under the traders' watchful eyes. Life aboard the slave ship *Creole* as described by its mate was similarly organized: "After putting to sea the Negro women were put in the afterhold of the vessel, and the men in the forehold, between these were stored the cargo of boxes of manufactured tobacco. The men were allowed to come on deck night and day if they wished, but it was the rule to whip the Negro men if they went in the hold with the women." Aboard the *Creole*, sex was apparently (and, it turned out, wrongly) deemed a greater threat than slave rebellion. Gonorrhea, according to slaveholding commonplace, was a disease "generally contracted among Negroes *en route* who are brought for sale." A number of different traders had their slaves aboard the ship, and segregating them by sex was a way to keep one slaveholder's slaves from diminishing the value of another's by passing a disease—or starting a pregnancy.[43]

Such careful attention sometimes placed traders in close proximity to their property. When slaves pulled up lame or got sick along the road, they traveled with the traders. Samuel Mitchell, who traveled south at the head of a coffle of eighty slaves, remembered that "some of the women were permitted occasionally to ride, but none of the men, unless sick." Likewise, aboard ships and steamboats, sick slaves were taken from the deck to their owner's state rooms. "His attention to her was as good as if she had been a white lady," remembered a traveler aboard a Mississippi River steamer of a slave trader and his slave.[44]

But consider again what Samuel Mitchell said about the coffle he led south: "some of the women were permitted occasionally to ride." Or what Zephaniah Gifford remembered of the *Creole:* two of the women "remained in the cabin on the voyage from Richmond to New Orleans." Those careful phrasings may have bridged brutal truths.[45] Compare those quotations to John Brown's memory of the experience of a woman in Starling Finney's coffle: "she was forced to get up into the wagon with Finney who brutally ill-used her, and permitted his companions to treat her in the same manner." Or Brown's comments on the practice of Theophilus Freeman's pen: "the youngest and handsomest females were set apart as the concubines of the masters." Or William Wells Brown's memory of his slave-trader master Walker and an enslaved woman named Cynthia: "On the first night we were aboard the steamboat, he directed me to put her into a stateroom he had provided for her, apart from the other slaves. I had seen too much of the workings of slavery not to know what this meant. I accordingly watched him into his stateroom, and listened to hear what passed between them. I heard him make his base offers and her reject them . . . but I foresaw too well what the result must be."[46]

The traders' rapes are the most extreme example of the brutal recognition of their slaves' humanity—the feelings and vulnerability upon which they registered their own violent power—that made up the traders' daily business. Indeed, in the day-to-day practice of the trade, traders' speculations on their slaves' humanity represented less a troubling philosophical contradiction—property treated as person—than a way of exploiting and disciplining slaves. The slave traders did not ignore or abolish the humanity of the people they categorized and compared and bought and sold. They used it. To protect themselves and their investment, the traders had to imagine the world from their slaves' perspective: to see geography and time and human connections and desire as their slaves did and to insinuate their surveillance and insert their discipline in every detail of the slaves' existence. It was amidst this constant invigilation and threat of violation that slaves in the trade came to know one another.

THE SLAVE COMMUNITY IN THE SLAVE TRADE

As the traders gathered the slaves they intended to sell, they brought together groups of people who were unknown to one another. Whether they were from all over Virginia, as were the slaves in the coffle that carried John Brown south, or from all over the South, as were the slaves Solomon Northup met in New Orleans, the slaves in the trade had been uprooted from the places and people that had defined their past identities.[47] In the weeks and sometimes months between sale into the trade and resale by a trader, slaves built the broken pieces of old communities and identities into new ones. Like the communities they had left behind, these communities were shaped within the framework of the very structures they opposed—a back-and-forth relation which fused power and resistance into a single process. The traders' fears, incentives, and threats—themselves responses to anticipated resistance—were woven into the very fabric of connection that bound slaves in the trade to one another.

For some, the sale into the trade was more than they could bear. Separated from the world that had given their lives meaning, some slaves were overwhelmed by the traders' brutality, the numbing privation of the slow southward march, and the terrifying contingency of lives put up for sale. To the social death experienced by those torn from their histories and identities and the physical death they faced in the killing fields of the lower South must be added the psychic deaths—the "soul murder"—that left many of the trade's victims with little will to resist.[48]

Within the narrow parameters afforded them by the watchful traders, many others struggled on. The slim favors the traders granted the "trustworthy" provided some slaves a chance to say good-bye or to try to carry a piece of the past into the trade. Those who were given the opportunity took the time to pack things to carry south with them: clothes, shoes, bed rolls, blankets, and perhaps a memento of their past lives. The clothes that William Grose's wife carried eight miles to give him as his coffle left for the south were a material reminder of the family and identity he had been forced to leave behind.[49] The Reverend William Troy portrayed the cruel rapidity of the sale of Martha Fields by invoking the image of her left-behind possessions. Fields, he wrote, "was taken early one morning, without time to get her clothes, hurried off to Richmond and sold to the highest bidder." Moses Grandy's memory of being parted from his wife was similarly mixed with the memory of the change he had in his pocket when he met the trader at the head of her coffle: "I asked leave to shake hands with her which he refused, but said I might stand at a distance and talk with her. My heart was so full that I could say very little . . . I gave her the little money I had in my pocket, and bade her farewell. I have never seen or heard of her from that day to this. I loved her as I loved my life."[50]

Many slaves who entered the trade knew they were being closely watched for signs of discontent. For some, the traders' spot estimations of their character offered opportunities for escape. Isaac Williams reminded a trader of his good behavior on entering the trade as he plotted his exit: "I came without any trouble and will *go* without any trouble," he told the trader. And when the trader, perhaps lulled by the slave's seeming pliability, left the gate to the pen open, that was exactly what Williams did. Sold to a trader, Edward Hicks similarly remembered imagining the world from the perspective of the man who had just bought him and then shaping his behavior to manipulate the trader's way of evaluating a slave's probability of flight: "I being so obedient, he thought I wouldn't run, but I determined to run if I could, for I thought that if I got to New Orleans I was at the shutting up place."[51] Lucy Delany's mother dutifully gained permission from a trader to return home "to gather her few belongings." When she entered the house, however, the older woman clasped her daughter to her breast and told her "that she was going to run away, and would buy me as soon as possible." Indeed, Delany's mother very quickly put that promise into effect: before long, Delany heard her mother had "made her escape." Like Williams, Hicks, and Delany's mother, Edmund must have seemed pliable enough when slave trader James White allowed him to go for his baggage accompanied only by a slave belonging to the trader. Once he was out of the trader's sight, however, Edmund gathered up his things and disappeared.[52] The escapees, however, were few; soon after sale, most slaves were bound into a coffle or loaded aboard a ship, where the opportunities to resist the traders were narrow and a misstep could be deadly.

In the coffles, slaves immediately set about the task of estimating one another—making social connections that could help sustain them and avoiding those that might compromise them. Building accurate accounts out of limited information was as much a problem for the slaves as the traders, and much of the initial information slaves had about one another was visual. A lot, for instance, depended on the way a slave came into the trade. The Reverend Alexander Helmsley drew a distinction between those who had to be forced, crying, into the traders' wagons and "some among them [who] have their minds so brutalized by the actions of slavery that they do not feel so acutely as others."[53] Helmsley, that is, retraced the same shortcut used by many of the traders when he estimated slaves as pliant or resistant based upon how they entered the trade.

Solomon Northup followed a similar path in his description of Eliza, a woman he met in a Washington, D.C., slave pen: "The woman . . . was arrayed in silk, with rings upon her fingers, and golden ornaments suspended from her ears. Her air and manners, the correctness and propriety of her language—all showed, evidently, that she had some-time stood above the common level of a slave. She seemed to be amazed at finding herself in such a place as that. It was plainly a sudden and unexpected turn of fortune that had brought her there. Filling the air with her complainings she was hustled, with the children and myself into the cell."[54] What is remarkable about Northup's later account is the density of the visual imagery he used in his initial portrayal of Eliza: her clothes, her carriage, her countenance. All of these were keys to esti-mating the identity of an unknown woman. It must, of course, be remembered that when Northup wrote his account of Eliza he was distant in time and space from the slave pen where he met her. But, no matter how he refigured his history in the meantime, Northup did his work in the familiar medium of the past: he described a way of seeing. And for Northup, ways of seeing were ways of surviving.

The Solomon Northup of *Twelve Years a Slave* was a deeply preju-diced person, certain of his own rectitude, suspicious and disdainful of most of his fellow slaves. He had grown to adulthood as a free person of color in New York before being kidnapped by slave traders and then sold to New Orleans, and held as a slave for twelve years until he managed to send word and arrange for legal action against his owner. His estimates of the difference between his own origins and those of his fellow slaves are inscribed on every page of his narrative: he comments on their table manners and intelligence, on their obsequity and their illiteracy. But behind all of Northup's disparaging descriptions of the character and capability of his fellow slaves is a single question often figured in visual terms: who could be trusted? Mary ("A tall, lithe girl, of a most jetty black, was listless and apparently indifferent. Like many of the class, she scarcely knew there was a word such as freedom")?

Lethe ("She was of an entirely different character. She had long straight hair, and bore much more the appearance of an Indian than a Negro woman. She had sharp and spiteful eyes and continually gave utterance to the language of hatred and revenge")? Or Robert ("I was hand-cuffed to a large yellow man, quite stout and fleshy, with a countenance expressive of the utmost melancholy . . . To this man I became much attached. We could sympathize and understand one another")?[55] Northup's descriptions are clearly racialized: Lethe and Robert have faces and interior lives; Mary, apparently, has neither. The racialized descriptions that punctuate *Twelve Years a Slave* may reflect Northup's pride in his northern origins and legal freedom, or the prejudices of his white amanuensis and abolitionist audience; or they may even hold the key to understanding why it took Northup so long to overcome his isolation and send word for help.[56] But whatever the origin of the specific descriptions, their general intent is clear: in the outward appearance of the slaves he met in the trade, Northup was seeking information about their inward relation to the system he was trying to escape.

Like the traders, slaves entering the coffles had to make mortally important estimations of people they had never met before. And like those made by the traders, the estimations slaves made of one another were made in a hall of mirrors where the standard signs of resistance or complaisance were well-known and manipulable. What looked like obvious resignation to the onlooking Northup might actually have been calculated appearance; behavior like Eliza's signified a resistant spirit to Northup, but it might have struck another slave as an insupportable arrogance. The initial anonymity that accompanied slaves into the trade, the anonymity reflected in Northup's largely visual reckonings of his fellow slaves, was edged with the suspicions of people for whom a mistaken confidence could be life-threatening. The community of slaves in the trade had to be carefully built; and in such an uncertain environment, not even Solomon Northup could afford to navigate by first impressions alone.

The circumstances under which slaves in the trade came to know one another were controlled by the traders. In the first days of the trade, the chain that bound them two-by-two, wrist-to-wrist and sometimes ankle-to-ankle, articulated many slaves' only connection to one another. When Charles Ball wrote about his first days in the trade, he specifically described only one other person: the man to whom he was chained. John Parker was equally clear in his memory of those to whom he was chained on his way to market. Between Norfolk and Richmond, he remembered, he was chained to an "old man" who "was kind to me, he made my weight of the chain as light as he could. He treated me kindly because I was brokenhearted on leaving my mother. He was the only human being who was interested in me." On the way south from Richmond, Parker was chained to a boy named Jeff. "He was smaller than I was," Parker remembered, "had never been away from his mother, blubbered and cried, until I kicked him to make him keep still." Parker continued: "As my cuffing only made him cry more I soon took pity on him. There was another boy larger than either Jeff or myself. One night this big boy took Jeff's dinner, just because he was bigger and stronger . . . I was on him like a hawk, punching and clawing him until he was glad to release Jeff's dinner."[57] Parker remembered a whole series of social relations—first filial then bullying then protective—lived across that slave-coffle chain.

Sex segregation likewise shaped slaves' experience of the trade. The slaves that Ball and Parker remembered from the coffles—the faces they gave to the trade—were male. Similarly, John Brown remembered the response to a rape in his coffle as strictly gendered: "Our women talked about this very much, and many of them cried and said it was a great shame." In many traders' coffles and pens, whatever communication there was between enslaved men and women occurred in secret. Henry Bibb spoke to his wife under the cover of darkness after she had been sexually assaulted and beaten by a trader who threatened to sell her child if she did not submit.[58] Like Brown's story, Bibb's reveals both the vulnerability and isolation of slaves in the trade and the fragile network of support they used to counteract the traders' power—vulnerable threads of connection slaves made beyond the limit of the traders' visual field.

As well as the bond that was articulated by the chain, slaves in the coffles shared a common culture. Many observers were struck by the fact that as slaves departed for the South they were often singing. Former slave Peter Bruner remembered that the slave traders whipped the slaves to make them sing as they left, and Sella Martin explained that the songs were meant to "prevent among the crowd of Negroes who usually gather on such occasions, any expression of sorrow for those who are being torn away from them." But, Martin continued, "the Negroes, who have very little hope of seeing those again who are dearer to them than life, and who are weeping and wailing over the separation, often turn the song thus demanded into a farewell dirge." The Reverend William Troy reported such an incident to an interviewer in the 1850s. A coffle of slaves, he remembered, "aroused me by singing about nine at night, passing my father's residence, singing, bidding farewell to all their friends."[59] These songs, then, were memorials for the communities the trade had destroyed.

But they were also the substance of the connections that slaves in the trade made with one another. As they sang songs they knew in common, slaves in the trade came to know one another. Songs could remind Christian slaves of transcendence and resistance and secular slaves of the deep structure of culture and commonality they shared with the slaves they met in the coffle.[60] Indeed, many of the songs slaves in the coffle must have sung—"Bound to Go," "Good-Bye, Brother," "Lay This Body Down," for example—were themselves accounts of imagined journeys which spun together temporal and spiritual imagery of loss and travel.[61] And even as their content helped to prepare slaves for the journey ahead, their meaning was not exhausted by that content: in singing these songs, slaves began to transform the coffle into a community.

Slaveholders, at least, sometimes saw an intention of subversion behind these songs. Never more clearly so than in Edenton, North Carolina, in December 1852. The town, William Pettigrew reported to a slaveholding correspondent, was still full of talk of a rebellion thought to have been planned by Josiah Collins's slaves in October. Those who had been implicated had been sold to a trader and gathered into a coffle when they broke out in song. "The town has been much shocked," Pettigrew wrote: "at the unbecoming manner in which Mr. C's Negroes Negroes [sic: perhaps Pettigrew was feeling surrounded] conducted themselves while there. Some of them were in prison while some were not: the former spent much of their time in singing and dancing, until Hempton the landlord threatened to confine them in the dungeon unless they were more silent; which they obeyed. One of their favorite songs was 'James Crack Corn I don't Care.' Their object was said to set their master at defiance, and to show their willingness to leave him . . . The good people of the place were rejoiced when they left, feeling apprehension of the insubordinate influence such conduct might have on their Negroes."[62]

There, reflected in the mirror image of a slaveholder's fears, is the importance of the songs slaves in the coffles sang as they traveled south. Commonly known songs could be quickened with the specific intentions of a new community. Whether they memorialized lives left behind, threatened those who carried them away, promised eventual salvation, or bemoaned present suffering, the songs slaves sang in the coffles were reminders of the slaves' cultural commonality and similar condition; the songs were the raw material of community. Seen this way, they represent less a timeless cultural commonality than the real-time ritual animation of an existing form with the substance of a new community: it was in the singing as much as the song that slaves in the trade came to know one another.[63]

The daily routine of the trade—traveling, eating, sleeping, and so on—deepened this commonality into personal familiarity. Charles Ball and Solomon Northup both gave disparaging accounts of the vigor with which other slaves in the coffle ate. For Ball, the voracious appetites of two women were evidence of their capitulation to slavery: "They appeared quite contented, and evinced no repugnance to setting out the next morning for their master's plantation. They were among the order of people who never look beyond the present day; and so long as they had plenty of victuals in this kitchen, they did not reflect upon the cotton field." For Northup, a description of the table manners of his fellow travelers provided the occasion to express his own race-tinged snobbery: "The use of plates was dispensed with, and their sable fingers took the place of knives and forks." For Winnifred Martin, the slave trade was shocking not for its manners but for its morals. Her son, Sella Martin, described her experience of the trade as she had described it to him. "Her own circle was small, and, for slaves, select," and so she was "sickened to the heart" by what she saw in the slave trade: the traders' lies and sexual predation and "the vice which was inseparable from crowding men and women together."[64] On the face of things, these quotations provide more evidence of the fact that a community of slaves in the trade was something that had to be built: the slave coffles were suffused with the same tensions and prejudices of gender, race, and sexuality that characterize many groups of people. By judging others, at least in retrospect, Ball, Northup, and Martin defined themselves.

Evident in their criticism, however, is also a trace of a dense communal life made up of shared time, common meals, and intimate proximity. In the interstices of the trade—out of the traders' sight, perhaps, or after dark, or when the coffles had traveled so far south that the traders relaxed their guard—slaves shared a common life that began to cut across the grain of the traders' silencing and sex-segregating discipline. Whether the substance of that life was social or sexual, whether, indeed, it was sympathetic or antagonistic, slaves were not alone in the trade. Through identification or enmity, they began to define communal identities out of a common life.

More than anything, the community of slaves in the trade seems to have been forged out of conversation. When Solomon Northup looked back on the time he spent in a Richmond slave pen awaiting shipment to New Orleans, he marked a moment with the memory of conversation: "while we were learning the history of each other's wretchedness, Eliza was seated in the corner by herself." And the content of these conversations, if the narratives are any guide at all, was largely autobiographical. As John Brown put it about a group of slaves joined to his Virginia slave coffle: "I soon learnt that they had been purchased in different places, and were for the most part strangers to one another and to the Negroes in the coffle." Even Solomon Northup, whose narrative represented other slaves in such powerfully visual terms, did not waste much time before building on his first impression. Of Robert, the man to whom he was chained in the trader's coffle, the man whose appearance so impressed him, Northup wrote, "it was not long before we became acquainted with each other's history."[65]

Robert, Northup related, had been born free in Cincinnati, kidnapped, and sold into slavery. Indeed, like Robert, most characters introduced along the way in ex-slaves' accounts of the trade came with a story, and those stories came from the time that slaves spent together in the coffles and slave pens, talking and getting to know one another. John Brown learned, for instance, that Critty had been forced to take a second husband when her first marriage did not produce any children, and that her owner had sold her to a trader when it became apparent that her unwillingness or infertility could not be overcome by his social engineering. Critty's identity (and even the cause of her death) in Brown's account was a reflection of the story she had told him: "her anguish was intense, and within four days from the time I saw her first, she died of grief."[66] As separated lovers, grieving parents, or orphaned children, as resigned victims or angry rebels, slaves in the trade made themselves known by telling their stories. During the weeks they spent in the ship holds, in coffles, and in the slave pens, the once anonymous slaves built a network of mutual recognition through communal remembering and retelling of the past.

Slaves in the trade, it should be added, did not self-consciously set out to overcome their isolation by forming "a slave community." The shape of the communities that developed in the slave coffles and pens were contingent upon the daily connections the slaves made to one another—connections that in the first instance might have been spiritual, biographical, cultural, moral, or sexual. And yet out of these everyday interactions, these contingent communities, some slaves managed to make alliances that helped them resist the trade. When the escaped slave Isaac Williams was interviewed in Canada, he remembered two of the men he had met in a Virginia dealer's pen: George Strawden, whose story Williams did not relate, and Henry Banks, who had been a fugitive for several months before being recaptured and sold into the coffle where he met Williams. When Williams ran away, he went with the man whose account of himself suggested a history of resistance, and he left the other man behind. "We were afraid to let George know," Williams explained, "for fear he would betray us."[67] Without a story to answer for his appearance of complicity with the trader (or perhaps his simple opacity), Strawden could not be trusted.

Amidst all of the deception and uncertainty that surrounded slaves' entry into the trade, it was hard to know whom to trust: subversion had to be carefully plotted and resistance came at the cost of suspicion. Charles Ball's caution in plotting to escape is a good example. When his coffle stopped to rest at a plantation in South Carolina, Ball noticed that the enslaved foreman overseeing work in the field where they were staying was wearing a piece of linen beneath his rough shirt. When asked about it, the foreman replied that the linen stanched wounds that had been inflicted after he had stolen some food. When Ball wrote his narrative, he set off the man's autobiographical story—the story the man told him as they talked—with quotation marks that span eleven pages, and then shifted quickly to an evaluation of the man's character: "his spirit was so broken and subdued that he was ready to suffer and bear all his hardships: not, indeed, without complaining, but without attempting to resist his oppressors or escape from their power."

As Ball later related it, "I saw him often whilst I remained at this place, and ventured to tell him once, that if I had a master who would abuse me as he had abused him, I would run away." Ball did not specify why saying so was "venturing," though he noted that he did so only once. Perhaps it was the simplest of conversational transgressions that led Ball to use such a word, a crossing over into impoliteness to insure that his own reputation was not flecked with the resignation of the man's beaten resentment. But Ball may have been venturing onto even more dangerous ground, raising the topic of running away as a concrete possibility rather than as a figure of psychological independence. The man's response was concrete enough: "I have heard there is a place called Philadelphia," he said, "where black people are all free, but I do not know which way it lies, nor what road I should take to get there; and if I knew the way how could I hope to get there?"[68] We may not trust that, thirty years after the fact, Ball remembered things exactly as they were said. But we can perhaps trust that he rendered the logic of conversation as he remembered it: he saw the man's scars, listened to his story, and they talked about running away.

Shortly after, on the night that he was sold—in the same kitchen with the two young women whose appetite he had so disdained—Ball met a man from the Northern Neck of Virginia, near the place of his own birth. "We soon formed an acquaintance," Ball remembered, "and sat up nearly all night." The man told Ball that he had often thought of running away, but knew the way only as far as Virginia, and was afraid that he would not be able to get to Philadelphia, "which he regarded as the only place in which he could be safe from pursuit of his master." Ball, who had lived in Maryland, had only an imperfect knowledge of the area "north of Baltimore," but "told him that I had heard that if a black man could reach any part of Pennsylvania, he would be beyond the reach of his pursuers." The man responded by telling Ball that he was planning to leave as soon as the corn in the fields was ripe enough to be roasted but before it had been taken in. He planned to travel only at night and to spend his days hidden in the woods. Ball spoke again of the North: "I advised him as well as I could as to the best means of reaching the state of Pennsylvania, but was not able to give him very definite instructions."[69] By that point, conversation had become conspiracy.

Ball's conversations allow us to eavesdrop on an underground network, set up and quickly dismantled, which circulated fragments of information about freedom and the North among those who could be trusted. And the differences between Ball's renderings of the two conversations hint at the signs of admission to such a community. When Ball mentioned running away to the beaten foreman, the man demurred, and the conversation ended with the man's vague knowledge of Philadelphia. In relating the conversation he had in the kitchen, on the other hand, Ball remembered the man from the Northern Neck broaching the topic of escape. Ball responded by saying what he knew of the North (more than he remembered telling the foreman), and then the other man related the specifics of his plan. The conversation ended with Ball providing "as well as I could" details about the North. Ball's memoir should not be mistaken for a literal rendering of what happened in the kitchen. But the structure of the discussion—the initial connection based on conversation and then the back-and-forth exchange of increasingly dangerous information—is something that can be read from Ball's subsequent account. After all, Ball had a good reason to remember the conversation: "This man certainly communicated to me the outlines of the plan which I afterwards put into execution and by which I gained my liberty."[70]

Solomon Northup's story of conspiracy was similarly structured. He remembered sitting at the bow of the slave ship talking to another slave named Arthur, who "said, and I agreed with him, that death was far less terrible than the living prospect that was before us." The broad topic of antislavery had been raised, and Northup outlined the steps by which it was built into a plan: "for a long time we talked of our children, our past lives, and of the probabilities of escape." That much was a history of the abuses of slavery and the desire for freedom—the same talk that Charles Ball had shared with the foreman—and it was conversation, not conspiracy. And then: "Obtaining possession of the brig was suggested by one of us." Once Northup and Arthur had crossed that line, their lives depended upon their actions and they proceeded with great care. "At length, with much care, Robert was gradually made acquainted with our intentions."[71]

Carefully, suspiciously ("There was not another slave we dared trust," wrote Northup), some slaves in the trade built everyday connections into conspiracies of resistance. Though Northup's plan was never put into action because Robert was soon infected with smallpox, other slaves in the trade were more successful. Beside southern roads (near Charleston in 1799, on the National Road in 1820, in rural Kentucky in 1829, in Virginia in 1834) or aboard slave ships (on a Mississippi flatboat in 1826 or at sea on the *Decatur* in the same year, and aboard the *Lafayette* in 1830), slaves who had met one another in the trade collectively and violently revolted against the traders.[72]

Perhaps most notable was the revolt of the slaves aboard the *Creole* in 1841. When the ship set out from Norfolk at the end of October, a shipment of tobacco destined for the Bahamas and 135 slaves (belonging to at least five different traders) destined for the slave market in New Orleans were packed beneath the deck. In the cabins above traveled thirteen seamen, three slave traders, and the captain's family. Around nine in the evening on November 7 the mate heard a suspicious noise in the hold where the women were kept, and he awakened one of the traders to check on the slaves. The trader lit a lamp and descended into the hold, where Madison Washington awaited him. There was a struggle; Washington slipped free and fought his way onto the deck. Somewhere, another slave fired a pistol, and at that moment Washington called out for the other slaves to join him. Eighteen rushed up from the hold and, as the ship's crew and slave traders ran onto the deck, set upon their captors with guns and knives. One white man, a slave trader named Hewell, was killed; the severely wounded captain, the rest of the crew, and the traders and white passengers saved themselves only by climbing onto the ship's rigging. As the mate fled into the sails, he thought he saw the slaves cutting the dead slave trader's throat before throwing him overboard.

Nineteen slaves, all male, took possession of the *Creole* that night. When the whites had been coaxed out of the sails, they were locked in the hold, where, in the style of the slave trade, they were forbidden to speak to one another. The other slaves, about 115 of them, were likewise locked in the hold. The leaders' initial plan was to sail for Liberia; but realizing the shortness of their supplies, they settled on sailing for Nassau. Some among them had heard of the story of the slaves aboard the *Formosa* who had been set free by the British when the ship ran aground in the Bahamas the previous year.[73]

Apparent in the *Creole* rebellion are the "infrapolitics" of the slave community in the trade—the generally invisible processes by which a group of strangers formed themselves into a resistant collective. In the week they had been at sea, nineteen slaves belonging to five different slave traders, most of them certainly strangers to one another, had managed to trust one another with their lives. Though it is ultimately unclear whether the nineteen rebels had tried to keep their plans secret from the others, tried unsuccessfully to convince them to join, or even, as the mate suspected, "been appointed by the others as chiefs," it is clear that their eventual action emerged, one way or another, out of a negotiation with all of the slaves in the hold. Indeed, it is hard to imagine that some among the 115 or so other slaves on the boat did not notice and help hide the fact that nineteen of the slaves were planning a revolt. Nor were the other slaves on the *Creole* the only slaves who might have been complicit with the nineteen slaves who took over the ship. The plan those nineteen men put into action was shaped around their broader knowledge of the Atlantic world—of the African colony of Liberia and the fate of a specific shipment of slaves that had run aground in the Caribbean the year before—a knowledge that must have been the product of the same underground network used by Charles Ball in plotting his escape. The information the slaves had received was good: in Nassau, all of those who had not participated in the revolt were allowed to go free almost immediately, and soon after the nineteen men who had seized the ship were freed as well. In the following days, when the traders incongruously encountered their former slaves walking in the streets of Nassau, they tried to coax them onto another ship bound for New Orleans. When that did not work, they took refuge in a more reassuring version of their business, dragging their ledgers of people and prices into court and suing their insurers for recovery of their losses.[74]

The formation of community in the slave trade—the creation of networks of support and sometimes resistance among individuals previously unknown to one another—began as something quite different: passing the time, engaging in conversation, offering isolated acts of friendship or succor. Indeed, the creation of "a slave community" in the slave trade was less a self-conscious project than an undesigned process by which a web of interconnection was spun out of a series of everyday interactions. There was nothing automatic about the formation of a community of slaves in the trade—the slave coffles and pens, indeed, were shot through with animosity and suspicion; yet out of these contingent interactions could be fashioned connections that could sustain slaves emotionally and help them circulate important knowledge about the trade. The revolts and runaways, of course, are the most obvious examples of the subversive connections that took root in the interstices of the slave trade. But even for the vast majority of the slaves who did not revolt or run away, the community of slaves in the trade provided information and support that slaves could use to their advantage when the traders began to make their pitches to the buyers who, flush with fantasies about purchasing a slave, entered their yards.

CHAPTER THREE

MAKING A WORLD
OUT OF SLAVES

Sнит in by herself on a dreary day in 1850, Miriam Hilliard found herself daydreaming about slaves. Hilliard's daydream was not about real slaves; it was far removed from the slave pens that were clustered on either side of the French Quarter in New Orleans, from the dusty coffles and cramped boats that carried the slaves southward to the market, from the brutal threats, the stripping, and the questioning hidden behind the walls of a yard into which no white woman of her position would ever pass. Instead, her daydream was about imaginary slaves: "It is raining so furiously this morning that even the belle of the ball's wish ('Oh that I had a million slaves or more, To catch the raindrops as they pour') would be of no avail."[1] This scrap of verse marks a common turn in the fantasy life of the antebellum South: Miriam Hilliard found a solution to her own problems—a fulfillment of her own desires—in the slave market.

For slaveholders like Hilliard, the slave market held dreams of transformative possibilities. Before they entered the slave market or inspected a slave, many slaveholders had well-developed ideas about what they would find there. These ideas had less to do with the real people they would meet in the market, however, than they did with the slaveholders themselves, about the type of people they could become by buying slaves. As they talked about and wrote about buying slaves, slaveholders mapped a world made of slavery. They dreamed of people arrayed in meaningful order by their value as property, of fields full of productive hands and a slave quarter that reproduced itself, of well-ordered households and of mansions where service was swift and polished. They dreamed of beating and healing and sleeping with slaves; sometimes they even dreamed that their slaves would love them. They imagined who they could be by thinking about whom they could buy.

MEN MADE OUT OF SLAVES

Traveling up the Red River in 1854, Edward Russell got into a discussion about slaveholders with a southerner. The southerner claimed to know how well the people of the North lived and assured Russell that in the South people did not live "half so well." "Planters," he continued, "care for nothing but to buy Negroes to raise cotton & raise cotton to buy Negroes." Russell would have been hard pressed to disagree. It was early February, the height of the slave-buying season; he had seen slaves sold at auction only a few days before. On either side of the boat he could see fields now barren of the cotton and sugar that slaves had harvested, packed, and shipped to market in the preceding months.[2] On the geography of those fields was imprinted the landscape of class and masculinity in the antebellum South—lesser men worked the sandy spits of infertile land between the river and joining creeks, greater men cultivated the more fertile land along the banks.[3] Among the white men who owned those fields, many were living lives of constant motion, moving west, gaining a stake, building it into a legacy, dreaming of growing old in a place far removed in space and class from the place of their origin.[4] As they grew up and moved on, these white men marked their progress by buying slaves, slaves whom Russell might have seen along the shore as he and his companion passed upward along the languid river.

Despite the tight circularity—Negroes, cotton, Negroes, cotton—outlined by the man on the boat, it would be a mistake to assume that "Negroes" (or even cotton) meant the same thing to every slaveholder. In the same way that a single automobile today might have vastly different personal meaning to a teenager, a wealthy suburban lawyer, or an isolated elderly person, in the nineteenth century, agricultural slaves (and their produce) had vastly different meanings to the white men of the South. According to their stage in life and social position, slaveholders had a number of ways to talk about slave buying. Imagining that they divined the hidden imperatives of "the market"—anticipating trends, seizing opportunities, and avoiding pitfalls, buying slaves to plant cotton and planting cotton to buy slaves—was indeed one way that white men thought about buying slaves.[5] But there were other ways of buying slaves and other dreams to be bought in the slave market. For many slave buyers, the dream of a never-ending cycle of purchase and profits was more than they could allow themselves to think of when they bought a first slave.

Take John M. Tibeats, for example. In the winter of 1842, in Rapides Parish along the Red River, Tibeats bought a man who was then called Platt but who turned out to be none other than Solomon Northup, the kidnapped free person of color from New York who recorded his experiences in *Twelve Years a Slave*. As Northup remembered him, Tibeats "was a small, crabbed, quick-tempered, spiteful man. He had no fixed residence that I ever heard of, but passed from one plantation to another, wherever he could find employment. He was without standing in the community, not esteemed by white men, nor even respected by slaves."[6] In Tibeats, Northup was describing the mobile and marginal nonslaveholding white men who lived all over the slaveholding South—figures of uncertain reputation and imperfect respectability. For men like Tibeats, buying a first slave was a way of coming into their own in a society that had previously excluded them.

Northup was probably the first slave Tibeats had ever bought, and so the sale marked Tibeats's passage from nonslaveholder to slaveholder. The market in slaves held the promise that nonslaveholders could buy their way into the master class, and the possibility that they might one day own slaves was one of the things that kept nonslaveholders loyal to the slaveholders' democracy in which they lived.[7] But Tibeats remained the holder of an incomplete share in the society of slaveholders—Northup's old owner still held a mortgage on the unpaid portion of Tibeats's new slave. Thus Tibeats was a man suspended in the midst of passage: the mortgage he owed extended his transition from nonslaveholder to slaveholder in a way that allows us to examine in detail the meaning of his movement into the master class.

Tibeats proved to be a hard master: he drove his new slave mercilessly from the break of the day and was still unsatisfied with his progress at its close. The progress Tibeats imagined—his own passage into independence and full citizenship perhaps—may have been more than any slave could have produced, but what finally brought things to a head was a dispute over a keg of nails. Tibeats had a contract to build a corn mill, kitchen, and weaving house for Northup's old master and had put Northup to work helping him (in all probability Solomon Northup was building the building that represented the final portion of his price). One night after work, Tibeats instructed Northup to get a keg of nails from the plantation overseer in the morning and start work on the last building. When Tibeats awoke he found Northup hard at work, but was not satisfied with the size of nails he was using. Northup tried to explain that the overseer had provided the nails, but Tibeats cursed him and went to get a whip. When Tibeats returned, he ordered Northup to strip for a beating. Northup refused, Tibeats attacked him, and Northup fought back, wresting the whip from Tibeat's hand, pinning the white man to the ground, and flogging his owner until his arm ached. And there they stood when the plantation overseer arrived: Tibeats, the owner, picking himself up off the ground; Northup, the slave, warily standing over him with whip in hand. Tibeats rode away to gather a gang, and when he returned he bound Northup—wrists, elbows, and ankles—and prepared to murder him. He would reassert his authority, his property right, over Northup by hanging him.[8] And Northup expected to die: he was a slave on the wrong side of his master, alone, easily disposed of.

Northup, however, did not die that day, for the plantation overseer intervened, reminding Tibeats that Northup was mortgaged to another man: to kill the slave would be to rob that man of his property. While this may have been merely a financial matter for Northup's former owner, for Tibeats it was a matter of the greatest personal urgency. When Tibeats prepared to murder Northup, he was staking his claim to full participation in the regime of racial slavery. He was a white man and a slaveholder: no slave should be allowed to attack him and survive. But Tibeats's assertion of the rights of mastery was constrained by his incomplete transition from nonslaveholder to slaveholder: although he was a white man, he could be publicly beaten by a slave under his command and still find himself on the wrong side of the law, because he was not the slave's owner. For nonslaveholding white men like Tibeats, buying a slave was a way of coming into their own in a society in which they were otherwise excluded from full participation, in which even the independent exercise of the privileges of their whiteness was constrained by the property regime of slavery.[9]

For Jefferson McKinney, a man who inhabited the same world as Tibeats, buying a first slave was an act of conscious self-transformation. In 1856 when he sat down to write to his brother about slave buying, McKinney had spent most of his life as a Red River overseer. He confessed that he had agreed to pay "a big prise," much of it yet to be paid, for the woman he had bought, but he went on to describe what he thought he had gained: "I have bin trying for seberel years to lay up money and find at the end of ebery year that I have sabed but little and probably being in debt will cause me to do without many things that I would otherwise buy and can do without."[10] For McKinney, the purchase of a slave was not the result of past frugality but the guarantor of such in the future. Buying a slave was a question of personal responsibility, and Jefferson McKinney was buying his way into the class of men who were responsible for themselves rather than to others. Jefferson McKinney had bought a slave in the hope of effecting the capitalist transformation of himself. McKinney's was a fantasy of economic independence and bourgeois self-control.

As McKinney transformed himself from dependent laborer to independent debtor, he was making a direct connection between the bodily capacity of the woman he bought and his own happiness that was ordinary by the standards of the antebellum South. "She is sixteen years old in May and is verry wel grone," he wrote to his brother, and on that growth he staked his own future: "If she should breed she wil be cheap in a few years and if she does not she wil always be a deer Negro besides it is getting time that I should begin to think of old age as my hed is past silvering and if eber I can get her paid for and then git a boy I intend then to quit Red River and return to St. Helena or somewhere East up the Mississippi Ribber and settle myself for life . . . Ower years of boyhood was spent together, the bloom of life far distant apart, but I hope it may be gods will for us to spend our aged years together."[11]

Like most first-time slave buyers, McKinney chose a lower price and the promise of reproduction when he decided to buy a young woman instead of a man.[12] The account he gave of his reasons, however, went well beyond the economic. The young woman's body was McKinney's future: he had made a match between her life cycle and his own; her purchase was to underwrite his happy old age; her reproduction—her "breeding" he would have said—held the promise that he and his brother might once again live like a family. For McKinney, the family he had left behind when he had followed his fortunes to the Red River could be put back together in the slave market.

As they made their way upward in southern society, slaveholding white men began to figure their slave buying as an investment, a choice. And as they put it (writing usually to older male relations), their choices were considered ones. "For a young man just commencing in life the best stock in which he can invest capital is, I think, Negro stock." That was Sam Steer in 1818 explaining to his uncle that "prudence" dictated a course apart from the older man's recommendation to buy stock in the Mississippi State Bank. He went on to include a proof of the theorem he proposed: "White Cotton can command from 2[0] to 30 cts per lb: Negroes will yield a much larger income than any Bank dividends."[13] Steer was making an account of himself before his rich uncle, accepting the terms of the older man's advice but revising the conclusion. Yet he was also a calculating young man, estimating his options, figuring the slaves he would buy into a first crop, cashing the crop in on an income. Steer's account of his slave buying to his uncle was also an account of his own financial coming of age.

So, too, for J. H. Lucus, who described his slave buying in a letter he wrote to his father in St. Louis from the South Bend of the Arkansas River. Lucas began with a summation, "I have been quite successful in the investment I made with the money you gave me." The letter continued, detailing how the younger Lucas had "bought five Negroes and entered a small tract at the land office with the view of improving that," how he had parlayed his investment in land and slaves into gain by selling the land and two of the slaves who had cleared it. With the money he had bought a plantation. His account of himself continued: "Since then I bought at auction a boy of 17 years of age for $1100, which makes me including a girl I got by my wife six likely slaves between 14 and 22 years of age all either natives of the country or acclimated by several years stay in this country, all trained to the culture of cotton."[14] "Which makes me," Lucas wrote—a figure of speech perhaps, but a revealing one. These masters of small worlds were men made out of slaves. Writing to older male relatives about the start they had made in the slave market, they translated the productive and reproductive labor of their (bought and imagined) slaves into images of their own upward progress through slaveholding society. These young men were writing themselves into the history of the antebellum social order—the lineal and patriarchal story of how their fathers' world would be reproduced over time and space.[15]

As they did so, they were able to distance themselves from the abject dependence upon their slaves that was so obvious in Jefferson McKinney's hopes that the woman he bought would "breed." The rising white men of the antebellum South wrote about slave buying in a way that showed they had the ability to wait or the wherewithal to move, depending on the deal they could make. They were not the type of men who got caught paying a "big prise." Rather, they bided their time and kept track of the market. They speculated. When James Copes was thinking about buying slaves, for example, he wrote to his brother to find out whether New Orleans would be a good place to buy in the spring. "There is a prospect of getting some this winter," he wrote during another year's speculation, "but they are not all young . . . and they will come very high, for the traders have been after them some time ago." Similarly, W. H. Yos wrote to his business partner that he had decided to buy only after careful consideration: "it seems to be a universal opinion here that they will be considerably higher this fall & entertaining a similar opinion myself I finally concluded to go it at a venture." Opinion was "universal," Yos concluded "finally," and then he moved quickly, "at a venture." Or Richard Tutt: "Negroes are selling very high here and I think by next fall will be much higher, specially if cotton keeps up at the present high prices."[16] As they bought, these men asked about season, city, and market; they went about their business with self-conscious rationality—asking others, explaining themselves, advising their friends, making sure they got it right.

The grammar of economic speculation, however, was not the only way that market-minded slaveholders talked about buying slaves. There was also the grammar of imagined necessity. "Will you be good enough to inform me candidly whether the present force will be enough to manage the crop and put up the buildings?" J. D. Conrad Weeks wrote to his brother David Weeks. If the logging was to be done, Robert Beverly informed his father, it would be "absolutely necessary" to have six or seven more men to do it. John Knight put it this way when he was trying to buy a carpenter, a blacksmith, and a midwife for the plantation he was building: "I must have them, and cannot get along without them, unless at considerable loss of time and money, and at a great inconvenience." Wealthy Thomas Butler similarly imagined slaves as the necessary solution to an objective problem when he wrote to his wife about his business in New Orleans: "I find it necessary to have a few hands more on my plantation to enable them to get on with the crops and carry on the brick yard at the same time."[17] According to the account he made of himself in the slave market, he was a rational man, a planter following the dictates of good sense. There was nothing else he could do.

In the planter's world of well-reasoned decisions, innumerable slaves could be bought to solve endless problems. More acres could be cleared and more cotton or sugar produced. Ditching and draining, clearing and fencing, hoeing and planting, cutting and packing—these tasks could be expanded infinitely. What could not be achieved through expansion might be done through intensification. Having coopers, carpenters, and bricklayers on the plantation could provide labor at just the moment it was needed and could solve problems as quickly as they arose, eliminating the time it took for outside laborers to be contacted and contracted. As men like Thomas Butler described their business, they objectified their desires into necessities—the crops and buildings themselves demanded that their owners buy more and more slaves. The exigencies with which they explained their choices were located not in the rising and falling prices of the slave market but in their fields and on their farms. Their self-explanations highlighted the productive rather than the consumptive aspect of their business. They were planters responding to necessity rather than slave buyers responding to opportunity.

There was, of course, nothing necessary about these choices except the language that described them: these men did not *have* to buy slaves. But to say that these invocations of necessity were imaginary is not to say that these planters misrepresented their motivation in their letters. Rather, it is to read the letters as if they were written by people who chose words carefully. The meaning Thomas Butler gave to his buying could not be encapsulated by the calculated speculation on the slave market that made W. H. Yos "go it at a venture," or the breathless optimism with which Sam Steer and J. H. Lucas solicited the approval of the older men in their families, still less with the chastened pride with which Jefferson McKinney paid his big price. As they explained the choices they made in the slave market, men like Butler were explaining themselves—giving cultural meaning to the economy in people upon which their lives (or at least their livelihoods) depended.

Another set of cultural meanings that slaveholders gave to their slave-market business dove-tailed well with the paternalist homiletics with which they increasingly defended slavery from its critics: managerial benevolence. A. G. Alsworth, an up-and-coming young man who was trying to negotiate a complicated bargain in which he would sell an old man in order to get enough money to buy some cattle and a young woman, described his business this way: "unless I can get a hundred head and a good girl that will make a wife for some of my boys in a few years I will not sell Spencer." In spite of the hard-headedness of his plans, Alsworth was making a tentative claim on the language of paternalism: he was doing it for his slaves, buying a wife for some of his boys. Likewise W. H. Yos, describing his decision to buy only men from a New Orleans slave trader: "I concluded in as much as he had a good selection of men to buy no women at all with hopes that we may buy them wives next year," Yos reported to his business partner.[18] Yos reached toward an account of his business that emphasized the needs of his slaves, not his own.

The synthesis of humanity and self-interest toward which these men groped was forged into a genre in the agricultural journals of the antebellum South. The "Management of Slaves" section of *DeBow's Review* included specifications for housing and provisioning slaves and arguments that neatness of dress was important in fostering "the health, comfort, and pride of a Negro, which should be encouraged by the owner." The immediate results of good treatment would be apparent to the slaves and to any neighbors who looked at them; the economic results apparent at harvest time; yield might be measured in cash or (public) credit. The "Duties of an Overseer" section put it more bluntly in 1856: "In conclusion, bear in mind that a fine crop consists first in the number and a marked improvement in the condition and value of the Negroes."[19] And *DeBow's*, as well as magazines like the *Southern Agriculturalist* and the *Southern Planter*, provided slaveholders with detailed instructions about diet, housing, work routine, and proper discipline which would make them successful slave farmers as well as slaveholders. These articles encouraged slaveholders to imagine themselves through the eyes of their fellow subscribers, to imitate the exemplary conduct described in the magazines in the hope that their actions might one day be thought worthy of public notice. Indeed, many of these articles were written in the first-person voice of a subscriber turned writer—the voice of an experienced planter passing on his practice to other men, pressing upon them the importance of scientific and humane management and establishing a shared public understanding of what it meant to be a leading slaveholder.[20] That was the type of slaveholder Thomas McAllister was, according to his overseer, "a very good master . . . a humane and indulgent man to his Negroes & careful of his Negroes," a planter whose virtues were expressed in his treatment of the people he bought in the slave market: "[he] don't want his new hands worked hard."[21]

And that was the type of slaveholder John Knight desperately wanted to be. In 1844, as he made plans for a plantation he had just bought, John Knight appended an exegesis of his intentions to one of the long lists of ages, sexes, and body parts that he sent to his father-in-law, who was buying slaves for him in Maryland. "This number (say 60)," he wrote, "will enable me to make a full crop on my land now in cultivation by working them very moderately and giving them every necessary indulgence." Knight was no stranger to the language of commercial necessity; his slave-market order seemed to grow up out of the land's need to be cultivated. But there was more to Knight's plans than simple planting. In subsequent letters Knight lovingly detailed his plans for his new slaves: their lodging ("I am now having built a number of first-rate additional Negroe quarters . . . where they can keep themselves clean, comfortable, and I hope Healthy"), their working conditions ("during the heat of the day, say from 11 O' Clock A.M. to 4 O'Clock P.M. they must be in their quarters or in the shade"), health care ("there is a good physician residing . . . on a removed but very convenient part of my plantation"), and oversight ("I derive much satisfaction from the knowledge that I have a humane and just manager to take charge of them").[22] With the exception of hiring the overseer, all of these plans were made and publicized before John Knight had even chosen or, still less, bought the slaves he was planning to treat so well. Along with an age-tiered and self-reproducing labor force to till his open land, John Knight was buying a fantasy of just and scientific management, of humane treatment and reciprocal benefit. There is no reason to doubt his sincerity; no reason to doubt, either, that by telling his father-in-law about the personal satisfaction he derived from his plans he intended to exchange his dream for a substantial reputation.

The distance between John Knight, with his lofty language of managerial benevolence, and John Tibeats, with his frustration at not being able to claim a full share of the brutal prerogatives of whiteness and mastery, measures the breadth of meanings that buying agricultural slaves had for white men. None of these men ever lost sight of the bottom line of their slave-market speculations: they were buying slaves to clear and till their fields, to plant and harvest their crops, to build their houses and their holdings. They bought more slaves to plant more cotton, and planted more cotton to buy more slaves. But their economic choices had broader cultural meaning. Some were outsiders buying their way into full participation in the political economy of slavery and white masculinity. Some were old men planning for the end of their lives or young men plotting their future. Some bought as brothers and fathers, sons and husbands. Some bought with the savvy of men on the make, others with the measured purpose of men long made. Some bought as businessmen, planters, or managers. As they narrated their upward progress through the slave market, slaveholders small and large were constructing themselves out of slaves. Whether slave buyers figured their independence as coming of age or coming into their own, as investment, necessity, or benevolence, it was embodied in slaves.

And as slaveholders moved upward through the social hierarchy, they gained access to ever more rarified fantasies of what it meant to be a white man and a slaveholder in the antebellum South. First-time slaveholders—Jefferson McKinney waiting for the woman he bought to breed, for example, or even J. H. Lucas accounting for the family money he had spent in the slave market—could not hide their reliance upon the people they bought. But as they bought ever more slaves, slaveholders were able to displace their reasons for buying slaves—the market, the land, and even the slaves themselves became the animating features of slaveholders' choices. That those who were most invested in the slave economy were best able to give alternative meaning to their dependence on slavery seems at first a curious paradox. On closer view, it becomes apparent that one of the luxuries that could be bought in the slave market was access to the master languages of slave buying, languages which transmuted the reality of dependence on slaves into the conventions of slaveholders' self-willed independence.

THE HOUSEHOLD AND THE SLAVE MARKET

Slaveholding white men relied upon slaves to do more than produce and reproduce the masculine economy of the antebellum South. Slaveholders relied on slaves to produce and reproduce slaveholding households. The outward face of a slaveholding household—the driver of the carriage, the greeting given at the door, the supervision of the child, the service at the table—was often a slave. And no less than their outward form, the internal lives of these households, the relations between their white slaveholding members, were shaped by slavery. By purchasing slaves for their wives and children, male slaveholders—for it was only men who went to the slave market—gave both a form and a function to their patriarchal authority. And yet the households over which these men presided were continually being transformed by the slaves they bought, and not always in ways that they could predict or control. Different imagined slaves answered different needs within any household, and the process of choosing what kind of slave to buy was a process of tallying and balancing the needs of various white family members against one another. In both their outward aspect and their inward character, the social relations that defined slaveholding households—between a household and the outside world and between the various white members of that household—were made material in the shape of a slave.

By law and by custom white women had little business being in the slave market. In Louisiana, a married woman had no right to buy or sell immovable property (slaves, under Louisiana law, were real estate) unless she had done one of three things: obtained her husband's permission to trade the property she had brought into the marriage; declared herself separate in property from her husband, thus gaining the right to trade in her own name and insulating herself from her husband's debts, though not necessarily physically separating herself from him; or, finally, gained the right to buy and sell freely without pulling shared property out of the marriage by getting a license to do business as a corporation. Even those few women who had the legal right to buy slaves did not go to the slave market to buy them: when women bought slaves, they found ways to participate in the market without going to the marketplace. Sarah Ann Allen, for example, did not go to the slave yard of the New Orleans dealer Walter Campbell when she bought a slave in 1849. Instead, her husband, Young D. Allen, from whom her property apparently was separate, went and bargained with Campbell, drew up the contract, and took it home (this was explicitly noted in the contract) for his wife to sign. Similarly, when Azelie Zerigue purchased an "axe-man" for her family's St. Bernard Parish plantation in 1850, it was not she who negotiated with New Orleans slave dealer John Buddy but her husband, Joseph Lombard, who was acting in a legal capacity as her agent.[23] The slave market was a site of perceived sexual and social disorder, not any place for a white lady to be. No less than for slaveholding men, however, the slave market was full of transformative possibilities for slaveholding women.

One of the many miraculous things a slave could do was to make a household white. Of course there were many white households in the antebellum South that subsisted without slaves, relying instead upon the labor of family members—husband, wife, and children working together in the fields. But there was something that made many white southerners, or at least white slaveholding southerners, uncomfortable about such households. J. D. B. DeBow, for example, could allow that nonslaveholding white households existed, but he could see them only as temporary steps in a natural commercial evolution toward slaveholding: "The non-slaveholder knows that as soon as his savings will admit, he can become a slaveholder, and thus relieve his wife from the necessities of the kitchen and the laundry and his children from the labors of the field."[24] DeBow did not allude to the possibility that his hypothetical nonslaveholder's wife might have been working in the field along with her husband and child, though such labor was as customary among nonslaveholding whites as it was customarily unmentionable among white slaveholders like DeBow.[25] By liberating them from work their slaveholding neighbors did not do, slave ownership promised nonslaveholding white women as full a transformation as it did their husbands and fathers. A slave could wash away the unspeakability of a woman's work in the field and bring a white household into being where previously there had been a conspicuous public silence. When Samuel Patterson wrote to his son about setting up housekeeping, he advised him that three things were necessary to make a household: a wife, a house, and a slave to work in it.[26]

Thus households—slaveholding and white—were conjured into being through slave-market speculations that were as personal as they were commercial. Edward and Lucy Stewart, living near Ponchatoula, Louisiana, in the 1850s, had just struggled through their first harvest on a new farm (they had been unable to get their potatoes out of the ground for want of a mule to pull the plow) when they turned their attention to buying a slave. Edward Stewart began by informing John Gurley, his friend and New Orleans agent, that he and his wife wanted "an orphan girl of eight or nine years of age . . . Lucy thinks she would prefer a girl to a boy."[27] With a slave to tend to gardening, drawing water, and chopping wood, Lucy Stewart would have been able to spend more time inside; her skin would no longer be darkened by the sun, her hands no longer roughened by the tools, her hair no longer blown into knots by the wind.[28] With a slave like the one she imagined, Lucy Stewart might be able to transform herself into a proper white lady.

But before Edward had time to seal the letter to his agent, the Stewarts had thought again: "we have decided that if a boy can be had at as low a price as a girl it will be better to get the former as he can be of equal service in the house while young and be of much more value out of doors as he gets older."[29] In contrasting the benefits of buying a boy to a girl, Edward Stewart made a distinction between the "service" promised by a domestic slave and the "value" promised by one who would eventually work in the fields. And the peculiar combination of value and service desired by him and his wife, the balanced demands of market and home, was to be found in a male body. The hopes the Stewarts had for their slave (and themselves) were keyed to the changing meanings they assigned his or her gender over the course of time: either a boy or a girl could help Lucy Stewart in the house, but a boy would grow into a man who would help Edward Stewart on the farm. Four days later, however, the Stewarts were at it again. "You will think we do not know our mind exactly," Edward projected, "as we have now concluded that it will be best to have a girl instead of a boy. Lucy quotes Christine [a slave woman] with her six or seven children as an example and I think that in after years a girl would prove most valuable."[30] So now, either a boy or girl could help Lucy Stewart in the house, but only a girl could eventually produce more slaves. The Stewarts were posed on the doorstep of their own future, unable to choose between sets of seemingly endless possibilities contained within the body of an eight-year-old child.

The slave the Stewarts imagined was to be a helper for Lucy; they could not yet afford to imagine buying slaves who would relieve Lucy entirely of her duties around the house, who would transform her from a mate into a mistress. And yet there were such slaves to be bought in the slave market: nurses, cooks, carriage drivers, spinners, seamstresses, servants, weavers, waiters, washers, and on and on. Amidst the public celebration of white male equality, it was difficult for slaveholding white men publicly to declare their superiority to their social inferiors, but the mark of distinction embodied in their slaves was unmistakable.[31] When a slave broker said of a customer "he is a man of means—he is well off," he was speaking from the experience of seeing the man buy slaves, referring to a type of social knowledge that was acted out every day in the finer households of the antebellum South. Another broker made the same point when buying for John Buhler: "Mr. Buhler wanted a good cook, but an indifferent one would not suit him." Buhler was saying of himself what another man said of John Baron: "[he] lives well and would not keep a bad cook." That was a reputation in a single sentence, an estimation of the man built out of the tone of his household and the service of his slaves—a reputation dependent upon the greeting given at his door and the slave-driven carriage that carried his family to church services and parties, a reputation dependent upon the washing and ironing, the cooking and cleaning, the slaving and serving.[32] Baron's gentility, like that of all of the slaveholders who bought domestic slaves, was made visible in the actions and abilities of his slaves. For the prosperous slaveholders of the antebellum South, domestic slaves were a necessity; one might compare the benefits of hiring or buying such a slave, but one could not do without.[33] Indeed, in a social sense, one could not *be* without.

The most perfectly turned performances of slaveholding class distinction were, of course, those of slaveholding ladies. The purchase of ever more slaves provided access to ever more rarified possibilities of feminine delicacy for the white women who watched over them. With a household full of domestic slaves, a white woman could skate lightly across the surface of daily exigency, her own composure unscathed by the messy process required to produce the pleasing tableau of her own life. Of course, these women were as much a part of that pleasing tableau as were the fine dinner parties, well-governed children, and crisply ironed shirts produced by their slaves—the leisure of these women was a part of the show as much as were the slaves who had been bought to create it. As they were replaced by slaves in the fields and moved inside to elaborate ever more accomplished performances of gentility and domesticity, these slave-made ladies perhaps more than anyone else marked out the class hierarchy of the antebellum South.[34]

The leisure and gentility of white women (itself produced by domestic slaves) was, in the public record of the antebellum South, credited to the reputations of their husbands. Male slaveholders often advertised to their correspondents and fellows in the slave market that they were buying slaves for their family members. By so doing they added a patina of patriarchal generosity—the ability to determine and provide for the needs of their dependents—to the social distinction they were buying in the slave market. John Knight, for example, made a public accounting of his slave buying in the following terms: "We find that we require another *female house servant*," he began his letter, "having to keep Jane exclusively as a nurse." The slave he imagined would be "of infinite advantage to Frances, who has necessarily been entirely too much confined (having the care of John B. and a pretty large family)."[35] Knight used the language of necessity, but the needs he described were domestic rather than economic. And they were Frances's: a house servant was "required" to relieve her confinement (itself necessary). He would provide.

A slave dealer remembered a buyer invoking his female family members in a similarly public accounting of his motive for buying a domestic slave: "I recollect that when plaintiff came to purchase her he stated to me that he wanted to buy her for one of his female relations."[36] Bruckner Payne framed a purchase in similar terms: "Mr. Payne said he wanted a little girl . . . to wait on his wife and do the sewing for a small family."[37] By publicly framing their purchases in terms of the needs of their white dependents, these men reframed the leisure of their wives as evidence of their own virtue—*their* wives would not have to wash or wait or nurse, they would see to that.

And, as they publicly went about providing for their wives and relatives, many slaveholders were buying for themselves a fantasy of provision that would amplify itself over time—even, perhaps, after they had themselves passed on. D. W. Breozeale's mind was on his own legacy when he wrote to his friend John Close about the slave market: "For my own part," he wrote, "should I ever get imbaressed it will be in purchasing Negroes as I wish to have a few more settled on my wife before I am carried off so that no future husband can spend them."

Breozeale was thinking about the frailty of his legacy and calming his fears about the future by thinking about buying slaves. He was going to the slave market to buy life insurance—a legacy that would insulate his family from the effects of his own death. For Breozeale, the slaves he bought in the market were a self-perpetuating part of an intergenerational chain of patriarchal provision: when he was gone, his slaves would take their place alongside those provided to his wife by her father: "I have saved all the slaves for her that I found with her (except one that died at very considerable expense)," he confided to his friend. Like the older man, he would be present in the bodies of his slaves long after he was dead and gone.[38]

A link between the generations of his family was something that J. F. Smith, like Breozeale, hoped to buy in the slave market. When he sat down to write to one of his friends, Smith had just—by his wife's "directions," he said—sold three women and their children. Perhaps their price was to help him pay for the farm he had recently bought and the house he had recently built, the sale of one type of future to pay for another. But as soon as the sale of the slaves was done, Smith was looking to the slave market for more. "If I can procure one or two good servants," he wrote, "we may expect to live in a little more satisfaction." He went on to explain what satisfaction he took from buying slaves: "I intend to purchase a girl of 18 or 20 years of age or a woman and children so that if I should be called away from my family they will at least have a comfortable home with servants sufficient without hiring and that will bring if sold double the original cost." While he made clear enough that he was acting on behalf of his family, Smith detoured around saying exactly what he meant by emphasizing the sunny results of his slave buying—"a little more satisfaction," "a comfortable home"—rather than the means by which such feeling would be produced. But his meaning was probably clear enough to the man who received the letter. The choice Smith posed was between a woman of childbearing age and one who already had children. J. F. Smith was buying a self-renewing slave force for his family; his provision would be perpetually embodied in the reproduction of the slaves he bought. Through the remarkable alchemy of the slave market, a legacy of white patriarchy could be passed on in the promise of black reproduction.[39]

No less than slaveholding men, slaveholding women experienced and expressed transitions in their own lives in relation to slavery. The dependence of slaveholding women on their slaves was expressed in a commonplace Isaac Jarratt passed to his cousin Betty: "I do think you and Sarah stand a chance to marry since Euclinda Wall has done so, but I fear it is . . . a bad chance without a show of some Negroes and Beauty, both of which is lacking with Sarah and unfortunately for you, you lack the Negroes."[40] Jarratt was a slave trader, a man well-acquainted with the way in which the traffic in slaves underwrote the traffic in (white) women, which in turn underwrote the reproduction of slaveholding patriarchy. Jarratt's recognition of the interrelation of the white marriage market and the black slave market, however, implied no identity of interest between slaves and slaveholding women. Far from it. Whatever their relation to slaveholding patriarchy, he implied, slaveholding women were like slaveholding men—made out of slaves.

As much as their external identities as ladies of distinction or suitable wives depended upon slaves, the internal lives of white women could also be reshaped in the slave market. For Miriam Hilliard, for example, thinking about what it meant to be a mother involved thinking about what it would mean to buy a caretaker for her child. "Isaac Henry kept me awake almost the whole of last night," she wrote shortly after the birth of her son. "I cannot conceive how a mother can rest satisfied to put her tender and helpless babes out to nurse. Who but a mother would patiently undergo the fatigue and sleepless nights which most generally have to be encountered?" Who but a slave, she found herself asking while visiting the family of Bishop Leonidas Polk two weeks later. "She has a faithful nurse (Negro) to whose care she abandons her babes entirely," Hilliard wrote of Mrs. Polk, "only when she has a fancy to caress them does she see them. Eight children and cannot lay to their charge the loss of a single night's rest. She is equally fortunate in having a housekeeper who . . . is everything she ought to be."[41] Mrs. Polk's caretaker filled Miriam Hilliard with wonder, if not with admiration. The well-rested Mrs. Polk, it seems, was leading Hilliard down the path from the household to the slave market.

Had Miriam Hilliard bought a slave, the transaction would likely have entered the public record under the same heading as John Knight's purchase of a nurse for his own wife and son: "patriarchal provision." Her husband would have gone to the slave market, advertised his beneficence by announcing that his intention was to buy a slave for his needy wife, and set about inspecting those available for sale. In the privacy provided by her diary, however, Miriam Hilliard could imagine a different set of meanings for her imagined slave. Still at the Polk's: "Our 'piece of perfection' kept us up the entire night. Mr. Hilliard got terribly out of patience—vowed this breaking of rest would kill him."[42] Can it have failed to occur to Miriam Hilliard, sitting in the house run by Mrs. Polk's slaves, stealing a moment for herself away from her crying child and raging husband, that buying a slave would emancipate her as a mother and a wife, that the inner life of her household (as well as its outward reputation) might be remade in the slave market? As useful as the patriarchal provision script was in describing slave sales in a way that knit together the authority of white men over both the political economy and the household economy, it could not fully contain the possibilities that a white woman like Miriam Hilliard might discern in the slave market—possibilities that might be subversive of domestic patriarchy, if not of slavery itself.

So it was with Kitty Hamilton. Hamilton had just been married when she asked her brother to buy her a slave. "I want a competent maid," she wrote to Louisiana from her new home in Vicksburg in 1856, "but do not wish to be in too great a hurry." A few months later, when Hamilton wrote to her father, action seemed a bit more to the point; her brother was sending a seamstress, but Hamilton was in the market for more than a seamstress. "Before long," she wrote, "I shall require two servants. Mrs. Lane is bad off for a washer & I should feel much better if I had some one who could do my washing."[43] Mrs. Lane was Kitty Hamilton's new mother-in-law, the mistress of the household in which she was living. It is not clear whether Hamilton was looking for a washer she could use to distinguish herself within the older woman's household or one she could offer as her own contribution to the greater good. What is clear is that Kitty Hamilton was relying on her father to help her renegotiate the terms under which she lived in her husband's household—she was buying a slave to do more than wash her dirty laundry.

If Kitty Hamilton bought slaves to help her define her relations with her in-laws, she was also using the slave market to help her define her relationship to her new husband. In November 1856 she wrote to her brother that the draft he had sent her had not arrived in time and she had been forced to borrow money from her husband. She did not dwell on the fact of the draft but sent it back with a request: "If Josh is sound

& well send him up to Vicksburg for me. I am not going to trust him to a Negro trader, but will sell him myself."[44] Hamilton's hope was that her father-in-law might be looking for a slave like Josh. Kitty Hamilton was trading furiously within a tightly bounded set of household economies. Worried about relations with her husband's relatives, she bought through her own family. In debt to her husband, she had her slave sent from her old home to her new one and tried to sell him to her father-in-law. Hamilton accepted the terms of the patriarchal-provision script: she did her slave buying through men, relying on the financial and practical support of her father, brother, and husband, and she stayed out of the slave pens and sold to a family member. But she also tried to dictate the terms of enactment for these pre-scripted roles. As well-grooved as was the process by which domestic patriarchy was reproduced out of chattel slavery, as axiomatic as was the rhetoric of masculine provision to the purchase of household slaves, buying a slave was still a social process, subject to the contrary inclinations and occasional subversions of all those involved.

Some white women went a step further than did Miriam Hilliard or Kitty Hamilton: they used slavery to dismantle patriarchy. The story of Polyxeme Reynes, a white woman of moderate means who lived in antebellum New Orleans, provides a view of the slippery capacity of some slaveholding women to fabricate independent identities in the slave market. Sometime after November 1843, Reynes used a few empty leaves at the beginning of her account book to write her commercial autobiography, "How I started to Work."[45] What followed was a chronicle of twenty transactions made between the end of 1833 and November 1843. The transactions were carefully indexed—First Sales, Sales made by Line, Jackson bought, Second acquisition on Congress Street, Jackson Sold, etc.—and described in loving detail.

As she remembered it to herself, Reynes began in 1833 by selling some of the clothes in her closet for forty dollars. With that money she bought muslin, lace work, and other articles out of which she made kerchiefs, dresses, and bonnets. These were sold in the street by her slave, Elyza. In the meantime, she had her slave Line selling beer and cakes (the cakes, she noted, she had made herself). By the end of the year her savings were considerable—she called them her "panier," her basket. Through 1835 Reynes expanded her enterprise. In August she bought, through an agent, a piece of ground on the Rue de Congres. In

November she paid for a formal accounting of how the $3080 she had brought to her marriage had been spent: "Reynes bought for me Elyza $1000, Betsi $300, Hemmok $1200," and they had, together, bought furniture for $460. The accounting may have meant that Polyxeme Reynes was being legally separated from her husband, a sign either of her commercial independence or of his insolvency. But Joseph Reynes remained active in her affairs. He had done the family's slave buying even when the money being spent was his wife's, and he continued to do so as her business grew beyond the bounds of his household. Also in November, Reynes later remembered, with the remaining $100 of her dotal money, "my husband bought in my name and with my promise to pay the Negro Jackson." Joseph Reynes paid the money down and brought the slave home, but the name on the note that promised the balance in eighteen months was Polyxeme Reynes. At the end of the month her husband gave her a gift—a horse and dray with which Jackson could "help me pay the $900 I paid for him." The money made by Jackson's work as a drayman went directly to pay her loan from the bank, which, she noted, as on every occasion when she borrowed money, was "paid before term."

Through the following years Reynes bought, sold, and rented land; prices and profits were detailed in the diary. And in those years she bought and sold slaves. Nina was purchased on February 17, 1836; again, Joseph Reynes did the slave buying and gave Polyxeme Reynes's promise to pay. This time no money changed hands; Polyxeme Reynes gave only her promise, which was partly backed by Nina herself: "The rent from my two small houses, and the work of Nina were designated to pay this sum."[46] Later in the same year she sold Jackson for one thousand dollars. "I gained at this affair a little less than three-hundred and fifty dollars, that is to say the fruit of his work during eight months," she later wrote.

At the back of the same volume in which she later wrote her commercial autobiography, Polyxeme Reynes kept her running accounts. It is in this list of receipts and expenditures that the depth of the meaning that the slave market had for Reynes is apparent. Much of her money was made into more money: by the end of 1836 she was no longer recording any income from work done by her slaves; money came instead from a rental property, the purchase of which had been underwritten by the sales her slaves made in the streets. But not all the money she made was reinvested. In May 1835 she recorded a small sum with the notation "expenditures for my children"; in November 1836 she bought presents for her children and clothes for herself; in January 1839 "a gold reliquary for my girl"; in 1841, amidst the growing depression, she gave her three children money to put in "their strongboxes."[47] As prominent as Joseph Reynes is in his wife's commercial autobiography, he is absent from her account book. Polyxeme Reynes had apparently established a separate economy within her husband's household.

Indeed, by the 1840s, hers may have been the only economy in the household. In the beginning, Joseph helped his wife get a start, fronting for her in slave purchases, giving her the horse and cart, and apparently lending her some money. In the twelfth entry of her diary (which, though undated, falls between those for June and August of 1836), Polyxeme Reynes recorded that she had repaid him the money he had advanced her for the purchase of Nina. That entry, like those before it in which Joseph Reynes appears, suggests a posture of patriarchal facilitation: he did not interest himself too deeply in her affairs but did what he could to help her out.

Rather than being the last of the entries detailing her husband's stewardship of her business, however, the twelfth entry may have marked the beginning of her support of him. Three months after she had repaid the outstanding debt, she was lending him money. When Reynes wrote her commercial autobiography, she did not include much about the years after 1836, years of depression. In March of 1843, she later recorded, "my husband having lost his position I began again to make sweets for my domestic to sell on the streets."[48] Polyxeme Reynes was beginning "her work" all over again, only this time it was she who headed the household. The fact that the money she gave her children was earmarked for their "strongboxes" provides a disquieting suggestion of the internal life of the Reynes household during the depression. But it is perhaps more telling that we cannot tell much at all about Joseph Reynes from the book left behind by his wife: long before she became the head of household, Polyxeme Reynes was using the slave market and her slaves' marketing skills to build herself an independent life within a household nominally headed by her husband.

The last entry in Reynes's autobiography marked the end of her enterprise. "In November 1843," she wrote, "I lost my slave Betsi."[49] The loss of Betsi was the occasion that seems to have spurred Reynes to write a narrative of her career. With Betsi, Reynes had lost her business and everything that slaves and the market had meant to her: her "work," her pride in paying her debts before term, her gifts to her children and herself, her support of her husband. And yet the entry is unclear. Did Betsi die or was she sold for the debts that had begun with Joseph and eventually engulfed his wife? Again, Reynes's silence is telling: it did not matter *how* Betsi was lost to Polyxeme Reynes, simply that she *was* lost. Any biographical interest Reynes might have had in Betsi the woman was apparently occluded by the desperate importance to her own biography of Betsi the slave.

Because even women as economically successful and legally independent as Polyxeme Reynes did not go to the slave market, the process by which they participated in slave buying was itself a renegotiation of the terms of domestic patriarchy. White women who chose slaves did so by a process that was as much a social relation with the man who bought for them as it was a commercial one with the man who sold to them. Recall the back-and-forth decision made by Edward and Lucy Stewart and Edward Stewart's sheepish admission to his agent that they had changed their mind again: he was a man who could not make up his mind on his own. Compare that to Isaac Jarratt, writing to his wife: "If you see Mr. Carson tell him I have left money and get him to buy such a girl as you want if he can get such a one."[50] Both families were smallholding white households, building class distinction out of domestic slavery, and in both families it was a man who would go to the slave pens, pay the money, and bring the slave home. The differences in the process, however, are as striking as the similarities: where Stewart could not conceal the fact that he was being told what to do, Jarratt told his wife that he was too busy and that she would have to find someone else to get her a slave.

Marriage was not the only patriarchal relationship that took daily shape through the process of buying slaves. When elderly Sidney Palfrey wrote to her brother-in-law, John Palfrey, she began by scolding him for returning to their seller two slaves she thought would have "suited" her. "I have," she added, "seen none that I like as well since." Palfrey, however, had not been going to the market herself: "The boys have not been able to procure me a servant," she wrote. "Alfred has been very kind and attentive to me and has been trying his best to procure me some servants. Charles is trying but both have failed so

far."[51] Those sentences stretched the social process of slave buying all the way from the "boys" in the marketplace to the old woman who compared their efforts (Alfred, very kind; Charles, trying) to the patriarch who was nominally overseeing the whole business. Tangles of obligation—between the "boys" and the old woman, between the patriarch and his brother's wife, between the man who got the letter and the "boys" of whom it spoke—were sorted, allotted, and discharged in the slave market.[52]

Twenty years later John Palfrey received a similar letter from his son, Edward. At issue was a joint purchase of slaves with a man called Tupper, who was the father-in-law of John Palfrey's daughter Sidney. Edward Palfrey wrote that he had passed on his father's slave-buying instructions, and noted that even before the purchase had been sealed the deal had afforded a small return: "It appears to afford Mr. Tupper great pleasure to think that his father and Sidney's had at last become acquainted."[53] Generation after generation, the Palfrey family was reproducing itself—lineally and laterally—in the slave market. How many slave families were being sacrificed to sustain this slave-buying genealogy is not mentioned in the family record. Of course, not every slaveholding family reproduced itself in the slave pens: gifts and inheritance were equally important means by which slaveholders used slave property to bind families and generations together. And so the point can be made about slavery generally: the links between the members and generations of slaveholding families often took the material form of a slave passed from one family member to another.

Built out of people who could be bought in the market, slaveholding households were advertisements for their masters, for their gentility and distinction, for the delicacy of their women, the tone of their lives, and the quality of their service. In the market, slaveholders could buy the slaves who could make a white woman into a lady by relieving her from work, who could give shape to white men's claims of social distinction by answering the door politely, polishing the silver table service, serving the right wine at the right time, by driving the carriage straight when the road was rough, ironing the shirts properly, and keeping the children quiet when there were guests in the house. In the slave market, male slaveholders could demonstrate their solicitude by buying slaves for their families, and they could provide for their own legacy by insuring that those slaves would be around to take care of their families

even after they had passed on. And in the slave market some slaveholding women, through the agency of a man, could renegotiate the terms of domestic patriarchy itself.

PAYING FOR MASTERY

The Old South was made by slaves. The fields cleared from the forests and the crops with which they were planted, the fine dinner parties and leisured white women, the expanding black population and the living legacies through which slaveholders reproduced their society over time, all of the things that made the South the South were accomplished through the direct physical agency of slaves. Yet through the incredible generative power of slaveholding ideology, the slave-made landscape of the antebellum South was translated into a series of statements about slaveholders: about their manly independence, their able stewardship of a family legacy, their speculative savvy, or their managerial skill, about their planter-class leisure and their luminous good cheer, about their well-ordered households and well-serviced needs, about their wise and generous provision for their families and their futures. Slaveholders became visible as farmers, planters, patriarchs, ladies, and so on, by taking credit for the work they bought slaves to do for them. Sometimes, however, it was not in the slave-made world that the slaveholders sought to make their virtues visible to everyone else but in the slaves themselves—in the fiber of their form, the feelings in their hearts, and the fear that the slaveholders could sometimes see in their eyes.

Usually, slaveholders bought slaves to do their work for them, but sometimes the slaves themselves were to be the slaveholders' work. John Brown, for example, remembered being traded to a doctor who had cured him of a mysterious illness. The doctor's intention was to use Brown for "a great number of experiments" concerning remedies for (forcibly induced) sunstroke, the effects of bleeding, and the depth of black skin (raised layer by layer by blistering). As Brown told it, the result for the doctor was quite a success: he made his reputation as a healer of sunstroke into a fortune by selling pills made of flour.[54] Dr. Robert Dawson was another man who thought he could buy a reputation for medical skill in the slave market. When Dawson first examined fourteen-year-old Martha in June 1858 he was being paid by the man who was trying to sell her. After Dawson had examined the girl—in the

kitchen, out of the sight of the other men—he reported that she had syphilis. "He said it was very bad—a pretty bad case," the prospective buyer remembered. The buyer was still willing to pay a thousand dollars "country paper" for Martha if the seller would guarantee her health, thus taking upon himself the risk that her condition would deteriorate, but the seller refused: he had bought Martha without guarantee and would sell her that way. Later on, the prospective buyer thought that Dr. Dawson had tried to extract a bit of cash from the expertise his examination demonstrated: "I think Dr. Dawson proposed that if I bought the Negro he would cure her for $50. I am not sure of this but think he did."[55] His offer rebuffed, Dawson bought Martha himself and spent the next three months trying to cure her. Dawson was gambling—and quite publicly, since a number of people knew she was sick—on his ability to heal her. Martha's body became the site of Dawson's demonstration of his confidence, and, when she died, the site of his failure.

Of course, these experiments were also speculations: a doctor like Dawson stood to make some money if he could buy sick slaves on the cheap and sell them for a greater sum (or figure out a way for others to do the same). But they were also claims on one of the most precious commodities in the antebellum South: the language of honor. Many historians have argued that the white male culture of the antebellum South was suffused by the idea of honor, the idea that appearances and reputation mattered above all else, even truth. When contradicted or "given the lie," slaveholders sometimes backed their reputations and opinions with their own lives, issuing a challenge and fighting a duel.[56] And in the slave market—as in the cock pit or the race track or the countless other sites where slaveholders contended with one another for precedence of reputation—slaveholding honor was daily measured out in cash as slaveholders put down their money to back their stated claims of expertise. Listen to a slave-market doctor named Johnston describing a disagreement with the slave dealer who had employed him to diagnose Critty and Creasy in Waterproof, Louisiana, in 1856: "Told Chadwick . . . that one or both of them were Consumptive. Chadwick would not believe it . . . Witness offered to bet in order to back his Judgment but Mr. Chadwick declined."[57] That, as much as any duel, was an affair of honor. Southern slaveholders may indeed have been willing to back their stated opinions with their substance, but those opinions were often about slaves and the substance ventured was often financial. It should go without saying that southern slaveholders spent a great deal more time buying and selling slaves than they did choosing seconds and choreographing duels; "affairs of honor" were more likely to be played out in the slave market than on the dueling ground.

Physicians were not the only white southerners who used slaves' bodies to advance their fantasies of mastery and potency. After Dr. Johnston had diagnosed Critty and Creasy, a man named Thomas R. Dixon bought them, though he had seen for himself that they were ill. It was "universally known in Waterproof" that Critty and Creasy were sick, and so in buying them Dixon was making a public statement: in the words of a pharmacist who questioned the wisdom of the purchase, "Mr. Dixon said that he could cure them."[58] His mastery, his ability to read their bodies, was not to be questioned. He backed it with his public promise to cure them and eight hundred dollars paid in cash.

The bargain Dixon was making, it turned out, was even more complicated than that, for he himself had no idea whatsoever how to cure Critty and Creasy. According to the report of a witness to the sale, he was counting on the skills of his wife: "They were speaking about their trade. Dixon said that one of the Negroes, the younger one, he knew to be unsound at the time of the purchase. That Mrs. Dixon had examined her previous to the purchase and thought that she could cure her. Mr. Dixon said that he had more faith in Mrs. Dixon's skill than he had in most of the doctors. Said that he knew what was wrong with her. That she had the stoppage of her monthly sickness that Mrs. Dixon could cure it without any difficulty . . . Said that the old one he did not consider worth much money but if the young one should live she would be worth 1000 dollars but there was some risk in curing her, but, for the fact of Mrs. Dixon's knowledge, he thought he had done well."[59]

Dixon was buying Critty to let her die and Creasy for his wife to cure. And he was bragging about it—about his savvy and his wife's ability, about the money he would save by buying a sick slave on the cheap (and not wasting his effort on a dying one), about a speculation that made him sharper than the slave trader and the knowledge that made his wife more reliable than the doctor, about the specialized knowledge of a woman's body he had gained from his wife, and about "the peculiar virtues of some kind of bark," which, made into tea, would bring back "the monthly courses . . . sometimes in twenty four hours" (though, as he knowingly confided, "it would be more prudent to bring on the courses more slowly by degrees").[60] Dixon was making sure that everybody in earshot knew that he knew what he was doing when he went in the slave market; he was tacking between "honor" and "the market," building his business into a reputation and backing his reputation with his business.

It soon became apparent how sick Critty and Creasy really were. And the Dixons started calling doctors, gradually expending the public credit they had hoped to gain in trying to save the people upon whom it depended. The diagnoses the Dixons got from the doctors were insults to their abilities wrapped in evaluations of their slaves. From Dr. McIlheney, who was asked to examine only Creasy: "Would not give anything for her." From Dr. Wilson, who examined both women: "Would not have given the funeral expenses as consideration for the two Negro women." With the brutal thrift of a slaveholding commonplace, the doctors spun reputation and speculation into a single evaluative economy: the Dixons could be judged by the way they bought slaves, and the judgment was not flattering. Still, even as Mrs. Dixon admitted to the doctors that "Mr. Dixon had been very badly swindled or rather Mrs. Dixon had been," the Dixons did not back out of the deal. Two weeks after the trade, after the Dixons had given way to the doctors, Chadwick offered to take the slaves back. "Mr. Dixon," a witness remembered, "said he did not think he could do it."[61] There was no legal reason, nor any discernible economic reason, why he could not, and yet the phrasing suggests an imperative. Dixon was being driven by the logic of the specific bargain he had made—by the investment of his reputation in his speculation, by the "honor" he had expended in the slave market—to stick with his purchase at any cost. For Dixon, apparently, reputation and speculation could be sundered only by the slaves' death; and when that eventually happened, rather than losing money along with face, Dixon sued, and the Supreme Court of Louisiana gave him his money back. He had not, after all, got what he had paid for.

If healing slaves' bodies was one way that slave buyers tried to extract reputation and honor from the people they bought, breaking their spirits was another. Solomon Northup wrote that Edwin Epps, to whom he was sold in 1843 after beating up his previous owner, John Tibeats, was known as a "'breaker,' distinguished for his faculty of subduing the spirit of a slave, as a jockey boasts of his skill in managing a refractory horse."[62] By putting the word "breaker" in quotation marks, Northup highlighted the recognizably social character of Epps's role, and by making the comparison between the breaker's reputation and that of another man's "boasts," Northup pointed to the pride with which Epps inhabited that role. Being a breaker was less a profession than a pose—a way of treating slaves and of talking to and about them, a way of building a reputation for indomitability out of brutality.[63]

How else can we understand Charles McDermott—who was told by the dealer who sold him Billy that the slave would "run and play off from his work," who had seen the scars on Billy's back inflicted by previous owners, who whipped Billy a dozen times for running away without thinking about returning him to the dealer—than as a man buying a reputation as a breaker?[64] How else can we understand Andrew Skillman—who "frequently" inquired about purchasing Henry, though the slave's character, "which was bad," was generally known, who said at the time of sale that he knew "the Boy had stolen goods and run off" but that he would not blame any Negro "for so doing when allowed the same liberty" as Henry had been allowed, who bought Henry though the slave was sold in chains from the jail, who asked Henry "if he would live with him" and removed the slave's chains "as soon as he bought him," who told Henry in the hearing of other white men "if he ran away from him once he would not run away again"—but as a man who sought honor among whites by publicly threatening his slave?[65] These men were demonstrating that they were not afraid of scars or chains or bad character, that the common caution of the slave market was expendable for men as forceful as themselves: they were buying the chance to match their will against that of a slave.

More than that: breakers were buying the chance to match their ability as masters against that of their neighbors. Skillman's comment that Henry's bad behavior had been due to his "liberty," his public removal of the chains applied by the previous owner, and his equally public threat to murder Henry if he ran away all drew rhetorical force from a slaveholders' commonplace: that the behavior of slaves reflected the ability of their owners.[66] Attributing Henry's bad behavior to his prior owner's lax management and proclaiming his ability to break Henry's spirit, Skillman was buying the chance to show that he was a better master—more discerning, more confident, more formidable, more *honorable*—than any other man around. At least he was so up to the point that Henry ran away, taking with him three of Skillman's other slaves. After that he was simply angry; and when he sued and the Louisiana Supreme Court ruled that he had got what he deserved, out of luck.

If healers tried to wring honor from their slave's bodies, breakers tried to wring it from their souls. Moses Roper remembered that his eventual buyer tried to inscribe his authority in Roper's mind long before he ever beat him: "Previously to his purchasing me, he had frequently taunted me, by saying 'You have been a gentleman long enough, and, whatever may be the consequences I intend to buy you.'"[67] Peter Bruner was similarly threatened when, after having run away and been captured, he was addressed by his owner's sister: "She said she wanted to buy me for the sole purpose of whipping me; she said if she could whip me and break me in she could stop me from running off."[68] A final example comes from William Wells Brown, who remembered that Robert More purchased John after a carriage the slave was driving had splashed him with mud with the "express purpose . . . to '*tame him.*'" This he did by chaining and beating John until the slave's limbs hung limp at his side. At that point, John had no value left but as a symbol of More's power. These slaves were bought to be broken, to be turned from unruly subjects into perfect symbols of their owners' will. Indeed, they were bought to be the embodied registers of the indomitability of that will, for the slaves themselves were the ultimate audience for their buyers' brutal performances.[69]

These slaves, then, embodied a type of public recognition—a type of honor—that could be beaten out of their backs. In buying them, slaveholders boasted that their own mastery would inhabit their slaves' every action. Their slaves would be extensions of themselves, the actions of the enslaved indistinguishable from the will of the enslavers. Slave breaking was a technology of the soul. Buying slaves to break them represented a fantasy of mastery embodied in the public subjugation of another, of private omnipotence transmuted into public reputation. In that way, it was not so different from paternalism.

As slaveholders progressed through stages of social standing by buying ever more slaves, they were able to accomplish another remarkable rhetorical inversion, perhaps one of the most remarkable of all time: they began to say they were acting on behalf of the people whom they had bought to act for them. That claim, like those based upon brutal subordination, was a reputation wrung from the soul of a slave, but it had a much nicer sounding name than slave breaking: paternalism. Indeed, the slave-buyer-as-paternalist was a recognizable enough figure to become a trope of proslavery fiction: the slaveholder who bought slaves in order to reunite families that had been divided by the disembodied power of the marketplace (often debts to a northern merchant). Buying slaves in these novels was a form of charity, a benevolence extended to the purchased on the part of slaveholders so attached to their slaves that they were willing to enter the unfamiliar and potentially contaminating confines of the slave pen to redeem their loved ones and treasured friends.[70]

An explicit balancing of the needs of master and slave, of commercial and paternal language, animated Richard T. Archer's slave buying as he described it to Joseph Copes. "I consider Negroes too high at this time," Archer began with a gesture of speculative savvy, "but there are some very much allied to mine both by blood and intermarriage that I may be induced from feeling to buy, and I have one vacant improved plantation, and could work more hands with advantage."[71] The vacant plantation was an objective necessity, but what was "feeling" worth? Archer was negotiating a complicated deal in which consideration for his slaves' needs, along with evaluation of the market and the need to work an open field, was tallied and entered into his relationship with Copes. By asking the question (and sharing it with Copes), Archer was figuring the slaves' needs alongside his own as he thought about buying them. Perhaps by sharing the dilemma with Copes he hoped to be better able to judge how another would balance the dictates of necessity and humanity; perhaps to be dissuaded from buying while still gaining credit for "feeling."

Feeling, then, could be bought, but only at a price. For a Louisiana slaveholder named Isett, feeling was behind his "intention to buy" William, the "principal inducement" being that William was "husband to one of his women." And for Isett the price was one thousand dollars. Later, in a courtroom where William was being portrayed as a runaway and a thief, Isett explained what he had been thinking when he had bought the slave. Had he known of the theft at the time the marriage was proposed, he would not have allowed William to marry his slave, "but after he did & had children by her he was willing to purchase him at $1000." "Had it occurred to him that the boy had been chg'd with that robbery he still would have given $1000 for him," he added to emphasize the tenor of the offer he had made for William.[72] Isett was saying that he did not know that William had been accused of a crime at the time he tried to buy him, but even if he had, it would not have made any difference. As he portrayed himself to the court, Isett was the kind of man who was willing to pay dearly for the satisfaction of keeping William's family together.

It was, of course, possible that, as he went before the court, Isett was still trying to rationalize the fact that he had paid a thousand dollars for a slave whom all of his neighbors thought was incorrigibly malign. But the terms in which he did so—a warmed-over account of his own paternalist generosity—were terms in which plenty of other slave buyers described the spirit with which they went to sale. Consummated, such a sale looked like this: "I am pleased to hear that the sale of the Negroes meets the approbation of yourself . . . not so much on my own account, as on the account of the Negroes, who were very anxious that I should own them, which was one of the greatest inducements to my purchasing, so far they appear perfectly contented."[73] That was slave buyer Thomas Maskell writing to slave seller Samuel Plaisted, getting a rebate—measured out in his slaves' esteem—on the price he had paid. His slaves' (imagined) affection was part of the purchase: he had bought himself a paternalist fantasy in the slave market.

The proslavery construction of slave-market "paternalism" was highly unstable: it threatened to collapse at any moment beneath the weight of its own absurdity. One could go to the market and buy slaves to rescue them from the market, but it was patently obvious even to the most febrile reader of proslavery novels that the market in people was what had in the first place caused the problems that slave-buying paternalists claimed to resolve. Some slaveholders solved this problem the same way they solved other problems: through ever more elaborate fantasies about the slave market. Writing in his private diary, for instance, Matthew Williams described his purchase of "a Negro boy" as "a new responsibility." He continued: "I bought him from a Negro trader. I feel satisfied that however inadequately I may discharge my duty towards this boy that he is better off with me than with the man from whom I bought him."[74] Carried with him into the slave market, Williams's paternalism was redemptive: the slave market was a bad thing in itself; sale to anyone was therefore better than sale to no one; Williams was doing the slave a favor, saving him from the market by buying him. Of course, Williams was a professor at South Carolina College, a man for whom it was perhaps a vocation to torture logic into self-congratulation. But he was far from being the only slaveholder to bewilder slave buying and paternalism.

John Knight's search for paternalism threatened to lead him into an endless series of trips into the slave market. When he received Jane (one of the people out of whom he was building his household), Knight also received a message from his father-in-law that his new slave had come to him at the cost of her own unwilling separation from her sister. As well as passing on the news, Knight's father-in-law was perhaps passing on the responsibility, for Knight immediately took up the issue: "If she still desires to come to this country, and reside with us in the vicinity of Jane, I authorize you to purchase her for me . . . If she is a faithful servant I will guarantee her a good master."[75] And, a year later: "We find that we require another female house servant . . . If Jane's sister can yet be bought as you advised me sometime since I should be very glad to own her as I could employ her to much profit."[76] Knight moved freely back and forth between considerations of his household's "requirements" and advertisement of his own good will.

It is not clear whether the person Knight's father-in-law eventually sent was Jane's sister. Her name was Ann, and the letter Knight wrote upon her arrival suggests both the father-in-law's bad faith in raising the issue of family separation in the first place and John Knight's dogged intention to do (or at least say—and often) the right thing in the slave market. Noting that Ann had arrived and was "pleased" with Natchez, Knight sent yet another slave-market request: "I wish you could purchase her brother for me for $700."[77] Knight's paternalism was pushing him deeper and deeper into slave buying. It is not clear how Knight's father-in-law would have read this request: perhaps as a reprimand for breaking up the family; perhaps as another effort to establish a reputation for good will. But however it was intended and however it was read, Knight's request was tendered wholly in the language of charity: he did not want a waiter or a hosteler or a carriage driver, he wanted Ann's brother.

To suggest that John Knight was trying to buy a reputation for charity along with his slaves is not to suggest that he did not care for his slaves' feelings. Indeed, he seems to have cared a great deal: he wanted his slaves to be happy, and he thought their happiness said enough about him that it would prove something to his father-in-law. Like the feelings expressed by Archer and Isett, Knight's feelings were heavily leveraged: he was extracting credit for good intentions out of incomplete purchases, out of transactions that might remain as imaginary as those in the novels. Knight was borrowing against feelings he had himself imagined for his future slaves—the happiness he was granting them—to prove the tenor of his offer. Through their own earnest incantations, practiced slave buyers like Knight portrayed themselves as charitable sojourners in the slave market, redeeming slaves rather than buying them.

Paternalism, then, was something slaveholders could buy in the slave market. Rather than being a prebourgeois social system or a set of rules by which slaveholders governed themselves, paternalism, like speculation, was a way of going about buying slaves, one answer among many that slaveholders gave to the question "What is slavery?" For every "capitalist" who wrapped the purchase of a slave in a detailed account of business cycle and material necessity, there could be a "paternalist" whose self-described motive in buying slaves was to treat them well or save them from the market. The point here is not to try to sort which of these representations were sincere and which were mendacious—slaveholders' real selves emerged only in real time and in confrontation with real slaves. The point, rather, is to emphasize the plasticity of slaveholding paternalism. Because it was a way of imagining, describing, and justifying slavery rather than a direct reflection of underlying social relations, because it was portable, paternalism was likely to turn up in the most unlikely places—in slaveholders' letters describing their own benign intentions as they went to the slave market.[78]

But the magic by which paternalism was produced in the slave market was hard to control. Once the slave market had been mixed in with paternalism, its capacity to produce a universal standard of comparison became indispensable to those who wanted to measure their own good will and attachment to their slaves. Listen to Chancellor Johnson of the South Carolina Supreme Court making a decree of specific performance in a case of disputed slave property (that is, arguing that an individual slave could not be replaced by a cash payment): "Can you go to the market, daily, and buy one like him, as you might a bale of goods, or a flock of sheep? No. They are not to be found daily in the market. Perhaps you might be able to find one of the same sex, age, color, height, and weight, but they much differ in moral qualities of honesty, fidelity, obedience, and industry, in physical qualities of strength and weakness, health and disease; in acquired qualities, derived from instruction, in dexterity in performing the particular labor you wish to assign him." One like him: Johnson's paternalism bordered on sentimentality. But it resided in the slave market. Johnson's brief on the behalf of the "fidelity, obedience, and industry" of specific slaves took the listener on a tour of the slave mart: the slaves lined out by sex and size around the walls of the pen; the visible differences in age, size, and complexion; the questions to determine moral qualities and intelligence; the inspections for health and tests of dexterity.[79] In Johnson's mind there was no more certain measure of a slave's pricelessness than the slave market, no more certain arena for demonstrating human singularity than that of universal comparison.[80]

The unstable antinomies of price and paternalism posed by Johnson were daily resolved into slaveholding commonplaces. "All those who live are above price," wrote a New Orleans agent to an absent owner who had been worried about the health of his slaves.[81] And here is John Knight expressing (as usual to his father-in-law) his paternalist devotion to Henson: "I need not say to you I never wish to purchase a slave to sell again. All I buy I expect to retain. Henson has proved a most invaluable buy to me, both in my store and house. I could get $1000 or more for him at a word, but, as I assured him, he never leaves me but for bad conduct."[82] Knight measured his paternalism in the slave market: not only could he buy slaves to treat them well, he could measure his attachment in dollars foregone. And he could use the threat of sale to guarantee that he would not have to treat his well-cared-for slaves otherwise. This rhetorical intermixture of market and paternalism could crystallize in an unmistakably material result: "I govern them in the same way your late brother did," Thomas Maskell wrote about the recently purchased slaves whose contentment figured so prominently in his own satisfaction, "without the whip, by stating to them that I should sell them if they do not conduct themselves as I wish."[83] That was a slave buyer's fantasy of paternalist mutuality being forced upon a slave through a disciplinary threat of resale—that was the slave trade as a technology of the soul.

Along with the social distinction, honor, and paternalism that could be wrung from the bodies and souls of the enslaved, slave traders were selling the buyers another fantasy: that other people existed to satisfy their desires. The word "fancy" has come down to us as an adjective modifying the word "girl," an adjective that refers to appearance perhaps, or manners or dress. But the word in its other meaning describes a desire: "he fancies . . ." The slave-market usage embarked from this second meaning: "fancy" was a transitive verb made noun, a slaveholder's desire made material in the shape of a little girl "13 years old Girl, Bright Color, nearly a fancy for $1135."[84] That was how slave dealer Phillip Thomas described a child he had seen sold in Richmond: an age, a sex, a complexion that were her own; a fantasy and a price applied in the slave market.

Buying slaves for sex or companionship was no less public than any other kind of slave buying. The slave market was suffused with sexuality: the traders' light-skinned mistresses, the buyers' foul-mouthed banter, the curtained inspection rooms that surrounded the pens. But more than anything, there were the high prices. The "New Orleans Slave Sale Sample" shows prices paid for women that occasionally reached three hundred percent of the median prices paid in a given year—prices above $1500 in the first decade of the century and ranging from $2000 to $5233 afterwards.[85] Contemplating prices like that, William Wells Brown wrote in his novel *Clotel*, "We need not add that had those young girls been sold for mere house servants or field hands, they would not have brought half the sum they did."[86]

The scene Brown was describing, the imaginative site of the "fancy trade," was an auction.[87] For, though "fancy" women were sold through private bargaining as well as public crying, the open competition of an auction—a contest between white men played out on the body of an enslaved woman—was the essence of the transaction.[88] The price paid, Solomon Northup remembered, was as much a measure of the buyer as of the bought: "there were men enough in New Orleans who would give five thousand dollars for such an extra fancy piece . . . rather than not get her."[89] The high prices were a measure not only of desire but of dominance. No other man could afford to pay so much; no other man's needs could be so substantially measured; no other man's desires would be so spectacularly fulfilled. And high prices were public knowledge, reported in newspapers and talked about by slaves and slaveholders alike. Lewis Clarke remembered that as a slave he had heard of "handsome girls being sold in New Orleans for from $2000 to $3000." And a Virginia slave dealer wrote to his partner in the 1850s: "There is here the highest field hand that has ever been sold in Richmond . . . he belongs to that man who bought that high priced Fancy at $1780."[90] "That man" had bought a reputation along with his slaves: he was known through the people he bought. His potency was gauged by his buying power.

Whether they were buying these high-priced women to be their companions or simply their toys, these slaveholders showed that they had the power to purchase what was forbidden and the audacity to show it off. To buy a "fancy" was to flirt publicly with the boundaries of acceptable sociability. John Powell, an editor of the New Orleans *Picayune*, for example, entertained his dinner guests at a house inhabited by his "Quadroon mistress" and the couple's child—their presence at the party showed Powell to be a man who was at once civilized and sensational. Theophilus Freeman, a New Orleans slave dealer, received visitors while lying in bed with Sarah Connor, a woman he had once owned. Through this carefully publicized intimacy with his own former slave, Freemen demonstrated his own freedom from convention—his liberation was made evident in her carefully displayed body.[91]

In the public transcript of the antebellum South, however, these performances of potency were often doubled back on themselves. When they stepped into the notary's office to register their stake in the high-priced women they had bought, slaveholders described them not as "mistresses" or "fancies" but as "cooks" or "domestics" or "seamstresses" or, most commonly, not at all.[92] The double discourse of fancy was reflected in the public assessments of those in the know. Joseph A. Beard, a man who earned his money by auctioning slaves, spoke of the child of George Botts, a slave dealer, and Ann Maria Barclay, Botts's former slave, this way: "a young girl who was generally supposed to be Botts' child though called Maria's sister." Louis Exinois preserved the same doubleness when describing a doctor who visited the house of an enslaved woman: "[he] appeared to be her friend or cher amie."[93] "Generally supposed," "appeared to be": both Beard and Exinois drew attention to the fact that they were speaking doubly, to the fact that there was a polite way of describing such things and another way of seeing them.

As with other forms of Victorian politeness, the rudeness lay with people who described things the way they saw them.[94] Asked in public about his relations with a family whom his uncle owned, Pierre Pouche of Pointe Coupée responded in a way that was at once defensive and accusatory: "I have had connexion with most of the females and am not ashamed to confess it, although I do not think the question pertinent, I would blush to steal but not to answer this question." Talk about such things, Pouche implied, was gossip; it reflected as badly upon the knower as the known. As Mary Chestnut put it, sex between slavehold-ing white men and their female slaves was "the thing we can't name." Thus was patriarchy defended by the silence of politeness, and by a kind of magical denial that allowed a white household to persist in its public performance, though its foundation had disappeared in practice: "Every lady tells you who is the father of all the mulatto children in everybody's household, but those in her own she seems to think dropped from the clouds or pretends so to think."[95] Slaveholders' "fancies" existed in a state of public erasure: they were unspeakable.

Behind the shroud of patriarchal prerogative, some slaveholders hid fantasies of domination that could be seen only by their slaves. Dr. James Norcom sneaked after his slave Harriet Jacobs, trapped her, and whispered his dirty fantasies into her ear. Robert Newsome bought Celia to replace his dead wife and raped her before they had returned from the slave market. Bruckner Payne, who had announced in the slave market that he was there to buy a slave to do some sewing for his wife, took Ellen Brooks to his plantation on trial and brought her back to the slave market so badly brutalized that she died two weeks later.[96] These secret slaveholders sought victims, not companions. In their most private moments, these men existed only in the slaves whose bodies provided the register for their secret desires and their evident power. By hiding their private desires from everyone but their slaves, they recapitulated the ultimate logic of the slave market: their phan-tasms of independent agency were built out of practical dependence upon people bought in the market—their selves were built out of slaves.[97]

The slave market was everywhere in the antebellum South. It sup-plied slaveholders' farms and households; it suffused their fantasies and figures of speech; it was incorporated into their social relations and their selves. Exigency, want, need, desire, wish, fancy, fantasy: answers to every one of these could be found in the slave market. All of the values associated with the antebellum South—the poses and the posturing, the whiteness and independence, the calculation and mastery, the hospitality and gentility, the patriarchy and paternalism, the coming of age and staging of obligation, the honor, brutality, and fancy—were daily packaged and sold in the slave market. All were embodied in slaves and turned out for display in the fields, farms, streets, and parlors of southern slaveholders. More than that, those values and the slaves bought to embody them were knitted together in countless letters, conversations, and court cases which gave cultural meaning to the economy in people. Sometimes that meaning was public—narrated, remarked upon, advertised. Sometimes it was secret—hushed, investigated, hidden. But always it depended upon the slaves.

As slaveholders became ever wealthier and their slave buying ever more elaborate, they became adept at covering their dependency on their slaves with a variety of very durable cultural languages that emphasized their own agency. They bought slaves to make themselves frugal, independent, socially acceptable, or even fully white; they acted in accordance with the necessities of their business or the exigencies of their households; they covered the contingency of their own identities in the capacious promises of paternalism, buying on behalf of the bought; they obscured the dependency of their fantasies with the brutality of their mastery. Using the ideological imperatives of slaveholding culture—whiteness, independence, rationality, necessity, patriarchy, honor, paternalism, and fancy—they produced, in the classic formulation, freedom out of slavery.

In doing so, however, they brought the slave market into their lives, their plans, and their reputations, for their self-amplifying fantasies could be made material only in the domain of the traders and through the frail and resistant bodies of their slaves.

2. As they were gathered by the traders to be sent South, many slaves knew that they would never see their friends and family members again. They entered the trade alone and unknown to the others with whom they traveled. Some marked the moment with mournful song. *Courtesy of the Chicago Historical Society.*

1. Slave traders all over the upper South gathered slaves in the summer months and shipped them south in the fall. Slave traders' advertisements like this one were a common sight in the upper South, just as those advertising the sale of the slaves the traders transported were common in the lower South. *Courtesy of the University of North Carolina Press.*

3. The traders measured the trade according to the double-entry standard of the marketplace. These pages from trader John White's account book record several of the hundred or so sales he might make in a single year of trading Missouri slaves down the Mississippi River. Smaller traders might reckon a year's business in the dozens. Of the two sale prices listed, the first is the total value of the sale and the second is the downpayment. *Courtesy of the Missouri Historical Society.*

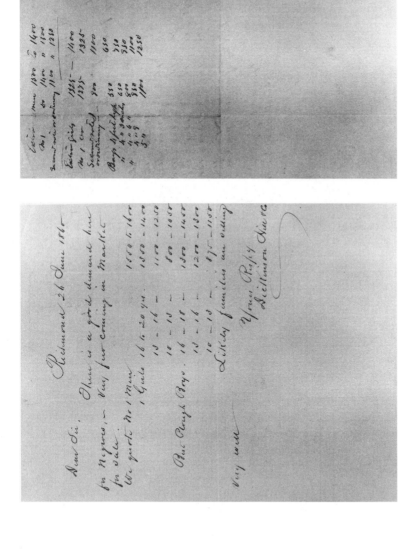

4. In order to track trends in the slave market, the traders packed their slaves into price categories by which they could be easily compared to one another and all manner of other goods. This slave-market circular was sent to subscribers by the Richmond firm of Dickinson, Hill & Co. On the back of the sheet, slave trader William Finney penciled his own estimates of the value of slaves in the summer of 1860, including a list of prices to be paid for "boys" based upon their height. *Courtesy of Rare Book, Manuscript, and Special Collections Library, Duke University.*

5. As they traveled south, men, deemed by the traders as most likely to escape, were chained together and put in the front of the line; women, unchained, walked behind. The traders' disciplinary practice shaped the connections the slaves made with one another as they traveled south. Those connections themselves sometimes grew into conspiracies and rebellions. *Courtesy of the University of North Carolina Press.*

6. For some, death was preferable to the slave trade. Their suicides made credible the threats of other slaves who resisted their owners' efforts to sell them by threatening suicide or self-mutilation. *Courtesy of the Schomburg Center for Research in Black Culture.*

7. While they were for sale in the market, slaves slept in jails within the slave traders' yards. Within the tightly controlled premises of the slave pens, slaves were nevertheless able to keep up connections and to share useful information about the trade. *Courtesy of the Library of Congress.*

8. This watercolor of a slave pen in New Orleans' downtown market was done shortly after the Civil War. The property had been used for selling slaves from the 1830s on and had been owned by such slave traders as Hope H. Slatter, Jonathan Wilson, and Joseph Bruin. *Courtesy of the New Orleans Notarial Archives.*

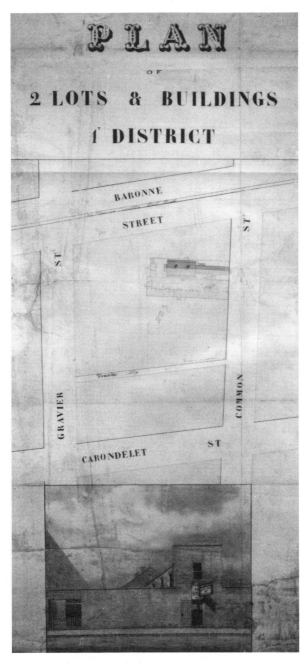

9. In the 1850s this slave pen in New Orleans' uptown market was owned by dealer Charles Lamarque. Next door was another slave pen. Down the street, an upholstery shop, a cotton brokerage, and a coffee house. Pietro Gauldi, "Two Lots on Common St." (10.14). *Courtesy of the New Orleans Notarial Archives.*

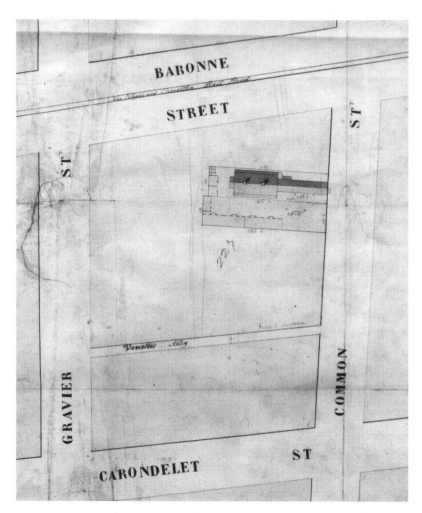

10. Commonly, fifty or a hundred people were held for sale in a space the size of a home lot. Their nights were spent in the jails (bottom edge of the diagram); their days were spent exercising in the yard or being examined in the showrooms in the main building. *Courtesy of the New Orleans Notarial Archives.*

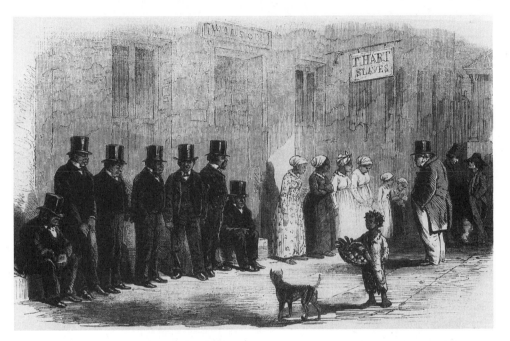

11. Before an 1852 law banned the practice, slaves in New Orleans were often sold on the street. Their uniform dress was calculated to obscure differences among them. Their varied postures, however, hint at different attitudes toward sale — attitudes that were, perhaps, designed to manipulate the buyers in the market to do what the slaves wanted them to do. *Collection of author.*

12. Although most of the slaves sold by the traders in New Orleans were not sold at auction, auctions were a common way of liquidating estates and settling debts. This painting of an auction in Richmond, where many of the slaves carried south were purchased by traders, shows that auctions were preceded by the same sorts of conversations and examinations that characterized the face-to-face bargains made in the traders' pens. *Courtesy of the Virginia Historical Society.*

13. This ad for a group of slaves to be sold at auction replays some of the sales pitches the traders made in the pens. Descriptions that look like qualifications might just as well be interpreted as fantasies of good living, pre-packaged by the seller for an eager buyer. *Courtesy of Hill Memorial Library, Louisiana State University.*

14. This picture from New Orleans shows a child being placed on a table so that buyers might better examine his joints with their hands and estimate his vitality as he was paced back and forth in front of them. *Courtesy of the Historic New Orleans Collection.*

15. John Brown was sold (by the pound) as a child in Georgia and as an adult in the yard of New Orleans trader Theophilus Freeman. He later escaped to London, where he wrote the story of his life, including his time in the slave trade. *Courtesy of the Schomburg Center for Research in Black Culture.*

16. The slave trade played a central role in the bustling economy of the lower South. Many of the slaves sold in New Orleans arrived in boats which carried the cotton and sugar produced by still other slaves to market on their return journeys. *Courtesy of the Historic New Orleans Collection.*

18. This portrait, entitled "Colonel and Mrs. James A. Whiteside, Son Charles, and Servants," gives some sense of the integral role that slaves played in the social identities of their owners. When these slaveholders sat for their portrait, they composed themselves out of slaves — their domestic slaves in the foreground and their slave-tended estate in the background. *Courtesy of the Hunter Museum of American Art, Chattanooga, Tennessee, Gift of Mr. and Mrs. Thomas B. Whiteside.*

HAULING THE WHOLE

WEEKS PICKING

17. Many of the slaves sold in the New Orleans market were put to work producing cotton in the fields of the lower South. The work was unfamiliar to most slaves from the upper South and they were punished when their production lagged. *Courtesy of the Historic New Orleans Collection.*

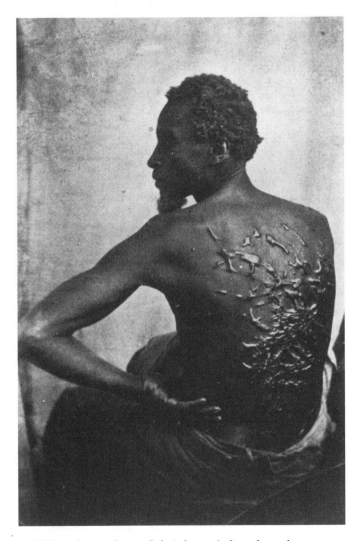

19. When slaves subverted their buyers' plans through unwillingness or simple inability, they were often brutally punished. Scars like these were used by buyers in the market to judge the "character" of the one who bore them. For slaves, however, the scars were better used as an estimate of the character of the one who inflicted them. Gordon, the man pictured here, was enslaved in Mississippi before escaping in 1863. *Courtesy of the Schomburg Center for Research in Black Culture.*

STATE OF LOUISIANA, ⎱
CITY OF NEW ORLEANS. ⎰

Be it known, THAT this day, before me, DANIEL ISRAEL RICARDO,
a Notary Public, in and for the City and Parish of New Orleans, State of Louisiana, aforesaid, duly commissioned and sworn, *Personally came and appeared,*

Calvin Morgan Rutherford of this City,
unmarried; —————————————————————

——————————— *Who declared that for and in conside=*
=ration of the price and Sum of Eight Hundred
Dollars to him in hand well and truly paid in ready
Money, the receipt whereof is hereby acknowledged he
does ———————————————————————

BY THESE PRESENTS, *grant, bargain, sell, convey, transfer, assign, and set
over,* with a full guarantee against all troubles, debts, mortgages, claims, evictions,
donations, alienations, or other incumbrances whatsoever,

unto Edwin Kingsbury Bryant Palso of this City
here present accepting and purchasing for himself his
heirs and Assigns and acknowledging delivery and
possession thereof a certain Negro man Slave for
life name Cæsar aged about Eighteen years, he
is fully guaranteed against the redhibitory vices and
maladies and defects prescribed by Law and is free
from incumbrance as will appear by reference to the
annexed Certificate of the Recorder of Mortgages
for this City and Parish dated this day ————
——————— *Said Slave was imported into this State by*
the present vendor and the State Tax has been duly
paid thereon as will appear by the annexed receipt

20. Under Louisiana law, slaves were real estate and their sale had to be officially
recorded in order to be legal. Southern archives are full of forms like these,
memorials of a time when slaves' lives could be forever changed as easily as a
piece of paper could be passed from one slaveholder's hand to that of another.
Courtesy of the Historic New Orleans Collection.

CHAPTER FOUR

TURNING PEOPLE
INTO PRODUCTS

Sₗₐᵥₑ ₜᵣₐ𝐃𝐄𝐑𝐒 were sometimes accused of selling people who were dead. J. B. Alexander, for instance, did not have time to get very far from the slave market with the slave he had just bought before a man whom he did not know walked up to him and "remarked to him that he had bought a dead Negro." Alexander asked the man what he meant. The man replied that he could see that "the boy was sick," too sick to be cured—already dead. The man, it turned out, was in a position to know dead slaves when he saw them. He had been a slave trader for almost thirty years.[1] The lawyers for the hapless Dixons invoked a similar set of images in the suit brought by the couple against the slave dealer who had sold them Critty and Creasy. As the Dixons' lawyers saw it, the trader was "an experienced jockey" who had resorted "to all of the nostrums and arts of his profession, such as cod liver oil, stimulants, etc. to fatten and keep up these dying consumptives until he could get them off his hands."[2] Essentially, they charged the dealer with sending the dead to market.

The imagery used by the lawyers—the imagery of forbidden nostrums and secret arts—had much more to do with the world of the occult than with the supposedly rational workings of the slave trade. But what served the lawyers for the Dixons as an accusation of improper conduct might have summoned up a vision of the perfect sale for a slave trader: an otherwise lifeless body quickened into motion by the magic of the market. By this dark magic, this necromancy, new people could be made out of the parts of old ones: slaves could be detached from their pasts and stripped of their identities, their bodies could be disciplined into order and decorated for market, their skills could be assigned, their qualities designated, their stories retold. Slaves could be remade in the image of the irresistible power of their salability—fed, medicated, beaten, dressed, hectored, and arrayed until they outwardly appeared to be no more than advertisements for themselves. The dead, their bodies disjointed from the past and their identities evacuated, would walk to sale.[3]

SLAVE MAKING

In the daily practice of the slave pens, slaves were treated as physical manifestations of the categories the traders used to select their slaves—No. 1, Second Rate, and so on. After gathering individuals into categories and attributing to those categories an independent existence in "the slave market" by which they could be compared to all other categories (and all other goods), the traders turned those categories around and used them to evaluate the individuals of whom they were supposedly composed.[4] Thus could slave trader J. M. Wilson walk into a Louisiana courtroom, declare himself "familiar with the prices of slaves in this market" (that is, with the price categories that traders used to do their business), and testify to the value of Clarissa and her family without ever having seen them. Similarly, slave trader J. W. Boazman could testify to the value of "Negroes bought about September 1851" in supporting a slaveholder's claim that the death of a woman he owned at the hands of a careless contractor had cost him a thousand dollars. Thus could slave trader David Wise testify to the value of a human eye: "Being asked if the girl had a filter on her eye if it would impair her value, he says it would impair its value from $25 to $40."[5] In switching the pronoun from "her" to "it," Wise revealed in a word what his business was about: turning people into prices. He used the tables of aggregates which *reflected* the market valuation of people to *project* that valuation.

The price tables made traders like Boazman and Wise capable of extraordinary feats of comparison, but it was their daily business to guide the buyers beyond comparison to selection: to get them to single out the one slave especially suited to their purposes from the many nominally similar slaves available in the market. In the daily practice of the slave pens, then, real slaves had a double relation to the abstract market in the traders' imaginations. On the one hand, they were to be transformed into exemplars of the category to which they had been assigned; but once the categories of comparison had been established and embodied, the slaves were supposed to become once again visible as individuals—comparable to all of those who inhabited the same category, yet different enough to attract a buyer's eye and seal the sale. This daily dialectic of categorization and differentiation was the magic by which the traders turned people into things and then into money.

Traders began to package their slaves for market before they ever reached the slave pens. As they neared their destination, the traders removed the heavy chains and galling cuffs from their slaves' arms and legs and allowed the slaves to wash and rest and heal. The traders shaved men's beards and combed their hair, they plucked gray hairs or blackened them with dye—the "blacking" that appears in their account books was perhaps intended for this purpose. Slave trader John White was clearer about what he did with the tallow he bought: it was "for the girls' hair."[6] The rituals of preparation continued once slaves had reached the market. In the slave pens the traders increased rations of bacon, milk, and butter, a fattening diet one trader referred to as "feeding up."[7] To keep the slaves' muscles toned, the traders set them to dancing and exercising, and to make their skin shine with the appearance of health, the traders greased the slaves' faces with "sweet oil" or washed them in "greasy water."[8]

The traders also hired doctors to visit their pens regularly. "Scarcely a day passes . . . but what I go to his establishment, it being on the road to my office," testified Dr. J. H. Lewis of J. M. Wilson's slave pen. Dr. John Carr spoke similarly of the slave yard owned by Hope H. Slatter in the 1840s: "is generally in the habit of calling there and sitting for an hour in the afternoon . . . he usually visited all the slaves." When Slatter's yard passed into the possession of Bernard and Walter Campbell, Carr continued as the yard's doctor: "was the attending physician at Campbell's establishment . . . is in the habit of visiting Campbell's establishment two or three times a day."[9] These accounts may be exaggerated, for these doctors had as much experience in the courts as they did in the slave market, and it was part of their ongoing business relation with the traders to emphasize the good care received by slaves in the pens. But even if they overstated the frequency and quality of their slave-market ministrations, it is clear that sick slaves in the pens often received professional treatment. At the time of his death and estate settlement, slave dealer Elihu Cresswell was carrying debts for having slaves' teeth pulled and providing them with medicine. In his account book John White recorded the twenty-five dollars he paid a physician to look after his slaves in 1845, and regularly noted prescriptions and treatment for slaves in the pens—chloride of lime, capsules, cupping, medicine. The New Orleans slave yards kept by Cresswell and Benjamin Screws both had separate rooms set aside for the sick. Fear of contagion more than charity might have motivated the traders' concern, but the separation of the sick was often accompanied by medical care. Frank, for example, was "nursed" back to health from yellow fever in slave dealer Calvin Rutherford's "private house," and Solomon Northup was treated for small pox in the hospital, as, according to an 1841 city law, all slaves suffering from infectious disease were to be.[10]

In the slave pens, however, medical treatment was a trick of the trade, nothing more. These expenditures were speculations like any others the traders made, tactical commitments to slaves' bodies that were underwritten by the hope of their sale. When that hope ran out, so seemingly did the traders' concern. John White's reckoning of his chances of curing and selling Harriet, for instance, can be tracked through the pages of his account book—capsules for Harriet on February third, cupping Harriet on the fifth, burial of her child on the fourteenth, brandy for Harriet on the sixteenth, burial for Harriet on the nineteenth, the sale of Harriet's surviving children on the twenty-first. Harriet was treated when it seemed possible to save her, comforted (or quieted) with alcohol when it did not, and buried when she died. Her children, less valuable than she had been, were not treated at all and were quickly sold when their care became the trader's responsibility and their presence in the yard a threat to his other property.[11] There was always an alternative to caring for sick slaves: selling them quickly.

Their bodies prepared, the slaves in the pens were packaged for sale. The traders' account books document their extensive daily attention to presentation: entries for dresses, shoes, stockings, and head coverings for the women; suits with undershirts, drawers, socks, boots, and sometimes a hat for the men. In October of 1857 John White bought forty identical blue suits for the men in his yard.[12] The clothes masked differences among the slaves; individual pasts and potential problems were covered over in uniform cloth. The sick and the well, those from far away and those from nearby, the eager, the unattached, and the angry—all looked alike in the trader's window-dressed version of slavery.

The clothes suggested not only comparability but also cleanliness and chastity. Eyre Crowe's famous drawing of slaves lined out for sale in New Orleans shows women with long-sleeved blouses and covered heads, men in black suits with top hats. Noting the kerchiefs tied around their heads "in a mode peculiar to the Negress," northern writer Joseph Ingraham pronounced the women he saw in the market "extremely neat and 'tidy.'" "Their appearance had little of the repulsiveness we are apt to associate with the slaves," wrote Robert Chambers, another northern visitor to the slave pens.[13] None of the poverty and toil that characterized the daily life of American slaves, none of the bareness that contributed so powerfully to the historical sexualization of black bodies, was immediately apparent in the slave market. These people were dressed as ideal slaves, exaggerated in the typicality of their appearance, too uniform, too healthy, too clean. Through the daily practice of the pens, individual slaves were turned into physical symbols of their own salability—nothing else about them was immediately apparent.

Except for the occasional whim or fancy. On the same page of the ledger book in which he recorded the prices of the steel rings and chain which he used to shackle the limbs of his slaves on the way south, Floyd Whitehead noted his purchases of the three gold rings and half-dozen "plated" ones he placed on their fingers when he sent them to market. John White bought a cravat and a "Boy's Fancy Suit" in 1857; in earlier years he had bought "trimmings" for men's pants and a shawl for a woman he was taking to Mobile to be sold. A. J. Walker sent enslaved women to sale wearing gloves.[14] These conceits were meant to draw a buyer's eye as he scanned a line of slaves, to suggest uncommon gentility, a paternalism of the "his-master's-clothes" variety, or an exotic fantasy. These obviously contrived appearances—self-revealing in their pretense—both perplexed the buyers' gaze and invited further investigation.

Their bodies treated and dressed, the slaves were turned out for sale divided by sex. "Men on one side, women on the other": the phrase runs through descriptions of the slave market like a leitmotif. "Here may be seen husbands separated from wives by only the width of the room, and children from parents, one or both," wrote John Brown, reenvisioning the family ties that were erased by the traders' practice.[15] Even when the traders kept track of family ties, they often severed them in the slave market. Of the seven slaves bracketed with the label "Overton purchase" in John White's "slave record" for 1846, two were sold together, one sent home as unsalable, and the rest sold individually in Louisiana, Tennessee, and Alabama. Families were likewise carefully bracketed on the bill of lading for a shipment of slaves received by Seraphim Cucullu in the winter of 1836. But they were indiscriminately separated as Cucullu sold them over the course of the spring. Cucullu's account-book record of the buyers of his divided slaves is a testament to the commitment of his employees to his instructions "that price might be the guide and to sell for the best of his interests."[16] That meant selling slaves the way the buyers wanted them, according to sex-specific demand rather than according to family ties.

The lengths to which slave traders could go in dismantling and repackaging slave families in the image of the market were limited by Louisiana law. The original *Code Noire* forbade the separation by sale of children under the age of ten from their mothers, and in 1829 the law was explicitly extended to outlaw the importation of thusly separated slaves.[17] While the 1829 law should not be ignored (it is a good example of slaveholders negotiating a hard bargain with their own consciences and of the tendency of paternalism to limit its already meager promises to protection of the very young), its effect should not be overemphasized. What the law did was to give legal credence to the categories according to which slave traders did their business. Who, after all, would favor a trade in motherless children? Not the slave traders. The vast majority of family-separating sales occurred in the upper South, out of the effective reach of the law. And the vast majority of these involved the removal of the parent; slave traders, especially those who traveled long distances, had little use for small children.[18] By the 1850s, as single women became a featured category of trade, orphaned children became a recognizable portion of the population in upper South slave communities.[19] Trader John White left four of Mary Cole's children (aged two to ten) behind when he took Cole and her three older children to New Orleans in 1846. Trader J. W. Boazman explained a similar choice this way: "servants are less valuable with children than without." But if the traders wanted to trade in children who had been separated from their mothers, there was little to keep them from adhering to the letter of the law by making orphans rather than finding them. It is hard to read slave trader David Wise's statement that "witness has often sold little children . . . " without wondering about his own role in the qualification he quickly added " . . . who had lost their mother."[20] The 1829 law, then, provided the maximal rhetorical effect with the minimal practical disruption of the slave trade. It stripped "the slave family" of its existing members, their history, their ties and affinities and substituted a more salable definition—a mother and a young child.

As well as packaging the slaves into salable lots, the traders packed them into racial categories. By the time they turned their slaves out for sale, the traders had transformed the market categories they used to talk to one another into the racial categories they used to talk to the buyers. In their back-and-forth market reports the traders described slaves as Prime, No. 1, No. 2, and so on, but on ninety percent of the Acts of Sale recorded by New Orleans notaries they used words like Negro, Griffe, Mulatto, or Quadroon.[21] These words were explicitly biological: they bespoke pasts that were not visible in the slave market by referring to parents and grandparents who had been left behind with old owners. But they did so by referring to something that the buyers would be able to see: skin color.

Brushed, dressed, and polished, divided by sex (or lamely protected by law), assigned a new history and a racial category, the people in the pens were lined out for sale by height: "The men were arranged on one side of the room, the women on the other, the tallest were placed at the head of the row, then the next tallest, and so on in order of their respective heights," remembered Solomon Northup.[22] Around the walls of the slave pens, the slaves were arranged to reflect the traders' buyer-tracking tables. As the slaves were hectored into line at the beginning of every day, there were no husbands or wives apparent among them, no old lovers or new friends; there were only men and women, field hands and house servants, Negro, Griffe, and Mulatto, tall, medium, and short.

Having done all they could to make real people represent the constructed categories of the marketplace, the traders began to try to turn them into money. Value in the slave market emerged out of the play of similarity with difference, the choice of one slave from among many similar slaves made a sale. To sell a slave, the traders had to peel back their own representations of commodified similarity and slip beneath them a suggestion of personal distinction that would make one slave stand out to a buyer who was trying to distinguish himself from all of the other buyers in the market. The traders had to make a pitch. In the slave pens, the traders pitched their slaves by telling stories that seemed to individualize and even humanize the depersonalized slaves. They breathed the life of the market into the bodies, histories, and identities of the people they were trying to sell, by using a simulacrum of human singularity to do the work of product differentiation.

The traders' reputation for buying the sick and malign on the cheap only to sell them at premium prices made it important for the traders to explain why the slaves were in the market in the first place.[23] Such as: "Sold for no fault of their own." This unasked-for excuse had specific variants, all of which shifted attention from slaves to their former owners. From an advertisement: "The Owner of the following named valuable Slaves being on the eve of departure for Europe." From Edward Sparrow's account of why he sent a man later alleged to have been alcoholic to be sold in the slave market: "Mrs. Sparrow expressed a wish that he should be sold here where his wife was." From the pitch made by a trader for a slave who had been once returned: "the party to whom he was sold had no fault except that the man was too much of a French Cook." From the explanation made by a trader about a man later alleged to have been once returned to him as a thief, drunkard, and runaway: "Did not take him back because he was a bad Negro, but because Forbes [the first buyer] was unable to pay for him." From a trader's account of why Jane, who was allegedly consumptive, had been returned after her first sale: "she was not a hair dresser, the lady was not pleased with her, that is the only reason I heard . . . for not keeping the girl."[24] These stories were neither wholly believable nor easily disproven; the former owners to whom they referred all questions were distant in time and space, unavailable to offer their own account. As a warranty the stories were useless; the traders were bound only by the stories they wrote down and signed. But as a warning to buyers, the pitches were perhaps more useful: the slaves' histories, not quite visible behind the shimmering tales told in the slave pens, belonged to the traders.

Some of the stories the traders told were quite simple, advertisements that were put forward as qualifications, accounts of past work through which buyers could view a certain future: first-rate cotton picker, experienced drayman, cooper, carpenter, cook, nurse, and so on. And some were more detailed: in the words of a slave trader's handbill, "Bill, Negro man, aged about 28 years, excellent servant and good pastry cook"; or, in the words of a witness to a trader's pitch, "[He] said that said slave was a first rate cook, a very good washer and could plait plain shirts very well & that Mr. Hewes would be satisfied in every respect with having purchased said Negress."[25] However brief, these lists of skills referred to the experience and judgment of former owners, to a past distant from the slave pens. But they insinuated themselves into the present as trustworthy representations of past experience, drawing whatever authenticity they had (enough to convince Mr. Hewes) from the constant babble of talk about slaves that characterized the social life of southern slaveholders. The traders were taking hold of slaveholders' fantasies about the slave market, wrapping them around the slaves they had for sale, and selling them back to the buyers as indications of those buyers' own good fortune and discernment

And the traders' pitches went well beyond work. They could spin a detailed fantasy out of a list of supposed skills: "Sarah, a mulatress, aged 45 years, a good cook and accustomed to housework in general, is an excellent and faithful nurse for sick persons, and in every respect a first rate character." Sarah, as sold, was gentility and paternalism embodied—good meals, a clean house, a companion who would wait faithfully by the bed of an ailing (vulnerable) owner. "Dennis, her son, a mulatto, aged 24 years, a first rate cook and steward for a vessel, having been in that capacity for many years on board one of the Mobile packets; is strictly honest, temperate, and is a first rate subject."[26] Dennis would bring with him a hint of riverboat grandeur: the plush seats and ornate surroundings; the graceful service and extensive menu; the pleasure of traveling first class.[27] And Dennis was trustworthy: he had worked on a boat but not run away; he might be hired out or given the run of the house. His purchase would make good sense; his service would be in good taste. And, though Dennis and his mother were put up for sale separately, they could be bought together by someone who cared enough to do so.

The slave traders could line their families out separately and then knit them together again in the sales pitch. They could package and sell the negation of their own way of doing business by offering the buyers a chance to rejoin families that had been sundered in the market. Slave-market paternalism thus replayed the plots of proslavery propaganda and fiction: the good-hearted slave at the side of the dying master; the slave who could be trusted to master himself; the slaveholder's saving interventions in the life of the unfortunate slave. As representations of individual slaves, the traders' pitches drew their authenticity from slaveholders' shared fantasies of gentility, reciprocity, and salvation. The traders' stories helped the buyers to mirror their shared fantasies in the individual slaves who stood before them, to imagine that they were distinguishing themselves through the purchase of the slave they chose.

There was a specific commercial variant to the slave-sale story in which the traders set aside bargaining to give the buyer some inside advice. The Virginia slave trader who sold Eden said that he was "so pleased" with Eden that he put the slave to work in the slave pen. He continued his description of Eden's virtues (that is, salability) by saying that the slave "always rendered a correct account to his master . . . and he was never chastised, and it is a rare case when a slave is sent six months to sell without being chastised."[28] Those who did not trust the traders' stories were sometimes allowed to take a peek into their business practice. James Blakeny literally opened his account books—where else would a trader unmask himself but in the counting room?—in trying to sell Mary Ellen Brooks to Bruckner Payne. Blakeny "told Payne he would sell her for $600 thereby losing her clothing and shipping costs" and exhibited a bill of lading to prove the price he had paid. Making a similar pitch, slave trader David Wise exhibited his own incentives when he told Clarissa's buyers "that he would dispose of the girl at a low price on account of her advanced state of pregnancy."[29] At the time Blakeny and Wise retold these slave-market stories, they were in Louisiana courtrooms being sued for knowing that the slaves they sold were mortally ill. In the courtroom, as in the slave market, the references to their own incentives were deployed by the traders to shield their motives from further scrutiny. "Negro Driver," "Southern Yankee," "Southern Shylock," they were called: what better proof of a trader's sincerity than an open accounting of what they had at stake?[30]

As they played their way back and forth between the stories told about every slave and the pitches they made for any slave, the traders sometimes had to refit their shopworn pitches to specific circumstances. Apparent ills required careful narration. A cough in the slave market was evidence of a present cold or past sickness—nothing serious, nothing incipient. Other ailments were similarly explained by being explained away: Sally's loose teeth—"they could have been pulled out with a person's finger"—were attributed to her excessive use of Calomel; the fit Henry had been seen having in the street was a result of his "pretending to be sick all the time"; Lewis's ruined knee was described by the broker at a probate sale as a "temporary twist received a few days previous while assisting others in covering a house"; Phillis's swollen leg was rheumatism, "nothing . . . it had never interfered with her work"; the swelling beneath Seraphine's skirt, which turned out to be a very large tumor, was described by the man selling her as evidence of her pregnancy.[31] These were minor ailments—some regrettable like Henry's fake fits, some laudable like Lewis's willingness to endanger himself in helping others—but all temporary. All of these stories emphasized circumstance in explaining apparent irregularity, and all of them provided buyers with the opportunity to demonstrate their abilities in the choice of their slaves: a little treatment, a little discipline—in short, a little mastery—and these slaves would be as good as new.

The traders had to be equally ready to spin unruly evidence of slaves' inward feelings back into the comforting conventions of proslavery rhetoric. When a woman who was missing two fingers mounted the stand in Richmond, the auctioneer quickly explained that the doctor had removed the first finger for a medical reason and she had herself cut off the second because it pained her. The disquieting specter of a woman who would choose to mutilate her hand rather than be sold was brushed over with the reassuring image of a slave so stupid and imitative that she would cut off one finger because the doctor had cut off another.[32] Anton Reiff, a visitor to New Orleans, remembered seeing a woman crying on the auction stand and recorded what he was able to learn about her in his diary: "Her master was in debt and was obliged to sell her to pay some mortgage. She had always lived with the family. She was about 35 years old. Her grief (to me) was heartrending. She wept most bitterly."[33] The loyal slave sold for her owner's debts: whether or not the story Reiff recorded was true, it was effective. The woman's tears became part of the auctioneer's pitch, and Anton Reiff, standing in the slave market, felt his heart rent by a convention of proslavery paternalism.

All of these stories may have been believed by the traders who told them; most of them may have been true, but their veracity is less important than their form. The traders' stories, redolent with the comforting commonplaces of slaveholding culture, guided the buyers' eyes to what they were supposed to see. The slave traders' stories suggested that the buyer of a particular slave would be a man with a sharp eye for the main chance, or a taste for the exceptional, or a singular capacity to do right. As they packaged their slaves in stories about the distant past, the traders were telegraphing suggestive accounts of the slaveholding futures that were for sale in the pens. Along with the virtues of their slaves, the traders were scripting those of their buyers.

Some of the people the traders sold were not slaves at all. Eulalie had been living as free for decades when she, her six children, and ten grandchildren were taken by force from their home in Pointe Coupeé, Louisiana, sold at auction in New Orleans, and then placed in a slave pen for "safe keeping." Euphémie and her seven children were held in a New Orleans slave pen, advertised for sale in the New Orleans *Bee*, and sold at public auction. She had been living as a free person for over twenty years. Though they lost years of their life to the slave traders, these women and their families had nearby friends and relatives who could help them reconstruct their histories and successfully sue to have their freedom restored on the grounds that whatever claim there was to their ownership had long since lapsed through disuse.[34] The hopes of other free people sold as slaves, however, were even more attenuated.

The shades of legality in which the traders dealt sometimes crossed into outright kidnapping. The list of those who managed to send word out of slavery must stand as a partial list of the kidnapped: John Merry, a free man from Illinois, was arrested as a slave in St. Louis and shipped to New Orleans to be sold; Solomon Northup, a free man from New York, was lured with lies to Washington, drugged, threatened with death, and put on a boat for New Orleans, where he was sold in the yard of slave dealer Theophilus Freeman; Albert Young was freed by his Alabama owner's will but nevertheless carried to New Orleans by the will's executor and sold to the New Orleans dealers McRae, Coffman & Co.; John Wesley Dunn, another free man, was charged with stealing

an "old coat" in Baltimore, jailed, sold to slave dealer Hope H. Slatter, and carried to New Orleans, where he was sold again. Messages sent by Merry and Northup reached their friends, and they were freed from slavery through the intervention of the courts. Young's suit also reached the courts, but his freedom was voided on the grounds that his emancipation was not legal under Alabama law. The letter Dunn sent for help may never have reached his father, to whom it was addressed.[35]

None of these stolen people could have been sold if their histories were known, so they were sold with new ones. These were only the most extreme cases of the creative power of the traders' market practice. Or, at least, they seem the most extreme, because lying about a slave's origins seems more abject than ignoring them, selling a person under an uncertain title seems more mendacious than selling with a clear title, and kidnapping a free person seems more shocking than selling a slave. But the extremity of these stories represents the regularity of what slave traders did every day for four hundred years, what they did hundreds of thousands of times during the antebellum period. Just as kidnapping made slaves of free people, the traders' packaging created slaves who did not previously exist out of the pieces of people who formerly did. By detaching slaves from their history and replacing human singularity with fashioned salability, the traders were doing more than selling slaves: they were making them.

Ultimately, however, the rites of the market had to be enacted by the slaves. From the time the buyers entered the yard in the morning to the time they left at night, the slaves were expected to enact carefully scripted roles. Solomon Northup remembered Theophilus Freeman hectoring his slaves to perform and "threatening" them with beatings if they stepped out of their assigned roles. In the slave pens, wooden boards with holes drilled through them or wide leather straps attached to a handle, were substituted for the mortifying lash, because paddles raised blisters but left no permanent scars. The traders' instruments of torture enforced the story they were trying to tell without leaving a trace of its source.[36] Northup also remembered Freeman "holding out various inducements," which left even fewer traces than beatings. The historian Michael Tadman has discovered that slaves were sometimes promised small cash rewards "if they would try to get homes and not do anything against the interest of their sales." As well as the entries for calico dresses and pantaloons, slave trader John White recorded regular

cash outlays to slaves to make sure that the costumes he had bought were inhabited with the right spirit. Northup remembered that Freeman used his slaves' own hopes to fund his inducements. Instructing Northup to hold up his head and look "smart," Freeman told Northup that he "might, perhaps, get a good master" if he "behaved."[37]

Throughout the day, the traders goaded the slaves into motion so that the buyers could better evaluate the way they moved. "Now hold up your head and walk pert . . . Quick—come—pert—only there already?—pert!" the antislavery journalist James Redpath remembered hearing a slave dealer's assistant bark at a slave. Around the walls of the pens, slaves were set into motion to prove their stamina and agility. Fredrika Bremer remembered seeing "forty or fifty" men walking up and down in front of a slave pen in Georgia. Robert Chambers remembered seeing slaves being asked to run across the sale room in Virginia. John Brown remembered slaves dancing, jumping, walking, leaping, tumbling and twisting before the buyers' eyes, showing off that they had "no stiff joints or other physical defects." The physician philosophers of the slave market admonished buyers to look even deeper. Juriah Harriss believed that constitutional unsoundness would become apparent as slaves were forced into motion before the buyers. Samuel Cartwright thought that slaves with "Negro Consumption" would be unable to ascend a flight of stairs without elevating their heart rates to a hundred and thirty or forty beats per minute.[38]

The traders instructed slaves to give ages that accorded with their polished bodies and to hide pasts that might make buyers wary. Slaves who had run away or been ill were told to hide their histories. Those who were being sold for their skills were told to "exaggerate their accomplishments." Slaves in the pens were instructed to appear happy and active, William Wells Brown remembered, "some were set to dancing, some to jumping, some to singing, and some to playing cards. This was done to make them seem cheerful as possible." Solomon Northup remembered that Theophilus Freeman "exhorted us to appear smart and lively" and provided Northup with a violin that he might give the others music to dance by. Following the conventions of antebellum racism, slaves were made to demonstrate their salability by outwardly performing their supposed emotional insensibility and physical vitality.[39]

These carefully prepared performances made it difficult for the buyers to sort representation from reality, and like other slave-import-

ing states, Louisiana had strong warranty laws designed to rebalance the relationship between seller and buyer.[40] The asymmetry of information in the slave market had been addressed in the Louisiana *Civil Code* by the law of redhibition, or "the avoidance of sale on account of some vice or defect in the thing sold." As a justice of the Louisiana Supreme Court put it in 1859, these laws were "evidently created as a matter of policy and . . . founded upon the difficulty which purchasers of slaves recently brought from another state experience in procuring proof of their bodily condition and the comparative ease with which the proof of that fact could be made by the vendors."[41] Specific provisions of the *Civil Code* limited actions for redhibition to those cases in which the problem was not apparent upon "simple inspection" and not explicitly exempted from the general warranty. The sales of slaves (and animals) could be voided for "vices" of either body or character. Leprosy, madness, and epilepsy were considered absolute vices of body, their bare existence sufficient cause to void a sale. Other diseases were considered in proportion to the disability they caused. Vices of character, as defined by Louisiana law, were limited to cases in which it could be proven that a slave had committed a capital crime, was "addicted to theft," or "in the habit of running away." A habit of running away was established by proving that a slave had run away "twice for several days, or once for more than a month." Warranty suits had to be preceded by an attempt at "amicable return" of the unwanted slave(s) and filed within one year of the date of purchase. Under an 1834 addition to the law, buyers of recently imported slaves did not have to prove that the "vice" was existent at the time of the sale if it became evident within two months (for questions of character) or two weeks (for illness or infirmity).[42]

These buyer-protection laws and presumptions could be overcome by specific declarations, which took the form of either a written statement of the maladies or "vices" that were specifically excepted from the warranty or simply a clause voiding the standard form of warranty ("guaranteed against the vices and maladies prescribed by law"). Such provisions, however, were comparatively rare, appearing on only six percent of the Acts of Sale notarized by buyers in the New Orleans market.[43] Most slave traders appear to have played the odds, preferring to sell risky slaves as sound ones and counting on the buyers' difficulties in returning a slave and filing a suit to make good their risk.

Returning slaves, after all, cost dissatisfied buyers even more money than they had already spent in the market: the cost of transportation for the slave, the buyer, and usually a sympathetic witness; the cost of having depositions taken or of getting people to court, including exceptional charges for expert witnesses like physicians; court costs and lawyers' fees; the possibility of losing. Indeed, the relative frequency with which buyers who lived at some distance from New Orleans appeared in court to sue slave traders suggests that the traders may have been choosing their targets carefully, identifying the out-of-town buyers for whom returning an unwanted slave would be the most difficult and steering them toward slaves about whom the traders themselves had suspicions.[44]

When dissatisfied buyers did make it back to the market, the traders sometimes raised other barriers. They refused to accept returns, which made buyers go to law; they deducted charges from the price of the slave or would take back slaves only if they were exchanged for new ones, the buyer paying a surcharge of a few hundred dollars; they temporized about whether the slaves were really unsound and put buyers off by asking them to wait until they returned for the next selling season or until slaves' diseases abated; they dodged buyers when they knew the year within which buyers had to file their suits was about to expire.[45] Again, the traders' behavior may have been influenced by the circumstances of the buyer. "Repeat players," slave traders who hoped to develop relationships with specific buyers or reputations in a region, may have been more likely to accept returns. Wealthy Louisiana planter Thomas Pugh, who yearly bought large numbers of slaves for his sugar plantations near Donaldsonville, Louisiana, certainly had no trouble in negotiating returns and exchanges with both John White and Theophilus Freeman.[46]

Though most buyers had to take more care than a man with the slave-market stature of Thomas Pugh, those who returned slaves to the pens usually had the law on their side, and many traders accepted returns rather than risking suits. One slave salesman stated that such a practice was a matter of course in the pen where he worked: "Mr. Slatter's instructions were never to misrepresent Negroes and to exchange them at any time rather than go to a lawsuit."[47] It is hard to imagine the man saying anything else—that Slatter told him to lie to customers, sell them sick slaves, and refuse to take them back, for example—with a thousand dollar suit hanging in the balance. But even if accepting returned slaves was not a hard-and-fast rule, it was a practice common enough to have generated a common resolution: slaves who had been returned to the traders were often resold to other buyers, sometimes for prices higher than the traders had received the first time around.[48]

No matter what they eventually did when faced with a returned slave, traders did the daily work of preparing and selling their slaves in the shadow of the law. The representations traders made in the marketplace could be subject to subsequent legal action; vices they managed to conceal at the time of sale could later emerge as the grounds for a suit; credulous buyer could turn sedulous litigant. The traders had to consider the law when they decided who to sell to whom. John White's slave record book listed a number of slaves as "in my hands unsold" at the end of every season. Some people the slave traders just could not sell.[49] Every year White's firm sent a few slaves back to central Missouri after unsuccessfully offering them for sale in New Orleans: five sent in 1846; six in 1851; five more in 1852.[50] No doubt those were small numbers to John White, who sold a hundred or more slaves in a season. But they were momentous decisions to the small number they affected. Slaves who could not be sold sometimes ended up in the places from which they had been taken in the first place, restored to their families and communities. "Sent home," one of White's entries reads.

The daily practice of the pens lay at the juncture of an unknown past and a promised future. As a justice of the Louisiana Supreme Court put it when considering the necessity of the enforcement of redhibition law: "The condition of a Negro at a trader's quarters, well dressed, well fed, unworked—in a word well cared for in every material respect for the express purpose of making a favorable impression on purchasers—is not necessarily a conclusive criterion of the future or the past condition and capability of that same Negro when undergoing the necessary hardships of ordinary slave service." The traders' daily business was to shape the real people they had in their hands to reflect the abstract market they had in their heads, and then to punctuate their categories of comparison with the value-producing practice of differentiation: the special clothes and spatial arrangement, the articulated human connections, the singular story. In the pens the traders medicated and fed and shined and shaved and plucked and smoothed and dressed and sexualized and racialized and narrated people until even the appearance of human singularity had been saturated with the representations of salability. This was the traders' version of necromancy—the magic that could steal a person and inhabit their body with the soul of another—the forcible incorporation of a slave with the spirit of a slaveholder's fantasy.

But though they went to great lengths to replace people with packaging, the traders did not have to fool anyone. Indeed, the traders could no more force their self-revealing representations upon a skeptical buyer than they could do their deadly business without the resistant bodies of living slaves. By replacing biography with salability, the traders did not have to do anything more than shape the discussion. Under the traders' watchful eyes, visible physical coordinates replaced invisible historical identities as the most accessible means for buyers to make their comparisons. Faced with the uncertainties of the slave pens, slave buyers turned to race as the best way to do the business of slavery.

CHAPTER FIVE

⟬ ✦ ⟭

READING BODIES AND
MARKING RACE

I<small>F YOU TAKE UP</small> a copy of Joseph Holt Ingraham's *The Southwest by a Yankee* (1835), you can follow the logic of a visit to the slave pens along the headings at the top of the book's pages: "The Slave Market," "Demeanor of the Slaves," "A Purchase," "African Inferiority." Ingraham was a self-described Yankee, and his account ostensibly resisted the white-supremacist logic it revealed: he followed an observation that "there was no expression indicative of intellect" in the slaves he examined in the market with the suggestion that no final "sentence" should be pronounced upon the mental capacity of slaves until they had been given the chance to develop themselves as free people.[1] Ingraham's flirtation with the slave market, however, was extensive. He made repeated visits to slave pens during his travels through the South, following buyers through their business, observing their gaze—"that singular look, peculiar to the buyer of slaves"—and recording their questions. And he looked for himself. He estimated slaves' "physiognomy," "looks," and "capacity for rapid movement" as a coffle passed him on a southern road, and "conversed with a great number" of the slaves he saw in the market. He was mistaken for a buyer by traders and for a slaveholder by slaves.[2] And when he sat down to record his experiences, he arrayed them in the order reflected by the headings: the market, the slaves he met there, the character of the race—that is, underlying system, daily practice, justifying ideology.

There is no more important question in American history than the one posed by Ingraham's account: the relation of slavery to race, of the process of economic exploitation to the ideology of racial domination. Historians have riddled that relation into various shapes. Some have argued that slavery was built out of race, that culturally based bias against "blackness" and a religiously determined desire to dominate "heathen" Africans underwrote the economic exploitation of the Atlantic slave trade and American slavery. Others have argued that slavery was first and foremost an economic system, that exploitation preceded racialization, and that racism—presumed inferiority—became important only when an existing system of social relations faced novel assertions of human equality. As the historian Barbara Jeanne Fields puts it, race was a particularly toxic "byproduct" of the southern mode of production in the "Age of Revolution." Recently, it has been suggested that both of these descriptions of the relation between economic exploitation and racial domination might be sharpened by attention to everyday life, to the specific historical sites where race was daily given shape.[3]

There were many such sites in the antebellum South, sites which, taken together, provide an outline of the region's white (male) public sphere. Church pulpits where ministers preached Biblical justifications of the enslavement of the "Sons of Ham" were such a site. So were medical and agricultural journals that argued questions about the ultimate unity of the races (monogenesis or polygenesis), the relative strength of the "pure" races and their hybrids, and the specific racial etiology of various diseases and behaviors; Louisiana physician Samuel Cartwright's designations of the physiological causes of running away, *Drapetomania*, and resisting, *Dysthesia Ethiopica*, were unsurpassed in this regard. So were the courtrooms, where cases concerning racial identity were argued in terms of blood quantums and behavior, and disputes concerning slaveholders' economic responsibility for the people they owned or sold were argued in terms of racial character and racist physiology. And then there were the countless visual stereotypes, racist jokes, and staged performances of hierarchy that punctuated daily life in the antebellum South.[4] But at no site was race more readily given daily shape than in the slave market.

MARKING RACE

When Richard Winfield went to the slave market to buy Elvira and Samuel Brown, he took James Calvitt along to help him see. As a witness remembered it, Calvitt had more experience in the slave market than did Winfield, and the sale went something like this: "The Negroes were called in and the girl was examined by Mr. Calvitt in the presence of Winfield. Winfield looked at the slaves. Calvitt asked the slaves some questions." Calvitt remembered the sale similarly. Winfield "looked" at Elvira and then Calvitt "put his hand where her breast ought to be and found nothing but rags." If he had been purchasing on his own behalf, Calvitt added "he would have made her pull her dress off." Soon after Winfield bought her, it became apparent that Elvira was mortally ill—the rags filled out a chest ravaged by consumption—and she died within a few weeks of the sale. Another witness to the sale drew a slaveholder's moral from the story: "Thinks Winfield a poor judge of slaves or he would not have purchased said girl. She is the first girl Winfield ever owned."[5] The observers described the nonslaveholder's inexperience as a matter of insight: Winfield was a poor judge of slaves. Indeed, comparisons of the depth of the slaveholder's insight with that of the nonslaveholder run through all of the descriptions of the sale: Calvitt "examined" while Winfield "looked"; Calvitt touched while Winfield stood by. Calvitt, by all accounts, could see things that Winfield could not.

Being able to see that way was a talent, and inexperienced buyers often took someone along with them when they went to the slave market. Friends, physicians, even slave dealers went to the slave market "at the request" of uncertain buyers.[6] These more experienced men examined the lots of slaves for sale in the market, reading their bodies aloud and helping buyers select the "likely" and the healthy from among them. The presence of these slave-pen guides hints at a masculine social world in which being a "good judge of slaves" was a noteworthy public identity, a world of manly one-upsmanship in which knowledge of slaves' bodies was bandied back and forth as white men cemented social ties and articulated a hierarchy among themselves through shared participation in the inspection and evaluation of black slaves. And as these white men watched one another examine and choose slaves, and as the slave-pen mentors helped inexpert buyers choose slaves, they daily reproduced and passed on the racial "knowledge" by which southern slavery was justified and defended.

A savvy slave buyer knew enough to try to look past the fancy clothes, bright faces, and promising futures lined up against the walls of the slave pens. Mississippi planter John Knight was presumably passing on the opinion of the "old planters" upon whom he regularly relied for advice when he sent his slave-market wisdom to his father-in-law. "The fact is," Knight wrote, "as to the character and disposition of all of the slaves sold by the traders, we know nothing whatever, the traders themselves being generally such liars. Buyers therefore can only judge the *looks* of the Negroes." The effects of the traders' practice—the invisibility of slaves' origins and the obscurity of their histories—and their reputation for dishonesty limited buyers' options as they tried to see through to slaves' pasts and prospects. In the absence of reliable information the buyers began with the physical coordinates of the people who stood before them in the pens.[7]

The axes of physical comparison used by the buyers were prefigured in the traders' practice. Slaves in the market were advertised by their sex, racial designation, age, and skill, and they were lined out for sale according to height. They were arrayed as physical specimens even as their origins, attitudes, and infirmities were covered over by the traders' arts. Buyers preferred darker to lighter people for work in their fields and lighter to darker people for skilled and domestic labor; they generally preferred slaves of "prime age" (between fifteen and twenty-five for laborers), although skilled slaves reached their prime at a later age (around thirty-five). Buyers favored men for work outdoors and women for domestic service; and they apparently paid higher prices for taller slaves.[8] As telling as they are, however, these broad correlations tell us very little about what buyers saw when they looked at slaves, about what was behind the "singular look" that so impressed Joseph Ingraham. What did skin color or sex or size mean to slaveholders?

Asked to explain what they looked for in a slave, most slave buyers would have responded with the word "likely." Today the word means probable, but as slave buyers used it was as much a description as it was a prediction. As they singled out the "likely" from among the many they saw in the pens, slave buyers made detailed inspections of people's bodies which went well beyond the traders' advertisements and the age, sex, and racial designation that were commonly recorded on an Act of Sale. The standard slave inspection, as one buyer described it, went like this: "my inspection was made in the usual manner: their coats being taken off and the breast, arms, teeth, and general form and appearance looked at." The whole process, according to another buyer, might take anywhere from fifteen minutes to half an hour, and bargaining might be stretched over three or four days. The inspections, at least at the outset, were public. The white male buyers in the yard mingled as they walked the rows of slaves; they observed the inspections made by one another and shared their own reckonings of particular slaves; they talked about and joked about the slaves standing before them.[9] All the while they invoked ever more elaborate notions of physiological meaning to make ever finer distinctions among the people they evaluated.

As the slaves were paraded before them, slave buyers began by reading the slaves' skin color, groping their way from visible sign to invisible essence. No doubt buyers were seeing skin color when they described a slave as "a Negro or griff boy," "a griff colored boy," "dark Griff color," or "not black nor Mulatto, but what I believe is usually called a griff color, that is a Brownish Black, or a bright Mulatto."[10] But in describing the blurred spectrum they saw before them, buyers used descriptive language that was infused with the reassuring certitudes of race. The words they used attempted to stabilize the restless hybridity, the infinite variety of mixture that was visible all over the South, into measurable degrees of black and white. They suggested that slaves' skin color could be read as a sign of a deeper set of racial qualities.

In the antebellum slave market, the buyers of field slaves boiled blackness down to a question of physical vitality. Slaveholders' broadest concern was with what they called "acclimation," and they endlessly expressed their preference for slaves who had survived the transition to the harsh conditions of lower-South slavery. When John Knight bought slaves, he looked for men and women from the swampy eastern shore of the Chesapeake Bay, which he thought would better prepare slaves for Louisiana slavery than the "more healthy" regions elsewhere in the upper South. Others would only buy slaves from Louisiana or Mississippi, the "Creole" slaves whom one slaveholder estimated were worth a full quarter more than slaves born elsewhere.[11] In the absence of reliable information about origins, however, skin color often served as a stand-in for acclimation. There are a litany of statements to the effect that the "blackest" slaves were the healthiest. From the published writings of Samuel Cartwright ("All Negroes are not equally black—the blacker the stronger") to the slave-market wish list sent by John Knight to his father-in-law ("I must have if possible the *jet black* Negroes, [they] stand this climate the best"), white men in the antebellum South talked to one another as if they could see slaves' constitutions by looking at their complexions.[12]

So far did slaveholders go in associating blackness and healthfulness that they believed that slaves changed color when they got sick. "Cannot tell her color because she did not look sharp," remembered Maria Piaja of the dying Mary Louise. According to Dr. G. E. Barton, dark-skinned slaves got whiter when they were ill. Barton bolstered his testimony that Elvira was consumptive at the time she was sold by referring to the observation that had led him to judge her unsound: "Her skin was a of a whiter color than was natural from the ordinary complexion of the girl . . . a decided whiteness about the lips and lightness and paleness about the face . . . gums and eyes pale pearly white." This slave-market commonplace was built into a law of nature by Dr. Cartwright: "Deviation from the black color, in the pure race is a mark of feebleness or ill health."[13] Blackness, then, was much more than a question of lineage. Indeed, blackness was much more than a question of color.

As they passed along the line of slaves, buyers evaluated field slaves on the basis of their growth and stature. Tracking age against size was particularly important to those who bought children and young adults. When he was thinking about buying the four children from whom one of his women had been separated, Alonzo Snyder asked about their ages and heights. At a distance, without actually seeing the slaves, Snyder was attempting to do what J. B. Poindexter did in a Louisiana court-room: estimate a slave's age and value on sight: "On looking at the Boy pointed out to him . . . in Court says that if this boy is 14 years old he is worth Eleven Hundred Dollars, but if he is seventeen years old witness thinks he would not be worth as much."[14] For Poindexter, who was a slave trader, putting a body in time was a way to measure the price a buyer would pay. In their efforts to tailor their slaves to the gaze of their customers, some traders selected young slaves according to tables that tracked size against price. William Chambers, a northern visitor to the Richmond market, remembered being handed a price-current which listed the prices for children according to height. On the back of a Dickinson and Hill price circular that priced slaves by market categories, slave trader William Finney sketched his own price list of the prices he would pay for "boys" five feet tall and under: three-inch increments matched by hundred-dollar increases. Slave trader Tyre

Glen literally paid for young men by the pound: "$600 for plow Boys, five to six dollars per pound, if the boy is very likely and ways 60 to 90 or 100, seven may be given, if you can get Ker's boy at seven, take him." John Brown remembered being measured that way, balanced against a saddle by a slave trader, priced, and sold.[15]

Fully grown, the slaves at the top of the traders' buyer-tracking tables would look like Edward, a man whom slave dealer Louis Caretta called "One of the best slaves in the state." Edward was, according to a man who saw him sold, "Stout and low statured. He was black and looked fat . . ." And, according to one who worked with him, "a big, strong, athletic fellow." Similarly, "the likeliest girl" slave trader A. J. McElveen "ever saw" was "Black, 18 years old, very near as tall as I am, no Surplus flesh, fine form." McElveen, indeed, seems to have weighed and measured every slave he bought. "She weighs 173 lbs, 5 feet 10 and three quarters inches high," he proudly reported of the woman.[16] The value of these slaves was outlined by their full physical presence, their size and their strength.

Buyers ran their hands over the bodies of the slaves, rubbing their muscles, fingering their joints, and kneading their flesh. Nathan Brown described a fifteen-year-old boy as "very interesting" after he had seen the slave placed on a table and walked back-and-forth so that those present could examine him "by feeling his joints." Similarly, Solomon Northup remembered that Theophilus Freeman "would make us hold up our head, walk briskly back and forth while customers would feel of our hands and arms and bodies, turn us about." The buyers were searching for taut muscles and hidden problems—broken bones, ossified sprains, severed tendons, internal injuries and illnesses. Listen to Joseph Copes apologizing to a friend for a slave he wanted the other slaveholder to hire: "small of stature, but wiry, strong, and tough."[17] Copes realized that the man's size was against him, and he tried to answer the objection he had imagined with a list of compensatory adjectives describing how the man would feel beneath a buyer's fingers.

The buyers took slaves' fingers in their hands, working them back-and-forth to insure they were, as Charles Ball remembered, "capable of the quick motions necessary in picking cotton." In his slave-market primer, "What Constitutes Unsoundness in the Negro?" Georgia slave doctor Juriah Harriss spent paragraphs on hands, advising slaveholders to look out for slaves who had lost "portions" of their hands or had manual "deformities arising from burns," both of which prevented "the dexterous handling of implements of labor." Asked in court to recall what their slaves' "hands" were like, slaveholders sometimes remembered missing digits: three different witnesses testified that Tom was missing his right forefinger, although they differed about which joint had been severed, the first or the second. Asked to remember William, both his seller and his overseer mentioned his hands. "Short arms and hands," said one. "His arms were short, hands small, and short fingers," said the other.[18] Quite literally, these men remembered William as a hand too small to pick cotton.

In a gesture that many observers connected with the practice of the horse trade, buyers thumbed their way into slaves' mouths to look at their gums and teeth. The whiteness of sick slaves first appeared in their mouths, according to Southern medical science. Samuel Cartwright saw the signs of "Negro Consumption" in the whiteness "of the mucous surfaces lining the gums and the inside of the mouth, lips and cheeks: so white are the mucous surfaces that some overseers call it the paper-gum disease." Cartwright's description suggests that he thought it routine for a slaveholder to pull back slaves' cheeks and finger their lips. And indeed slave trader A. J. McElveen referred to teeth again and again in the letters he wrote to his boss: "Very badly whipped but good teeth"; "Likely except bad teeth"; "very likely, has good sense, fine teeth."[19] McElveen may have been choosing slaves in the same way he would have chosen a horse: judging their age by the condition of their teeth. Or, more simply, McElveen may have been looking at teeth and gums because he knew that his buyers would. The rote practice of the market could produce its own standards of comparison: teeth did not need to be a practical sign of anything in particular to be compared to one another.

When they were described at all, field slaves' faces were evaluated as signs of physical vitality. For Samuel Cartwright, for instance, visage and complexion were interchangeable outward signs of blackness and inward health. "The blackest Negroes were always the healthiest, and the thicker the lips and the flatter the nose, the sounder the constitution," he wrote. John Knight sounded almost gleeful when he prefaced the list of body parts he wanted his father-in-law to buy him in the slave market with the phrase "no matter how ugly the faces."[20] It was the instrumental value of these bodies that mattered to the buyer, their size and shape, the color and the ages, the comparability of parts and durability of attributes—not the faces.

The spectrum of slaves ran in two directions along the walls of the slave pen: men on one side, women on the other. The bodies of those bought to work in the fields were comparable but not entirely fungible. W. H. Yos, comparing the men and women he found in the market, found the men "more likely" and put off buying women for another year—in the short run he could compare men to women, but in the long run he would have to have both. A similar perspective shows through John Knight's plantation plans, which stipulated that his slaves be "half men and half women . . . young say from 16 to 25, stout limbs, large deep chests, wide shoulders and hips, etc." Knight's list of body parts ran male and female attributes together, describing a body that was to be, like his slave force, half and half: men and women bought to work in the fields were comparable in any instance but they had to be sexed and balanced in the aggregate.[21] Having, like Knight, broken people down into parts, slaveholders could rebalance their attributes in the quest for slaves like those trader Samuel Browning called the "right sort" for the lower South. "Likely young fellows, stout girls the same and Black," was how Browning described the slaves who would sell best in Mississippi. Virginia trader Hector Davis similarly headed his slave-market tables with "Best young men" and "Best black girls." Likely young women were not the same as likely young men, but likely young black women might be. If she was destined to be a field hand, being "black" was better; it made an enslaved woman look more like the men alongside whom she would work in the fields. In evaluating female slaves, the traders were imagining composite slaves, matching the vitality they attributed to blackness with the vulnerability they expected from femaleness to make a better slave.

As well as comparing women to men, buyers compared women to one another. They palpated breasts and abdomens, searching for hernias and prolapsed organs and trying to massage bodies into revealing their reproductive history and capacity. Women passed through their "prime" interest to the slave traders at an earlier age than men. Males predominated in the slave trade among slaves over the age of nineteen; below that age, females did. Behind the aggregates lie the assumptions that slaveholders inscribed upon the bodies they bought. When Hector Davis set up his parallel categories of "Best" for young men and young women, the "best" men were those aged nineteen to twenty-four, the "best" black women were those aged sixteen to nineteen. A. J. McElveen made the terms of comparison explicit in a letter describing two slaves he had bought. "A boy large enough to plow," he wrote, outlining the labor against which a boy's body was to be judged, and "a Girl large Enough to nurse."[22] These sex-specific age categories reflected different evaluations of which capacities of the human body made a slave useful: production in the case of males and reproduction in the case of females. Putting it scientifically, one might say that slaveholders emphasized full physical growth for males and menarche for females.

But putting it as a slaveholder would, one might say that buyers were concerned that their female slaves be "breeders." Even without the eugenic implications it has taken on in the twentieth century, the word is an ugly one. It contains within it a history of crass incentives to reproduction and occasional unwanted matings to which many slaveholders subjected their female slaves.[23] The apparent absence of evidence that a large number of slaveholders focused solely on breeding slaves for the market should not obscure the fact that in their evaluations of the women they bought to work in their fields, slaveholders reduced consideration of gender difference to the medical consideration of generative capacity. The reduction of femininity into reproduction was ultimately embodied in the figure of the enslaved nurse and midwife—the woman who cared for and often suckled not just her mistress's offspring but those of other slave women who had to return to the fields shortly after giving birth. As described by John Knight, such a woman would be "a good, sound, intelligent, middle-aged woman of experience, not only for midwifery purposes, but as a constant nurse for [the children on] my plantation. That they may be properly taken care of and attended to regularly especially in absence of their mothers at work in the fields."[24] As he built his plantation, Knight was building a composite Mother: one midwife and nurse evaluated according to age and experience who would take care of the children produced by many women whose own bodies would be evaluated solely according to their physical and reproductive capacity.

Repeatedly, in the parlance of the slave market, slaveholders "stripped" the slaves to the waist so that they might have a closer look: "stripped the girl and made a careful examination"; "examined the boy

very particularly . . . stripped the boy and examined him . . . stripped all the boys . . . and this boy appeared to be the finest of the lot." Buyers and traders alike used the word "stripped" as if they had done it themselves—literally unbuttoned their slaves' clothes and pulled them off: "I stripped the boy and examined him several times."[25] Slave buyers began undressing their slaves by asking them to roll up the legs of their pants or lift up their skirts so that their legs might be examined for ulcers and varicose veins produced by incipient illness. As the slaves removed their coats and frocks and shirts, buyers inspected their naked bodies minutely, looking for what they called "clear" or "smooth" skin, skin unmarked by signs of illness or injury. Buyers avoided those whose bodies showed signs of diseases like scrofula—"the narrow chest, prominent shoulders . . . and relaxed muscular tissue"—or evidence of the cupping and blistering used to cure a recent illness, like the "blister mark" discovered on the breast of a Virginia woman by a slave trader, or the marks on Dempsey's arm, "three scars of deep cuts which . . . had injured the arm and much weakened him."[26]

More than anything, however, they were looking for scars from whipping. As Solomon Northup explained, "scars upon a slave's back were considered evidence of a rebellious or unruly spirit, and hurt his sale." As they worked their way from inflicted scars to essential character, buyers fixed slaves in a typology of character according to the frequency, intensity, and chronology of the whipping apparent on their backs: "not whiped"; "a little whipt"; "some scars upon her shoulders . . . produced by the whip"; "considerably scarred by the whip"; "the back of the girl had been cut pretty severely"; "he had many old stripes and scars on his body and head"; "she is very Badely whipped [but] the whipping has been done long since"; "she had marks of the whip not perfectly healed but did not appear to have been severely whipped."[27] Looking at the scars, slave buyers created whole stories for the people who stood stripped in front of them: perhaps if the scarring was very light the offense had been minor, perhaps if it was very old the vice had been whipped out of the slave. The buyers thought they could read slaves' backs as encodings of their history.

In 1828 the state of Louisiana had experimented with another method of making the slaves' history visible: they required traders who brought slaves over twelve years of age into the state to bring with them a certificate of good character signed in the slave's place of origin by two

or more freeholders. Ultimately, these certificates assured slave buyers of little more than the fact that at least three people might be lying to them, and the law was repealed in favor of the total prohibition of importations following Nat Turner's rebellion in 1831.[28] Made early in the history of the interstate slave trade, the law requiring certificates of good character marks a first attempt to do the work that later slaveholders did through stripping and examining slaves' bodies. Confronted by slaves distant in time and place from their origins and reputations, the Louisiana legislators tried to trace their way backward through the trade along a chain of reputable white men. By the time the trade was reopened in 1834, however, such an effort had been abandoned. Buyers for the rest of the antebellum period sought information about slaves' pasts in the pattern of scars that were traced across their backs.

In so doing they reproduced in the slave market a set of ideas about slave character that was central to the medical and racial philosophy of the antebellum South. In southern courtrooms and medical journals, slaves' misbehavior was often attributed to an inward disposition of character, which meant that there was something invariably, inevitably, perhaps biologically "bad" about the slave. Jim, for instance, was said to have "the habit" and "the character" of "taking his master's horses out at night and riding them without leave."[29] This line of thinking was reflected in redhibition law, which defined the commission of murder, rape, theft, or "the habit of running away" as evidence of a "vice of character." Slave "character" was likewise treated as an immutable fact by physician Samuel Cartwright, who held that running away and "rascality" were the misidentified symptoms of mental diseases with physiological cures—the most notable of which was getting slaves to work harder so that they would breathe harder so that their brains would get more oxygen.[30] As they traced their fingers across the scars on the slaves' naked backs, buyers were looking for the causes rather than the consequences of bad behavior; they were looking for, as North Carolina planter William Pettigrew put it, "deformity" of character.[31] Cartwright's famously bizarre views were simply a dressed-up version of a slave-market commonplace: slaves' bad behavior was a matter of nature.

And sometimes contagion. Slaveholders like William Weaver of Virginia worried that their slaves' moral failings might be infectious. Weaver was dissuaded from purchasing a slave accused of incest by the

following advice: "you should not have such a slave about you. He would not only trouble you—but would pollute your other Negroes." Even more threatening than contagious moral failings, however, were disciplinary problems. Upon finding out that his recently bought slave, James Allen, had once been free, John Knight began to worry not so much about the legality of holding such a slave, still less about the morality, but about the consequences for his other slaves. "I fear he will be troublesome and will infect the rest with discontent and insubordination." "Indeed," he added ominously, "I think he has already sown some of the seeds of both." Knight's first impulse was to sell Allen to a trader, the very solution adopted by Louisiana slaveholder John Bisland. Writing to the agent who had brokered the sale of an unruly slave for him, Bisland expressed his disappointment at the low price but was relieved that the sale was completed at all when he thought about "what the consequences might have been to the rest of my Negroes." Similarly, in a letter South Carolina slaveholder Thomas Fleming wrote from Charleston, he explained that January had been sold for running away and because his owner "fears the influence he may have on the rest of his slaves in incouraging some to do the same." In a social order based on intimidation, nothing was more fearful than a fearless slave.[32]

All the buyers had to do to protect themselves was ask to look at the slaves' naked bodies. As slave dealer Maurice Barnett put it: "whenever a purchaser at auction or private sale wishes to have the Negro examined they are always allowed to do so." And yet asking was not as easy as it looked, for an incongruous modesty bordered the slave market, especially in the case of women. One slave buyer, explaining in court why he did not make a full examination of a woman he bought, said that "the room was somewhat unfavorable to make a very close inspection." Lining the slave pens and auction houses were screens and dressing rooms that isolated the stripping and examining from the rest of the buyers' activities. Solomon Northup remembered that "sometimes a man or woman was taken back to the small house in the yard, stripped, and inspected more minutely."[33] These set-apart rooms were at once protective and suggestive. They hinted that there was something shameful about stripping slaves even as they invited the buyers to do so. And the modesty being protected was certainly not that of the slaves.

As they went about their slave-market business, slaveholders mapped their own forbidden desires onto slaves' bodies—particularly when the buyers were, as they invariably were, male and the slaves being examined were female. In Richmond, where buyers crowded behind the screen to undress and examine male slaves, "the women were more tenderly dealt with. Personal examination was confined to the hands, arms, legs, bust and teeth," according to Charles Weld.[34] When Fanny's buyer found that she had gonorrhea, he returned her, loftily declaring that the disease "was not discoverable by simple inspection." Referring to a buyer who had bought a herniated woman and then sought to return her, a justice of the Louisiana Supreme Court declared for the record that the discovery of such a malady in the slave market would have required "a peculiar kind of examination which is not generally resorted to in relation to Female slaves unless some suspicion is raised by their looks and appearance."[35] Buyers had to ask to look below a woman's skirt, and to ask they had to have a reason. Fernando Lemos might have wished to examine Seraphine, but he did not ask to do it. When he noticed the swelling beneath her skirts, Lemos had presumably been told the same thing that the auctioneer who was selling her had been told: Seraphine was pregnant. It was not until after he bought her that he discovered a large tumor "which appeared cicatriced, which indicated that the same swelling had taken place before and had been operated on, it was about two inches from the groin." Those were the words of a doctor testifying on Lemos's behalf. Trying to prove that her "defect" was not an apparent one, he located it in a place that Lemos could not be expected to have found it: beneath her skirt.[36] A similar boundary between ordinary and extraordinary inspections was apparent in the testimony that Dr. James Clarke, a slave dealer's doctor under cross examination, gave about the venereal disease for which Cynthia was returned: "The disease . . . is such a one as would escape observation without a special examination was made for it and generally any venereal disease would escape the eye of anyone but a physician." [37]

Once they had found a way to ask, however, buyers gave free reign to their curiosity. James Redpath described the "inner room" at Dickinson, Hill & Co. (also in Richmond): "The slaves—the males—were there . . . stripped naked, and carefully examined." As he described it, however, only one of the women sold that day was stripped: "She was 'warranted sound and healthy,' with the exception of a female complaint, to which mothers are occasionally subject, the name and nature of which was unblushingly stated. She was taken into the inner room, after the bidding commenced, and there indecently *'examined'* in the presence of a dozen or fifteen brutal men." Redpath highlighted the public accounting of the medical concerns which got the woman into the room, but he went on to detail the "brutal remarks and licentious looks" that accompanied her return. The stated concern about the woman's capacity for reproduction served as public cover for a much more general interest in her naked body.[38] The careful stories buyers used to explain their actions were revealing denials of something everybody knew: that for white men, examining slaves, searching out hidden body parts, running hands over limbs, massaging abdomens and articulating pelvic joints, probing wounds and scars with fingers, was erotic. The buyers were getting closer to the bodies of slaves than any practical consideration could justify.

The rituals of the slave pens taught the inexperienced how to read black bodies for their suitability for slavery, how to imagine blackness into meaning, how to see solutions to their own problems in the bodies of the slaves they saw in the market. Gazing, touching, stripping, and analyzing aloud, the buyers read slaves' bodies as if they were coded versions of their own imagined needs—age was longevity, dark skin immunity, a stout trunk stamina, firm muscles production, long fingers rapid motion, firm breasts fecundity, clear skin good character. The purposes that slaveholders projected for slaves' bodies were thus translated into natural properties of those bodies—a dark complexion became a sign of an innate capacity for cutting cane, for example. Daily in the slave market, buyers "discovered" associations they had themselves projected, treating the effects of their own examinations as if they were the essences of the bodies they examined. Passed on from the experienced to the inexperienced, from the examiners to the on-lookers, the ritual practice of the slave pens animated the physical coordinates of black bodies with the purposes of slavery.

Slave-pen blackness held another meaning for slaveholders: it brought the outlines of slaveholding whiteness into sharper relief. The gross physical capacity of the slave was a rough background for the graceful motion of the slaveholder; all the talk about black "breeders" set off the elaborate rituals of white courtship; and the violation of black bodies emphasized the inviolability of white ones. Through shared communion in the rites of the slave market—the looking, stripping, touching, bantering, and evaluating—white men confirmed their commonality with the other men with whom they inspected the slaves.

And yet, through the same gaze and beneath the same probing fingers, slaveholders were looking for a different set of (projected) qualities—qualities that were not, like those they attributed to their black field hands, opposite of the qualities they ascribed to themselves but, rather, were proximate to their own whiteness. The traders' efforts to codify that strain of proximate whiteness produced the antebellum South's most detailed racial taxonomy. Whereas the categories of the United States census were limited to "black" and "mulatto," the traders' detailed categories—"Negro," "Griffe," "Mulatto," "Quadroon," and so on—attempted much more precise measurement of imagined portions of "black" and "white" blood. And whereas the courts limited their own detailed investigations of blood quantum and behavior to drawing a legal line between "black" and "white," the traders' categories preserved a constant shifting tension between blackness and whiteness—a tension that was daily measured, packaged, and sold in the slave market.[39]

As with blackness, slave-market whiteness was not simply a matter of skin color. To begin with, like blackness, it looked different on male bodies than on female ones. Over nine tenths of those advertised by a skill that was nondomestic—coopers, carpenters, draymen—were male. And light-skinned men were three times more likely to be assigned those jobs than were dark-skinned men.[40] Like Monday, who was labeled "mulatto" and sent to be trained as a cooper at the age of twelve, these men had been assigned a skill on the basis of their skin color. Indeed, slaveholders often "naturalized" the association of skill with skin color by attributing a particular mechanical or technological aptitude to successive generations of men from a single family, then training those men in this trade, and finally concluding from the success of the successive generations in learning that trade that the family had a natural predisposition to being, say, iron workers.[41]

No less than the field hands with whom they were sold in the market, the bodies of skilled slaves were interpreted as physical maps of their own commercial potential. Jacob, for instance, was a carpenter, who was described by his overseer as "six feet two inches high" and having "a scar below his left eye and the little finger of his hand (right) is off."[42] Jacob's body, much like the dark-skinned and unskilled people driven by the same overseer, was intelligible in terms of labor (the right hand that could hold a tool only loosely) and brutality (the left-eyed scar across from the overseer's own right hand). Like the supposed predisposition of "black" slaves for field work, the natural propensity of skilled slaves for their work was treated as if it were physically manifest in the outward appearance of their bodies. These bodies, however, aged differently than bodies set to work in the fields. The most expensive skilled slaves were men of about forty-five years old, well-past their full physical prime as a laborer but old enough to have mastered the intricate skills of their trade.[43] Their development was measured along the axis of their skill and intellectual development rather than their physical vitality.

Indeed, these men's presumed capacity for development sometimes made them seem threatening to slaveholders. Henry Bibb, whose skin was by his own account very light, remembered that he spent months in the New Orleans slave market before being sold. "No one would buy me for fear I would run away," he later wrote. Anticipating an examination by a prospective buyer, Bibb projected the evaluation previous buyers had made: "he would have doubtless brought up the same objection that others had brought up—that I was too white; and that they were afraid I could read and write; and would never serve as a slave but run away." Bibb, in fact, was ultimately able to keep his family together in the slave market, because the presence of his wife seemed to a buyer to diminish his high risk of running away. The association of masculinity with resistance and of whiteness with intelligence made light-skinned men like Henry Bibb as threatening to some slaveholders as their skills made them valuable to others. This worry tended to reduce their value overall. Whereas light-skinned women commanded a premium price in the market, light-skinned men did not.[44]

It was on those light-skinned women that the eyes of buyers looking for domestic servants usually lingered. Over three quarters of the people advertised for sale as domestic servants were female,[45] and a disproportionate number of light-skinned women were chosen for these roles—an association typified by a slave trader's 1859 letter that put color before even qualification: "the girls are Brownskin and good house girls."[46] Sex, color, and domestic service were powerfully associated in minds of slave buyers. This is not to say that all domestic slaves were women or that all female domestic slaves were light-skinned—neither was the case. But taken altogether, the statistics show that just as those seeking field slaves associated darkness with masculine productivity, those buying household slaves associated lightness with feminine domesticity.

A word that comes up again and again in slaveholders' descriptions of the bodies of the light-skinned women they bought to work in their houses is "delicate." Alexina Morrison, for example, was described as "rather slender and delicate" by her former owner. Jane's in-between body seems to have been visually tailored to her in-between color: "a Griffe woman of medium size of delicate appearance." And Mary Ellen Brooks, who was sold as a house servant, was said to be light-skinned and "delicate." The descriptions of Jane and Mary Ellen Brooks come from court cases in which their health at the time of sale was at stake, and the witnesses who gave these descriptions had a stake in telling a story that emphasized infirmity. The repetition of the word "delicate," however, rather than, say, "sickly" or "puny," hints at a world of positive meaning made explicit by slave dealer Theophilus Freeman as he contemplated Eliza's stolen daughter Emily. "There were heaps and piles of money to be made for such an extra fancy piece as Emily would be," Freeman enthused, "She was a beauty—a picture—a doll—one of your regular bloods—none of your thick-lipped, bullet-headed, cotton [pickers]."[47] Freeman made explicit the assumption behind all these descriptions: these bodies were useless for production.

All of their race science and all of their superstition made slaveholders suspect that the whiteness in their female slaves made them ill-suited for the daily rigors they demanded of dark-skinned women. Indeed, in southern medical science, light skin ("mulattoism," slaveholders would have said) was associated with infertility; arguing from analogy, and putting all empirical evidence aside, writers often argued that "mulattoes," like the mules from whom they took their name, were unable to reproduce themselves.[48] Unproductive in the field and unprolific in the quarter, these women were the embodied opposites of the laborer/breeders slaveholders sought as field hands.

Those searching for domestic slaves paid attention to different body parts than did those looking for field slaves. Maria Donald, in reference to a thirty-year-old woman whom she had seen advertised, wrote "that age would suit us very well as we would like to have a cook with good eyesight." For Maria Donald, age was a diagnostic of fine motor skills rather than general vitality or reproductive history: cleaning vegetables and boning fish did not require good health but they did require acute eyesight. A different set of concerns fixed Clarissa's body with meaning. The slave dealer who sold her remembered her as "very far from being a good looking woman, disfigured by the loss of her front teeth."[49] Clarissa's missing teeth were visually rather than medically problematic: hers was a body that was to be bought (or not) for appearances, and in the case of domestic servants, faces mattered.

The bodies of men bought to work in slaveholders' households were described according to the same set of race and gender conventions. Writing about a man who had been sent from the fields to work in her household, Virginia slaveholder Elizabeth Powell described his body as if it were in the midst of a material transformation: "Henry is right awkward as you might imagine but I think he will do very well. He seems to be very willing to learn and if his limbs were about half their present length I think he would be much more graceful—but he seems very much at a loss to know what to do with his hands." The long arms that had served Henry well in the field were a nuisance in the house; and whatever use his hands had been in tending tobacco, they were not much account without the animating spirit of service that Elizabeth Powell expected from her household servants. Indeed, as the historian Brenda Stevenson has shown, Powell was taking it upon herself to discipline Henry's body to fit his new job.[50] A similar set of concerns shows through a Louisiana slaveholder's description of his runaway slave Sam: "a bright mulatto, tolerably well grown for his age, with very long arms, rather disproportioned to his height and large feet, rather modest when spoken to; voice somewhat effeminate, his upper teeth a little projecting and slightly decayed which will be readily seen when he laughs."[51] Sam's body was remarkable because of its ill proportion rather than its incapacity; his tooth decay, like Clarissa's missing teeth, was a matter of disfigurement rather than disability. Indeed, his mouth was of singular interest to his owner. His modest effeminacy was, perhaps, an outward marker of his innate suitability for domestic work, and his laughter a sign of the interiority that set him apart from other slaves.

As slaveholders looked over the people they bought to cook their meals, wash their clothes, and wait on their tables, they elaborated fantasies about their slaves' interior lives and intellectual capacity. John

Knight's new "errand boy," for instance, was "smart" and "intelligent." A man who had thought of buying Agnes remembered her as "a girl of unusual good sense." And Celestine was remembered in her owner's household for her mood: "she was always gay and singing." But the inner life slaveholders imagined for their domestic slaves went well beyond their mental acuity or their actions. Mary Ellen Brooks, who was variously described by the men who sold her as "delicate," "intelligent," "well-suited for a house servant," "fancy," and "a mulatto," was provided with a mattress on which to sleep in the slave market. The practice, one of the traders later recalled, was "usual with house servants." Similarly, Madison, "mulatto" by designation, was put to work as a cabin boy on the steamboat that carried him to the New Orleans market. The captain of the ship described Madison as "genteel" and explained that the slave "did not like to associate with the others, and it was on this account that he was kept about the cabin." The ship captain, like the slave trader who provided Mary Ellen Brooks with a mattress, attributed sensibilities and preferences to Madison that matched his own. He imagined that Madison desired a social proximity to whites commensurate with his imagined racial proximity—in other words, he saw Madison as a shadowed version of himself. And all of this in spite of the fact that Madison's presence in the cabin was, literally, on the captain's account: he had paid Madison's owner a dollar a day for the slave's service.[52]

Like the association of light-skinned men with skilled work, the association of light-skinned women with domestic service was sometimes framed as a matter of biological descent. The young woman whom John Knight hoped would complement his "intelligent" errand boy was to be, like his own wife and daughters, "well-bred." He would perhaps have jumped at the chance to have a woman like the one Kitty Hamilton hoped to obtain: "I should very much like to own Frank," she wrote to her father, "her mother is a most excellent character & she is of a good breed."[53] The breeding that buyers talked about in relation to female household slaves was different from the rough talk about "breeders" that occurred elsewhere in the slave market. Buyers' descriptions of house slaves, like their descriptions of their slaveholding friends and neighbors, used phrases like "well-bred" and "good breeding" in a way that combined family heritage, reputed good character, and socialized physical bearing into a single stream of analysis.

In addition to outward delicacy and inward gentility, the racial gaze of the slaveholder projected sexual meaning onto the bodies of light-skinned women. Phillip Thomas simply described a woman he had seen in Richmond as "13 years old, Bright Color, nearly a fancy for $1135." An age, a sex, a color, a price, and a fantasy. A longer description of Mildred Ann Jackson ran along the same lines: "She was about thirty years old. Her color was that of a quadroon; very good figure, she was rather tall and slim. Her general appearance was very good. She wore false teeth and had a mole on her upper lip. Her hair was straight." Jackson's body was admired for its form, for its delicacy and detail. Slave dealer James Blakeny made the density of the traffic between phenotype and fantasy explicit when he described Mary Ellen Brooks: "A very pretty girl, a bright mulatto with long curly hair and fine features . . . Ellen Brooks was a fancy girl: witness means by that a young handsome yellow girl of fourteen or fifteen with long curly hair." For slave buyers, the bodies of light-skinned women and little girls embodied sexual desire and the luxury of being able to pay for its fulfillment—they were projections of slaveholders' own imagined identities as white men and slave masters.[54]

And so, at a very high price, whiteness was doubly sold in the slave market. In the first instance the hybrid whiteness of the slaves was being packaged and measured by the traders and imagined into meaning by the buyers: into delicacy and modesty, interiority and intelligence, beauty, bearing, and vulnerability. These descriptions of light-skinned slaves were projections of slaveholders' own dreamy interpretations of the meaningfulness of their skin color. Indeed, in the second instance, it was the buyers' own whiteness that was being bought. In buying these imagined slaves, they were buying for themselves ever more detailed fantasies about mastery and race. The qualities they projected onto their slaves' bodies served them as public reflections of their own discernment: they were the arbiters of bearing and beauty; their slaves were the show pieces of their pretensions; their own whiteness was made apparent in the proximate whiteness of the people they bought.

Ironically, these expensive flirtations with racial proximity, these commodifications of projected and imagined whiteness, were under-written by the slaveholders' ideology of absolute racial difference. The saving abstraction "black blood"—later codified in law as the "one-drop rule"—held the power to distinguish nearly white people from really white people. Hence, perhaps, the attention to imperfection: Sam's lisp and the decayed teeth you could see when he laughed; the mole over Mildred Ann Jackson's lip or the false teeth she had in front; the length and awkwardness of Henry's arms. These physical details were sallied forth to mark the boundary of difference between the authentic whiteness of the slaveholders and the almost-whiteness of their slaves. Visible on the face of things, these tiny imperfections preserved the tension between the underlying blackness and the asymptotic approximation to whiteness which made these slaves salable. As long as enslaved whiteness was legible as imitation, money could be made from the synergetic whiteness of slaveholder and slave.

Some slaves, however, were "too white to keep." That was how Edmund was described by the man who had sold him from Tennessee. The man's hope was that such a sale would make it more difficult for Edmund to escape from slavery, but, as it was, New Orleans suited the slave well: within a day of arriving in the city, Edmund had slipped unnoticed onto a steamboat and disappeared. So, too, Robert, who boarded the steamboat that carried him away from slavery and New Orleans as a white man. "I should have thought he was of Spanish origin," remembered one of his fellow passengers, "he was a man of clear skin and dark complexion." But more than the way Robert looked, the other passengers remembered the way he acted: "he was very genteely dressed and of a very genteel deportment"; "he had more the appearance of a gentleman than a plebeian"; and, almost every witness noted, "usually seated himself at the first table, high up, and near the ladies." Robert, it turned out, had once been a waiter, and he used the skills he had learned as a slave, the gentility and sociable palate of the server, to make his way into the confines reserved for the served. Alexina Morrison was likewise "too white." That is how she was described by the man who sold her in New Orleans, and indeed she proved so to be: blue-eyed and flaxen-haired, she escaped from her buyer and sued him for her freedom in the courts of Louisiana. One after another, her supporters came into court to testify that she was white in "her conduct and her actions."[55]

Robert made it as far as Memphis before being arrested and sent to the slave market in New Orleans, where he very shortly died. Morrison was luckier: she was judged white by three Louisiana juries and lived as free while her case made its way through the courts, until the Civil War made the point moot. Edmund seems also to have made it to freedom.

No one who testified in the case brought to assign responsibility for his loss could even tell what boat he had used to escape. More than the escapes, which were few, however, it is the performances that are telling. At the margin, where enforced mimicry shaded into subversive performance, it was clear that the racialized salability of the slave market—whether is was blackness or proximate whiteness that was being sold—had to be acted out by the slaves.

The effect of these performances is evident at a century and a half's distance in slaveholders' descriptions of the slaves they bought, descriptions that lurched through a range of incompatibles as they tried to pack the infinite variety of physical bodies into the standardized racial categories of the slave market. William was "very black" if you asked his overseer, "not perfectly black, but dark brownish" if you asked his owner. Clarissa seemed "mulatto or copper colored" to the doctor who made a postmortem examination of her body; a neighboring slaveholder, however, had thought her "a Griff colored woman." Major was "dark brown" according to a man who had supervised him in a factory, but "black" according to a man who had supervised him on a farm. Polly was "whiter than quarteroon" according to one man who had owned her, and "a bright mulatto" according to another. Hubbard was "a tolerably dark Negro of a Sugar Bread complexion" if you asked one of the men who witnessed his sale, but he was "a kind of dark Griff, or copper colored" if you asked the dealer who sold him. Madison, finally, was "a genteel, good looking boy . . . permitted to wait on the passengers" aboard the steamboat, but in the slave market he was "free from any blemish, he was a muscular, strong looking boy and very heavily set."[56] The range of difference between these descriptions suggest that the racialized bodies these buyers thought they had discovered in the slave market were, in fact, being produced by their examinations—not in the sense that there was no physical body standing there until a buyer described it but in the sense that the racialized meaning of that body, the color assigned to it and the weight given to its various physical features in describing it, depended upon the examiner rather than the examined.

Indeed, these differing descriptions seem to reflect in miniature the presumptions of the broader economy in black and white: William seemed darker to the man who worked him in the field everyday than to the man who owned him but did not supervise his work; Clarissa seemed lighter to a man who saw her dead than she did to a man who had judged her healthy; Major seemed darker when he worked with slaves in the field than he did when he worked with white men in the factory; Polly seemed whiter to the man who discovered that she was a free woman kidnapped from Alabama than to the man who had traded her as a slave; Hubbard seemed lighter to the man who had talked to him every day in the slave pens than he did to the witness who had only seen him sold; Madison was judged according to aesthetics and attitude by the man who put him to work as a waiter, but according to size and strength by the man who sold him as a cooper. Employment, health, countenance, clothes, conversation, desire, any number of things might have guided slaveholders' imaginations as they looked at slaves' bodies. Which is to say that slaves' bodies were shaped and shaded by what the traders were selling and what potential buyers were seeking.

So powerful, indeed, was the acquisitive gaze of the slaveholder that slave-market "blackness" or "whiteness" could occasionally be produced in opposition to the phenotype of the body to which they were applied. Many a person with light skin was nevertheless set to work in the fields, described perhaps like Andy Foster as "a mulatto boy with coarse features, large bone, stout made and rather awkward appearance," or like Bob as "a dark mulatto, raw-boned and muscular" and "a dark rough looking Negro." These men might have been instructed in the market, as was light-skinned, literate Henry Bibb, "to act very stupid in language and thought" but to "be spry" when told to move about—to perform slave-market blackness in order to make themselves more salable.[57] Many dark-skinned women, likewise, were bought to be sex workers or house servants. Indeed, although most dark-skinned women in the slave trade did not become domestic slaves, the majority of domestic slaves were dark-skinned, since light-skinned women were comparatively rare in the market and very expensive. The "blackness" or "whiteness" associated with particular types of slavery could be mapped onto slaves' bodies according to coordinates other than color—gender, size, shape, visage, and conversation, for instance. And then those bodies could, like young Henry's awkward arms, be disciplined to yield the meaning they had been assigned. As they compared the people in the market to one another, slaveholders broke physical bodies into pieces and traded them back and forth. The vitality associated with blackness might cancel out the vulnerability associated with femininity in the search for a field hand, while a "bright disposition" might lighten a dark-skinned woman in the search for a domestic servant; a "rough" face might darken a light-skinned man, while "effeminacy" might lighten a dark-skinned one; an outwardly dull demeanor and the presence of wife and child might make a light-skinned man seem less likely to run away; and so on. In the slave market, buyers produced "whiteness" and "blackness" by disaggregating human bodies and recomposing them as racialized slaves.

The racism of the slave pens, however, was less an intended effect than a tool of the trade. To paraphrase the historian Barbara Jeanne Fields, the business of the slave pens was the buying and selling of slaves, not the production of wide-ranging ideas about racial proximity and inferiority. The buyer's most immediate interest in detailing an account of a slave's racial characteristics was getting a lower price. And the more accomplished he was at using the verities of antebellum racism to detail "faults and failings" of the slaves in the market, the less he could expect to pay for the slave he wanted to take home. When Virginia slaveholder Virginia Shelton wanted to reduce the value of the slaves in her uncle's estate so that she could afford to buy them for herself, for example, she did so through a detailed account of their inherited disabilities: "Lucy has been the mother of thirteen living children, of whom four only are living now; four others died with decided consumption between the ages of fifteen and twenty-five, and some of the others had something like it. John, Lucy's husband and the father of her two youngest children, died of consumption and all of his family go the same way. Jefferson . . . when he was growing up strained himself so much in lifting logs that he was diseased for a number of years and I presume is so now. Besides he drinks. Charley, of course, is scrofulous, though his mother's family were healthy, he takes it from his father's family. Margaret's weak arm ought to be considered and the present state of Frances' health."[58] Shelton, of course, had precisely the type of information that had been hidden from slave-market buyers by the process of the trade: a detailed biographical account of the slaves' health and history. In the absence of such information, buyers critiqued the slaves according to the physical details they uncovered through examination. Describing a man he had seen in the market but not bought, William Dickson remembered that "his underlip fell down too low—he appeared to keep his mouth open—his lips was thick and his fingers too short to be a good cotton picker which were objections if witness had been going to purchase."[59] Dickson used the conditional: these were not objections *to* purchasing, they were instead objections *if* he had purchased—they were part of the process of purchasing. Defect by defect, buyers could run slaves down until they could afford them. So it was that slave traders had to be so concerned with parts, that trader J. E. Carson demanded a price reduction when he bought the woman with the scar blistered onto her breast; that trader A. J. McElveen would worry that a slave's missing toe would be "an objection to his Selling," or that that slave trader David Wise could unflinchingly value a missing eye at twenty-five dollars.[60]

Whether they bought slaves at public auctions or in private bargains made in the traders' pens, by vocalizing their objectifying examinations, by reading slaves' bodies aloud, buyers gained market leverage. Perhaps as importantly, they also gained respect in the slave market. "Marks were criticized with the knowing air assumed by horse dealers, and pronounced to be the results of flogging, vermin, or scrofula," remembered Charles Weld of the Richmond slave market.[61] By showing off what they saw, buyers established their authority as good judges of property, their "knowing air" warned the traders of their discernment and underwrote their offers with their body-reading ability. Charles Ball remembered watching a buyer make such a play on a country road. The trader who was carrying Ball south began by offering to sell at a price that was dressed up as a sacrifice: "as they were not able to keep up with the gang he would take twelve hundred dollars for the two." The purchaser, Ball remembered, offered nine hundred, and when his offer was rejected "many faults and failing were pointed out in the merchandise. After much bargaining, and many gross jests on the part of the stranger, he offered a thousand dollars for the two, and said he would give no more."[62] In the buyer's effort to get a lower price, the dirty jokes and detailed criticism were of a piece: they demonstrated the buyer's familiarity with the slave business and lent credibility to his offer. His ability to read slaves' bodies and make dirty jokes, his facility with the terms of slave-market racism, underwrote the hard bargain he drove with the trader.

And it was through hard bargains like the one that Ball described— through detailed physical examinations and publicized accounts of racial knowledge—that white men in the slave market cemented attach-

CHAPTER SIX

ACTS OF SALE

In 1852 the Second Municipality of the city of New Orleans passed a law that forbade the exposure of slaves for sale on the sidewalks in front of the slave pens. "Scarcely anyone desires to pass such places," the *Daily Orleanian* explained, "while to the ladies it is like running the gauntlet to be exposed to the prying, peering gaze of lengthened lines of grinning Negroes of both sexes." And if the slaves could look at the ladies with the same penetrating gaze they received from the slave buyers, they could also echo the bawdy banter of the traders: "They hardly await the passing of persons before their extended lines, ere they commence making their comments and these eke out lengthy and amusing conversation for each other."[1] As well as being remarkable for its sexualized imagery of peering and prying, the newspaper's account is important for what it communicates about the daily life of the slave market: exposed for sale, slaves were looking and talking back. At the moment of their performance, the slave traders' carefully choreographed pageants were being interrupted by slaves' unruly subjectivity.

Put that way, the worrisome scene on the street seems a displaced reminder of what could happen inside the pens. On the economic margin—at the point where the slave market that slaveholders carried around in their heads was faced with the real person they hoped to take home from the market—objectification could dissolve into projection, anxiety, and finally dependence. As the traders prepared them for sale

ments to one another and sorted themselves into a hierarchy of ability. By sharing out their knowledge of the mysteries of blackness, they made their claim for respect among their white peers. Indeed, in their public performance of their expertise—for example, in the passing on of the sly confidence relayed to Joseph Ingraham by a Natchez slave buyer that there was a peculiarly soft spot at the base of a slave's "ancle"—slave buyers expressed their own barely concealed desire for the attention and admiration of the white men with whom they bought slaves.[63]

If necromancy was the slave market's magic, race was its technology. Just as the magic of alchemy based its claims on the scientific techniques of chemistry and mineralogy, the necromancy of the slave pens was founded on the technology of biological racism. Without any reliable knowledge about the histories or identities of the people they met in the market, buyers turned to physical examination as the best method of comparison. In the slave market, the physical coordinates of human bodies—size, skin color, scars, physical carriage, and so on—were made meaningful through the application of slave buyers' medical, managerial, aesthetic, and sexual concerns. In the slave market, the racial ideologies by which slaveholders organized their society were put to work doing the hard work of differentiating commodities and negotiating prices.

As the experienced guided the eyes of the inexperienced, slaves' bodies were made racially legible. The buyers' inspections, the parts they fingered, the details they fetishized, and the homosocial connections they made with one another gave material substance to antebellum notions of "blackness" and "whiteness" and outlined for observers the lineaments of a racial gaze. Out of the daily practice of slavery, they reproduced the notions of race that underwrote the system as a whole.

Many of the observers in the pens, however, were not white, and the conclusions they drew from watching the buyers' inspections were quite different from those drawn by a man like Joseph Ingraham. For the slaves in the market, the examinations were revealing accounts of the buyers themselves, accounts that allowed them to guess what a buyer was looking for and, sometimes, to shape a sale to suit themselves.

and the buyers examined them, slaves in the market became accustomed to presenting themselves as commodities. But as they did so, they also looked out for themselves, estimating the people who examined them, assessing the advantages of particular buyers, and presenting themselves accordingly. As the buyers proceeded through ever more intimate examinations of the slaves, the slaves could manipulate ever subtler signs to guide them.

INFORMATION

The daily routine of the slave pens—the preparations, the examinations, and the constant contingency of being for sale to anyone who cared to buy—alienated slaves from their own bodies. William Wells Brown conveyed this experience with the image of slaves forced to dance to a merry fiddle while "their cheeks were wet with tears." For Brown, those tears marked the distance between two selves, one outwardly presented by the traders and one inwardly preserved by the slaves. Other slaves recalled a similar doubleness when they described the experience of being sold. J. D. Green, whose narrative was entitled *Narrative of the Life of J. D. Green, a Runaway Slave from Kentucky, Containing an Account of his Three Escapes 1839, 1846, and 1848,* remembered with no small irony his slave-market self being described as "above all free from the disease of running away." John Brown remembered "not being very well pleased to hear myself run down" as a buyer tried to knock a few dollars off his price. Henry Bibb so distanced himself from his own sale that he described the time he spent in the New Orleans slave pens in the third person: "They were exposed for sale . . . they had to be in trim . . . they were made to stand up straight . . . they had to answer as promptly as they could and try to induce the spectators to buy them."[2] More than literal renderings of slaves' specific thoughts at the time of their sale, these memories should be read as accounts of their double consciousness. Each contains a recognition of what a slaveholder saw—a dancing body, a pliant slave, a run-down little boy, a well-disciplined lot of slaves—alongside a marker of the slave's separation from his or her buyer's evaluation. They describe the divided meanings of salable bodies—once from without, once from within.

In practice the distinctions were difficult to maintain: the motions slaves made, the food they consumed, and the clothes they wore literally incorporated them with their enslavement. Slaves in the market could not avoid being pushed out of any stable self-definition and into the space between person and thing. But if—to adopt for a moment the terms of the nineteenth-century discussion—it was ultimately impossible to leave behind the enslaved body to take flight in an unfettered soul, it was equally impossible to sell the slave without also selling the soul. In this boundary-blurring doubleness was the obscenity of the slave market: people forced to perform their own commodification. But there was also opportunity. Slaves in the market were in the position to watch themselves enact assigned roles, and to subvert the traders' elaborate presentations by bending buyers' perceptions around their own purposes. By knowing what slaveholders were looking for, slaves could turn their own commodification against their enslavement.

The daily business of the slave pens, of course, was manipulating buyers. All of the feeding, clothing, caring for, and preparing had that single goal in mind, and slaves in the market were carefully instructed about how to present themselves to buyers—about what would sell and what would not. As the traders pitched them to the buyers, the slaves learned more. Charles Ball, for instance, heard two traders evaluating his potential. He was, they said in his hearing, worth about a thousand dollars "to a man making a settlement, and clearing a plantation." Ball's bodily vitality would be what a buyer was looking for. Other slaves picked up hints from the way they were dressed. John Parker guessed that he was to be sold as a house servant because his market clothes set him off from the other slaves in the pen: civility rather than strength would entice a likely buyer. And light-skinned Henry Bibb, remember, was told by his seller to "act stupid in language and thought," to perform slave-market blackness in order to entice a buyer who might otherwise have been put off by his light skin.[3] The traders' pitches, threats, and hectoring promises charged their slaves with enacting the slave buyers' fantasies. But they also provided slaves with a detailed account of buyers' system of signs, of how slave buyers read appearances. By the time the buyers entered the pens, the slaves knew a lot about them.

The buyers brought more information with them when they came. Although one of the conceits of the southern ruling class seems to have been the idea that slaveholders were invisible and that therefore they could parade around naked, drink too much, argue, and discuss the most intimate affairs of their business and personal lives without making themselves vulnerable to on-looking slaves—they were not. When the buyers came into the pens, they were subjected to careful scrutiny. Josiah Henson remembered this as "the anxious scanning of the purchasers' faces" that accompanied every sale. Solomon Northup remembered that behind the slaves' apparent anxiety was an estimating gaze. He introduced the account he gave of his eventual buyer as a "description of his personal appearance and my estimation of his character at first sight." As Northup also suggested, a slave buyer's "character" was of central concern to those facing sale. Of a buyer who looked him up and down in the market, Charles Ball later wrote, "I never saw a human countenance that expressed more of the evil passions of the heart than did that of this man, and his conversation corresponded with his physiognomy." Likewise, in his fictionalized account of the slave market in *Clotel*, former trader's assistant William Wells Brown introduced a slave buyer with the following words: "the very appearance of the young southerner pointed him out as an unprincipled profligate."[4]

These memories, though they might subsequently have been embellished or exaggerated, reveal the outline of slave-market physiognomy. Faced with people whom they had never met—people who appeared in isolation from the histories that might have made their actions seem predictable—slaves behaved in the same way buyers did. They depended upon their discernment. The facial valuations made by the enslaved were not necessarily more dependable than those of the slavers, although they might have been. Buyers, after all, had less reason to mask their intentions than did some slaves, and slaves' life-long vulnerability to white brutality often provided them with the experience of what John Brown called "a long habit of studying the expression of countenance" born of being "forced to watch the changes of my master's physiognomy, as well as those of the parties he associated with, so as to frame my conduct in accordance with what I had reason to believe was their prevailing mood at any time."[5] But in any case, there was more to the buyers' appearance than their faces.

Unlike the slaves in the market, whose dress was calculated to obscure individual difference, the slave buyers' clothes were consciously calculated to express their individuality. Nineteenth-century drawings and paintings of southern slave markets reproduce a visual code that must have been apparent to slaves (and traders) as soon as the buyers entered the yard. Buyers in full black suits stand beside those with multicolored (ocher crossed with orange plaid) pants, men with stiff top hats next to those whose hats had wider brims and softer shapes, those with walking sticks next to those with whips, those with rings, watch chains, ties, cravats, and other signs of wealth alongside those without.[6] This visual grammar was put into prose by traveling observer William Chambers, who identified a buyer who caught his attention in Richmond as "wide awake" in reference to the style of hat the man wore. Similarly, John Brown included the fact that one of the men who inspected him wore "a long shabby blanket coat" in a list of features that ended with the summation, "I did not like the looks of him."[7]

As the buyers began to bargain, the slaves could learn more. Slaveholders gained credibility in the market by attaching reasons to their offers, and often slaves stood by as sellers and buyers argued back and forth about the value of a slave, anchoring their opinions in accounts of the hidden failings or evident advantages of a given body. Dennis Donovan remembered that he was standing with a slave named Ben, "talking with the boy," when Benjamin Huntington walked up and started to talk to him about Ben, asking "if he was a good boy" and whether he was healthy.[8] The discussions they had in front of the slaves revealed the buyers' criteria, but they also occasionally revealed the buyers themselves. The buyers, after all, were showing off as they tried to match themselves with the person they bought. Charles Ball remembered watching a buyer announce himself and his intentions for the person he hoped to buy: "a thin sallow man" rode up to the house where Ball's coffle was staying and said "that he wished to get a good field hand, and would pay a good price for him." The information that Ball overheard could perhaps have been divined by another method, but the knowledge obtained by Solomon Northup as he listened in on a slave-pen bargain was more precious: "One old gentleman, who said he wanted a coachman, appeared to take a fancy to me. From his conversation with [the slave trader] Burch, I learned he was a resident in the city."[9] To Northup that piece of information held a treasured hope.

The more minute the buyers' attention, the greater the opportunity for the slaves. John Brown remembered that the buyers who asked him questions ended up giving him answers: "I was careful, however, to draw out the buyers, in order to learn what they wanted me for; which I judged by the questions they put to me."[10] The argument might be extended indefinitely: Can you drive a coach? Cook a bird? Wield an ax? Have you nimble fingers for picking cotton? Strong arms for cutting cane? Breasts for nursing a child? All of these questions, asked in conversation and examination, were also answers, accounts of a buyer's needs, their purposes, and their origins. Buyers in the slave pens were trading information about themselves for information about the slaves.

Much of the information that slaves in the pens gained about slave buyers would have been useless without a broader local knowledge: about the circumstances of slavery in New Orleans as opposed to those in rural Louisiana, for example, or about the differences in the labor regimes on cotton plantations (often brutal) and sugar plantations (often fatal), or the reputed differences of character between Creole, American, and Indian slaveholders. Slaves who were from places as far away as Missouri and Maryland may not have had such information when they entered the pens in New Orleans, but they could certainly have obtained it while they were there. The networks of connection and support that slaves forged during their time in the trade could be used in the slave pens to make local knowledge social knowledge, to make sure that slaves in the pens had a meaningful context in which to situate their information about specific slave buyers.

Though they were surrounded by high walls and overseen by brutal masters, the slave pens were permeated by slave-borne information. William Wells Brown, for instance, had served out his term as the hired assistant of a Mississippi River slave trader when he paid his sister a last visit in the St. Louis slave pen where she was awaiting shipment to New Orleans. Brown, who had spent his year with the trader preparing slaves for sale and instructing them what to say to potential buyers, could not save his sister from the trade, but he was in a good position to tell her about it, to prepare her for the traders who would carry her south and the buyers she would meet in New Orleans.

Brown's visit to his sister was probably by special favor of a familiar trader, but many slaves went in and out of the pens as a matter of routine. When Brown had worked for the dealer, for instance, he regularly passed in and out of the gates of the pens. As slave dealer Thomas Frisby explained to a court full of people who were apparently unin-formed about the daily practice of the slave trade: "It is usual to have a boy a kind of a head over the rest of the Negroes, to send on errands and to send him with slaves placed in their keeping with their baggage and their clothes." No doubt these stewards were hard for some of the slaves in the trade to trust. But as well as being agents of the traders, these men could act as the agents of the enslaved, providing a remote link to the city outside the slave pens. Henry Bibb remembered giving the steward in a Louisville slave pen a shilling to buy him a watermelon. John Brown, in New Orleans, got steward Bob Freeman to buy him tobacco. When the enslaved steward found that Brown had money, he "induced" the slave dealer to allow the two to go out of the pens together on errands. Later, when he needed information about the buyers in the yard, Brown remembered, "I began to draw Bob."[11]

It was, however, not only the stewards and their friends who were able to pass in and out of the pens. After all, it was one of the jobs of the stewards, Frisby told the court, to go *with* slaves to pick up their baggage or belongings. Some slaves slept in one place and were marketed in another. Slave dealer John Womack remembered that when he sold slaves for Thomas Hundley, "Hundley fed his boys at his own Home; I only saw them half the day at my show room." And recall that when Samuel Hite, the slave dealer and sometime bartender who plied his business on the streets of New Orleans, got close to making a sale, he sent word for a slave to be walked out from the pens.[12] In fact, the same commercial imperatives that underwrote the tight discipline and micro-surveillance inside the slave pens sometimes provided slaves with an opportunity to experience the world outside the pens without supervision. Testimony in the case brought to settle the affairs of deceased slave dealer Elihu Cresswell suggests that many of the slaves in Cresswell's pen were hired out. Slave dealer David Wise testified that Cresswell tried to hire out a group of slaves in his yard "as much as possible." Frank, who had been shipped from Texas and sent to sale in C. M. Rutherford's New Orleans slave yard, was, like the slaves in Cresswell's yard, hired while he was on sale. For Frank, the dismal routine of line-ups and examinations was punctuated by the anonymity of urban slavery. During the time that he was being offered for sale, Frank daily left the slave yard to go work at a New Orleans dry goods store, where he stocked shelves alongside the store's white employees. Reluctant to lose the regular income Frank provided them, income which could perhaps cover the cost of his room and board at Rutherford's pen, the enslaved man's owners had hired him out as they tried to sell him. For his part, Frank was reluctant to leave his job even for the ten days (spent in the pen) it took him to recover from yellow fever. He preferred spending his days abroad in the city—unloading goods at the levee, perhaps, listening to slaveholders talk about business and slaves, watching the free people of color in the street and walking among them.[13]

As well as information about the general practice of the slave trade, the character of lower South slavery, or black life in New Orleans, experienced slaves in the pens could provide newcomers detailed information about the process of sale from beginning to end. Mixed in among the out-of-state slaves boarded by the interstate traders in the yards were slaves who had been sent to the market from less distant origins. Indeed, among the slaves in the yards there were generally a number of slaves who had already been sold. In testimony that was admittedly self-serving, one New Orleans slave dealer estimated that he "almost invariably" sold slaves to New Orleans residents on a trial basis. While that probably overstated the practice, slaves were commonly sold on trial to buyers from both the city and the country. And they were commonly (though not as commonly) returned to the pens after being tried in a new environment.[14] They came back to the pens, that is, with a local knowledge of slavery, of what lower-South buyers wanted and what they did not.

The provisions of redhibition law put other slaves (and their experience) back in the pens. John White's *Slave Record* indicates that two to four percent of the slaves he sold were typically returned to him; in 1851, however, the figure was fifteen percent.[15] These slaves were returned to the pens with a knowledge of the process of sale from beginning to end, of a buyer's method in selecting, trying, and disqualifying a slave. In most cases this knowledge probably would have been useful as an account of slave buyers in general, but the antebellum South was sometimes a small enough place that slaves in the pens might sometimes have known quite a bit about an individual buyer before he even entered the yard. Over the course of a few months at the beginning of the 1850s, for instance, John Buhler of Baton Rouge bought and returned some fifteen slaves from the various local dealers who kept their slaves in a common pen. After a few of these transactions, Buhler must have been well known to the slaves in the pen; his situation and expectations were certainly common knowledge among those whom he had tried and returned but also perhaps among the other slaves in the pen who could have heard about him from those who were returned. In fact, by the time he finished buying, Buhler was being offered a man whom he had long since sent back in exchange for a woman whom he was seeking to return.[16] If nothing else, slaves returned under buyer-protecting warranty laws would have been recognizable to those who remained in the pens. They did not need to tell their stories to communicate their experience: there was a way out of a sale which led back to the pens.

If they had wanted to tell their stories, however, they could have. Even within the close confines of the slave pens, slaves found room to escape, if only for a moment, their sellers' watchful gaze. Some slaves talked right past the traders. Eulalie and her family, for instance, were remembered by slave trader L. M. Foster as having spoken French "with the other slaves in the yard." What they had said, he could not report. "He doesn't understand that language," read a court reporter's summation of his testimony on the matter.[17] It might have been harder to get away with whispering in English than talking in French: whispering looks suspicious. For whispering, however, there was always the nighttime.

As John Brown remembered it, the discipline of the slave pens relaxed between the time the last buyer left the yard at six o' clock and the time the slaves went to bed at ten o' clock. Slaves had these hours to themselves. It was during this time that Solomon Northup learned the stories of his fellow slaves and Henry Bibb stole a moment alone with his wife, from whom he was separated during the day. At another time in another jail, Bibb used darkness to cover a conversation he had with two slaves who called to him from the outside, asking directions to Canada. So, too, for Sally, who had just laid down one night in the slave pen when she heard a man she knew calling to her through the bars of a window. He had come to tell her that the traders had gone out for the evening and that she might escape over the fence when the fires in the yard burnt down.[18] These are remarkable conversations, conversations worth remembering and recording in a published narrative of slavery, but the slaves in the pens must also have had more mundane ones about the traders' temper and tricks or the appearance and attitude of the day's buyers—conversations that inverted the slaveholders' gaze by mocking it, analyzing it, and sometimes using it.

When slaves looked at a particular buyer, they could do so with an informed eye to their own future. Among the many poisoned outcomes faced by slaves in the pens, some were worse than others. As Charles Ball remembered it, the prospect that he would be sold to the rough looking man who was bargaining for his price, for instance, "struck terror" into his heart. Solomon Northup, by contrast, remembered hoping that the man who was examining him would seal the bargain. Northup had overheard that the man was from New Orleans and "very much desired that he would buy me for I conceived it would not be difficult to make my escape from New Orleans on some northern vessel." John Brown similarly wanted to be sold to a man from up the Mississippi River because upriver was the direction of freedom. And Henry Bibb wanted to be sold to an Indian because he thought it would be easier to escape from an Indian than a white man. Besides, the man "wanted me only for a kind of body servant to wait on him—and in this case I knew that I should fare better than I should in the field." Writing *Clotel*, William Wells Brown neatly summed both the signs of difference between buyers evident to slaves in the pens and the social character of the process of interpreting those signs. In the voice of Mrs. Devant, Brown described a slave's perspective on a buyer like this: "I observed a tall young man, with long black hair, eyeing me very closely, and then talking to the trader. I felt sure that my time had come, but the day closed without me being sold. I did not regret this, for I had heard that foreigners made the worst of masters, and I felt confident that the man who eyed me was not American."[19]

Like Brown's fictional account, those of the narrators have the acuity of hindsight: there is no way of knowing if Charles Ball really felt "terror" at the moment of his sale or if Henry Bibb actually thought that he could escape from the Indian the moment he saw the man. But like other evidence from the slave narratives, these stories bear the trace of the slave pens, of a way of seeing and using information which reflects a history that has remained invisible to many historians. In the interstices of the slave-pen routine there were ways for slaves to gather and spread knowledge about the traders and the buyers. As the traders instructed them in how to represent themselves as salable, the slaves learned about slaveholders' system of slave-buying signs; as the buyers looked them over and asked them questions, the slaves looked back and came to their own conclusion about the prospects held by a given sale. Each step in commodification was also a step in perception. Meanwhile, the same incentives that governed the rest of the traders' practice provided small spaces for its subversion. The effort the traders saved by buying a steward to prepare their slaves for sale, the time they saved by sending their slaves to pick up their own baggage, the money they saved by hiring slaves out while they were offered for sale, the sales they made on trial and the returns they accepted to avoid legal action all provided ways for slaves in the pens to gather and spread a useful local knowledge of the trade. Without the opportunity to use it, of course, the information that slaves in the pens gathered and shared would have been useless. It was, however, the daily business of the slave traders and the daily practice of the slave buyers to give the slaves a chance to shape their own sale.

OPPORTUNITY

The impersonality of the slave market, where they knew neither the traders nor the slaves, forced buyers into reliance upon the people they were buying. The slaves in the pens, after all, were the best authorities on their histories, bodies, and behavior: they knew what kind of work they could do, whether they had run away, or if they had been sick. And so as they tried to sort the one "likely" slave from the many in the market, the buyers asked the slaves questions. Their questions were about slaves' histories, ages, origins, health, attitudes, and abilities, and they were designed to help them read the slaves' bodies and place them in a meaningful biographical context by revealing the life stories that had been hidden by the traders. Of course, only a fool would believe a story told in the slave market. The traders' reputation for sharp dealing was well-known, the slaves' vulnerability to those who choreographed their sale obvious. As Charles Weld remembered it, "little value was apparently attached to the answers of the slaves."[20] Buyers' conversations with slaves were layered with efforts to form alliances, suggest threats, and see through to the truth, and their concern was as much with peeling back the traders' misrepresentations as with the literal answers the slaves gave to their questions. In the slave market, business was fraught with all the manipulation, negotiation, and uncertainty of human interaction.

Almost all of those who described the buyers' practice referred to their questions about the slaves' ages. Charles Weld, for example, remembered that buyers took "considerable pains" to "ascertain their ages." The task was considerable because, as Weld reported, many slaves did not know their own age. In the antebellum South, biological time often remained the property of slaveholders, who recorded slaves' birthdates in their own commercial records and revealed them only at Emancipation.[21] But even slaves who knew how many years they had been alive were often assigned a new age by the traders, and the buyers could safely assume that they would try to avoid punishment by answering any inquiries as they had been instructed. To learn what they wanted to know about biology, the buyers sometimes tried to use the slaves' biographical time. William Wells Brown, for example, described the buyers asking slaves to break their lives down into periods spent with particular owners or in particular places and then summing the slaves' broken biographies into a total to see if it matched their advertised ages.[22] The buyers could not count on getting honest answers in the slave market, but they might hope to get revealing ones.

Those in search of skilled slaves asked about the accuracy of the traders' representations. When David Campbell described his slave buying in a letter he wrote to his wife, he carefully distinguished between what he saw for himself, what the trader had told him, and what he had heard from the slave: "I saw a tolerably good looking man today, who is said to be a house servant, and he told me he could drive a carriage." Other questions asked in the market seem similarly calculated to fathom the difference between the traders' promises and the slaves' hidden pasts: "Can you make shirts?" "Betty, can you cook?" "Did you drive your master's carriage?"[23] These questions forced slaves in the market either to underwrite or undermine the traders' accounts of their accomplishments: if they told a displeasing truth, they might be immediately punished; if they told the traders' lies, they might later be held accountable.

As the buyers picked over the slaves' bodies for signs of illness or injury, they asked the slaves questions about their health. Louis Hughes remembered that as a child he was asked by a slave buyer "if I could remember having the chickenpox, measles, or whooping-cough. I answered yes. Then he asked me if I wanted to take a little walk with him." As well as information about the slaves' medical history, the buyers asked for information about their current condition. Joseph Ingraham remembered buyers in the Natchez market asking slaves about their appetites. Similarly, in Richmond James Redpath overheard a slave-holder asking a slave to assess himself in the language of the market: "You all sound?" The buyers were guaranteed honest answers to these questions only as far as they could persuade the slaves that they might buy them and hold them accountable for what they said in the market, but even if slaves lied about their health, it might be revealed in their answers. "She was suffering when purchased with a cough," wrote one doctor of a slave whom he had treated, "and spoke in a low, compressed, stridulous voice apparently with great effort. This state was said to be a 'bad cold' of a few days standing."[24] Looking back on the sale, the doctor could see what the buyer had missed: the woman's literal answers were less reliable than the voice in which she gave them.

The buyers also asked the slaves to tell the stories behind their scars. James Redpath remembered that when the woman with missing fingers was paraded before the buyers in Richmond, she was asked, "Didn't you cut your finger off kase you was mad?" W. H. Yos apparently asked a similar question of two men whose backs were "considerably scarred by the whip." Having seen their scars, he nevertheless decided to purchase them, basing his decision on "their appearance and talking with them about the cause, &c."[25] By asking the slaves questions, Yos was brought to seeing good slaves where he might otherwise have seen bad characters. Buyers used slaves' answers to slot them into prefabricated stereotypes—in these cases the defiant hellion or the misused but faithful slave—within their larger categories of comparison. They reflected the slaves' answers through the prism of their supposed ability to know and categorize racial others.

As they talked to the slaves, buyers sometimes used the forms of polite conversation to do the business of speculation. Most simply, as Frederick Douglass remembered it, the buyers would "impudently ask us if we would not like to have them for masters." Charles Ball remembered being asked "if we would like to live with them, if they would purchase us" and also remembered giving an answer which reveals much about the question: "we generally answered in the affirmative." Audible behind the smutty tone of the buyers' insincere solicitude was a test: how pliable are you, how willing to act a pleasing part? Other questions came similarly wrapped. Buyers, for example, asked slaves about left-behind homes in a tone that might have indicated concern but masked a complicated speculation on the disciplinary effect of the slave trade. Slaves who had been carried far from their homes, after all, were thought to be less likely to run away. Dr. D. S. Rogers, for example, bought Davy only after he had been assured that the young man was from Mississippi and had been in New Orleans just a few days. As important as distance could be attachment, particularly when the slave standing before the buyers was young and male. "Have you a wife?" was one of the questions buyers repeatedly asked in the Natchez market, according to Joseph Ingraham. Henry Bibb, whose youth, gender, and exceptionally light skin suggested to buyers that he might run away, explained that evidence of attachment could make some slaves more salable. Speaking of his trader's decision to sell him in a lot with his wife, Bibb wrote: "for fear he might not get me off at so great an advantage, as the people did not like my appearance, he could do better by selling us together."[26]

Slave buyer David Campbell gave a fuller account of the calculation that lay behind the surface of conversation in describing to his wife a man whom he had seen in the market but not bought for fear that the man would run away. "He seemed an honest fellow, for he said that he would tell me no lie about it, he loved a Julep in the morning," Campbell wrote, "But he was between thirty and forty years of age and had a wife. He seemed not unwilling that I should purchase him, but I apprehended that he would immediately run away."[27] All the way through the account he sent to his wife, Campbell maintained a distinction between seeming and being: he thought he was being hustled and he located his doubt in the man's age and his marriage—the slave had been separated from his wife of longstanding and would be likely to run away (immediately) to return to her. As he put it to his own wife, he—the model slave buyer—looked beyond the man's self-advertised honesty and worked a paternalist line of questioning about the man's family into a hard-headed evaluation of the slave's intentions.

Like David Campbell, other buyers thought they could peel away the semblance of the slave market and discern the authenticity that lurked in predictable answers. John Knight thought he could look into a slave's heart. Writing about Frances, who had been banished from Maryland for an unspecified crime, Knight offered that he would pay full price for her if he could "feel fully satisfied that there was no danger to be apprehended of her repeating her recent crime or of committing any other equally bad." But how to know, how to recognize a "naturally wicked disposition, if such she have?" Simple: Knight would ask her. "When she arrives here and we shall see and have a conversation with her," he wrote, "we can probably be better able to judge."[28] Unless Knight thought that Frances would come right out and threaten him, he was talking about looking behind the literal meaning of her words to find a deeper meaning, about reading her mind—though he probably would have called it her soul—from her conversation. That was something that happened to Henry Bibb all the time. "After conversing with me," Bibb wrote of the slave traders and cotton farmers who examined him while he was on sale in New Orleans, "they have sworn by their Maker that they would not have me among their Negroes; and that they saw the devil in my eye; I would run away &c."[29] Bibb did not need to tell the slaveholders those things; they could, they thought, see them by watching him answer their questions.

And so, though they could never be sure of the answers, slave buyers asked a lot of questions. As they ran through what Solomon Northup called "the usual questions propounded by purchasers," the buyers tried to make the slaves divulge any information that the traders were trying to hide.[30] They were hoping to build alliances with the slaves, to pester and cajole them into being honest, to intimidate them and fool them, and finally to look right through them. From question to question they were trying to make the slaves' humanity serve their speculations by using the forms of conversation to peel away the artifice of the market. And from answer to answer, the slaves were guiding their way.

SHAPING THE SALE

Slaves were the information brokers in the slave market. Anonymous, they stood at the center of the slaveholders' bargains, between imperfectly known pasts and unpredictable futures, between traders who depended upon them to market their commodified selves and buyers who relied upon them to reveal their "real" ones. They knew what the traders wanted them to say and what the buyers wanted to hear. And they knew whether they fit the traders' representations and the buyers' expectations—whether they were sickly or skilled, whether they had thoughts of escape or revolt. Using these pieces of information, slaves could create themselves in the slave market, matching their self-repre-

sentations to their own hoped-for outcomes. Sometimes, at enormous risk, they shaped a sale to suit themselves.

Their choices were hedged by violence on either side. Most slaves probably did not believe the traders' pledges to sell them to good masters if they were well behaved—they knew that prices meant more than promises in the slave market. But they also knew that they would be punished if the traders could tell that they were not representing themselves as they had been instructed. The traders' present threats, however, had to be balanced with the knowledge that dissatisfied buyers might later hold slaves responsible for the answers they gave in the pens. Caught between the traders and the buyers, the slaves made tacit alliances that were both necessary and risky. Interviewed in 1892, L. M. Mills described his own slave-market dilemma in the third person: "When a Negro was put on the block he had to help sell himself by telling what he could do. If he refused to praise himself and acted sullen, he was sure to be stripped and given thirty lashes. Frequently a man was compelled to exaggerate his accomplishments, and when his buyer found out that he could not do what he said he could he would be beaten unmercifully. It was pretty sure a thrashing either way."[31] Like Mills, slaves in the pens were interposed between bargainers—pre-sented on the one hand and examined on the other—who made their expectations and intentions brutally clear. And like Mills, slaves in the market had to calculate their behavior: discouraging a sale might lead to an immediate beating, encouraging it too much might lead to vio-lence down the road. L. M. Mills described shaping one's own sale as a dangerous necessity, a Hobson's choice—"a thrashing either way." And yet he also described a situation in which the business of slaveholders was *necessarily* done through the agency of their slaves, a situation of grave danger but also of great opportunity.

Henry Bibb's case was extreme. After months in a New Orleans slave pen where the buyers thought they could see the devil in his eyes, Bibb was sent out to find himself a master. Given the chance to choose, Bibb proceeded much as the buyers he had met in the pens. Of the man who eventually bought him, Bibb later wrote, "When I approached him, I felt much pleased at his external appearance." Satisfied with his estima-tion of the potential buyer, he represented himself in answers that compensated for the threat of flight encoded in his exceptionally light skin. He told the man that he was happily married to a woman who was

also for sale (which was true), that he was illiterate (which was not true), and that he had only run away once (which was half true). Convinced by Bibb's answers and perhaps taken in by Bibb's willingness to lend a little of the truth about his history of flight to the credibility of his lies about literacy, the man bought Bibb and his family. Bibb was mistaken in his own estimation (he had supposed the man to be a Christian, but later pronounced him to be "one of the basest hypocrites that I ever saw") but certain in his manipulation.[32]

Slaves in the pens had less room to maneuver than did Bibb on the street, but it did not take much space to shape a sale. Small signs meant a lot in the slave market. Buyers were searching for vitality and responsiveness and often used the words "lively" or "active" to describe the slaves they desired. To manipulate the buyers' minute attention, traders tried to discipline their slaves into postures of strength and readiness. Whether intentionally or not, the slaves sometimes undermined their efforts. As Henry Thomas explained about why he was so long in selling in New Orleans, "nobody there liked my countenance at all—no one would give a cent for me." Lucy, whose owner thought her "low spirited situation" responsible for his inability to sell her, was sent home from the slave market unsold. "Assure her," the owner wrote to the slave dealer, "that I will keep her myself or sell her in Falmo." Unwilling or unable to sell herself, Lucy was returned to the neighborhood where she would be happier and presumably more salable. Lucy's depression—her murdered soul—was a recognizable enough feature of the slave pens to be a commonplace explanation for difficulty in selling a slave.[33] As John Brown remembered it, "A man or a woman may be well in every respect, yet their value be impaired by a sour look, or a dull vacant stare, or a general dullness of demeanor."

For Brown, however, it was easy enough to animate a slave-market commonplace with a slave-pen strategy. In describing his own time there, he inverted the roles of seeker and sought, using the buyers' own strategies as a tool in *his* effort to find a suitable owner: "I had not yet found a purchaser. One reason of this was that McCargo and Freeman demanded a heavy price for me, but also in some measure because I did not care to speak up for myself, so that my looks did not recommend me to buyers."[34] Slaves like Brown knew that buyers were using simple social cues, attempting to look through their bearing to discern their

character. By modulating their responses and adjusting their carriages, slaves could bend the buyers' perceptions to fit their own purposes.

Buyers who thought that they could read slaves' minds by looking at their faces made their market method vulnerable to the vagaries of human interaction—deception, manipulation, and misunderstanding. John Parker: "I made up my mind I was going to select my owner so when anyone came to inspect me I did not like, I answered all questions with a 'yes' and made myself disagreeable."[35] As Parker remembered it, he inhabited the set-piece conversations of the slave market with a subversive literalism, marketing himself in a dead-pan tone that undermined the meaning of the words he used. He met the slaveholders at the margins of their questions, answering the inquiries implicit in the questions in one voice while explicitly answering them in another. That slave traders often referred to slaves who were "either sick or deceitful," refused to "talk up right," or needed "correcting" suggests that not all slaves were as successful as John Parker in escaping the traders' attention as they doubled their answers upon themselves.[36] It also suggests that many tried.

Most slaves did not have to take the risks that Parker took to steer the buyers' eyes. Recall the buyers in Richmond who asked the enslaved woman why she had cut the fingers off one of her hands: had they been diseased? had she done it by accident while working at a dangerous job? had she willfully tried to destroy her own value? What those buyers saw depended upon what she said, or perhaps how she said it. And recall also W. H. Yos explaining that he had bought two severely scarred slaves because he had been convinced "from their appearance and from talking with them about the causes &c." that they posed no threat of resistance.[37] Yos bought the slaves on their own recommendation. Slaves could choose their buyers by retelling (or not) the well-known stories slaveholders used to choose among the slaves in the market. The more detailed the buyers' questions about their bodies, the greater the opportunity for slaves to create themselves according to their own preferences.

At times, the slaves' role in undermining their own sales drove the traders to distraction. One exasperated Virginia trader wrote to another in the 1850s, "I heard Coleman tell some men who were looking at him the reason his hair was out it was because he had been cupped. You must stop that. I forgot to tell you in Montgomery. I never was able to find the cup marks." Similarly, from South Carolina in the same decade: "Mr. Oakes, James is cutting up . . . I could sell him like hot cakes if he would talk Right. You may blame me but I tell nothing on him but the fact and Dr. Weatherly will tell the same. The boy is trying to make himself unsound. He says he wore a truss in Charleston. I think it would be best to see his former master and know the facts." Or from New Orleans: "I have just got rid of your man Lawson . . . the hardest selling Negroe I ever sold and the worst talker he stuck out to the last that he was not healthy."[38] Searching for signs of a disease they thought they might never find, these traders found themselves caught in the trap they had set for the buyers: unable to trust the slaves but uncertain about dismissing their answers.

Questions about skills and experience further involved slaves in determining the outcome of their sale. "The boy says he can make a panel door," gushed one expectant slave dealer about the self-proclaimed skill that he thought made Isaac salable. John Jones, apparently, was less forthcoming. "I was convinced that John Jones has been deceiving us with respect to his qualifications," wrote John Knight about his suspicion that the recently purchased Jones had under-represented himself in the slave market, and, he proudly continued, "one of the new hands just arrived . . . says he knew John well and that he has always been employed in shoeing horses, stamping plows & was a good hand at such work."[39] Whether Jones lied because he had simply tired of being a blacksmith, wanted to reduce his value, or wished to avoid sale entirely, it was only the untimely appearance of a history he thought he had left behind that prevented him from living out his life in the role he had chosen in the slave market.

Finally, some slaves tried to shape their own sale by advertising their feelings. Moses Roper told a buyer directly "that I would, on no account, live with him if I could help it." A Madame Beauvais of New Orleans did not buy Virginia "because she had said she would not come with her." Mary, sold to a woman who lived in the sugar parishes of Louisiana, ran away before she could be carried away from New Orleans. When she was captured, she said "that she was willing to stay with anyone who would purchase her in the city, but would not return to the country." "Whereupon," the Supreme Court recounted in a case arising from the sale, "negotiations were set on foot" for sale to a resident of the city. Other slaves called upon the prospective purchasers to buy them only with their families. As slave buyer Maria Williams remembered it, Henry gave a very specific response to a common slave-market question when he was sent to be tried in her neighbor's home: "I enquired whether he was willing to be sold, he said he did not desire to be sold without his wife."[40] Henry, in effect, was threatening to run away if the man did not buy his wife. Slaves who were brave enough to meet insincere questions with a sincere response built upon the accreted experience of the slave market with unwilling slaves—the actions of those who had come before them lent a desperate credibility to their own threatened resistance.

Other slaves challenged the buyers to back their oft-expressed concern for slaves' families with their behavior in the slave market. Joseph Ingraham overheard a slave in the Natchez market asking a buyer "would you be so good as to buy Jane?" and pointing out his wife so that the slaveholder could examine her for himself. Slaves' requests to be sold with their family members were often edged with desperation: "Please, master, buy Emily. I can never work anymore if she is taken from me; I will die," Solomon Northup remembered Eliza saying as she pleaded to be sold with her daughter; "Oh! master, master! buy me and my children with my poor husband—do, pray," J. D. Green remembered a woman calling from the auction stand to the man who had just bought her husband, Rueben.[41] This was not freedom: slaves like Eliza were forced to retail themselves according to one of the governing fictions of the slave market—that the buyers were there to rescue them from the traders. But it was hope: some, like the unnamed man in the Natchez market, were saved from separation through their own intervention. Others, like Eliza and Emily, like Reuben and Sally, were literally beaten apart.

The closing of a deal, however, was not the closing of a sale. "Almost invariably" was the way one slave dealer described the frequency of selling on trial within the city of New Orleans. The advantages for the buyers of taking a slave on trial, which could last anywhere from an afternoon to a few months, were many. Buying on trial gave slaveholders time to test the fit between the person they imagined and the one they were about to buy; it gave those who bought for a business a chance to spread the responsibility of evaluating and choosing slaves among their partners; and it gave white women a chance to participate in slave buying without going to the slave market. Slaves, especially cooks, nurses, and seamstresses, had skills that were best evaluated by the slaveholding women to whom they would answer, and their sales were often consummated outside the pens. "It was understood," remembered one broker, "that I should take the slave to his house for his wife to see her." Thomas Butler sealed the bargains he made for field hands in the pens but planned to try to get the woman he was buying for his wife sent out to his plantation for "some time on trial." Buying on trial also allowed slaveholding women like Mrs. Fernando Lemos to participate in the degrading rituals of the slave market in the comfortable confines of their own drawing rooms. A doctor who had visited the Lemos household remembered Mrs. Lemos asking him "how he liked a Negro girl in the room. Witness said very well, that she appeared nice and neat. The lady then raised the petticoat on the right leg of the girl, which appeared swollen."[42] But if buying on trial allowed slaveholders an opportunity to extend the slave market in time and space, it also gave slaves an opportunity to examine their buyers and choose whether to match or subvert their evident expectations.

We cannot know how many slaves took the opportunity offered by a trial period to shape their own sale. We cannot, for example, taste the food prepared by an unnamed cook who was sent to a country plantation and quickly returned to the city. We cannot compare the rural product to the urban one and cannot know if it was a slaveholder's delicate palate or a slave's subtle strategy that undid the deal. Nor is there any way to tell if Daniel, sold on trial as a house servant to Spire Haggerty of Texas, was really deaf or was just pretending. He seemed deaf to Haggerty, who had to yell at him to be heard aboard the steamboat that carried them away from New Orleans. But a slave dealer's employee remembered him otherwise: "I saw and talked to him every day from sometime in March until he was sold."[43] Either Haggerty was lying, the employee's testimony suggested, or Daniel was shamming. The man's testimony, of course, might not have been true, but it was meant to be credible: what we can tell is that Daniel had the space to shape his sale if he had wanted to. That, apparently, is what Harriet Tubman did. Tubman was sent on trial to a woman who soon, in the words of the ex-slave's amanuensis, "got tired of Harriet, as Harriet was determined she should do, and she abandoned her intention of buying her and sent her back to her master."[44]

Other slaves sent on trial tried to seal deals rather than undermine them. Richard, for instance, had long been employed in a New Orleans coffee house, where, one man who knew him later testified, he had been "thought to drink." When he was taken on a trial basis from the auction house where he had been sent for sale to another coffee house (owned by William Stoppenhagen), Richard was quick to seize the opportunity; a slaveholder later recalled seeing Richard "talking to Stoppenhagen to buy him." Alexina Morrison made a similar pitch when Andre Hutt carried her out to his house from the slave market so that his wife could see her. As Hutt later remembered it: "My wife looked at her and was not pleased, said she was not such a girl as she wanted, the girl tried to persuade my wife to buy her . . . I had a general conversation with the girl about her qualities as a cook, washer, ironer, etc. She said she was first rate at all, that she was not well at the time, but soon would be, and that when well she was a stout healthy girl, and manifested a great anxiety for me and my wife to buy, in fact my wife had almost to drive her out of the kitchen to get rid of her."

Morrison was trying to avoid being exported to New Orleans, where she would later claim that she was the kidnapped child of white parents, unjustly sold into slavery. Hutt was trying to convince a Louisiana court that if Morrison was really a free white woman, she had ample time to say so. "During all this time," he testified, "the girl set up no claims to freedom, she had ample opportunity to do so, as we were going from and returning to the store, a distance of one half or three-quarters of a mile."[45]

Legal testimony has a partisan purpose and cannot be taken as a transparent account of what happened in a given situation. But because partisan, it is meant to be convincing, to quicken a common understanding of the possibilities inherent in a particular situation. Hutt thought it believable that Alexina Morrison would try to shape her sale by trumpeting the qualifications the traders used to market her. Indeed, Hutt thought it equally believable that Alexina Morrison, if she had really been free and white, would have subverted her sale by saying so—these things could happen. My argument follows Hutt's: the space was available for slaves to shape their own sale when they were sold on trial—these things could happen.

Indeed, under the law of redhibition, they often did.[46] According to the Louisiana version of the law, a slave sale could be contested in court up to one year after it was sealed in the market. Slaves could go on shaping their sale long after dealer and buyer had agreed to terms and filed an Act of Sale with a notary public. When a newly bought slave like William "said he was sick," the result was often a redhibition case. And because the legal definition of "defect" hinged upon the duration of an illness or the frequency of a forbidden behavior, those who brought these cases under redhibition law often depended on the slaves in question for information. Robert Mills, for instance, made his case that Mariah's shortness of breath while working dated from before he had purchased her: "she says it has been the case ever since she had the scarlet fever some three years ago." Likewise, the overseer who worked Dempsey depended upon the slave's own account of his medical history and physical capacity when he testified before a Louisiana court that Dempsey was unsound. Dempsey, he said, had a bad back "arising the Negro said from an injury he had sustained in the back from a Waggon passing over him." Hoping to bolster his employer's case for return, the overseer added a sentence which suggested that Dempsey himself might have encouraged the owner to file suit: "I can only say that the said Dempsey told me that he had been sold two or three different times and was as often returned."[47] But Dempsey, whose autobiographical stamp is so evident in the medical and commercial histories provided by his dissatisfied owner, was not around for the end of the trial he had done so much to bring about. By that time he had escaped—bad back and all.

Though it is clear that they were reshaping their buyers' bargains with the stories they told about themselves, it is not known whether Dempsey or Mariah or William were shamming or sick, whether they were telling the truth about being sick and hoping for mercy or lying and hoping for return. What is clear, however, is that slave dealers spent a lot of time worrying that the slaves they sold would intentionally undermine bargains sealed in the pens. A. J. McElveen, for instance, advised his boss not to accept Didry's return because the woman was faking her illness: "As for old Didry . . . she will always lie up. She is no more sick than women are generally. Mr. Oakes don't take her back unless he has her examined by a Doctor." About another slave who had been returned by a dissatisfied buyer McElveen was even more economical in his evaluation: "The fact is the boy has told lies." As L. E. Hooper said to a Louisiana court in an effort to prove that a slave he had sold had not been sick at the time of the sale: "Negroes are very apt to have an excuse not to work." Or as a Louisiana judge wrote in declaring that a carpenter who could not work wood might still be a carpenter, apparent inability "might on the part of the slave be owing to obstinacy or perverseness."[48] The court could not take the chance of letting a delicate deal between slaveholders be disrupted by a slave's crude trick.

That much was the quotidian racism of the antebellum regime: any illness could be seen as an excuse, any inability an occasion for brutality. But the traders' anxiety about the slaves they sold went well beyond the idea that they were shamming illness to avoid work. Sometimes, the traders thought, the slaves were intentionally trying to undermine their own sale. Tyre Glen, for instance, suspected that a slave he had sold to a slaveholder called General May was faking an illness because he was unsatisfied with the terms of his own sale. "The Negro," he explained to his partner, "I expect is unwilling to Live with May and that his object is to sham the note." Soon after, Glen found himself on the other side of the same story when he tried to return a slave whom he believed was ill. "Peter Layner was here on yesterday he refuses to take the Negro back and says she was sound when he sold her tho sayd he had onst swaped her to a Saml Smith 4 or 5 years since that she then fained to be sick and he rescinded the contract tho he can prove by 50 persons that she was sound when he sold her." Essentially, the man said, the slave dealer was being taken in by a trick the slave had tried before. Another dealer made a similar evaluation as he instructed his partner about how to dispose of two slaves who had been sold and returned: "I don't want you to sell them to anybody back there because if you do they will always brake up your sales through bad talking."[49] These slave traders, with their constructions of intentional commercial disruption—sham the note, break the sale—and recidivism born of experience—she did it before, they will always do it—thought that their slaves were intentionally meddling in their business. Not only that: they thought they knew why.

To explain their suspicions, slave sellers sometimes referred to slaves' opinions of their own sale. Slave seller Manuel Lopez, for instance, tried to answer Louis Caretta's charge that the woman Lopez had sold him was insane by referring to her opinion of the sale. "I had a talk with Caretta in which I told him that Esther did not like to be sold and to have a new master, and having on the contrary a great anxiety to remain in my family's house maybe she would make some excentricity and that the only thing to be done was to have her flogged and that everything would go strait." When Henry was returned to him for fits, slave dealer

J. W. Boazman's response was not to take him back but to threaten him: "he could cure all & the damned rascal is playing off," Boazman said. In supporting the court case that grew out of his refusal to accept Henry's return, Boazman later suggested that Henry was faking it because he had a wife in New Orleans and was to be sold to an owner who lived outside the city—a suggestion that was perhaps supported by Henry's escape before the case came to trial. Not only did slave sellers refer to slaves' opinions of their own sales when they were trying to explain their behavior afterwards, the courts in Louisiana occasionally accepted these stories as the most likely explanation for a slave's behavior. When Nelly's dissatisfied buyer alleged that she had epilepsy, for example, witnesses representing her former owners replied that her crying and rolling on the ground "was from dissatisfaction" with her new owners rather than any organic affliction. The Supreme Court sided with the seller, apparently concluding that Nelly was trying to arrange for her own return. In the Louisiana courts, slaveholders were willing to hang the outcome of thousand-dollar court cases on the argument that apparent ailments should be understood as signs of hidden intentions, that buyers who tried to return their slaves had fallen prey to their own property, and that slaves were shamming to reshape their own sale. Not only were slaveholders making law out of the imagined intentions of their slaves, they were arguing that their slaves knew the law and were using it to their own advantage.[50]

It was a reasonable argument. The slaves they sold, after all, had seen slaves returned by unhappy buyers before. And slaves were present, as one slave dealer testified in court, when dealers and dissatisfied slaveholders haggled over the duration of slaves' ailments, the causes of their behavior, and the terms under which a sale might be rescinded. Indeed, slaves sometimes demonstrated a detailed understanding of the terms under which they had been sold. When Palmyra ran away from her new owner, for instance, she went to the slave yard, where she asked the slave dealer "to take her back." In his own description of the daily routine of the slave pens, John Brown made explicit reference to the law that governed his own sale when he explained to his readers that a slaveholder who sold a "guaranteed" slave was obliged to refund the money if that slave ran away. Henry Bibb described the result of a warranty case between slaveholders as a personal triumph when he concluded the story of his time with a couple from whom he had repeatedly escaped: "They got sick of their bargain, and returned me back into the hands of my sellers." And listen to the half truth that Bibb told the man on the street when he was sent out to sell himself: "I never told him that I had been a runaway longer than one month—neither did I tell him that I had not run away more than once in my life; for these questions he never asked me."[51] Apparently drawing his knowledge from questions he had been asked in the slave pens, Henry Bibb described his fugitive past in precisely the terms used by the state of Louisiana to define a "habit" of running away—once for more than a month or twice for less than a month.

To say that Henry Bibb shaped his own sale and to suggest that he might have known the law of slavery and manipulated that too is to embed the slave market, the central symbol of slavery's inexorable brutality, in a history of opposition and manipulation. The argument should not be overstated. Slavery ground on in spite of Bibb's mastery of the man on the street or John Parker's spiteful tongue, in spite of the fact that the traders could not present their wares nor the buyers investigate them without offering slaves a chance to undermine their purposes, in spite of those who presented brushed up selves to desired buyers, begged to be sold with family members, or endured threats and risked beatings to seize a slim chance of escape. The history of the antebellum South is the history of two million slave sales. But alongside the chronicle of oppressions must be set down a history of negotiations and subversions. To be sold with family members rather than apart from them, to be sold to a rich buyer rather than a poor one, to be sold into the anonymity of the city rather than the isolation of the country, to work in the house rather than the field—all of these were outcomes sought and obtained by slaves in the pens. Placed on a scale between slavery and freedom or judged according to a theory that accepts revolution as the only meaningful goal of resistance, these slave-shaped sales do not look like much: as many skeptics have put it, "after all, they were still enslaved."[52] But placed between subordination and resistance on the scale of daily life, these differences between possible sales had the salience of survival itself.

The antislavery of the slave pens, of those who opposed slavery where they met it, where distance or surveillance or attachment made escape impossible, where state power and a hopeless deficit of armed force made rebellion suicidal, transmits today an important reminder about the extent to which the histories of domination and resistance are inextricably intertwined. They are two sides of a single history. The worshipful admiration of the aesthetics of domination which has seethed through so much recent work in the humanities—the thrilling fear that the world is built out of the phantasmic dreams of the powerful, their language and categories and objectifying gaze—must be cooled with the recognition that dreams, even the dreams of powerful people, must be made material if they are to come true.[53] And in the slave market, slaveholders' dreams could not come true without slaves—without people who could look back, estimate, manipulate, and sometimes escape.

CHAPTER SEVEN

LIFE IN THE SHADOW OF THE SLAVE MARKET

WHEN THEY REACHED into their kit of images to represent a slave, antebellum printers had only two options. One was a plate depicting a male slave with a bag on a stick slung over his shoulder; the other was a female slave with a traveling bag held out in front of her. Both slaves were in motion. Thus the same stereotypes (for that is what the printers' plates were called) were used in the advertisements placed by slave traders hoping to attract buyers and by slaveholders hoping to track down lost or runaway slaves.[1] Maybe buyers should have seen in this repetition a cautionary, if unintentional, reminder of the subversive humanity the slave traders tried so hard to hide: the slaves who could be bought in the market were the same slaves who could run away; the vessels of slaveholders' fantasies could also disrupt them; the men and women out of whom the Old South was being made could also unmake it.

In the slave market the destinies of slaveholders and slaves were fused into a volatile interdependence. Life in the shadow of the slave market was framed by the tension between the fantasies the slaveholders purchased in the market and the real people they brought home from the pens. For slaveholders, the sealing of a sale was the moment when their hopes were realized, and they bragged about their slaves and showed them off. For slaves, sale marked another kind of beginning. As they left the pens, they began lives bounded by a new set of expectations—those encoded in the price paid for them in the market—in an unfamiliar setting.

MAKING THE OLD SOUTH

Sold slaves walked out of the market and into a field of possible mistakes. From the moment they were sold, their lives were measured against a buyer's slave-pen fantasy, itself constantly refreshed through phrases such as "my New Orleans Negroes" or "the Negroes my father purchased of Taylor," which slaveholders might use six months or a year after a sale.[2] The price paid for slaves in the market represented a set of expectations that were ultimately inaccessible to them: they did not have the chance to look at their owners' lovingly detailed plantation diaries, the day-by-day records that tracked the activity and productivity of each slave in the field and summed them into a progressive contribution to the great nineteenth-century ideology of "improvement." Nor did they have a chance to read their owners' letters or be made privy to their dreams, to envision from above the imagined futures that were to be wrung gradually from their bodies. But these shadowy expectations took daily shape as grand plans were divided into assigned tasks that were themselves broken into disciplined motions until the whole world must have seemed to throb with slavery—with the shouts of owners railing about distinctions that only they could understand; with the hushed and hurried advice of slaves who had already survived their "seasoning"; with the quick hiss of the lash and the low baying of hounds that marked the boundaries of the permissible; with loneliness, uncertainty, and fear.

As recently sold slaves reached the places that would become their new homes, their eyes scanned the surroundings for portents of what was to come. Charles Ball remembered that "it was with great anxiety that I looked for the place which was in the future to be my home." Solomon Northup, who remembered that he thought continually of escape as he traveled from the market, cataloged a succession of modes of transportation—steamboat to train to footpath—and a sense of increasing isolation as he walked home with his new owner. Northup also had a detailed memory of the richness of his new owner's home ("it was two stories high, with a piazza in front. In the rear of it was also a log kitchen, poultry house, corncribs and several Negro cabins. Near the house was a peach orchard, and gardens of orange and pomegranate trees"), of several small kindnesses afforded him by his new owner in the days just after his sale, and of the welcoming appearance of the man's other slaves, who came out to meet him as he arrived.[3]

Henry Bibb's first impression was gloomier. Bibb immediately noticed that the other slaves on his new owner's plantation were "poor, ragged, stupid, and half-starved," victims of a meager diet and a cruel work regime. As in his description of the slave pen, Bibb continued in the third person: "The food allowed them per week, was one peck of corn for each grown person, one pound of pork, and sometimes a quart of molasses . . . The overseer's horn sounded two hours before daylight for them in the morning, in order that they should be ready for work before daylight. They were at work from daylight until after dark, without stopping but one hour to eat or rest, which was at noon. And at the busy season of the year they were compelled to work just as hard on the Sabbath, as on any other day . . . My first impression when I arrived on the Deacon's farm were that he was far more like what people call the devil than he was like a deacon." Charles Ball's account of his first day out of the market was similar: "The next morning I was waked, at the break of day, by the sound of a horn which was blown very loudly . . . In a few minutes the whole of the working people, from all of the cabins, were assembled; and as such it was now light enough for me distinctly to see such objects as were about me, I at once perceived the nature of the servitude to which I was, in future, to be subject . . . The overseer then led off to the field, with his horn in one hand and his whip in the other; we following—men, women, and children promiscuously—and a wretched looking troop we were. There was not an entire garment among us."[4] The elements of these descriptions are common to many others: slaves judged their new owners by the way their old slaves looked, by the quality and extent of the provisions and clothing the slaveholders provided, by the length of the work day, the difficulty of the work they demanded, the leisure time they allowed, and by the violence of their temper.

For many recently sold slaves, work had a fearful character. Faced with unfamiliar tasks (clearing trees, picking cotton, and cutting cane were all foreign to most slaves from the upper South) or uncertain expectations, they had to guard every motion.[5] For Louis Hughes, sold south to Mississippi from Virginia, the most distressing task was sweeping and dusting for his new mistress. The new work, he remembered, was "awkward to me at first . . . I dreaded this work, for I always got my ears boxed if I did not or could not do the work to suit her." Moses Grandy spoke similarly of the work he did for a man named Jemmy Coats. "Because I could not learn his way of hilling corn," Grandy remembered, "he flogged me naked with a severe whip, made of a very tough sapling; this lapped around me at each stroke; the point of it at last entered my belly and broke off, leaving an inch and a half outside."[6] For others, the delicate action of the hand necessary to pick cotton or the sharp eyes needed to spot a worm on a tobacco leaf, the sheer endurance it took to make it through a day of cutting cane or the delicate palate required to season to a slaveholder's taste—all were fraught with dangers.[7]

According to Solomon Northup, who was soon sold from a man whom he respected to one whom he could not abide, unfamiliar work under a new master could take on a terrible character. His excruciatingly detailed description of cotton picking emphasized its unfamiliar motions and the prospect of being held accountable to an utterly foreign measure of productivity:

> One morning . . . Epps appeared at the cabin door and, presenting me a sack, ordered me into the cotton field. At this time I had no experience whatever in cotton picking. It was an awkward business indeed. While the others used both hands, snatching the cotton and depositing it in the mouth of the sack, with a precision and dexterity that was incomprehensible to me, I had to seize the boll with one hand, and deliberately draw out the white, gushing blossom with the other. Depositing the cotton in the sack, moreover, was a difficulty that demanded the exercise of both hands and eye. I was compelled to pick it from the stalk where it had grown. I made havoc also with the branches, loaded with the yet unbroken bolls, the long cumbersome sack swinging from side to side in a manner not allowable in the cotton field. After a most laborious day I arrived in the gin-house with my load. When the scale determined its weight to be only ninety-five pounds, not half the quantity required of the poorest picker, Epps threatened the severest flogging . . . The number of lashes is graduated according to the nature of the case. Twenty-five are deemed a mere brush,

inflicted, for instance, when a dry leaf or piece of boll is found in the cotton, or when a branch is broken in the field; fifty is the ordinary penalty following all delinquencies of the next higher grade; one hundred is called severe: it is the punishment inflicted for the serious offense of standing idle in the field.[8]

Northup's description of his first day in the cotton field is a catalog of unfamiliar motion and unremitting discomfort: his hands fumbling awkwardly at the delicate bolls, his eyes straining in the sunlight, the bag dragging heavily on his sweating shoulder, leaving a trail of broken branches and crushed bolls in his wake. Under Epps's job-scaled (and often actuated) threats, the unfamiliar requirements of the cotton field worked their way into Northup's consciousness until his body seemed to turn against him—failing him in every motion, paining him in every extremity.[9]

The terror must have been especially acute for those who had been sold as sound even though they were sick (as was Northup when he went into the field that day) or disabled. A few days after she was sold in New Orleans, Phillis told her new owner's sister about the pain in her leg and revealed a limb that was swollen with a tremendous tumor. Phillis, however, "was always unwilling that Mrs. Hewes or any of the family should see the limb." For Phillis, the possibility of receiving medical care and relief from work seemed less likely than receiving a beating for having stood by silently while her condition was misrepresented by her seller. Similarly, Mary Louise, whose syphilis pained her so badly that she could hardly stand, said nothing about it for two or three weeks after she was purchased. When the pain finally became too much to bear, she told her buyer's sister and some of the free women of color who worked with her in the house. When one of the latter "asked her why she did not tell her master and mistress she said she was afraid." Her fears were probably justified. In a court case that grew out of another sale, a Louisiana doctor testified that when he was called to treat a woman similarly afflicted with gonorrhea, he found that rather than being cared for, she had been "neglected and roughly used" and "had the marks of the whip not perfectly healed." The specter of women being brutally punished for having a sexually transmitted disease is perhaps a measure of both slave buyers' unwillingness to look beneath women's skirts in the slave market and of their frustration at

not being able to possess their female slaves utterly. But men, too, felt the dread of being held responsible for concealing their diseases in the slave market. Recently purchased and chronically consumptive, Jim was cursed by the doctor who treated him for concealing his condition from his buyer: "Damn it, boy, yours is not a case of yesterday," said the doctor. It is perhaps impossible to gauge the terror felt by these sick slaves, or by one in the situation in which Daniel allegedly found himself after his sale. Sold as fit though he may have been deaf, he might have faced his new master's increasingly agitated commands without any way of knowing what it was he was being told to do.[10]

Many slaves took flight from their new owners shortly after they were sold.[11] Charles, who had been sold as a "fine pastry cook" and a "very good body servant," ran away from his new owner when he was sent to work in the field. Similarly, thirteen-year-old Celestine, who had worked for several years as a cook in the houses of various New Orleans free women of color, took flight shortly after she had been beaten by a white male buyer who found her cooking inedible and her manners impudent. Changed work conditions also seem to have shaped the decisions of several of the slaves bought by Augustus Walker. Walker, his neighbors testified, was a much harder man than the slaves' previous owner had been, and it did not surprise them that several of the slaves ran off after a short time in his possession. For Charles, who was remembered by a free man of color with whom he worked as always having wet clothes "because he could not retain his urine," the decision to flee his new owner must have been an effort to escape constant humiliation and misery.[12] For these slaves and many others who ran away from new owners, sale marked a moment when slavery suddenly became unbearable, when changed conditions made escape, with all its dangers, seem preferable to living a life assigned in the slave market.

When they ran away, slaves often traced a path backwards toward their past lives. After his escape, William was overtaken on the road to slave trader Samuel Woolfolk's plantation; his owner apparently knew that he would try to return to the family he had been forced to leave behind when he was sold. Similarly, Eden ran away after he was sold, against his stated wishes, to a man who lived on the other side of the Mississippi River from a woman whom he visited. The Act of Sale by which Harry's ownership was transferred contained an exception, noting that it was expected that "he would absent himself to visit his wife."

Some, like Henry Bibb, Charles Ball, and John Brown, escaped their new owners for a lasting freedom. Others made a different kind of escape. Within hours of her sale, Agnes drowned herself and her young daughter in a "waterhole 150 or 200 yards from the house" of the man who had sold her. When ten-year-old Ben first escaped, he ran back to the slave yard from which he was sold. He was able to hide there about three weeks (presumably with the help of the loved ones to whom he had returned) before being discovered and sent back to the man who had bought him. A few weeks later he was dead in a nearby river, having "plunged in and drowned himself."[13]

For most of the slaves sold by the traders, however, escape was part of their daily lives in slavery. Sold as a carpenter though he couldn't do the work, Lafortune was "drunk almost every night." Bought as a caretaker, Celestine took her new owner's children with her when she went to visit her friends among the servants at her old owner's house.[14] As many scholars have noted, the majority of slaves spun transcendence out of everyday activities: singing, praying, or playing; hunting, fishing, and trapping; taking off at night or taking it easy during the day; or just talking, telling stories, and passing the time that slaveholders thought belonged to them.[15]

Those who had been sold by the traders soon set about reconstructing the communities and social identities that had been fractured by the trade. As, over time, more women were traded through the domestic slave trade, the settled character of slave communities in the early nineteenth-century upper South was gradually transferred to the lower South. By the 1850s, slave communities in Louisiana had more even sex ratios and were more family-centered than they had been in any of the previous decades.[16] Within this historical cycle of dissolution and reconstruction were many individual cycles of social death and rebirth. In the weeks after they had been sold, many of the slaves bought by John Knight recovered identities they had been forced to leave behind by asking to be called by their given names rather than the names they had been assigned in the trade. "'Milly Head,'" Knight wrote, "says that is not her name but that it is 'Amelia Armstrong.'" He continued, "The girl 'Rachel' says her name is not 'Rachel' but 'Emily Sheppard' and 'Jerry Gooding' says his proper name in 'Jerry Sims' . . . 'Mama Smith' says her name is 'Eliza Smith.'"[17] In this snapshot of power relations in the shadow of the slave market, we can see John Knight's slaves beginning the process of reclaiming their history and identity from their buyer. As is particularly evident in the case of Eliza Smith, who made clear that she did not want her buyer (who had possibly separated her from her family and likely had designs upon her reproductive capacity), to call her "Mama," Knight's slaves were trying to make themselves known on their own terms, trying to reclaim pieces of the lives that had been stolen from them by the trade.

The shattered pieces of old lives could not be carried into the future as easily as a remembered name, and the process of rebuilding communities and identities at the end of the trade was generally slow and painful. As was the case with many of the slaves he met in the trade, Solomon Northup was able to provide both detailed physical descriptions and extensive biographies of the slaves he met on the farms and plantations of his various owners. Northup said of the slave Abram: "Abram was tall, standing a full head above any common man. He is sixty years of age, and was born in Tennessee. Twenty years ago, he was purchased by a trader, carried into South Carolina, and sold to James Buford of Williamsburgh County in that state. In his youth he was renowned for his great strength, but age and unremitting toil have somewhat shattered his powerful frame and enfeebled his mental faculties."[18] The socialization process in the slave quarter was not always smooth. As soon as she arrived at the home of her new owner, a woman bought by Henry Haynes "quarreled with the other Negroes" and from that time on she had to go to the river to do her own washing as "no other would wash her clothes."[19]

The sign by which Haynes' new slave was excluded from the community of his other slaves—no one would do her washing—hints at the reciprocity through which slave communities were structured. Sick in the days after her sale to the point that she sometimes vomited blood, Betsy was nevertheless put to work washing by her new owner, Nicholas Zimmer. As a woman who lived in the Zimmer household remembered it, Betsy was able to make it through the day only with help from Zimmer's other slaves: "There is a very good washer woman at Mrs. Zimmer's and Betsy could not wash as well as her. Betsy washed in the same tub with the other slave, but all the clothes she washed were washed afterward by the other."[20] A similar exchange of small kindnesses marked Charles Ball's transition to his new home in South Carolina. Sold south from Maryland and unaccustomed to cotton culture, Ball remembered the humiliation of his first day of picking in gendered terms. "I hung down my head, and felt very ashamed of myself," Ball later wrote, "when I found that my cotton was so far behind that of many, even of the women, who had heretofore regarded me as one of the strongest and powerful men of the whole gang." On his first day in South Carolina, however, Ball had been assigned a place to sleep in the cabin of an enslaved family owned by his master, and it was there that, through the dislocation of a new work routine, Ball was able to sustain his sense of himself as an able worker and a man. Though he had nothing to contribute to the family that first night, he made his hosts a promise: "I would bring all my earnings in the family stock, provided I might be treated as one of its members, and be allowed a portion of the proceeds of their patch or garden." Ball continued, "This offer was very readily accepted, and from this time we constituted one community as long as I remained among the field hands on this plantation." Before long Ball was able to use his skill at making bowls and ladles to make money which he combined with money of Nero, the head of the houschold, to buy molasses for "our family" and winter coats for "Dinah [Nero's wife], ourselves, and the children."²¹ As well as extending their hospitality to Ball, Nero and Dinah had provided him with a share in the leadership of their family—our family, Ball called it—and a share of the social role as patriarch and provider that he had been forced to leave behind in the upper South.

In the interstices of slavery, in moments stolen from their owners' demands or the wretchedness of their own situation, those sold by the traders rebuilt themselves and their communities in the shadow of the slave market. Through the gradual exchange of kindness and consideration, through praying together, telling their life stories and singing shared songs, through work and leisure, uprooted slaves became transplanted members of the slave communities of the lower South. And through their daily efforts to forge a set of commonalities on the underside of slavery, they reproduced their culture over time and space—over the decades of antebellum slavery and the expanding ambit of the slaveholders' regime.²²

UNMAKING THE OLD SOUTH

It was perhaps less an irony than an axiom of the master–slave relationship that sold slaves were the first audience for the poses that their buyers tried to put on after the slave market. Dr. Samuel Cartwright's "Directions for Treatment of Negroes" advised those who had recently purchased slaves to imagine themselves from the perspective of their property and to shape themselves to the task of making a good impression: "Coming therefore to a new and strange country, among stranger Negroes and finding that they had plenty to eat and only moderate work to perform and had an impartial protector in their overseer, who would see that they were not imposed on, they as a matter of fact will naturally become contented and happy and, when they get sick, that happy and contented vein of humor running through them will often keep them up, through hard spells of sickness that would kill dejected, desponding, and dissatisfied Negroes."[23] There were well-known reasons for not working new hands too hard, allowing them to get accustomed to the labor regime and disease environment before subjecting them to its full rigor, for example. But when these reasons were put to the slaves, they came wrapped as if they were gifts from the master. Solomon Northup remembered that the brutal Edwin Epps said he would spare Northup a beating on his first night "in consideration of my being 'a raw hand.'" Slave buyers like Epps were trying to impress themselves upon their new slaves: they were fair-minded men—impartial, considerate—who expected hard work and good behavior in return for their benevolence. As in the case of the account of himself that Epps provided Northup, presentations of slaveholder paternalism were often edged with the threat of violence. Recall that when Andrew Skillman bought Henry, he immediately removed the slave's chains, telling him that "if he ran away from him once he would not run away again."[24] Such grand gestures were designed to make a lasting impression on the slaves for whom they were performed, to familiarize them with the roles that their buyers had scripted for themselves—benevolent manager, tough-but-fair disciplinarian, steadfast slave breaker—and to make clear the costs of failing to play along.

As well as trying to impress their new slaves (and to reiterate their expectations to any of their old slaves who might have been watching), slave buyers used the moment of purchase to refigure their relations with other slaveholders. Indeed, one of the ways white men made friends with one another was by talking about the slaves they had just bought or sold. Franklin Matthews, for instance, was aboard the steamship *J. W. Downes* when a friend of his introduced him to a third man,

J. B. Alexander. As a bridge over their unfamiliarity the men started talking about slaves. "Upon being introduced," Matthews remembered, "we all three commenced speaking of the prices of and sales of Negroes in New Orleans and Mr. Alexander remarked . . . to me that he was just from New Orleans and that he had purchased some Negroes." That made Alexander interesting (at least to himself), and as he continued about the boat he kept on trading his experience in the slave market for the recognition of the men he met: he introduced himself to a man whose name he had overheard because he had met a man with the same name in the slave market; he told another man (apparently selected at random) that he had just bought slaves in New Orleans.[25] Alexander was seemingly all over the ship, introducing himself to people he had never before met and talking to them about buying slaves. His insistence illuminates the role that talk about the slave market played in the relations between white men in the antebellum South. By buying a slave, Alexander had bought himself a public stake in the world of white men: he was a man who was worthy of notice. As Alexander scoured the boat for other men to whom he could tell his story—men whose notice he desired—he was playing a leading role in one of the daily rituals by which white men defined their place at the center of life in the antebellum South.[26]

What is even more remarkable, perhaps, is that as he frantically shuttled around the boat, representing himself to his new friends as a player in the slave market, Alexander was fully aware that the life was ebbing from the body of one of the slaves he had just bought in the market, an eleven-year-old boy who lay in his stateroom, dying of cholera. Perhaps Alexander was trying to cover for an uncertain performance in the slave pens—concealed beneath the sick boy's shirt were the patterned blisters of a recent cupping—with a lot of big talk about the slave market. For he surely knew how these conversations went: more than simply talking about their slaves, slaveholders were supposed to show them off. Solomon Northup remembered that on the way home from New Orleans his new owner stopped for dinner at the house of one of his neighbors. After the two men had dined, they came out to the yard to look at the slaves. "Martin," Northup remembered of the neighbor, "came out and took a look at us, asking Ford the price of each, if we were green hands, and so forth, making inquiries in relation to the slave market generally."[27] As Northup's buyer showed off his recently purchased slaves and answered his friend's questions, he was also asking questions about himself: did I do the right thing? would you have done the same thing?

Other purchasers had other intended audiences for their slave-borne success stories. After his sale, Louis Hughes was literally presented to his buyer's family: "Boss took me into the house and into the sitting room, where all the family were assembled, and presented me as a Christmas gift to the madam, his wife."[28] As soon as they had purchased their new slaves, slaveholders set about the task of refiguring their relations with other whites—whether they were friends, family members, or simply on-lookers—in the image of slaves they had bought in the market. Indeed, as well as being a marker of the extent of slaveholders' trespasses upon the identities of the people they bought, the practice of making slaves take their owners' last names or the possessive tags by which slaves were commonly identified (Ford's boy or Richardson's Lucy, for instance) were markers of the extent to which slaveholders' identities were merged with those of their slaves. Wherever Ford's boy went, so too did Ford's good name (and often his legal responsibility).[29]

When these exhibitions of newly purchased slaves went well, they were remembered like this: "When my brother bought the slave he brought him to me and told me of his purchase. I examined the boy and told him that the boy was very likely." Or this: "when Fox had bought her, I expressed my regret at not having been able to purchase her myself." Or from the perspective of a slave, Charles Ball: "One of the young ladies said they had come to look at me and see what kind of boy her pa had brought home. The other one said I was a very smart looking boy."[30] Slaves propped up their buyers' post-sale performances of the varieties of slaveholding masculinity. Through the exhibition of their new slaves these men—the able brother, the worthy adversary, the providing father—came into a higher form of public being.

But when a slave show did not go well, it could be embarrassing. The first thing that Charles Bienvenu said to Edward Marin when he saw the man Marin had just bought was that he "didn't like the cough of the slave at all." That must have been quite a come-down for Marin, who had been told by the trader who brokered the sale that he was taking home "one of the strongest Negroes in the state." Robert Nash Ogden, who had bought William as a sound slave, must have felt equally caught out when a man who saw them together walked up and ominously asked if the slave had been up "to his old tricks" yet. The purchase of a slave was a public occasion—a spectacle—and as well as giving the buyer property rights in the person they bought, it gave onlookers a certain kind of property in the buyers: the right to judge them by their slaves. When Jeremiah Stillwell showed Alexander English the woman he had bought to help out his wife, English was unimpressed. "The girl appeared to be an unsound subject," he remembered, and he said as much to his own wife in front of Stillwell. When he heard that his neighbor Josiah Taylor was back from the slave market, planter Robert Montgomery of Plaquemines Parish walked down the levee to meet him. "Then Capt. Taylor came on the Levee," Montgomery later recalled, "I asked him what Black Boy he have on board. He answered that the boy belong to him . . . I observed that the Boy was sick." And J. B. Alexander, remember, was greeted with an even more economical evaluation. When he boarded the *J. R. Downes* with his new slave, a man he did not know walked up and "remarked to him that he had bought a dead Negro."[31]

The litany of comments continued when disappointed slave buyers sought medical treatment for their sick slaves. Medical practitioners often wrapped their diagnoses of slaves in an evaluation of their buyers. When Thomas Dixon went to the pharmacist to buy medicine for his sick slaves, the man, before dispensing anything to treat them, "asked him how he could make such a bargain & buy sick Negroes." Dr. A. G. Trask's evaluation of Joseph Young's new slave was similar: "Came to the conclusions the boy would die . . . and told Mr. Young he had made a bad bargain." Likewise, the doctor whom Archibald Palmer hired to examine his recently bought (and chronically ill) slave, Jim, offered his diagnosis of the buyer before speaking about the slave: "Returned to the house of Palmer," he remembered, "and told Palmer that in his old age he was making some beautiful bargaining."[32] As well as emphasizing the extent to which slaveholders' own reputations depended upon the evaluations that others made of their slaves, these quotations underscore the extent to which the culture of the slave pens was a part of the wider public culture of the slaveholding South. On plantations and aboard steamboats, in public bars and private homes, observers reproduced the slave-pen cult of expertise that measured white men by their ability to judge black slaves.

Much more was at stake in these transactions, however, than the reputation for sharp dealing of an old man like Archibald Palmer. When slaveholders bought slaves, they were remaking themselves in the slave market. And when they brought those slaves home, they brought the residue of that setting—the uncertainty, the dependence, the deception—into their own lives. When the former shopkeeper John Knight finally populated the model plantation he had lovingly imagined in the letters to his father-in-law with real slaves from the market, he encountered a world of human frailty and resistance that seemed to catch him unawares. The slaves of his imagination were healthy, happy, hard-working, and grateful for the solicitude with which he had set about designing their lives; those he actually bought were only human, and his fantasy turned out to be no more durable than the slaves who were expected to embody it.

Knight kicked off his career as a planter in a tone of rosy optimism about his new slaves: "Of course," he wrote in June of 1844, "I shall accompany them from this place to the plantation and see them all installed in their new homes." Within a few days, however, Knight began to make minor yet disquieting discoveries about the people he had bought. One of the men turned out to have once been free—a threat, Knight thought, to the docility of the rest of his slaves and a violation of the laws of Louisiana that forbade keeping people who had once been free as slaves within the state. There were other nagging doubts: a couple of the slaves had been sold with false names and told him so, and few others turned out upon closer inspection to be sick—a woman with swollen feet and suspended menses, a man who said he had been having attacks of "the gravel" (gall stones) for several years before being sold, a girl who had seemed sound at first but had a "trifling appearance" on closer inspection. Still, Knight remained chipper: "After having seen all of them now very often & talked with them, I again say I consider them, as a lot, first-rate—far superior to most plantation lots in this country."[33] Riding out on his horse to watch his slaves toil in the field, John Knight was observing his own progress—and, it seems likely, imagining that his neighbors were doing the same—in that of his slaves.

Over the next year, however, Knight's optimism began to weather. By August several of his slaves had run away and two had died in the field, victims, he thought of an incautious overseer who worked the slaves too hard, "contrary to my positive orders." By November two more slaves had died and more slaves had run away. Though he could temporarily insulate himself from responsibility by blaming his overseer, Knight was gradually having to face the fact that his demands were killing or driving off the slaves he had so long anticipated managing and caring for. By the beginning of the following May he had come to expect his slaves to "fly the track & run off again" at the "most pushing time of the crop." By the end of that month, the only dream that John Knight had left for his plantation was getting a good price for it: "I do assure you that I am heartily sick and tired and disgusted with planting, especially so far as Negroes are concerned, and I would gladly sell out tomorrow, aye today, if I could satisfactorily." By the end of the year he had done just that, selling his plantation and all his slaves under the condition that "the said John Knight is not to warrant and guarantee the *health* of any of said Negroes, mules, horses, oxen, etc."[34] Overworked, sick, and recalcitrant, John Knight's real slaves were both less resilient and less pliable than those he had imagined when he planned his plantation.

Although not all failures were as catastrophic as Knight's, the dissolution of his plantation fantasy was emblematic of the frustration slaveholders often faced in the months after they returned from the market. Those, like Knight, who went to the slave market with dreams of expansion, efficiency, and profit were often disappointed by the medical and managerial problems posed by slaves unfamiliar with Louisiana's pathogenic environment and resistant to the labor regime of lower-South slavery. Those, like J. F. Smith, who bought slaves for his wife and daughters in the hope that a self-reproducing slave force would extend his patriarchal provision long after he died made plans dependent upon decisions made in the slave quarters rather than the slave market. Those, like Gerald Chretien, who bought enslaved artisans sometimes found themselves setting complicated tasks for men like Lafortune who, Chretien later realized, was only "capable of executing work when marked out to him." Those, like Robert Nash Ogden, who bought slaves to drive their fancy carriages to town occasionally ended up on the road, walking home after a bruising ride. Those, like James McHatton, who bought a cook to improve his lifestyle and reputation for good living could find their gentility contested by a woman like Jane, who refused to cook, quoted the Bible to justify refusing to take her medicine, and cried incessantly for the children she had been forced to leave behind in Kentucky. Those, like Jeremiah Stillwell, who bought nurses to relieve their wives, care for their children, and keep their households orderly could find their children "becoming attached" to a woman like Mary, whom Stillwell described to a friend as "a drunkard and a whore." Those, like Miriam Hilliard, who wanted "a million slaves or more to catch the raindrops as they pour"—or, failing that, a nurse to quiet her crying child and spare her the ill-temper with which her husband arose from a sleepless night—were liable to be undone by a woman like Jane, who was put up for sale, in the words of her seller, "because she was very saucy: she had too much jaw" or by one like Kitty, who, in the words of a man who saw her sold, "knew too much." Even those who, like sugar planter Thomas Pugh, bought their slaves by the dozen and had no idea of the names of the people who worked in their fields could be forced to recognize the intimacy of their dependence upon their slaves when illness or flight disrupted the careful columns of profit and loss through which they measured their mastery.[35] Whatever their purpose in buying slaves, slaveholders made themselves subject to the health, ability, and behavior of the people they bought, people who mouthed off, slowed down, slipped away, fought back, got sick, and sometimes died.

But these episodes were more than mere inconveniences. Like anyone else, slaveholders depended upon the world to be relatively constant: they depended upon being in the same bed, answering to the same name, and tasting the same food in the same way when they woke up as they had when they went to sleep. And like anyone else, slaveholders also depended upon their property to help them keep themselves constant over time—they oriented themselves around the expectation that they would have the same things and the same rights over those things when they woke up as they had when they went to bed.[36] For slaveholders, of course, some of those things were people, and when their slaves ran off or got ill or resisted, the smooth surfaces of slaveholders' lives were ruptured by the unfathomed frailties and motivations of their slaves. Indeed, the awkwardly reflexive constructions they used to describe their slaves' escapes—"the slave who absconds steals himself," "he would absent himself," and so on—make it sound as if the body they thought they had bought had been repossessed by an unseen soul.[37] A complete list of such ruptures would be a negative image of the world as slaveholders imagined it should be: there was coughing keeping the slaveholders awake when there should have been quiet, or quiet when there should have been the singing of a healthy slave; there was dust where the patio should have been swept or a bone where there should have been a clean breast; there was a place in the line headed out to the field where there should have been a slave, or an absence when there should have been a hand to guide the plow, and so on.[38] At the moments when it became apparent that something was not right—missing, disordered, out-of-joint—these people who were making themselves out of slaves must have realized that they might also be unmade by slaves. This is not to say that when their slaves misbehaved, got sick, or ran away, slaveholders were completely unmade, cut loose from any recognizable identity. It is, however, to say that they were forced into roles quite different from the ones they had selected for themselves in the slave market: unsuspecting dupe, inexperienced fool, naive victim, frustrated slave breaker.

Whether their slaves were sick, resistant, or simply unskilled, slaveholders often beat them for not living up to the expectations that had been attached to them in the slave market. When it became apparent within a few months of their purchase that they could not keep up with the other slaves in the field, Charles Kock's overseer apparently broke Michael Perry's ribs and beat William Diggs so mercilessly that Diggs, in a futile attempt to escape, jumped in the bayou and drowned. Likewise, soon after his sale, Madison, who was sold as a cooper though he could not make a barrel and sold as healthy though he was consumptive, was struck seventy or eighty times by his buyer's grown son. He could not be sure, but from the sound of it, a witness thought the weapon had been an ox whip. Billy refused to work in the kitchen though he had been sold as a cook, and when he was sent to the field he ran away. Repeatedly. Each time he was brought back, he was beaten—at least a dozen times in all before his buyer finally decided to sue for the slave's return. Twelve-year-old Monday was beaten because his lupus made his nose run onto the dinner napkins when he was setting the table—"my wife whipped him because he was nasty, his nose was running," explained his master.[39] Punishment reminded those whom they owned, and anyone else who might have been watching, that buyers would not allow real slaves to behave differently from imagined ones.

The extremity of the violence with which slaveholders responded to disappointment suggests the intimacy of their dependence upon their slaves. Fugitive slave Lewis Clarke put it this way: "As for whipping, a slave don't get whipped according to his crime, but according to the ambition of his master."[40] As Clarke explained it, the extent of slave-holders' violence was an index of their personal investment—their ambition—in the behavior of their slaves. The greater the transforma-tive hopes slaveholders took with them to the slave market, the more violent their reactions to the inevitable disappointment of their efforts to get real slaves to act like imagined ones. By punishing slaves for not fulfilling the roles assigned them in the slave market, slaveholders violently reasserted the identities they had bought their slaves to em-body: they were people of refinement even if their slaves were nasty, undisciplined, or rude; they were the arbiters of a genuine illness, a good day's work, or a well-made barrel. If they had to, they would use brutality to close the distance between the roles they imagined for themselves and the failings of the slaves they bought as props for their performance.

The piteous image of a twelve-year-old child beaten because he could not stop his nose from running onto the dinner napkins was not, as some scholars would have it, a violation of the mutuality of master and slave. It was, instead, the essence of that grim mutuality: the natural result of slaveholders' inevitable failure to live through the stolen bodies of their slaves. In the face of the frailty or resistance of those whom they had bought—publicly caught between their own fantasies of self-amplificat-ion and the reality of their dependence—slaveholders often responded with shocking brutality. Only through the threat of violence could slave-holders enforce their slave-market fantasies on the people they bought and reinscribe their status as masters and mistresses. This pervasive vio-lence belies the influential claim that slaveholders were able to exact a sort of unwitting consent from their slaves, a "hegemony" which shifted the terrain of conflict between master and slave away from sites that threatened the system of slavery itself.[41] For people made out of slaves, there was no terrain of conflict with their slaves that did not represent a fundamental threat: their slaves' resistance was internal to themselves, and they maintained their dominance through force. The only slave buyers who could be assured of getting what they wanted in the slave market were the ones who bought slaves in order to torture them.

When they found their slaves unable to bear the hopes that were loaded onto their backs, some slaveholders quickly abandoned them. January was left to die in the jail where he was placed after his seller refused to accept his return: neither party to the suit about his sale wanted to compromise his interest by having use of the slave during the course of the trial. Similarly, it was unknown to Madison's owner at the time his redhibition suit came to trial whether Madison was dead or alive: he had refused to provide for a slave whom he hoped to return. Agnes and her child Virginia were left floating in the waterhole where they had drowned themselves because their seller was afraid that by pulling their bodies out of the water he would compromise himself in any suit resulting from her death.[42] These slaves, abandoned for their prices, were reminders to all of the inexorability of the chattel principle, of the willful incapacity of their owners to imagine a world in which enslaved people were anything other than the often fragile, sometimes resistant, but ultimately disposable vessels of slaveholders' desires.

THE PUBLIC RECORD

For most buyers and slaves, this was the future that began when they left the slave market: the contest between slaveholders' efforts to bother or beat their slaves into performing their fantasies and the slaves' collective will to approximate, subvert, or resist. This was the everyday history of slavery. When they could not bother or beat their slaves into approximating their fantasies, however, some disappointed slave buyers extended the moment of sale by going to court. Under Louisiana law, these legal contests were mediated by a legal standard encoded in a word that sounded as wholesome and simple as the slave business was brutal and complex: "prudence." As long as they had cared for their slaves "as might be expected of the prudent father of a family" between the time they bought them and the time they tried to return them, slave buyers were entitled to the broad protections of the law of redhibition.[43] That meant that slave buyers who sued usually won—the law, after all, was designed to protect buyers from traders. But it also meant that litigants in redhibition suits often found themselves being measured against the explicitly paternalist standard of the state's property law: sharp-dealing slave dealers often found that their best defense was to accuse the buyers of mistreating the slaves they had bought.

"Prudence" was variously conjured into meaning, but defining it almost always involved a review of the character and abilities of the slaveholder who had brought the suit in the first place. When he was sued for selling a woman infected with gonorrhea, slave trader John White responded in court that any disease the woman had was "the result of the cruel and outrageous and barbarous treatment" she had received from her buyer. Likewise, lawyers for Joseph Cucullu argued, anything wrong with a group of slaves purchased by Augustus Walker was due to the "stern treatment" they had received after being sold to him. Such testimony was often elicited through questions that were quite broad—"had the Negro man Charles . . . when you first saw him or afterwards, any bruises or contusions on his head or any part of his body? Is it to your knowledge that sufficient care was taken of said Negro man Charles while sick?" But these legal forms—fishing expeditions, really—could sometimes yield answers that were quite specific. No, a witness for slave buyer Andrew White had to testify in court, it would not be "prudent if a Negro laboring under an affliction you have described were kept at the plough in the field constantly." Yes, a friend of Henry Haynes had to admit reluctantly, Haynes had "told him that if the girl died she was his loss as his wife had imprudently sent her to wash after he had given her calomel." Maybe, a man who had helped Carmelite Bocod buy a slave had to say, "he is not sufficiently acquainted with [the buyer] to say what sort of disposition or temper she had."[44] Not all of these accusations of improper conduct stuck (although those levied against Augustus Walker, Andrew White, and Henry Haynes did—all three men lost their cases), but in a culture obsessed with honor and appearance, an accusation of rape, cruelty, or even simple inattention could be as discomfiting as the proof that it was true.[45]

Accusations of mistreatment were often bolstered by questions about the condition of slaves' bodies. Doctors who testified about slaves' health at the time of their sale were often also asked about their treatment in the months after the sale. Asked to testify about the tumor on Seraphine's leg, for instance, the physician hired by slave buyer Ferdinand Lemos also had to admit that he had seen the scars on her back. Called to treat Fanny's venereal disease, another doctor "concluded that she had been neglected and roughly used . . . she had the marks of the whip not perfectly healed but did not appear to have been severely whipped." Others who had seen the slaves after their sale were also called to testify to their mistreatment or decline. In an effort to prove that thirteen-year-old Celestine had run away because of bad

treatment rather than bad character, the lawyers for her seller called a woman who testified that she had seen the child when she was "recently whipped and marked with the blows of the whip and had blood on her clothes." Joseph Cucullu called Augustus Walker's neighbors into court to testify that rather than being sick at the time of their sale, Walker's slaves had "got poor" since he bought them. "They are," one of them testified, "pitiful in their persons . . . their trail bear the marks of overbearing work, even their walk is heavy." These slave buyers found themselves being judged (indeed, Augustus Walker literally found himself on trial for criminal mistreatment of his slaves) by the same somatic signs that they had used to measure the slaves when they bought them. Put another way, in these cases slaves' scars, carriage, and condition were read according to the method of the slave quarter—as a measure of the master—rather than according to that of the slave pen.[46]

The identities of those who testified must have been almost as troubling to some slaveholders as the testimony they gave. When he was accused of bloodying thirteen-year-old Celestine, Joseph Pilié was the city surveyor of New Orleans; the women who testified to his brutality were free women of color who lived nearby. One of the men who gave testimony against Augustus Walker had once worked for the slaveholder as an overseer. He testified that Walker worked his slaves from four in the morning to ten at night and sometimes struck them as many as three hundred blows at a time. He concluded his testimony by saying that he was certain that if Walker had not been stopped from planting, he would have ruined himself in a very short time: the man, the overseer testified, had no business being a planter. Asked about the possibility that his next door neighbor Samuel Slater might have abused Madison, S. S. Rice testified that "The character of the plaintiff is that of a hard and cruel master and that is witness's opinion and that of many of his neighbors." Only on cross examination did Rice add that he was not on good terms with Slater, believing that the other man had wronged him in the past.[47] These court cases, then, gave social inferiors, disgruntled former employees, and resentful neighbors a chance to exact a measure of revenge from the litigants. As awkward for the slave buyers, perhaps, was the fact that they had to find other neighbors, employees (often the physicians they hired to treat their slaves), and onlookers to rebut these charges.[48] Rather than being publicly credited for their slave buying, the plaintiffs in redhibition suits found themselves taking on more

obligations, turning their reputations inside out as those who were supposed to be witnesses *to* their mastery or management or skill or civility or whatever instead became witnesses *for* those qualities.

More than that, dissatisfied slave buyers often found themselves relying on their slaves. It was, of course, a settled principle of southern jurisprudence that slaves (and, in most cases, blacks) were not allowed to testify in cases concerning whites. And though slaves were sometimes exhibited in court, most of the information presented in redhibition cases about their character or condition came from other sources. When they were asked about a slave's "inherent vices," overseers answered with accounts of labor time lost to convalescence or escape, low production, and so on. Physicians followed the same basic template: asked about pains that only the slaves could feel, they gave answers that focused on the outward signs of inward infirmity—accelerated heart rate, heavy breathing, swelling, lesions, suppuration—or if the slave in question had died, they read their dissected bodies aloud.[49] The efflorescence of careful forms was the result of a difficult project: getting information about slaves' bodies and pasts without asking them—describing slaves' inward experience while maintaining their outward legal silence.

And yet time and again it became apparent that slaveholders had silent partners in their legal speculations. Many suits on the grounds of infirmity began when the slaves themselves told their new masters about their illnesses. But buyers were often reliant on slaves for the preparation as well as the initiation of their suits. It was very common in the courts of antebellum Louisiana for slaves' own accounts of the duration of their illnesses to be introduced (through the testimony of a consulting physician usually) as evidence in legal actions between the parties to their sale. For example: "it is dropsy and she is suppressed since three or four years as he understands from her . . . That by the examination he has found that she is suppressed, but that he knows from her it is since four years past."[50] As well as asking them about the facts of their cases, slaveholders used slaves to help them find white deponents to testify to those facts. As John Knight contemplated returning a slave he had bought, he asked questions which helped him reconstruct the past that had been hidden from him in the slave market: "he says he had frequent attacks of the gravel within one or two years; and that Docr. McGill of Jefferson, near Frederick [Maryland] attended him

during an attack and took a stone from him." Similarly, when Archibald Palmer sued slave dealer Humphrey Taylor, he was able to reconstruct his sick slave's lost medical history by talking to his slaves: "Knowing the physician who had attended the boy (as told by the boy), Dr. Wallace, was dead, was the reason why he addressed his letter to Inman Horner on the subject. The way in which the former owner was found was from the other Negroes purchased by Palmer from Taylor."[51]

Slaves could likewise assist their buyers in piecing together an account of past transgressions necessary to establish a "vice" of character. When Hosea George sued Moses Greenwood for selling him J. W. West, he based part of his case on the account West had given of his prior life. "From the Negro's statement," George's overseer testified, "he was carried to Texas, ran away, and went back to the Cherokee Nation." When that was struck from the record, West reframed it to give the story he told a more suitable provenance: "All I know: He is a runaway from his own statement and from those who profess to know him. They spoke of him as a runaway and that he did actually run away from Hosea George."[52] Willingly or under threat of punishment, these slaves helped their owners prepare redhibition cases involving their own sales.

And, in one of the more incredible contradictions that characterized the law of slavery, the courts of Louisiana occasionally allowed testimony about slaves' statements at the time of their sale to be figured into the law that governed their owners. When slave dealer J. W. Boazman was sued over Henry's fits, his courtroom response was to call upon auctioneer Joseph Beard to testify that Henry's illness was a sham: "I had a conversation with the boy," Beard recalled, "he appeared sulky and said he had a wife in town and would not be sold in the country." Similarly, Eden's declaration to the other slaves in the yard at the time of his sale that he would not stay with the man who bought him—"The slave was talking with the rest saying that he would not go across the River"—was used as evidence that Eden was in the habit of running away.[53] The law of sales was being shaped around the intentions and notions of justice expressed by the property involved.

While slave buyers had a great deal more access to their slaves and thus a great deal more control over what they could be made to say, slaves' shadowy testimony was sometimes used by sellers against buyers. When Charles Kock sued slave dealer Hope H. Slatter, the slave dealer defended himself by alleging that the brutality of Kock's overseer was responsible for the evident incapacity of the slaves in question. Slatter prepared his case by sending one of his slave salesmen to Kock's neighborhood to ask questions: "was in the neighborhood of plaintiff's plantation in January 1847," Francis Jump testified, "and inquiring about Mr. Pike the overseer of the plaintiff ascertained by general reputation that he was a most cruel man to slaves. He spoke to a dozen persons on the subject and all concur in stating so to be his reputation." The dealer's lawyer then called Kock's overseer and apparently asked him the following questions: Did you strike Michael Perry with the loaded end of a whip, thus breaking his ribs? Did you beat William Diggs so severely that he jumped in the bayou and drowned? The overseer answered that he did not, but it remained the case that Perry's ribs *were* broken and Diggs *had* drowned in the bayou and that the only witnesses to what had happened were the overseer and Kock's other slaves. These questions, asked in the knowledge that the charges they made would be denied, nevertheless telegraphed their point through the specificity of the allegations they contained: among the dozen people who had testified to the brutal treatment received by Michael Perry and William Diggs were Kock's other slaves. Conversations between Hope Slatter's agent and Charles Kock's slaves were not a matter for legal record in the antebellum South: we can only speculate about them. Not so for the conversations between slave seller Joseph Cucullu's witnesses and the slaves of dissatisfied slave buyer Augustus Walker. As he detailed Walker's brutality—an ailing woman whipped every day for two months, slaves imprisoned with their hands bound so that it was impossible for them to eat—slave seller Cucullu's witnesses used information they had "received from Mary Louise a Negro woman slave of Augustus Walker."[54] In the voice of their seller's witnesses, in the court that protected their buyer's interests, Augustus Walker's slaves testified against their owner.

It was perhaps the feats of imagination encouraged by such testimony—masters viewed through the projected opinions of their slaves—that provided the best definition of the standard of "prudent" care demanded by Louisiana's redhibition law. As a witness for one buyer put it, "he treated his slaves very well . . . believes those Negroes were very well satisfied with him."[55] Every court case involving a disputed slave sale threatened a small-scale recapitulation of the logic of the market it governed—a market in which the relations between white people depended upon the actions and opinions of black slaves. Through their resistance, their frailty, and, finally, their testimony, slaves inscribed their stories and their own notions of justice on their masters' legal history.

In the image of a slaveholder's history registered in the eyes of a slave resides the ultimate nature of the slave market. In the slave pens, the ethereal fantasies of the slaveholding regime were daily converted into the material shape of sold slaves. Those slaves were sold to be the vehicles of their masters' history, of their political economy, their patriarchal domesticity, and racist ideology. More than that, whether it was brutally lashed across their backs or lovingly implanted in their minds, those slaves were supposed to give witness to that history, to recognize and record their masters' virtues, plans, and power. The slaves, however, often proved unwilling vessels for their buyers' dreams. They had to be terrorized or beaten into the roles that had been assigned them in the market; they acted according to a different script and recorded a different history. Day after day, the history of slavery, the terrible interdependence of master and slave, of destinies implacably opposed and yet hopelessly intertwined, was renewed in the slave market.

SOUTHERN HISTORY AND THE SLAVE TRADE

THE HISTORY OF the antebellum South was made (and occasionally unmade) in the slave pens. There, through the black arts of the trade, people were turned into products and sold at a price; there, human bodies were stripped, examined, and assigned meaning according to the brutal anatomy lessons of slaveholding ideology; there, slaveholders daily gambled their own fantasies of freedom on the behavior of people whom they could never fully commodify; there, enslaved people fashioned communities and identities that enabled them to survive one of the most brutal forcible dislocations of human history; and there, sometimes, slaves were able to shape a sale to suit themselves. In the slave market, slaveholders and slaves were fused into an unstable mutuality which made it hard to tell where one's history ended and the other's began. Every slave had a price, and slaves' communities, their families, and their own bodies were suffused with the threat of sale, whether they were in the pens or not. And every slaveholder lived through the stolen body of a slave.

In the half century before the Civil War, the back-and-forth bargaining of slaveholder and slave was repeated two million times in a pattern that traced the outline of southern history. Central to this history was the role played by the interstate trade in the transformation of the South from a declining tobacco economy stretched along the eastern seaboard to a thriving cotton economy that reached westward as far as

Texas. Right behind the soldiers and squatters who, during the first quarter of the nineteenth century, began to drive the Indian inhabitants of the lower South into the arid plains of the West came the slave traders and the coffles of people who, through their labor and reproduction, transformed those rich and emptied lands into "The Cotton Kingdom" in the century's second quarter. Of the million or so slaves who moved southwest and transformed the depopulated forests of the deep South into the richest staple-producing region of the world, two thirds were carried there by slave traders.[1]

The transformation of the slaveholders' economy brought with it a transformation of the lives of the slaves upon whom it depended. Most important were the separations. The trade decimated the slave communities of the upper South through waves of exportation determined by slaveholders' shifting demand—first men, then women, and finally children became featured categories of trade. As they were driven south and west by the people they called "soul drivers," those slaves carried with them the cultural forms—the songs, the stories, the family names, and the religion—out of which they forged the commonalities that supported their daily struggle against slavery. By the time of the Civil War, southern slaves had a common culture that stretched from Maryland to Texas, a spirited mirror-image of the pattern traced by the trade in their bodies. Indeed, as war broke out, settled communities and rebuilt families were beginning to emerge at the trade's southern outlet.[2]

Even as it transformed the geography of both white and black life in the South, the criss-crossed pattern of the slave trade knit the political economy of slavery into a cohesive whole. Long after intensive tobacco farming had eroded the fertility and profitability of the slave-cultivated fields of the Chesapeake, the slave trade enabled Virginia and Maryland planters to retain their ties to the political economy of slavery. As much as anything else in the years leading up to the Civil War, the planters of the Chesapeake were slave farmers who held onto their wealth and status by supplying the cotton boom with the offspring of slaves idled by the decline of tobacco. Even as the political economy of slavery moved south and west, the slave trade bound the diverging fortunes of the emerging regions of the South into mutual benefit. Indeed, in the 1850s, when for a time it seemed that the upper South was being overtaken by a renewed tobacco boom, the trade began to flow northward as well as southward.[3]

As important as the trade was in the spatial expansion of slavery, the slave trade also played a crucial role in the reproduction of the slave-holding regime over time. Even when the prosperous slaveholders of the antebellum South did not produce their legacies through the direct purchase of slaves for their heirs, they relied upon that market to provide the standard of comparison (the dollar values) according to which they divided their estates. The everyday role of the slave market in the reproduction of the southern social order, however, was far less abstract than that: it was in the slave market that the rising men of the antebellum South built the stakes that had been provided them by their forebears into legacies of their own. And it was in the slave market that the political economy of slavery daily deepened the roots of its own support among southern whites as nonslaveholders were turned into slaveholders. Indeed, as they faced the sectional conflict that threatened to end history as they knew it, southern politicians considered radical measures to insure that nonslaveholders would support the regime of slavery into the future. In the same series of conventions that led to secession and in the same journals and newspapers that carried news of the rising political conflict to the white citizens of the South, slavehold-ing politicians considered reopening the African slave trade in order to lower the price of slaves and increase the proportion of slaveholders within the population. "That minute you put it out of the power of common farmers to purchase a Negro man or woman to help him in his farm or his wife in the house," wrote one Louisiana editor in support of reopening the African trade, "you make him an abolitionist at once."[4] The future of slavery, the editor argued, could be bought in the slave market.

That future, it became increasingly apparent, would come to pass (or not) in the West. Over the course of the antebellum period, the incen-diary value of cotton, the wayward dreams of migrating slaveholders, and the ruthless efficiency of the slave trade had pushed slavery to the outer limits of "the South." First in Missouri, then in Texas, and finally in Kansas and Nebraska, political conflict over slavery was increasingly defined by the question of how far west it would be allowed to spread. With every slave sold from the declining eastern seaboard to slavery's expanding western frontier, the South pushed the nation a step closer to its ultimate showdown over slavery.[5] And, once again, it was perhaps less an irony of history than an axiom of historical process that the sharpest critics of "the Slave Power," the abolitionist critics of slavery who would provide their own push toward Civil War, armed themselves with arguments that had been produced along the leading edge of slavery's expansion.

For all of the smoothing over and covering up that characterized their daily activities, the slave pens provided a remarkably clear exposition of the nature of slavery—a person with a price. There were, of course, other available definitions, other answers to the question "What is slavery?"answers that emphasized production or paternalism or politics or violence. And there were other places to go to see slavery: plantations where the slave mode of production was visible in the fields; white churches and universities across the South where the spiritual and moral benefits of slavery were floridly proclaimed; northern and European cotton-finishing factories where the full reach of "the slave economy" was daily evident; the halls of Congress where the influence of the "Slave Power" was tallied in a series of compromises between "North" and "South" which outlined the political history of the antebellum period. Increasingly, however, and with revolutionary effect, opponents of slavery argued that slavery was best seen in the slave market.

It had not always been so. The central document of early abolitionism, Theodore Dwight Weld's *American Slavery As It Is* (1839), had very little to say about the slave market. It was, instead, a catalog of bodily tortures. Drawing upon southern newspapers and runaway advertisements which sought to identify escaped slaves by their mortifying injuries, Weld was able to draw back the veil that protected "the peculiar institution" from critical eyes. Slavery for Weld was a system of unchecked brutality, made grotesquely visible on the suffering bodies of the slaves.[6] Even today, in an age inured to violence by movie-made brutality, *American Slavery As It Is* is hard to read. And yet nineteenth-century slaveholders were quick to develop an answer to this critique of slavery's inhumane brutality. The maimings and the rapes were isolated episodes, they argued, and they set about publicizing the "paternalist" reforms that would restore to the system of slavery its good name. They broke the system of slavery into hundreds of thousands of isolated sets of human relations between individual masters and individual slaves and argued that the violence of slavery was a matter of generally benevolent human relations gone awry, of the personal failings of particular owners, of bad masters who gave slavery a bad name, not an inevitable feature of the system itself.

Thinking about the slave trade, however, made possible an entirely different account of the relation between master and slave. J. W. C. Pennington described his motivation for writing his narrative of slavery this way: "My feelings are always outraged when I hear them speak of 'kind masters,' 'Christian masters,' 'the mildest form of slavery,' 'well fed and well clothed slaves' as extenuations of slavery." Pennington did not deny that such things existed, but he thought that they were misleading forms taken by a more fundamental relation: "The being of slavery, its soul and its body, lives and moves in the chattel principle, the property principle, the bill of sale principle; the cart-whip, starvation, and naked-ness, are its inevitable consequences," he wrote. Sale from a good master to a bad one, from the "mildest form of slavery" to the "worst of which the system is possible," from the "favorable circumstances" of slavery in Maryland, Virginia, and Kentucky to the killing fields of Alabama, Mississippi, and Louisiana was, in Pennington's formulation, "the legitimate working of the great chattel principle." "It is no acci-dental result," he continued, "it is the fruit of the tree. You cannot constitute slavery without the chattel principle—and with the chattel principle you cannot save it from these results. Talk not about kind and Christian masters. They are not masters of the system. The system is master of them."[7] Through an outline of the philosophy and practice of the slave trade, Pennington was able to convey the complicity of all slaveholders (no matter their individual merits) in the most brutal results of the system of slavery.

Through his exegesis of "the chattel principle" Pennington placed the slave trade at the center of the abolitionist critique of slavery; other former slaves accomplished the same thing through telling the stories of their own experiences in the trade. Charles Ball, William Wells Brown, Solomon Northup, and John Brown all included lengthy dis-cussion of the slave trade in their published narratives. Lewis Clarke (along with William Wells Brown) lectured extensively about the trade. Henry Bibb concluded his narrative with a list of his owners and the prices they had paid for him: "In 1836 'Bro.' Albert Sibley of Bedford, Kentucky, sold me for $850 to 'Bro.' John Sibley, and in the same year he sold me to 'Bro.' William Gatewood of Bedford, for $850. In 1839 'Bro.' Gatewood sold me to Madison Garrison, a slave trader of Louisville, Kentucky, with my wife and child—at a depreciated price because I was a run away. In the same year he sold me with my family to 'Bro.' Whitfield, in the city of New Orleans, for $1200. In 1841 'Bro.' Whitfield sold me from my family to Thomas Wilson and Co., black-legs. In the same year they sold me to a 'Bro.' in the Indian Territory. I think he was a member of the Presbyterian Church."[8] Like Henry Bibb, who outlined his own history of slavery with a series of sales sealed between supposedly Christian slaveholders, these survivors put the slave trade at the center of their account of what slavery was and what was wrong with it.

Join to their efforts those of white abolitionists like William Lloyd Garrison, who emblazoned the masthead of *The Liberator* with an engraving of an auction stand labeled with the sign "Slaves, Horses, and other Cattle to be sold at 12 O' Clock," of traveling observers like Fredrika Bremer, Charles Weld, and Frederick Law Olmsted, who went to the slave market rather than the cotton field or legislative chamber when they wanted to see "slavery," and, finally of Harriet Beecher Stowe, who, taking a page from Pennington, articulated the connection between the kindly but ineffectual Kentucky slaveholder Mr. Shelby—"a man of humanity" she called him—and Louisiana's brutal Simon Legree by putting the family-separating trade plied by the heartless "slave driver" Haley at the center of *Uncle Tom's Cabin*.[9] Carried north by the escapees, the indigenous antislavery of the enslaved South—the ideology of "the chattel principle" as it was represented in slaves' stories and songs about the trade—was reworked into a central element of the northern abolitionist critique of slavery.

The crude spectacle that was daily on view in the slave pen—a human body publicly stripped, examined, priced, and sold—thus became an image that stood for the whole of slavery. The daily process of the trade provided a template through which opponents of slavery could establish the connections between the upper South and the Lower, between kind masters and brutal ones, between slaveholders' loose talk about their affection for their slaves and the unmistakable material reality of a person with a price. By thinking their way through the slave trade, critics of slavery like Pennington could articulate the links that joined individual slaveholders to the broader system and argue that the essence of slavery lay in the worst of its abuses rather than the rosiest of its promises. The daily process of the slave pens created a type of knowl-

edge about the nature of slavery that was indispensable to its critics—the information necessary to dismantle the proslavery argument
was produced along the leading edge of slavery's history.

That history ended in 1865. The slave pens themselves were boarded
up and closed for a time—all signboards advertising slaves for sale in
Union-held New Orleans were taken down on January 1 of 1864—and
the pens were later sold. They became boarding houses and cotton
brokerages; on the site of one of the largest there is now a bank.
Through those gates had passed the people who made the history of the
antebellum South—the traders who had outlined that history with their
market time and speculative maps, the buyers who had filled in the
traders' outline with the fantasies through which slaveholders made
sense of the world, and the slaves themselves, in whose fallible bodies
and resistant wills the history of the antebellum South had finally been
made material.

And when slavery was over and the slave market was closed, former
slaves and slaveholders alike found themselves marooned on a shoal of
history. The longings of slaveholders to hold onto the past as it receded
from their grasp are well-documented: their reactionary paternalism,
their lost-cause politics of nostalgia, and the coercive labor discipline
they began to enforce through the state. Well-known, too, is the dis-
belief they experienced, the sense of betrayal they talked about, when
their slaves left them behind. For many former slaves, it was likewise
too late to go back—not to slavery or the slave market but to the places
and families they had been forced to leave behind. They faced a future
that was at first defined only by what it was not: in the words of the
freedom song "Many Thousands Gone," "No more auction block for
me, no more driver's lash for me, no more peck of corn for me, no
more mistress call for me." Some placed newspaper advertisements for
lost family members and took to the roads in an effort to travel backwards in time to the families, friends, and places they had known
before the trade. Others stayed where they were, seizing the first
chance that many of them had ever had to make their marriages legal
and to make up their own minds about the relationship of their households to the wider markets for labor and goods. Still others pushed on
in search of a brighter future—first toward southern cities and later
westward and northward in search of freedom.[10] In 1865, their history
began again.

ABBREVIATIONS

NOTES

ACKNOWLEDGMENTS

INDEX

ABBREVIATIONS

DU   Duke University, Archives and Special Collections, Perkins
       Memorial Library
HNO   The Historic New Orleans Collection
LSU   Louisiana State University, Lower Mississippi Valley Collection,
       Hill Memorial Library
MHS   Missouri Historical Society
RASP   Records of Antebellum Southern Plantation on Microfilm (Kenneth
       M. Stampp, ed.)
TU   Tulane University, Archives and Special Collections,
       Howard-Tilton Memorial Library
UMC   University of Missouri, Western Historical Collection, Elmer Ellis
       Memorial Library
UNC   University of North Carolina, Southern Historical Collection
UNO   University of New Orleans, Supreme Court of Louisiana
       Collection, Archives and Special Collections, Earl K. Long
       Library

NOTES

Introduction: A Person with a Price

1. Albert E. Fossier, *New Orleans, the Glamour Period, 1800–1840* (New Orleans, 1957), 26–30, 35–40; Robert C. Reinders, *End of an Era, New Orleans, 1850–1860* (New Orleans, 1964), 30–35.

2. City of New Orleans, Treasurer's Office, Census of Merchants, 1854; City of New Orleans, Street Commissioner's Office, Census of Merchants, 1855, New Orleans Public Library, Louisiana Collection; Fossier, *New Orleans, the Glamour Period*, 161–165; Reinders, *End of an Era*, 67. Downtown, the traders were grouped around the corner of Esplanade and Moreau (now Chartres); those above the Quarter were scattered through an area about three blocks square around the corner of Baronne and Gravier Streets.

3. See, e.g., Fredrika Bremer, *The Homes of the New World*, Mary Howitt, trans. (New York: Harper Brothers, 1853), I, 373, 493; II, 202–205, 535; Frederick Law Olmsted, *The Cotton Kingdom: A Traveler's Observations on Cotton and Slavery in the American Slave States* (New York: Alfred A. Knopf, 1862), 228–230.

4. *Perkins v. Shelton*, unreported Louisiana Supreme Court case #5654 (1859), testimony of D. M. Matthews, UNO.

5. City Council of New Orleans, *Report of the Sanitary Commission of New Orleans on the Epidemic Yellow Fever of 1853* (New Orleans, 1854); Fossier, *New Orleans, the Glamour Period*, 11–12, 35–40; Reinders, *End of an Era*, 93–96; for the size of the lots, generally about 50' x 100', see Act of Sale John Gilbert Coles to Walter L. Campbell, recorded before Edward Barnett, June 19, 1857; Act of Sale Littlefield to James B. Diggs, recorded before William Boswell, February 7, 1832; Act of Sale Jules Macé to Henry Slatter, recorded before Achille Chiapella, January 28, 1845; Mortgage Joseph Bruin to Widow Donovan, recorded before Edward Barnett,

April 6, 1867; Plan of Two Lots and Buildings in the First District, P. Gauldi, April 14, 1855 (10.14); Third District Site Plan by Pilié and DePouilly, February 8, 1866, Orleans Parish, Louisiana, Notarial Archives Research Center (NAOP).

6. Building Contract between Hope H. Slatter and Charles Pride, recorded before Edward Barnett, June 6, 1848 (44/663); Building Contract between Walter L. Campbell and William Armstrong and James Riggin, recorded before Edward Barnett, June 19, 1857 (63/314); see also Building Contract between Charles F. Hatcher and Henry D. Rilee, recorded before August Commandeur, August 13, 1859 (1/89); Leases of Property, Marie Rainbauld (Widow Journu) to Thomas Boudar and John Hagan, May 19, 1847, and May 21, 1847, recorded by Edward Barnett; Building Contract between Maire Rainbauld (Widow Journu) and Etienne Derepas, May 31, 1847, recorded by Edward Barnett, NAOP; plan of Two Lots and Buildings in the First District, P. Gauldi, April 14, 1855 (10.14); Third District Site Plan by Pilié and DePouilly, February 8, 1866, NAOP.

7. James A. Rawley, *The Transatlantic Slave Trade: A History* (New York: 1981), 22–23, 55–57, 70–84, 132–141, 247–260, 284–294; David W. Galenson, *Traders, Planters, and Slaves: Market Behavior in Early English America* (Cambridge: Cambridge University Press, 1985); Patrick Manning, *Slavery and African Life: Occidental, Oriental, and African Slave Trades* (Cambridge, 1990), 99; John Thornton, *Africa and Africans in the Making of the Atlantic World, 1400–1680* (Cambridge, 1992); Gwendolyn Midlo Hall, *Creole Africans in Colonial Louisiana: The Development of Afro-Creole Culture in the Eighteenth Century* (Baton Rouge, 1992); Robin Blackburn, *The Making of New World Slavery: From the Baroque to the Modern, 1492–1800* (London: Verso, 1997).

8. The baseline estimate of the trade was 9.5 million, tallied in Phillip D. Curtin, *The Atlantic Slave Trade: A Census* (Madison, 1969). That number has since been revised upward. See, e.g., Manning, *Slavery and African Life*, 37 (ten million), and Rawley, *The Transatlantic Slave Trade*, 428 (over eleven million).

9. Rawley, *The Transatlantic Slave Trade*, 303–306.

10. Rawley, *The Transatlantic Slave Trade*, 283–306; Joseph Miller, *The Way of Death: Merchant Capitalism and the Angolan Slave Trade, 1730–1830* (Madison: University of Wisconsin Press, 1988), 314–442; See also Stephanie Smallwood's brilliant 1999 dissertation from Duke University entitled "Salt-Water Slaves: African Enslavement, Migration, and Settlement in the Atlantic World of the Late Seventeenth Century."

11. On the closing of the African trade and the early years of the domestic slave trade see Steven H. Deyle, "The Domestic Slave Trade in America," unpublished Ph.D. dissertation, Columbia University, 1995, 20–44; W. E. B. DuBois, *The Suppression of the African Slave Trade to the United States of America, 1683–1870* (New York: Longmans, 1904); Ira Berlin, "Time, Space, and the Evolution of African Society in British Mainland North America," *American Historical Review*, 85 (1980), 44–78; and Michael Tadman, *Speculators and Slaves: Masters, Traders, and Slave in the Old South* (Madison: University of Wisconsin Press, 1989), 12, 133–178.

12. Tadman, *Speculators and Slaves*, 12–21; Deyle, "The Domestic Slave Trade in

America," 17–70. See also Timothy H. Breen, *Tobacco Culture: The Mentality of the Great Tidewater Planters on the Eve of Revolution* (Princeton, NJ: Princeton University Press, 1985); Allan Kulikoff, *Tobacco and Slaves: The Development of Southern Cultures in the Chesapeake, 1680–1800* (Chapel Hill: University of North Carolina Press, 1986); Allan Kulikoff, *The Agrarian Origins of American Capitalism* (Charlottesville: University Press of Virginia, 1992), 226–263.

13. Tadman, *Speculators and Slaves*, 12. Tadman's indispensable work provides estimates of both the total number of "migrant" slaves and the proportion of those migrations which involved interstate sale. The migration numbers Tadman provides are as follows: 42,482 for the 1790s; 68,641 for the 1800s; 123,221 for the 1810s; 154,882 for the 1820s; 287,831 for the 1830s; 188,863 for the 1840s; 250, 637 for the 1850s. Tadman has established that, between 1820 and 1860, sixty to seventy percent of this total migration occurred through the slave trade.

14. Frederic Bancroft, *Slave Trading in the Old South* (Baltimore: J. H. Furst and Company, 1931), 339–364; Roger W. Shugg, *Origins of Class Struggle in Louisiana: A Social History of White Farmers and Laborers* (Baton Rouge: Louisiana State University Press, 1939), 86–88, 153–157; Laurence Shore, *Southern Capitalists: The Ideological Leadership of an Elite, 1832–1885* (Chapel Hill: University of North Carolina Press, 1986); Deyle, "The Domestic Slave Trade in America," 80–98. On the dimensions of slave economy generally see also Robert W. Fogel and Stanley L. Engerman, *Time on the Cross: The Economics of American Negro Slavery* (Boston: Little Brown & Co., 1974), and Robert W. Fogel, *Without Consent or Contract: The Rise and Fall of American Slavery* (New York: W. W. Norton & Co., 1989).

15. Tadman, *Speculators and Slaves*, 130; Lawrence J. Kotlikoff, "The Structure of Slave Prices in New Orleans, 1804–1862," *Economic Inquiry*, 17 (1979), 498; and H. Freudenberger and J. B. Pritchett, "The Domestic United States Slave Trade: New Evidence," *Journal of Interdisciplinary History*, 21 (1991), 471–475; Deyle, "The Domestic Slave Trade in America," 117–119. For insurance, see Todd L. Savitt, "Slave Life Insurance in Virginia and North Carolina," *Journal of Southern History*, 43 (1977), 583–600; Eugene D. Genovese, "The Medical and Insurance Costs of Slaveholding in the Cotton Belt," *Journal of Negro History*, 45 (1960), 141–155; and Judith Kelleher Schafer, *Slavery, the Civil Law, and the Supreme Court of Louisiana* (Baton Rouge, 1994), 103–104, 164–165. For examples of life insurance see policy for Caesar Rivers, sold by dealer Alexander Hagan (along with Ceasar Rivers) to John Randolph on January 16, 1855, John H. Randolph Papers, LSU; Phillip Thomas to William Finney, January 24, 1859 ("it is very sickly here among the Negroes, 1 or two dies every day. I am having all I by insured"), William A. J. Finney Papers, RASP. For examples of transportation insurance see *McCargo v. Merchants' Insurance Co.*, #5123, 10 Rob. 334 (La. 1845), *McCargo v. New Orleans Insurance Co.*, #5146, 10 Rob. 202 (La. 1845); for duties and taxes see "An Ordinance to Establish a uniform rate of Taxes and Licenses on Professions, Callings, and Business, and on Carriages, Hacks, Drays, and other Vehicles"; and "An Act to Increase the Revenue of the State of Louisiana," Mayoralty of New Orleans, approved March 26, 1842, and December 20, 1855; Thomas Curry, ed. *A New Digest of the Statute Laws of the*

State of Louisiana (New Orleans, 1842), vol. 1, 34 (auctioneers); *State v. J. A. Beard*, #5809, 11 Rob. 243 (1845); *Heres* [collector of state taxes] *v. Powell*, #1808, 6 La. Ann. 586 (1851); *City of New Orleans v. Kendig* [Bernard], Unreported Louisiana Supreme Court Case #5201 (1857); *City of New Orleans v. Kendig* [Benjamin], Unreported Louisiana Supreme Court Case #5280 (1858); *City of New Orleans v. J. A. Beard*, Unreported Louisiana Supreme Court Case #5282 (1858), UNO.

16. For local sales see Deyle, "The Domestic Slave Trade in America," 12–141; for state sales see Thomas D. Russell, "South Carolina's Largest Slave Auctioneering Firm," *Chicago-Kent Law Review*, 68 (1993), 1241–1282.

17. For the mechanics of the trade see Bancroft, *Slave Trading in the Old South*, Tadman, *Speculators and Slaves*; and Deyle, "The Domestic Slave Trade in America."

18. W. E. B. Du Bois, *Black Reconstruction in America: An Essay toward a History of the Part Which Black Folk Played in the Attempt to Reconstruct Democracy in America, 1860–1880* (New York: Russell and Russell, 1935).

19. See Marion Wilson Starling, *The Slave Narrative: Its Place in American History* (Washington, D.C.: Howard University Press, 1988).

20. Elizabeth Clark, "The Sacred Rights of the Weak: Pain and the Origins of the Humanitarian Sensibility," *Journal of American History*, 82 (1995), 463–493; Nell Irvin Painter, *Sojourner Truth: A Life, a Symbol* (New York: W. W. Norton & Co., 1996), 151–280.

21. See Annette Gordon-Reed, *Thomas Jefferson and Sally Hemmings: An American Controversy* (Charlottesville: University Press of Virginia, 1997).

22. William Wells Brown, "Lecture," reprinted in *Four Fugitive Slave Narratives* (Reading, MA: Addison-Wesley Publishing Company, 1969), 82.

23. William L. Andrews, *To Tell a Free Story: The First Century of Afro-American Autobiography, 1760–1865* (Urbana: University of Illinois Press, 1988); John Sekora, "Black Message/White Envelope: Genre, Authenticity, and Authority in Antebellum Slave Narratives," *Callaloo*, 10 (1987), 482–515; Hazel V. Carby, *Reconstructing Womanhood: The Emergence of the Afro-American Woman Novelist* (New York: Oxford University Press, 1987), 20–61; Painter, *Sojouner Truth*, 151–280.

24. I have not used the WPA narratives for two reasons: (1) because those whose testimony was recorded in the 1930s would generally have been too young to recollect the level of detail about the slave trade that the nineteenth-century narrators provided; (2) because I believe the rhetorical situation of the interview by a white recorder in the 1930s South to have been a great deal more inhibiting than that which characterized the production of the abolitionist narratives.

25. This is not to suggest that the "experience" of slavery existed outside of the cultural, religious, and political terms through which slaves imagined it in the South, only that those terms were not reducible to those promulgated by white-dominated antislavery in the North. On "experience" see Joan Scott, "The Evidence of Experience," *Critical Inquiry*, 17 (1991), 773–797.

26. I differ from some recent readers of nineteenth-century narratives in that I believe these traces to be quite common. Readers of the narratives often assume that the power relations between editors and amanuenses on the one hand and ex-slaves

on the other hand were clear, that antislavery whites rode rough-shod over the formerly enslaved people whose stories were being told. It would be foolish, as recent work on the subject makes clear, to underestimate the power of intimidation or moralism wielded by these antislavery whites over people who were often dependent upon antislavery societies for both their living and their slim hope of purchasing relatives in the South. But I would not want to ignore the possibility that the narrators themselves had some bargaining power in their negotiations with their editors: the power of their own authenticity, of having seen and experienced the slavery that abolitionists spent all of their time thinking about but could never really risk seeing. The interviews Benjamin Drew did among escaped slaves in Ontario during the 1840s, which I use extensively below, seem to me to gesture in the direction of this hidden history. Slaves in those interviews repeatedly referred to the scars on their bodies in order to authenticate their testimony. These allusions surface in the interviews as part of the process of authentication: the reader sees the scars through Drew's eyes as evidence of the veracity of the story being told, a white readership trusts the slave through the mediation of a white observer. But in the making of the interview they might have had quite a different meaning: before a white man who was asking them questions that only they could answer, a man who was not himself scarred, and who had not himself been a slave, the scars supported a standpoint from which formerly enslaved people could speak their own stories.

27. See Darline Clark Hine, "Female Slave Resistance," in Filomina Chioma, *Black Women Cross-Culturally* (Cambridge: Cambridge University Press, 1981).

28. On warranty law generally see Thomas D. Morris, *Southern Slavery and the Law, 1619–1860* (Chapel Hill: University of North Carolina Press, 1996), 102–131; Andrew Fede, "Legal Protection for Slave Buyers in the U.S. South: A Caveat Concerning *Caveat Emptor*," *American Journal of Legal History*, 31 (1987), 322–358; Ariela Gross, "Pandora's Box: Slave Character on Trial in the Antebellum Deep South," *Yale Journal of Law and the Humanities*, 7 (1995), 267–316. On Louisiana see Schafer, *Slavery, the Civil Law, and the Supreme Court of Louisiana*, 127–179.

29. See Schafer, *Slavery, The Civil Law, and the Supreme Court of Louisiana*. My debts to Marie Windell, the curator of the collection, and to Professor Schafer are enormous, evident in the footnotes on almost every page of this book.

30. See, generally, Peter Brooks and Paul Gewirtz, eds., *Law's Stories: Narrative and Rhetoric in the Law* (New Haven: Yale University Press, 1996). For the slave-holding South see William Fisher, III, "Ideology and Imagery in the Law of Slavery," *Chicago-Kent Law Review*, 68 (1993), 1051–1086; Gross, "Pandora's Box," 267–316; and Walter Johnson, "Inconsistency, Contradiction, and Complete Confusion: The Everyday Life of the Law of Slavery," *Law and Social Inquiry*, 22 (1997), 405–433.

31. See Pierre Bourdieu's concept of *habitus* in Bourdieu, *The Logic of Practice*, Richard Nice, trans. (Stanford, CA: Stanford University Press, 1990), 52–65.

32. On the way in which antebellum social relations were built out of letters see Steven M. Stowe, *Intimacy and Power in the Old South: Ritual in the Lives of the Planters* (Baltimore: The Johns Hopkins University Press, 1987), 1–4, and Richard

Bushman, *The Refinement of America: Persons, Buildings, Cities* (New York: Vintage, 1992), 215.

33. Louisiana law was unlike that of other southern states in that slaves were generally considered "real" rather than "personal" property. While this made little difference in the daily process of a sale or of slavery itself, it made a dramatic difference in the production of the historical record. Legally speaking, sales of real estate are not valid unless transacted on paper and registered; sales of personal estate may be legally binding even if they are agreed to by word of mouth (or "parol"). This means that the historical record of the slave market in Louisiana is much more complete (and much more accurate) than that of any other state (where some sales may have been officially recorded while others were not). On the property-law status of slaves see Schafer, *Slavery, the Civil Law, and the Supreme Court of Louisiana*, 21–27; Thomas D. Morris, *Southern Slavery and the Law, 1619–1860* (Chapel Hill: University of North Carolina Press, 1996), 61–80.

34. See Walter Johnson, "Writing the History of the Atlantic Slave Trade in the Age of Global Capital: Some Speculations on Time, Temporality, and History," forthcoming in *Amerikastudien/American Studies.*

1. The Chattel Principle

1. William Johnson interviewed in Benjamin Drew, ed., *The Refugee: A Northside View of Slavery* (1846), reprinted in *Four Fugitive Slave Narratives* (Reading, MA: Addison-Wesley, 1969), 19; the phrase also appears in Harriet Jacobs, *Incidents in the Life of a Slave Girl, Written by Herself*, Jean Fagin Yellin, ed. (1861; Cambridge: Harvard University Press, 1987), 13; a similarly framed threat—to make a slave into "riches without wings"—appears in Josiah Henson, *An Autobiography of Rev. Josiah Henson*, in *Four Fugitive Slave Narratives*, 50.

2. J. W. C. Pennington, *The Fugitive Blacksmith: Or Events in the Life of James W. C. Pennington* (London, 1849), iv-vii.

3. Michael Tadman, *Speculators and Slaves: Masters, Traders, and Slaves in the Old South* (Madison: University of Wisconsin Press, 1989), 147–171; see also Brenda Stevenson, *Life in Black and White: Family and Community in the Slave South* (New York: Oxford University Press, 1996), 224.

4. Peter Bruner, *A Slave's Adventures toward Freedom* (Oxford, Ohio, n.d.), 13; John Brown, *Slave Life in Georgia: A Narrative of the Life, Sufferings, and Escapes of John Brown, a Fugitive Slave Now in England*, L. A. Chamerovzow, ed. (London, 1855; Savannah, GA: The Beehive Press, 1991) 21; Elizabeth Keckley, *Behind the Scenes: or Thirty Years a Slave and Four Years in the White House*, in Henry Louis Gates, Jr., ed., *Six Women's Slave Narratives* (New York: Oxford University Press, 1988), 21. See, generally, Wilma King, *Stolen Childhood: Slave Youth in Nineteenth-Century America* (Bloomington: Indiana University Press, 1995).

5. Henry Clay Bruce, *The New Man: Twenty-nine Years a Slave and Twenty-nine Years a Free Man* (York, PA, 1875), 14. Brown, *Slave Life in Georgia*, 7.

6. Elizabeth Powell Conrad to Burr Powell, December 25, 1829 (?), quoted and

analyzed in Stevenson, *Life in Black and White*, 198; Moses Grandy, *Narrative of the Life of Moses Grandy, Late a Slave in the United States of America* (Boston, 1844), 7; *Pilié v. Ferriere*, #1724, 7 Mart. (N. S.) 648 (La. 1829), testimony of Mary Ann Poyfarre and Celeste, UNO; *Bloom v. Beebe*, #5921, 15 La. Ann. 65 (1860), testimony of Catherine Klopman and L. Klopman, UNO.

7. On the material incorporation of bodies with social relations, see Norbert Elias, *The Civilizing Process: The History of Manners*, vol. 1 (New York: Pantheon, 1978); Paul Connerton, *How Societies Remember* (Cambridge, UK: Cambridge University Press, 1989), 72–104, and, generally, Judith Butler, *Gender Trouble: Feminism and the Subversion of Identity* (London: Routledge, 1990).

8. Bruce, *The New Man*, 20.

9. Thomas Johnson, *Twenty-Eight Years a Slave, or the Story of My Life in Three Continents* (Bournemouth, 1909), 2.

10. Thomas H. Jones, *The Experience of Thomas H. Jones Who Was a Slave for Forty-Three Years* (Worcester, 1857), 2, 31; Lewis Hayden, quoted in Harriet Beecher Stowe, *A Key to "Uncle Tom's Cabin," Presenting the Original Facts and Documents upon Which the Story Is Founded* (Boston, 1853), 154–155, italics are in the original.

11. Thomas Maskell to Dr. Samuel Plaisted, August 8, 1838, Samuel Plaisted Correspondence, LSU.

12. Bruce, *The New Man*, 102–103; George Johnson interview in Drew, ed., *The Refugee*, in *Four Fugitive Slave Narratives*, 36. See also Andrew Jackson, *Narrative of the Sufferings of Andrew Jackson of Kentucky* (Syracuse, NY, 1847), 8. On the widespread use of sale and separation as a method of slave discipline see Norrece T. Jones, Jr., *Born a Child of Freedom, Yet a Slave: Mechanisms of Control and Strategies of Resistance in Antebellum South Carolina* (Hanover, NH: University Press of New England, 1990), 37–63, and Stevenson, *Life in Black and White*, 159, 179–180, 231, 237, 240, 249.

13. On the importance of family and community to slaves' efforts psychologically and practically to resist slavery, which will also be developed below, see John W. Blassingame, *The Slave Community: Plantation Life in the Antebellum South*, rev. ed. (New York: Oxford University Press, 1972); Herbert G. Gutman, *The Black Family in Slavery and Freedom, 1750–1925* (New York: Vintage, 1976); Leslie Howard Owens, *This Species of Property: Slave Life and Culture in the Old South* (New York: Oxford University Press, 1976); Thomas L. Webber, *Deep Like the Rivers: Education in the Slave Quarter Community, 1831–1865* (New York: W. W. Norton & Co., 1978); Charles Joyner, *Down by the Riverside: A South Carolina Slave Community* (Urbana, IL: University of Illinois Press, 1984); Deborah Gray White, *Ar'n't I a Woman? Female Slaves in the Plantation South* (New York: W. W. Norton & Co., 1985); Jones, *Born a Child of Freedom, Yet a Slave*; and Stevenson, *Life in Black and White*.

14. Lewis Clarke, *Narrative of the Sufferings of Lewis Clarke during a Captivity of More than Twenty-Five Years Amongst the Algerines of Kentucky* (Boston, 1845), 84; Jacob Stroyer, *My Life in the South* (Salem, 1890), 40; Henson, *Autobiography*, in *Four Fugitive Slave Narratives*, 34. See also Kate E. R. Pickard, *The Kidnapped and the*

Ransomed: Being the Personal Recollection of Peter Still and His Wife "Vina" after Forty Years in Slavery (New York, 1856), 149; interviews with George Johnson, Edward Hicks, and Robert Nelson in Drew, ed., *The Refugee*, in *Four Fugitive Slave Narratives*, 36, 182, 260. The idea of "social death" is borrowed from Orlando Patterson, *Slavery and Social Death: A Comparative Study* (Cambridge: Harvard University Press, 1982), and elaborated in Igor Kopytoff, "The Cultural Biography of Things: Commoditization as Process," in Arjun Appaudurai, ed., *The Social Life of Things: Commodities in Cultural Perspective* (Cambridge: Cambridge University Press, 1986), 64–91, and Akhil Gupta, "The Reincarnation of Souls and the Rebirth of Commodities: Representations of Time in 'East' and 'West,'" *Cultural Critique*, 22 (1992), 187–211.

15. On waiting for sale as the "temporality" of African-American slavery see Michael Hanchard, "Afro-Modernity: Temporality, Politics, and the African Diaspora," *Public Culture*, 11 (1999), 245–268.

16. F. R. Southmayd, ed., *Digest of the Ordinances and Resolutions of the Second Municipality* (New Orleans: Wm. H. Toy, 1848), 143, 363 (quotation); John Calhoun, ed., *Digest of the Ordinances and Resolutions of the Second Municipality of New-Orleans in Force May 1, 1840* (New Orleans: F. Cook & A. Levy, 1840), 356; *Digest of the Ordinances and Resolutions of the General Council of the City of New Orleans* (New Orleans: J. Bayon, 1845), 28; Winfield Collins, *The Domestic Slave Trade of the Southern States* (New York: Broadway Publishing Company, 1904), 126–128.

17. Daniel Hundley, *Social Relations in Our Southern States* (New York, 1860; reprinted Baton Rouge, 1960), 139–149. For the figure of the trader and the nature of slavery see Tadman, *Speculators and Slaves*, 111–210.

18. Hundley, *Social Relations*, 140–142. For the proslavery version of capitalist transformation see Eugene D. Genovese, *The World the Slaveholders Made: Two Essays in Interpretation* (Middletown, CT: Wesleyan University Press, 1969), 119–244.

19. See Tadman, *Speculators and Slaves*, xix-xxxvii, 111–221; Brenda Stevenson, *Life in Black and White*, 178.

20. For collateral credit see Richard H. Kilbourne, *Debt, Investment, Slaves: Credit Relations in East Feliciana Parish, Louisiana, 1825–1885* (Tuscaloosa: University of Alabama Press, 1995), 58–73; and Thomas D. Morris, *Southern Slavery and the Law, 1619–1860* (Chapel Hill: University of North Carolina Press, 1996), 122–123. For investment banking funded by mortgaged slaves see share-buying mortgages to the Citizen's Bank of Louisiana with inventories of slaves dated June 17, 1837 (uncat. ms. 81–65-L), November 6, 1837, September 18, 1843, Auguste Tête Papers, and May 24, 1844, Special Collections, HNO. For estate divisions see priced slave list of 'Negroes belonging to the Estate of Mrs. S. B. Evans,' 1857, Nathaniel Evans Papers, LSU. For family members trading in their future shares in the slaves of living relations see bill of sale dated June 28, 1851, Hickman/Bryan Papers, UMC. The idea that slave values were the capital upon which the southern economy was based is an axiom of the literature on Reconstruction—see, for instance, Gerald Jaynes, *Branches without Roots: Genesis of the Black Working Class in the American South, 1862–1882* (New York: Oxford University Press, 1986)—but is peculiarly

absent from antebellum studies of slavery. Almost without exception, antebellum historians treat slavery as a labor system without acknowledging that it was also a system of capital accumulation. This blindspot, I believe, is the result of an over-rigid model of the distinction between capital and labor more appropriate to the industrializing North than the enslaving South.

21. William Welhan, Plantation Book, LSU; Leonidas Spyker Diary, 1857, LSU; Pleasant Hill Plantation Record Book (Amite County, Mississippi), E. J. Capell Papers, LSU. For the idea of a "good crop" including an increase in the value of slaves, as it was reflected in southern agricultural magazines and the quotation, see James Oakes, *Slavery and Freedom: An Interpretation of the Old South* (New York: Alfred A. Knopf, 1990), 139–143.

22. Henson, *Autobiography*, in *Four Fugitive Slave Narratives*, 16–17; Isaac Williams and Christopher Nichols interviews in Drew, ed., *The Refugee*, in *Four Fugitive Slave Narratives*, 37–38, 48; Stevenson, *Life in Black and White*, 249; Brown, *Slave Life in Georgia*, 15; *Ogden v. Michel*, #5127, 4 Rob. 154 (1839), plaintiff's brief, UNO; Grandy, *Narrative*, 15; Lucy Delany, *From the Darkness Cometh the Light, or Struggles for Freedom* (St. Louis, n.d.), 21; *Cohn v. Costa*, No. 5252, 15 La. Ann. 618 (1860), testimony of Francois Terralon, UNO; Pennington, *The Fugitive Blacksmith*, vi; Henry Crawthorn and Mrs. Harry Brant interviews in Drew, ed., *The Refugee*, in *Four Fugitive Slave Narratives*, 180, 260; Frederick Douglass, *Narrative of the Life of Frederick Douglass* (1845; New York, 1963), 20.

23. T. D. Jones to Eliza, September 7, 1860, Butler Papers, LSU.

24. See, for instance, Henson, *Autobiography*, in *Four Fugitive Slave Narratives*, 16–17; Pickard, *The Kidnapped and the Ransomed*, 66–76; Isaac Mason, *Life of Isaac Mason, as a Slave* (Worcester, MA, 1893), 12; Jones, *The Experience of Thomas H. Jones*, 29.

25. Clarke, *Narrative*, 31; interview with Williamson Pease in Drew, ed., *The Refugee*, in *Four Fugitive Slave Narratives*, 88; Harriet Newby to Dangerfield Newby, August 16, 1859, in John Blassingame, ed., *Slave Testimony: Two Centuries of Letters, Speeches, Interviews, and Autobiographies* (Baton Rouge: Louisiana State University Press, 1977), 118.

26. Mason, *Life*, 35; interview with Charles Peyton Lucas in Drew, ed., *The Refugee*, in *Four Fugitive Slave Narratives*, 74.

27. Clarke, *Narrative*, 31; William Still, *The Underground Railroad: A Record of the Facts, Authentic Narratives, Letters, etc. Narrating the Hair-breadth Escapes and Death Struggles of the Slaves in their Efforts for Freedom, as Related by Themselves and Others, or Witnessed by the Author* (Philadelphia, 1872), 1, 46, 48, 62, 66; interviews with Charles Peyton Lucas and David West in Drew, ed., *The Refugee*, in *Four Fugitive Slave Narratives*, 74, 60, see also 106, 111, 127, 128, 148.

28. Tadman, *Speculators and Slaves*, 188; White, *Arn't I a Woman?* 70–71; Stevenson, *Life in Black and White*, 181, 253, 256.

29. Grandy, *Narrative*, 5. For a similar story of negotiations by a slave in the woods aided by those who remained behind see interview with Isaac Williams in Drew, ed., *The Refugee*, in *Four Fugitive Slave Narratives*, 39.

30. Interview with Edward Hicks in Drew, ed., *The Refugee*, in *Four Fugitive Slave Narratives*, 182–183.

31. *Walker v. Sanchez*, #4485, 13 La. Ann. 505 (1858), letter from Lev. Washington to Augustus Walker, April 27, 1853, UNO.

32. Interview with Madison Jefferson, in Blassingame, ed., *Slave Testimony*, 222; interview with Alexander Hamilton in Drew, ed., *The Refugee*, in *Four Fugitive Slave Narratives*, 124; Clarke, *Narrative*, 76.

33. See Elizabeth Clark, "The Sacred Rights of the Weak," *Journal of American History*, 82 (1995), 463–493; Karen Sanchez-Eppler, *Touching Liberty: Abolition, Feminism, and the Politics of the Body* (Berkeley: University of California Press, 1993).

34. William Arick to Joseph Copes, May 6, May 16, and June 8, 1849, Copes Papers, TU.

35. Grun. B. Davis to Joseph Copes, December 5, 1844, Copes Papers, TU.

36. Grandy, *Narrative*, 11.

37. Charles Ball, *Fifty Years in Chains: Or, The Life of an American Slave* (New York, 1859), 10–11.

38. William Green, *Narrative of Events in the Life of William Green* (Springfield, 1853), 3; Grandy, *Narrative*, 6; Bruce, *The New Man*, 102; Jane Crisswell to Joseph Copes, February 4, 1857, Copes Papers, TU.

39. The error of not allowing for any difference between slaves' outward allegiance to their owners' ideology and their strategic use of that ideology for their own purposes is often attributed to Eugene D. Genovese in *Roll, Jordan, Roll: The World the Slaves Made* (New York: Vintage, 1974), although it is much more clearly evident in Bertram Wyatt-Brown in "The Mask of Obedience: Male Slave Psychology in the Old South," *American Historical Review*, 93 (1988), 1228–1252.

40. See Suzanne Lebsock, *The Free Women of Petersburg: Status and Culture in a Southern Town, 1784–1860* (New York, 1984), xix; for a more roseate portrait than this one see Catherine Clinton, *The Plantation Mistress: Woman's World in the Old South* (New York: Pantheon Books, 1982). The role of slaveholding women as intercessors was, to some degree, formalized in Louisiana property law, which required married men to gain the written consent of their wives (recorded by a Notary Public in a room where the husband was not present) to sell any of the family's real estate, including slaves. While the normal function of this law was to prevent unscrupulous husbands from selling off the property their wives had brought into the marriage, it also provided slaveholding women a chance to impress their own feelings upon the sale of the family's slaves.

41. Thomas G. Clemson to Francis Pickens, October 7, 1850, Francis Pickens Papers, DU; interview with Mrs. Harry Brant in Drew, ed., *The Refugee*, in *Four Fugitive Slave Narratives*, 243.

42. James Phillips to Mary Phillips, June 20, 1852, in Blassingame ed., *Slave Testimony*, 95–99.

43. Fatima [by her master] to Ziba Oakes, April 14, 1857, quoted in Tadman, *Speculators and Slaves*, 168.

44. See, for instance, Bertram Wyatt-Brown, *Southern Honor: Ethics and Behavior*

in the Old South (New York: Oxford University Press, 1982); Steven M. Stowe, *Intimacy and Power: Ritual in the Lives of the Planters* (Baltimore: Johns Hopkins University Press, 1987); Kenneth S. Greenberg, *Honor and Slavery: Lies, Duels, Noses, Masks, Dressing as a Woman, Gifts, Strangers, Humanitarianism, Death, Slave Rebellions, the Proslavery Argument, Baseball, Hunting, and Gambling in the Old South* (Princeton: Princeton University Press, 1996).

45. Lewis Stirling, Sr., to Lewis Stirling, Jr., January 10, 1843, Stirling Papers, LSU.

46. Interview with Williamson Peace in Drew, ed., *The Refugee*, in *Four Fugitive Slave Narratives*, 88.

47. Thomas G. Clemson to Francis W. Pickens, October 7, 1850, Francis Pickens Papers, DU. Clemson, remember, had pulled Daphny and her family out of the sale and let them sell themselves as a consideration for their service and of the fact they had been a gift from Calhoun.

48. Interview with Charity Bowery, in Blassingame, ed., *Slave Testimony*, 265; Keckley, *Behind the Scenes*, 28–29; Solomon Northup, *Twelve Years a Slave*, Sue Eakin and Joseph Logsdon, eds. (Baton Rouge: Louisiana State University Press, 1968), 31.

49. Sella Martin, "Narrative," in Blassingame, ed., *Slave Testimony*, 707–708; James L. Smith, *Autobiography of James L. Smith* (Norwich, 1881), 39–40; interviews with Thomas Johnson and Rev. William Troy in Drew, ed., *The Refugee*, in *Four Fugitive Slave Narratives*, 249, 267.

50. Quoted in Stevenson, *Life in Black and White*, 250.

51. See, especially, Stevenson, *Life in Black and White*, and King, *Stolen Childhood*.

52. Interview with Ann Garrison, in Blassingame, ed., *Slave Testimony*, 215; John Wesley Dunn to Charles Dunn, January 3, 1845, HNO; interview with Charles Brown in Drew, ed., *The Refugee*, in *Four Fugitive Slave Narratives*, 243–248; T. D. Jones to Eliza, September 7, 1860, Butler Papers, LSU; Jane Dennis to Eliza October 6, 1861, Butler Papers, LSU.

53. William Wells Brown, *Narrative of William Wells Brown: A Fugitive Slave, Written by Himself* (1847), in Gilbert Osofsky, ed., *Puttin' on Ole Massa* (New York: Harper & Row, 1969), 193, 210.

54. James L. Smith, *Autobiography*, 32.

55. Interview with Charles Brown in Drew, ed., *The Refugee*, in *Four Fugitive Slave Narratives*, 246–247; Clarke, *Narrative*, 71, 76.

56. John Dixon Long, *Pictures of Slavery in Church and State* (1857), quoted in Lawrence Levine, *Black Culture and Black Consciousness: Afro-American Folk Thought from Slavery to Freedom* (New York: Oxford University Press, 1978), 14–15.

57. Stevenson, *Life in Black and White*, 180–183.

58. On imagined communities and particularly on the salience of communities constructed through the remembrance of an anonymous representative figure—for instance, The Tomb of the Unknown Soldier—see Benedict Anderson, *Imagined Communities: Reflections on the Origin and Spread of Nationalism* (London: Verso, 1983).

59. Sella Martin, "Narrative," in Blassingame, ed., *Slave Testimony*, 705–706.

60. My argument is with Genovese, *Roll, Jordan, Roll*, especially 597–598, where it is argued that personalized conflicts with slaveholders detracted from, rather than providing the foundation for, collective resistance to slavery. My perspective is indebted to James C. Scott, *Weapons of the Weak: Everyday Forms of Peasant Resistance* (New Haven: Yale University Press, 1985); James C. Scott, *Domination and the Arts of Resistance: Hidden Transcripts* (New Haven: Yale University Press, 1990); and Robin D. G. Kelley, *Race Rebels: Culture, Politics, and the Black Working Class* (New York: The Free Press, 1994), especially 1–13, 35–75.

2. Between the Prices

1. John White, *Slave Record*, 1851–1852, UMC.

2. On the interstate trade see Fredric Bancroft, *Slave Trading in the Old South* (Baltimore: J. H. Furst and Company, 1931); Michael Tadman, *Speculators and Slaves: Masters, Traders, and Slaves in the Old South* (Madison: University of Wisconsin Press, 1989), and Steven Deyle, "The Domestic Slave Trade in America," unpublished Ph.D. Dissertation, Columbia University, 1995.

3. Wendell Stephenson, *Isaac Franklin: Slave Trader and Planter of the Old South* (Baton Rouge: Louisiana State University Press, 1938), 22–52, 68–93; Robert Evans, "Some Economic Aspects of the Domestic Slave Trade, 1830–1860," *Southern Economic Journal*, 27 (1961), 329; William Calderhead, "The Role of the Professional Slave Trader in the Slave Economy: Austin Woolfolk, A Case Study," *Civil War History*, 23 (1975), 195–211; Donald Sweig, "Reassessing the Human Dimensions of the Interstate Slave Trade," *Prologue: The Journal of the National Archives*, 12 (1980), 5–22; John White, *Slave Record*, UMC; see also *Rist v. Hagan*, #4503, 8 Rob. 106 (1844), testimony of Alexander Hagan, UNO.

4. Evans, "Some Economic Aspects of the Domestic Slave Trade," 329; William A. J. Finney Papers, RASP; Jarratt/Puryear Papers, RASP.

5. Generally, for the predominance of the rural trade see Evans, "Some Economic Aspects of the Domestic Slave Trade," 329; Deyle, "Domestic Slave Trade," 119–122. Specifically, see Samuel R. Browning to Archibald Boyd, December 2, 1848, December 19, 1848, June 4, 1849, August 5, 1849, August 22, 1849, August 28, 1849. Archibald Boyd Papers, RASP.

6. Tadman, *Speculators and Slaves*, 153; Deyle, "Domestic Slave Trade," 2.

7. *Coot v. Cotton*, #2410, 5 La. 12 (1831), testimony of J. B. Desbois, Samuel Woolfolk, Daniel Talbot, and Joseph Price, UNO; *Rist v. Hagan*, #4503, 8 Rob. 106 (La. 1844), testimony of Alexander Hagan, UNO; *Bank of Charleston v. Hagan*, #464, 2 La. Ann. 999 (1847), testimony of A. Mosie, UNO; John White, *Day Book*, UMC; Herman Freudenberger and Jonathan Pritchett, "The Domestic United States Slave Trade: New Evidence," *Journal of Interdisciplinary History*, 21 (1991), 447–477; Robert Fogel and Stanley Engerman, eds., *The New Orleans Slave Sample, 1804–1862*, database available from the Inter-University Consortium for Political and Social Research.

8. Evans, "Some Aspects of the Domestic Slave Trade"; Laurence Kotlikoff, "The Structure of Slave Prices in Antebellum New Orleans, 1804–1862," *Economic Inquiry*, 17 (1979), 503; Tadman, *Speculators and Slaves*, 70–71; Freudenberger and Pritchett, "The Domestic United States Slave Trade," 447–477. Economic historians differ over the weight that should be given to (upper-South) supply and (lower-South) demand in determining the reasons for the seasonality of the trade.

9. Featherstonhaugh quoted in Stephenson, *Isaac Franklin*, 46. Italics in the original.

10. Joseph Ingraham, *The Southwest by a Yankee* (New York: Harper Brothers, 1835), vol. 2, 235; *Hitchcock v. Harris*, #1935, 1 La. 311 (1830), testimony of Samuel K. Page, UNO.

11. Freudenberger and Pritchett, "The Domestic United States Slave Trade," 467–472; Stephenson, *Isaac Franklin*, 50; Deyle, "Domestic Slave Trade," 99; Louis C. Hunter, *Steamboats on the Western Rivers: An Economic and Technological History* (Cambridge: Harvard University Press, 1949), 490.

12. See Charles Ball, *Fifty Years in Chains: Or the Life of an American Slave* (New York, 1859), 29–92; John Brown, *Slave Life in Georgia: A Narrative of the Life, Sufferings, and Escapes of John Brown, a Fugitive Slave Now in England*, L. A. Chamerovzow, ed. (London, 1855; Savannah, GA; The Beehive Press, 1991), 18–21; Solomon Northup, *Twelve Years a Slave*, Joseph Logsdon and Sue Eakin, eds. (Baton Rouge: Louisiana State University Press, 1968), 41–50; *McCargo v. The Merchants' Insurance Company of New Orleans*, #5123, 10 Rob. 334 (La. 1845), UNO; *McCargo v. New Orleans Insurance Company*, #5146, 10 Rob. 202 (La. 1844), UNO; *Andrews and Hatcher v. Ocean Insurance Company*, unreported case #5213 (1844), UNO; *Lockett v. Firemans' Insurance Company*, unreported case #5214 (1844), UNO; *Hagan v. Ocean Insurance Company*, unreported case #5218 (1844), UNO; *Johnson v. Ocean Insurance Company*, unreported case #5219 (1844), UNO; *Lockett v. Merchants' Insurance Company*, unreported case #5164 (1844), UNO.

13. See *Stewart v. Sowles*, #725, 3 La. Ann. 464 (1848), testimony of Theophilus Freeman, UNO; John White, *Slave Record*, UMC.

14. *City of New Orleans v. Kendig*, unreported case #5201 (1858), testimony of J. F. Wood, UNO; Richard Randall Tansey, "Bernard Kendig and the New Orleans Slave Trade," *Louisiana History*, 23 (1982), 159–178.

15. New Orleans City Treasurer's Office, 1854 Census of Merchants manuscript, New Orleans Public Library, Louisiana Collection (my thanks to Jonathan Pritchett for bringing this valuable document to my attention); John White, *Slave Record*, 1846, sales of Margery White, Math Duplisse, Betsey Buckner, America Brown, and Mahala (numbers 145, 162, 166, 167, 169), UMC; *Succession of Cresswell*, unreported case #3521 (1854), UNO; *Stewart v. Sowles*, #725, 3 La. Ann. 464 (1848), testimony of William Morgan and Theophilus Freeman, UNO; see also *Slater v. Rutherford*, #1021, 4 La. Ann. 382 (1849), UNO; *Person v. Rutherford*, #3585, 11 La. Ann. 527 (1856), UNO.

16. *Farmer v. Fisk*, #5248, 9 Rob. 351 (1842), testimony of S. N. Hite, UNO; *Cornish, f.w.c. v. Shelton*, #4642, 12 La. Ann. 415 (1851), testimony of Mrs. Pierre

Weeks, f.w.c., UNO; *Winn v. Twogood*, #2920, 9 La. 422 (1836), testimony of Robert Wright, UNO; *Brabo v. Martin*, #2458, 5 La. 275 (1833), testimony of Réné Salain, UNO; *Cohn v. Costa*, #6252, 15 La. Ann. 612 (1860), Louis Caretta, UNO. See also *Hill v. White*, #4489, 11 La. Ann. 170 (1856), letter from Oscar Hamilton, UNO; Douglas to William Hamilton, March 3, 1857, William Hamilton Papers, LSU.

17. *Marvin v. Michel*, unreported Louisiana Supreme Court case #5298 (1858), testimony of Charles Prince, UNO; *Stewart v. Sowles*, #725, 3 La. Ann. 464 (1848), testimony of H. B. Kenner, D. W. Bowles, UNO.

18. *Barclay v. Sewell*, #4622, 12 La. Ann. 262 (1851), testimony of William Wilz, UNO; *Nixon v. Boazman and Bushy*, Act of Sale from McMurdo to Matilda Bushy underwriter for Bernard Kendig, #3485, 11 La. Ann. 750 (1856), UNO; *Folger v. Kendig*, unreported case #5337, testimony and cross examination of J. W. Boazman, UNO.

19. *Allen v. Campbell*, #1849, 5 La. Ann. 755 (1850), testimony of James Blakeny, UNO; *Stewart v. Sowles*, #725, 3 La. Ann. 464 (1848), testimony of H. B. Kenner, D. W. Bowles, UNO.

20. *Stewart v. Sowles*, #725, 3 La. Ann. 464 (1848), testimony of Theopilhus Freeman, UNO; *Coot v. Cotton*, #2410, 5 La. 12 (1831), testimony of Daniel Talbot, James Payne, and Richard Ferril, UNO; John R. White, *Slave Record*, 1858, UMC; J. S. White, Account Book manuscript, Chinn Collection, MHS. Compare sales of Selia Samuels, Ellen Duncan, Catherine Smith, Bettie Smith, Ashley Fulkerson, Jane Corder, and Rhody. The fact that all of the inconsistencies favoring John White's book involved the sale of young women suggests to me that he found that the prices in this sector of the market were higher than expected and thus afforded a good opportunity for graft. For (much smaller) inconsistencies favoring the apparent partner's book see the sales of Roxana Longacre, Charlotte Barker, and Henry White. Thanks to Greta Reisel at the Missouri Historical Society for her help in tracking down the account book of John White's partner, J. S. White; unfortunately, the relationship of the two Whites to one another remains obscure.

21. *State v. J. A. Beard*, #5809, 11 Rob. 243 (1845), J. A. Beard Account Book, January 1 to March 7, 1843, UNO; *City of New Orleans v. J. A. Beard*, unreported case #5282 (1858), UNO; Francis Rives Account Book, 7, 16, Francis Rives Collection, DU; Edward Stewart to John Gurley, November 28, December 28, 1858, John Gurley Papers, LSU; Slave Auction broadside, March 13, 1838, mss. 44, f. 86, HNO. See also Bancroft, *Slave Trading in the Old South*, 312–338; Tadman, *Speculators and Slaves*, 102; Thomas Russell, "South Carolina's Largest Slave Auctioneering Firm," *Chicago-Kent Law Review*, 68 (1993), 1241–1282.

22. Tadman, *Speculators and Slaves*, 192–200.

23. *Peyroux v. Hagan*, unreported Louisiana Supreme Court case #964 (1849), UNO; Stephenson, *Isaac Franklin*, 11-21; *Coulter v. Cresswell*, #2734, 7 La. Ann. 367 (1852), testimony of J. W. Boazman; *Nixon v. Boazman and Bushy*, #3485, 11 La. Ann. 750 (1856), testimony of J. W. Boazman, UNO; Judith Kelleher Schafer, "Theophilus Freeman," in *A Dictionary of Louisiana Biography*, Glenn R. Conrad, ed. (Lafayette, LA: Center for Louisiana Studies, 1998), I, 323.

24. Harriet to Isaac Jarratt, October, 19, 1835; Isaac to Harriet Jarratt, November 9, 1835, and December 1, 1835, Jarratt/Puryear Papers, RASP.

25. Otis Bigelow "Recollections," quoted in Bancroft, *Slave Trading in the Old South*, 102–103; John Brown, *Slave Life in Georgia*, 101; John White, *Day Book*, *passim*, UMC.

26. *Stewart v. Sowles*, #725, 3 La. Ann. 464 (1848), testimony of Richard Murphy, UNO; *Coot v. Cotton*, #2410, 5 La. 12 (1831), testimony of John Sturges, Arthur Hughes, and letter from Cotton to Coot dated February 7, 1830, UNO.

27. Thomas B. Jackson to William Crowe, January 31, 1837, William Crowe Papers, DU; Tyre Glen to Isaac Jarratt, December 29, 1833, Tyre Glen Papers, RASP; Phillip Thomas to William Finney, January 6, 1859, January 30, 1859, February 2, 1859, William A. J. Finney Papers, RASP.

28. For buying and selling in a single market see Tansey, "Bernard Kendig and the New Orleans Slave Trade," 158–178. For brokerage see John White, *Slave Record*, 1846, sales of Margery White, Math Duplisse, Betsey Buckner, America Brown, and Mahala (numbers 145, 162, 166, 167, 169), UMC; *Succession of Cresswell*, unreported case #3521 (1854), UNO; *Stewart v. Sowles*, #725, 3 La. Ann. 464 (1848), testimony of William Morgan and Theophilus Freeman, UNO; see also *Slater v. Rutherford*, #1021, 4 La. Ann. 382 (1849), UNO; *Person v. Rutherford*, #3585, 11 La. Ann. 527 (1856), UNO. For buying for a specific buyer see *New Orleans Gas and Light Company v. Botts*, #4545, 9 Rob. 305 (1844); *Campbell v. Botts*, #1436, 5 La. Ann. 106 (1850); and *Lynch and Wiesman v. McRae*, unreported Louisiana Supreme Court case #270 (1850), UNO. For buying a list for a known buyer see A. and A. J. Walker, "Account Book," 1853–54 season, Walker Account Book, UNC.

29. A. S. Dillon to William Powell, December 31, 1840, William C. F. Powell Papers, DU; Phillip Thomas to William Finney, January 24, 1859, and Zack Finney to William Finney, January 30, 1860, William A. J. Finney Papers, RASP. See also Richard Puryear to Isaac Jarratt, January 30, 1830, and Tyre Glen to Isaac Jarratt, December 29, 1833, Jarratt/Puryear Papers, RASP.

30. See, for gender, A. R. Jones to Isaac Jarratt, January 11, 1834, RASP; A. S. Dillon to William Powell, December 19 and 30, 1840, William C. F. Powell Papers, DU; Zack Finney to William Finney, January 30, 1860, William A. J. Finney Papers, RASP; for age, "Scale of Valuations," undated, Tyre Glen Papers, RASP; for height, price list on back of Dickinson and Hill slave price circular, June 26, 1860, in William A. J. Finney Papers, RASP; William Chamber "Journal" reproduced in Fredrick Law Olmsted, *Cotton Kingdom: A Traveler's Observations on Cotton and Slavery in the American Slave States* (New York, 1862), II, 374; for weight, Tyre Glen to Thomas Glen, January 9, 1836, Tyre Glen Papers, RASP; Phillip Thomas to William Finney, July 26, 1859, William A. J. Finney Papers, RASP; for skin color, Samuel Browning to Archibald Boyd, August 28, 1849, Archibald Boyd Papers, RASP; Phillip Thomas to William Finney, January 24, 1859, November 28, 1859, William A. J. Finney Papers, RASP.

31. Tyre to Thomas Glen, January 9, 1836, Tyre Glen Papers, RASP; Thomas B.

Jackson to William Crowe, January 31, 1837, William Crowe Papers, DU; Dickinson and Hill price circular, August 25, 1850, William A. J. Finney Papers, RASP.

32. On commodities see Karl Marx, *Capital* (New York: International Publishers, 1967), vol. 1, 43–145; Igor Kopytoff, "The Cultural Biography of Things: Commoditization as Process," in Arjun Appaudurai, ed., *The Social Life of Things: Commodities in Cultural Perspective* (Cambridge: Cambridge University Press, 1986), 64–91; and Margaret Jane Radin, *Contested Commodities* (Cambridge: Harvard University Press, 1996).

33. Newton Boley to William Crowe, February 7, 1842, William Crowe Papers, DU; Tyre to Thomas Glen, January 9, 1836, Tyre Glen Papers, RASP; Phillip Thomas to William Finney, January 20, 1859, January 12, 1860, William A. J. Finney Papers, RASP.

34. Jacob Stroyer, *My Life in the South* (Salem, MA, 1898), 40.

35. Henry Bibb, *Narrative of the Life and Adventures of Henry Bibb, An American Slave, Written by Himself* (1845), in Gilbert Osofsky, ed., *Puttin' on Ole Massa* (New York: Harper & Row, 1969), 95; interview with Isaac Williams in Benjamin Drew, ed., *The Refugee: A Northside View of Slavery* (1846), in *Four Fugitive Slave Narratives* (Reading, MA: Addison-Wesley Publishing Company, 1969), 41.

36. Richard Puryear to Isaac Jarratt, March 3, 1834, Jarratt/Puryear Papers, RASP; Northup, *Twelve Years a Slave*, 43; John Brown, *Slave Life in Georgia*, 17; Ball, *Fifty Years in Chains*, 29. See also Sella Martin, "Narrative," in John Blassingame, ed., *Slave Testimony: Two Centuries of Letters, Speeches, Interviews, and Autobiographies* (Baton Rouge: Louisiana State University Press, 1977), 704–705; Stephenson, *Isaac Franklin*, 46; Bancroft, *Slave Trading in the Old South*, 283. On the gendered character of running away see Deborah Gray White, *Ar'n't I a Woman? Female Slaves in the Plantation South* (New York: W. W. Norton & Co., 1985), 70–71.

37. Martin, "Narrative," in Blassingame, ed., *Slave Testimony*, 704. See also Stroyer, *My Life in the South*, 40; interview with Levi Douglas and James Wright in Blassingame, ed., *Slave Testimony*, 303, and Isaac William and Edward Hicks interviews in Drew, ed., *The Refugee*, in *Four Fugitive Slave Narratives*, 42, 182.

38. Ethan Allen Andrews, *Slavery and the Domestic Slave Trade* (New York, 1836), 142–143; *Coot v. Cotton*, #2410, 5 La. 12 (1831), testimony of James Cook, UNO; *McCargo v. The Merchants' Insurance Company of New Orleans*, #5123, 10 Rob. 334 (La. 1845), UNO; Ball, *Fifty Years in Chains; Or, The Life of an American Slave* (New York: H. Dayton, 1859), 59.

39. *McCargo v. New Orleans Insurance Company*, #5146, 10 Rob. 202 (La. 1844), UNO; *Andrews and Hatcher v. Ocean Insurance Company*, unreported case #5213 (1844); *Lockett v. Firemans' Insurance Company*, unreported case #5214 (1844), UNO; *Hagan v. Ocean Insurance Company*, unreported #5218 (1844), UNO; *Johnson v. Ocean Insurance Company*, unreported case #5219 (1844), UNO, *Lockett v. Merchants' Insurance Company*, unreported case #5164 (1844), UNO; Featherstonhaugh quoted in Stephenson, *Isaac Franklin*, 46.

40. *Coot v. Cotton*, #2410, 5 La. 12 (1831), testimony of Levi Jacobs, UNO; *Rist v. Hagan*, #4503, 8 Rob. 106 (La. 1844), testimony of Alexander Hagan, UNO.

41. S. W. Tod deposition quoted in J. Winston Coleman, "Lexington's Slave Dealers and Their Southern Trade," *Filson Club History Quarterly*, 12 (1938), 7; Ball, *Fifty Years in Chains*, 36–41; Richard Puryear to Issac Jarratt, March 3, 1834, Jarratt/Puryear Papers, RASP.

42. Bibb, *Narrative*, in Osofsky, ed., *Puttin' on Ole Massa*, 108; John Brown, *Slave Life in Georgia*, 95; Bigelow, "Recollections," quoted in Bancroft, *Slave Trading in the Old South*, 102–103.

43. *McCargo v. New Orleans Insurance Company*, #5146, 10 Rob. 202 (1845), testimony of Zephaniah Gifford, UNO; *White v. Guyot*, #5086, 4 Rob. 108 (1843), testimony of Walter McEvers, UNO. The traders' view of pregnancy will be discussed below. The shipboard separation of slaves by sex was standard practice in the Atlantic slave trade.

44. *Armour v. Huie*, #3554, 14 La. Ann. 346 (1840), testimony of Samuel Mitchell, UNO; *Coulter v. Cresswell*, #2734, 7 La. Ann. 367 (1852), testimony of Jonathan M. Clifton, UNO. See also *Alexander v. Hundley*, #5276, 13 La. Ann. 327 (1858), testimony of Dr. James S. Sandige, UNO.

45. *Armour v. Huie*, #3554, 14 La. Ann. 346 (1840), testimony of Samuel Mitchell, UNO; *McCargo v. New Orleans Insurance Company*, #5146, 10 Rob. 202 (1845), testimony of Zephaniah Gifford, UNO.

46. John Brown, *Slave Life in Georgia*, 18–19, 95; William Wells Brown, *Narrative of William Wells Brown: A Fugitive Slave, Written by Himself* (1847), in Gilbert Osofsky, ed., *Puttin' on Ole Massa* (New York: Harper & Row, 1969), 194–195.

47. The literature on slave communities is large. Some of the most influential and important examples are: John W. Blassingame, *The Slave Community: Plantation Life in the Antebellum South* (New York: Oxford University Press, 1972); Eugene D. Genovese, *Roll, Jordan, Roll: The World the Slaves Made* (New York: Vintage, 1974); Herbert G. Gutman, *The Black Family in Slavery and Freedom, 1750–1925* (New York: Vintage Books, 1976); Lawrence W. Levine, *Black Culture and Black Consciousness: Afro-American Folk Thought from Slavery to Freedom* (New York: Oxford University Press, 1977); Albert Raboteau, *Slave Religion: The "Invisible Institution" in the Antebellum South* (New York: Oxford University Press, 1978); Charles Joyner, *Down by the Riverside: A South Carolina Slave Community* (Urbana: University of Illinois Press, 1984); White, *Ar'n't I a Woman?*; Sterling Stuckey, *Slave Culture: Nationalist Theory and the Foundations of Black America* (New York: Oxford University Press, 1987); Margaret Washington Creel, *"A Peculiar People": Slave Religions and Community-Culture among the Gullahs* (New York: New York University Press, 1988); Norrece T. Jones, Jr., *Born a Child of Freedom, Yet a Slave: Mechanisms of Control and Strategies of Resistance in Antebellum South Carolina* (Hanover, N.H.: University Press of New England, 1990); Brenda Stevenson, *Life in Black and White: Family and Community in the Slave South* (New York: Oxford University Press, 1996). A recent body of work (to which I am greatly indebted) has added to these works a sense of the daily processes by which communities are built out of shared cultural forms. See Sidney Mintz and Richard Price, *The Birth of African-American Culture* (Boston: Beacon Press, 1992); Gwendolyn Midlo Hall, *Africans in Colonial Louisiana: The Development of Afro-Creole*

Culture in the Eighteenth Century (Baton Rouge: Louisiana State University Press, 1992); Paul Gilroy, *The Black Atlantic: Modernity and Double Consciousness* (Cambridge: Harvard University Press, 1992); Robin D. G. Kelley, "'We Are Not What We Seem': The Politics and Pleasures of Community," in his *Race Rebels: Culture, Politics, and the Black Working Class* (New York: The Free Press, 1994), 35–54.

48. Nell Irvin Painter, "Soul Murder and Slavery: Toward a Fully-Loaded Cost Accounting," in Linda K. Kerber, Alice Kessler Harris, and Kathryn Kish Sklar, eds., *U.S. History as Women's History: New Feminist Essays* (Chapel Hill: University of North Carolina Press, 1995), 125–146.

49. Harriet A. Jacobs, *Incidents in the Life of a Slave Girl, Written by Herself*, Jean Fagan Yellin, ed. (1861; Cambridge, MA: Harvard University Press, 1987), 82; interview with James Smith (by Henry Bibb) in Blassingame, ed., *Slave Testimony*, 277; interview with William Grose in Drew., ed., *The Refugee*, in *Four Fugitive Slave Narratives*, 57. See also *Hill v. White*, #4489, 11 La. Ann. 170 (1856), UNO; and Tadman, *Speculators and Slaves*, 48.

50. Interview with Rev. William Troy in Drew, ed., *The Refugee*, in *Four Fugitive Slave Narratives*, 249; Moses Grandy, *Narrative of the Life of Moses Grandy, Late a Slave in the United States of America* (Boston, 1844), 11.

51. Interviews with Isaac Williams and Edward Hicks in Drew, ed., *The Refugee*, in *Four Fugitive Slave Narratives*, 42, 182, italics in the original; see also interview with Levi Douglas and James Wright in Blassingame, ed., *Slave Testimony*, 303.

52. Lucy A. Delany, *From the Darkness Cometh the Light, Or Struggles for Freedom* (St. Louis, n.d.), 22; *Hill v. White*, #4489, 11 La. Ann. 170 (1856), testimony of J. J. Green, UNO.

53. Interview with Reverend Alexander Helmsley in Drew, ed., *The Refugee*, in *Four Fugitive Slave Narratives*, 25–29.

54. Northup, *Twelve Years a Slave*, 30.

55. Northup, *Twelve Years a Slave*, 38–39.

56. On reading slave narratives see William L. Andrews, *To Tell a Free Story: The First Century of Afro-American Autobiography, 1760–1865* (Urbana: University of Illinois Press, 1988); John Sekora, "White Message/Black Envelope: Genre, Authenticity, and Authority in the Antebellum Slave Narratives," *Callaloo*, 10 (1987), 482–515. The evaluation of Northup's isolation was made by Margaret Washington at the Center for the Humanities, Wesleyan University, February 4, 1996.

57. Ball, *Fifty Years in Chains*, 30; John Parker, "Narrative" manuscript, 5–6, Rankin-Parker Papers, DU. On enslavement and violence between enslaved people see Brenda Stevenson, "Distress and Discord in Virginia Slave Families, 1830–1860," in Carol Bleser, ed., *In Joy and in Sorrow: Women, Family, and Marriage in the Victorian South, 1830–1860* (New York, 1991), 103–124; Painter, "Soul Murder and Slavery," 125–146.

58. John Brown, *Slave Life in Georgia*, 19; Bibb, *Narrative*, in Osofsky, ed., *Puttin' on Ole Massa*, 112.

59. Peter Bruner, *A Slave's Adventures toward Freedom* (Oxford, Ohio, n.d.), 11;

Martin, "Narrative," in Blassingame, ed., *Slave Testimony*, 705; Rev. William Troy interview in Drew, ed., *The Refugee*, in *Four Fugitive Slave Narratives*, 249.

60. See, generally, Levine, *Black Culture and Black Consciousness;* Albert J. Raboteau, *Slave Religion: The "Invisible Institution" in the Antebellum South* (New York: Oxford University Press, 1978); Stuckey, *Slave Culture.*

61. See William Francis Allen, *Slave Songs of the United States* (New York: A. Simpson & Co., 1867).

62. William Pettigrew to James C. Johnston, December 23, 1852, William Pettigrew Papers, UNC. See also related letters in the Pettigrew Papers: Josiah Collins to William Pettigrew requesting a secret meeting—interesting in itself in that it implies that most meetings between slaveholders were not considered secret—and Pettigrew's reply, October 21, 1852; William Pettigrew to his brother, December 24, 1852; and James Johnston to William Pettigrew, December 27, 1852, where Johnston lauded Pettigrew for going home "to protect your and your brother's Negroes and to prevent the ridiculous stories that were in circulation which were all heard by the Negroes from having an improper effect on them."

63. See Kelley, "We Are Not What We Seem," in his *Race Rebels*, 35–54, and Gilroy, *The Black Atlantic.*

64. Ball, *Fifty Years in Chains*, 102; Northup, *Twelve Years a Slave*, 42; Martin, "Narrative," in Blassingame, ed., *Slave Testimony*, 706.

65. Northup, *Twelve Years a Slave*, 38, 39; John Brown, *Slave Life in Georgia*, 17.

66. John Brown, *Slave Life in Georgia*, 18.

67. Interview with Isaac Williams in Drew, ed., *The Refugee*, in *Four Fugitive Slave Narratives*, 42.

68. Ball, *Fifty Years in Chains*, 79–92.

69. Ball, *Fifty Years in Chains*, 102–104.

70. Ball, *Fifty Years in Chains*, 104.

71. Northup, *Twelve Years a Slave*, 44.

72. Deyle, "Domestic Slave Trade," 214–216.

73. Howard Jones, "The Peculiar Institution and the National Honor: the Case of the *Creole* Slave Revolt," *Civil War History*, 21 (1975), 29–31; *McCargo v. The Merchants' Insurance Company of New Orleans*, #5123, 10 Rob. 334 (La. 1845), testimony of Zephaniah Gifford and decision of the Supreme Court, UNO. See also *McCargo v. New Orleans Insurance Company*, #5146, 10 Rob. 202 (La. 1844), UNO; *Andrews and Hatcher v. Ocean Insurance Company*, unreported case #5213 (1844); *Lockett v. Firemans' Insurance Company*, unreported case #5214 (1844), UNO; *Hagan v. Ocean Insurance Company*, unreported #5218 (1844), UNO; *Johnson v. Ocean Insurance Company*, unreported case #5219 (1844), UNO, *Lockett v. Merchants' Insurance Company*, unreported case #5164 (1844), UNO. The fact that both Madison Washington and Solomon Northup were acting as slave traders' slave-overseeing "stewards" at the time they plotted revolts suggests the possibly subversive role of the "stewards," a point that will be taken up in greater detail in chapter six.

74. Jones, "The Peculiar Institution and the National Honor," 41; *McCargo v.*

The Merchant's Insurance Company of New Orleans, #5123, 10 Rob. 334 (La. 1845), testimony of Zephaniah Gifford, UNO.

3. Making a World Out of Slaves

1. Miriam Badger Hilliard Diary, January 20, 1850, TU.

2. Edward Russell, Journal, Jan. 31, Feb. 3, 4, 1854, HNO. For cotton and sugar culture see Ulrich B. Phillips, *Life and Labor in the Old South* (New York: Little Brown and Co., 1929).

3. Stephanie McCurry, *Masters of Small Worlds: Yeoman Households, Gender Relations, and the Political Culture of the Antebellum South Carolina Low Country* (New York: Oxford University Press), 5–36.

4. James Oakes, *The Ruling Race: A History of American Slaveholders* (New York: Vintage Books, 1982).

5. My thoughts on the impossibility of separating "the market" from "the culture" of the antebellum South owe much to Jean-Christophe Agnew, *Worlds Apart: The Theater and the Market in Anglo-American Thought, 1550–1750* (Cambridge: Cambridge University Press, 1986), as does the idea that "the free market" is itself an ideological production.

6. Solomon Northup, *Twelve Years a Slave*, Joseph Logsdon and Sue Eakin, eds. (Baton Rouge: Louisiana State University Press, 1968), 74.

7. Eugene Genovese, "Yeoman Farmers in a Slaveholders' Democracy," *Agricultural History* 49 (April 1975), 331–342; Oakes, *The Ruling Race*, 229–232; Harry L. Watson, "Conflict and Collaboration: Yeomen, Slaveholders, and Politics in the Antebellum South," *Social History*, 10 (1985), 273–298. McCurry's *Masters of Small Worlds* provides a brilliant analysis of yeoman allegiance to slavery in the planter-dominated lowcountry of South Carolina. For my purposes, however, McCurry's definition of "yeoman" is misleading. McCurry has argued that small (less than ten slaves and 150 acres of cultivation) slaveholders should be classed with nonslaveholders as "yeomen" and "self-working" farmers. McCurry does this to highlight two things: that on holdings of this size the labor of white dependents—wives and children—was required along with that of black slaves to attain a sufficiency; and that a sufficiency was all that such farmers were interested in anyway. The first point will be treated below. The second, I believe, rests on a question of intentions upon entering the market—the evanescent distinction between being *in* and *of* the market, or the difference between what McCurry calls a "foray" to reinforce nonmarket values (i.e., reproducing the household over time) and market values (cash income). It is my view, elaborated below, that slaveholders of all magnitudes bought slaves to reflect both of these sets of values, but that in so doing they were making themselves up in the market—becoming of it by being in it, not necessarily as a producer but as a consumer. Relatedly, I believe that the most sensible way to understand class difference among whites in the antebellum South is along the axis of slave ownership. By my lights, someone who owned nine slaves and a hundred acres of land

would be a substantial slaveholder, and a person with a great deal of money invested in human, agricultural, and cultural capital.

8. Northup, *Twelve Years a Slave*, 79–81.

9. On whiteness as entitlement and property see Cheryl I. Harris, "Whiteness as Property," *Harvard Law Review*, 106 (1993), 1709–1791. On the relation between slaveholding, nonslaveholding, whiteness, violence, and property see Walter Johnson, "Inconsistency, Contradiction, and Complete Confusion: The Everyday Life of the Law of Southern Slavery," *Law and Social Inquiry*, 22 (1997), 405–433. See also McCurry, *Masters of Small Worlds*, 92–130.

10. Jefferson McKinney to Jeptha McKinney, April 21, 1856, Jeptha McKinney Papers, LSU.

11. Jefferson McKinney to Jeptha McKinney, April 21, 1856, Jeptha McKinney Papers, LSU.

12. McCurry, *Masters of Small Worlds*, 50.

13. Sam Steer to William Minor, Feb. 23, 1818, William Minor Papers, LSU.

14. J. H. Lucas to John B. C. Lucas, n.d., John B. C. Lucas Papers, MHS.

15. See Kenneth Lockridge, *On the Sources of Patriarchal Rage: The Commonplace Books of William Byrd and Thomas Jefferson and the Gendering of Power in the Eighteenth Century* (New York: New York University Press, 1992).

16. James Copes to Joseph Copes, July 14, 1835, and August 24, 1857, Joseph Copes Papers, TU; W. H. Yos to Owen Cox, May 7, 1847, Owen Cox Papers, LSU; Richard Tutt to J. S. Tutt, February 4, 1839, James Tutt Papers, DU. For more advice see Samuel Steer to William Minor, August 6, 1818, Minor Papers, LSU; J. F. Carter to Farish Carter, November 20, 1852, and Maria Donald to Ben, January 20, 1851, Farish Carter Papers, UNC; A. F. Burton to his brother and sister, January 14, 1861, W. Burton Papers, UNC.

17. J. D. Conrad Weeks to David Weeks, Feb. 3, 1828, Weeks Family Papers, LSU; Robert Beverly to Robert Beverly, Aug. 28, 1832, and Aug. 20, 1833 quoted in Ira Berlin and Philip Morgan, eds., *Cultivation and Culture: Labor and the Shaping of Slave Life in the Americas* (Charlottesville: University Press of Virginia, 1993), 59; John Knight to William Beall, June 24, 1844, John Knight Papers, RASP; Thomas Butler to Ann Butler, April 30, 1830, Thomas Butler Papers, LSU.

18. A. G. Alsworth to Joseph Slemmons Copes, November 18 and December 13, 1856, Joseph Slemmons Copes Papers, TU; W. H. Yos to Owen Cox, May 7, 1849, Owen Cox Papers, LSU.

19. Robert Collins, "Management of Slaves," *DeBow's Review*, 17 (1854), 422; "Duties of an Overseer," *DeBow's Review*, 18 (1855), 345.

20. See James Oakes, *Slavery and Freedom: An Interpretation of the Old South* (New York: Alfred A. Knopf, 1990), 140–143.

21. *McAllister v. Freeman, Burtin & Co.*, #405, 20 La. Ann. 205 (1868), testimony of Michael Carrigan, UNO.

22. John Knight to William Beall, February 10, May 9, and June 24, 1844, John Knight Papers, RASP.

23. *Allen v. Campbell*, #1849, 5 La. Ann. 755 (1850), plaintiff's petition and

testimony of J. Walton Gray, UNO; *Lombard v. Jacobs,* #2158, 6 La. Ann. 396 (1851), plaintiff's petition and brief to the Supreme Court, UNO. By the time the Supreme Court decided the latter case, Joseph Lombard had died and his widow was legally identified as "widow of Joseph Lombard," which is why the case bears his name. See also *Bocod v. Jacobs,* #2101, 2 La. 408 (1831); *Ogden v. Michel,* #5127, 4 Rob. 154 (1839); *Perche v. L'Admirault,* #4613, 1 Rob. 365 (1842); *White v. Slatter,* #943, 5 La. Ann. 27 (1849); *Dixon v. Chadwick,* #4388, 11 La. Ann. 215 (1856); *Wright, Allen & Co. v. Railey,* #5731, 13 La. Ann. 536 (1858), UNO.

24. Quoted in Oakes, *Slavery and Freedom,* 95.

25. McCurry, *Masters of Small Worlds,* 72–91, 121–129; see also Victoria Bynum, *Unruly Women: The Politics of Social and Sexual Control in the Old South* (Chapel Hill: University of North Carolina Press, 1992), 47–49.

26. S. F. Patterson to R. S. Patterson, January 10, 1854, Samuel Patterson Papers, DU.

27. Edward Stewart to John Gurley, December 19, 1858, John Gurley Papers, LSU.

28. On the changes a slave brought to nonslaveholding households see Oakes, *Slavery and Freedom,* 94–95. On the association of nonslaveholding white women with hard work (and its bodily manifestations) see Bynum, *Unruly Women,* 47–49.

29. Edward Stewart to John Gurley, December 19, 1858, John Gurley Papers, LSU.

30. Edward Stewart to John Gurley, December 23, 1858, John Gurley Papers, LSU.

31. McCurry, *Masters of Small Worlds,* 121–129.

32. *Bloom v. Beebe,* #5921, 15 La. Ann. 65 (1860), testimony of L. Klopman; *Buhler v. McHatton,* #3448, 9 La. Ann. 192 (1854), testimony of Henry A. Castle; *Hewes v. Baron,* #1641, 7 Mart (N.S.) 134 (1828), testimony of L. M. Reynard, UNO. For "the weighty social implications" of carriages see Winthrop Jordan, *Tumult and Silence on Second Creek: An Inquiry into a Civil War Slave Conspiracy* (Baton Rouge: Louisiana State University Press, 1993), 10–11; for sewing see, *White v. Slatter,* #943 5 La. Ann. 27 (1849).

33. See Maria Donald to Ben, January 20, 1851, Farish Carter Papers, UNC.

34. McCurry, *Masters of Small Worlds,* 121–129. For the practical dependence of white women's social identities on women of color see Elsa Barkley Brown, "Polyrhythms and Improvization: Lessons for Women's History," *History Workshop,* 31 (1991), 85–90.

35. John Knight to William Beall, February 16, 1835, John Knight Papers, RASP.

36. *Perkins v. Shelton,* unreported Louisiana Supreme Court case #5654 (1859), testimony of R. W. Lang, UNO.

37. *White v. Slatter,* #943, 5 La. Ann. 27 (1849), testimony of James Blakeny, UNO.

38. D. W. Breozeale to John Close, December 12, 1822, John Close Papers, LSU.

39. J. F. Smith to James Tutt, April 19, 1845, James Tutt Papers, DU. On

slaveholders' anxiety about reproducing their society see, generally, Lockridge, *The Sources of Patriarchal Rage*. See also Kathleen M. Brown, *Good Wives, Nasty Wenches, and Anxious Patriarchs: Gender, Race, and Power in Colonial Virginia* (Chapel Hill: University of North Carolina, 1996).

40. Isaac Jarratt to "Cousin Betty," undated, Jarratt/Puryear Papers, RASP.

41. Miriam Badger Hilliard Diary, January 20, February 4, 1850, TU.

42. Miriam Badger Hilliard Diary, February 7, 1850, TU.

43. Kitty Hamilton to William B. Hamilton, April 8, 1856, and William S. Hamilton, July 21, 1856, William S. Hamilton Papers, LSU.

44. Kitty Hamilton to William B. Hamilton, November 17 and 27, 1856, William S. Hamilton Papers, LSU.

45. Quotations throughout this section are my translations of Reynes's diary and account book, which is in French. Polyxeme Reynes Diary and Account Book, Joseph Reynes and Family Papers, LSU.

46. In the first entry in the diary, Nina is referred to as working for Reynes in 1834. My guess is that Nina was hired at that time and not purchased until 1836. It is also possible that Reynes got ahead of herself when she sat down to write the diary, which was, after all, written many years later. The first seems the simpler explanation; the second is suggested by the way the diary seems to have been written. It begins in a rush of an entry which covers 1834, then there is a table of contents which details every subsequent entry, and then there are more entries dealing with 1834. Subsequent entries are rigidly chronological. This suggests to me that Reynes started writing, made it as far as the purchase of Nina (1836 in this formulation), realized that she was leaving some things out, and started over in better order. Polyxeme Reynes Diary and Account Book, Joseph Reynes and Family Papers, LSU.

47. Polyxeme Reynes Diary and Account Book.

48. Polyxeme Reynes Diary and Account Book.

49. Polyxeme Reynes Diary and Account Book.

50. Issac to Harriet Jarratt, February 10 and 13, 1839, Jarratt/Puryear Papers, RASP. See also R. W. Baker to Joseph Copes, March 8, 1851, Joseph Slemmons Copes Papers, TU.

51. Sidney A. Palfrey to John Palfrey, March 14, 1836, Palfrey Papers, LSU.

52. A similar story probably lies behind the undated "List of Slaves purchased by A. F. Conrad and C. M. Conrad for Mrs. Mary Weeks." Weeks was a rich widow living in New Iberia, Louisiana; Alfred and Charles, the Conrads, were relations of both Weeks and Palfrey and lived in New Orleans.

53. Edward Palfrey to John Palfrey, August 24, 1857, Palfrey Papers, LSU. The first Sidney Palfrey died in 1839.

54. John Brown, *Slave Life in Georgia: A Narrative of the Life, Sufferings, and Escapes of John Brown, a Fugitive Slave Now in England* (London, 1855; Savannah, GA; The Beehive Press, 1991), 40–43.

55. *Virgin v. Dawson*, #854 (Monroe), 15 La. Ann. 532 (1860), testimony of John W. Hooler (direct, cross, and re-examination) and R. Burns, UNO.

56. On honor generally see Bertram Wyatt-Brown, *Southern Honor: Ethics and Behavior in the Old South* (New York: Oxford University Press, 1982); Stephen M. Stowe, *Intimacy and Power: Ritual in the Lives of the Planters* (Baltimore: The Johns Hopkins University Press, 1987); Kenneth S. Greenberg, *Honor and Slavery: Lies, Duels, Noses, Masks, Dressing as a Woman, Gifts, Strangers, Humanitarianism, Death, Slave Rebellions, the Proslavery Argument, Baseball, Hunting, and Gambling in the Old South* (Princeton: Princeton University Press, 1996). In spite of the importance of their work for its brilliant evocation of the peculiar frequency with which slaveholding white men killed one another over seemingly trivial disagreements, I differ from these historians in that I do not think that there was a totalized cultural system—a set of a tacitly agreed-upon rules which lay just behind everyday behavior—called "Honor." Instead, I think that "honor" was a cultural language which could be applied to various situations; it was one way, among others, of describing motives and narrating differences of opinion. Nor do I think that evidence of "honor" talk in the antebellum South can be used to define that society as essentially precapitalist (cf. Greenberg), an argument which depends upon deriving an account of the economic "base" through a totalizing account of its ideological "superstructure." The market, I am arguing, was one of the places where slaveholders demonstrated their honor, and gambling their money was one of the ways in which they backed their reputations with their substance.

57. *Dixon v. Chadwick*, #4388, 11 La. Ann 215 (1856), testimony of Dr. Johnston, UNO.

58. *Dixon v. Chadwick*, #4388, 11 La. Ann 215 (1856), testimony of Dr. Johnston, Edward Lennox, and John W. Cole, UNO.

59. *Dixon v. Chadwick*, #4388, 11 La. Ann 215 (1856), testimony of E. A. Abercrombie, UNO.

60. *Dixon v. Chadwick*, #4388, 11 La. Ann 215 (1856), testimony of E. A. Abercrombie, UNO. The fact that both this case and *Virgin v. Dawson* deal with gynecological health suggests to me that the arcane medical knowledge the buyers wished to express was particularly embodied—below a woman's waist. That was, we will see, a region of the body that was generally out of bounds to slave buyers, and so these were public claims of expertise in things that remained mysterious even to many of those who regularly bought slaves. This seems equally reflected in Dixon's comparison of his wife's ability to that of male physicians, which seems to me to reflect the longstanding conflict between midwives and physicians over sexual and reproductive health. See Kathleen Brown, "'Changed . . . into the fashion of a man': The Politics of Sexual Difference in a Seventeenth-Century Anglo-America Settlement," *Journal of the History of Sexuality*, 6 (1995), 171–193, and Laurel Ulrich, *A Midwife's Tale: The Life of Martha Ballard, Based on Her Diary, 1785–1812* (New York: Alfred A. Knopf, 1990).

61. *Dixon v. Chadwick*, #4388, 11 La. Ann 215 (1856), testimony of Dr. McIlheney, Dr. Wilson, and William McCullough, UNO.

62. Northup, *Twelve Years a Slave*, 138.

63. The familiarity of the "slave breaker" as social role—and the figure of Edward

Covey, the man who tried to break Frederick Douglass, is particularly important in this regard—has led to a commonplace misapprehension that being a slave breaker was generally a matter of profession rather than reputation. Perhaps it was in the case of Covey. It is my contention, however, that the rhetoric of slave breaking was much more widespread than any recognizably professional role—that slave breakers were ordinary rather than exceptional figures among slaveholders.

64. *McDermott v. Cannon*, #5706, 14 La. Ann. 313 (1859), testimony of J. W. Boazman and F. Withers, UNO.

65. *Dunbar v. Skillman*, #1575, 6 Mart (N.S.) 539 (La. 1828), testimony of Robert J. Nelson, Kendall Dunbar, and George Long, UNO.

66. Ariela Gross, "Pandora's Box: Slave Character on Trial in the Antebellum Deep South," *Yale Journal of Law and the Humanities*, 7 (1995), 281–288. See also George Frederickson, *The Black Image in the White Mind: The Debate on Afro-American Character and Destiny, 1817–1914* (New York: Harper & Row, 1971).

67. Moses Roper, *A Narrative of the Adventures and Escape of Moses Roper from American Slavery*, originally published 1834 (New York: Negro Universities Press, 1970), 71.

68. Peter Bruner, *A Slave's Adventures toward Freedom* (Oxford, Ohio: n.d.), 33.

69. William Wells Brown, *Narrative of William Wells Brown: A Fugitive Slave, Written by Himself* (1847), in Gilbert Osofsky, ed., *Puttin' on Ole Massa* (New York: Harper & Row, 1969), 186. See Robert Reid-Pharr, "Violent Ambiguity: Martin Delany, Bourgeois Sadomasochism, and the Production of a Black National Masculinity," in Marcellus Blount and George P. Cunningham, eds., *Representing Black Men* (London: Routledge, 1996), 73–94.

70. See, for example, J. Thornton Randolph [Charles Jacobs Peterson], *The Cabin and Parlor: or, Slaves and Masters* (Philadelphia, 1852); Mary H. Eastman, *Aunt Phillis's Cabin; or, Southern Life as It Is* (Philadelphia, 1852); Baynard R. Hall, *Frank Freeman's Barber Shop: A Tale* (New York, 1852). The shared publication date indicates that these novels were intended to respond to *Uncle Tom's Cabin*, which had placed the slave trade at the center of the critique of slavery.

71. Richard T. Archer to Joseph Slemmons Copes, March 3, 1854, Joseph Slemmons Copes Papers, TU.

72. *Ogden v. Michel*, #5127, 4 Rob. 154 (1839), testimony of Isett, UNO.

73. Thomas Maskell to slave seller Samuel Plaisted, August 8, 1838, Samuel Plaisted Correspondence, LSU.

74. Matthew Williams Diary, October 11, 1850, Matthew Williams Papers, DU.

75. John Knight to William Beall, March 1, 1834, John Knight Papers, RASP.

76. John Knight to William Beall, February 16, 1835, John Knight Papers, RASP.

77. John Knight to William Beall, October 9, 1835, John Knight Papers, RASP.

78. For the debate about the relation of slavery, capitalism, and paternalism see Eugene D. Genovese, *The Political Economy of Slavery: Studies in the Economy and Society of the Slave South* (New York: Vintage, 1967); Oakes, *The Ruling Race*; Elizabeth Fox-Genovese, *Within the Plantation Household: Black and White Women in the Old South* (Chapel Hill: University of North Carolina Press, 1988); Oakes,

Slavery and Freedom. Rather than accepting the categories of this debate—both sides of which treat economic change as if it were outside and strictly determinative of culture and treat slavery as if it were one thing all the way through, either capitalist *or* paternalist—I have concentrated upon the meanings that slaveholders themselves attached to the slave market. This is not to say that buyers' self descriptions existed outside the material context in which they traded. Indeed, it is to emphasize, as I do in Chapter 7, that those who bought from the traders brought the uncertainty and chicanery of the market into their lives. For my perspective see Stuart Hall, "The Toad in the Garden: Thatcherism among the Theorists," in Lawrence Grossberg and Cary Nelson, eds., *Marxism and the Interpretation of Culture* (Urbana: University of Illinois Press, 1988), 35–73. For the use of paternalist language in the slave property law of the South see Thomas D. Morris, *Southern Slavery and the Law, 1619–1860* (Chapel Hill: University of North Carolina Press, 1996), and Johnson, "Inconsistency, Contradiction, and Complete Confusion," 413–415.

79. *Young v. Burton* (1841), quoted in Morris, *Southern Slavery and the Law,* 116.

80. On price and pricelessness see Igor Kopytoff, "The cultural biography of things: commoditization as process," in Arjun Appadurai, ed., *The Social Life of Things: Commodities in Cultural Perspective* (Cambridge: Cambridge University Press, 1986), 64–91.

81. In the original: "Tout ce qui vivres est a hors de prix." Auvignac Dorville to M. St. Geme, May 4, 1855, St. Geme Papers, HNO.

82. John Knight to William Beall, February 16, 1835, John Knight Papers, RASP.

83. Thomas Maskell to Samuel Plaisted, August 8, 1838, Samuel Plaisted Correspondence, LSU.

84. Phillip Thomas to William Finney, July 26, 1859, William A. J. Finney Papers, RASP.

85. Robert Fogel and Stanley Engerman, *New Orleans Slave Sample*, database available from The Inter-University Consortium for Social and Political Research. Using the same data, Laurence Kotlikoff has concluded that such high prices were more often paid in the 1810s and 1820 than after, and attributed them to free black people buying their relatives. Laurence J. Kotlikoff, "The Structure of Slave Prices in New Orleans, 1804–1862," *Economic Inquiry,* 17 (1979), 496–517.

86. William Wells Brown, *Clotel: or, the President's Daughter: a Narrative of Slave Life in the United States* [1853] (New York, 1969), 208.

87. And, not coincidentally, an auction in New Orleans, which was itself the imaginative site of the "fancy trade."

88. For "fancy" women sold in private sales see *White v. Slatter,* #943, 5 La. Ann. 27 (1849), and *Fisk v. Bergerot,* #6814, 21 La. Ann. 111 (1869), UNO. Both of these cases will be discussed below.

89. Northup, *Twelve Years a Slave,* 58.

90. Frederic Bancroft, *Slave Trading in the Old South* (Baltimore, 1931), 38, 50–51, 328–334; Lewis Clarke, *Narrative of the Sufferings of Lewis Clarke during a Captivity of More than Twenty-Five Years among the Algerines of Kentucky* (Boston, 1845), 85; Phillip Thomas to William Finney, December 24, 1859, William A. J. Finney Papers, RASP.

91. Anton Reiff, "Journal," 23, Anton Reiff Journal, LSU; *Dunbar v. Connor,* unreported Louisiana Supreme Court case #1700 (1850 and 1851), testimony of Samuel Powers, UNO.

92. Fogel and Engerman, *New Orleans Slave Sample*; John Blassingame, ed., *Slave Testimony: Two Centuries of Letters, Speeches, Interviews, and Autobiographies* (Baton Rouge: Louisiana State University Press, 1977), 506; B. A. Botkin, ed., *Lay My Burden Down: A Folk History of Slavery* (Chicago: University of Chicago Press, 1945), 122–123.

93. *Barclay v. Sewell,* #4622, 12 La. Ann. 262 (1857), testimony of Joseph A. Beard, UNO; *Dunbar v. Connor,* unreported Louisiana Supreme Court case #1700 (1850 and 1851), testimony of Louis Exinois, UNO.

94. Karen Halttunen, *Confidence Men and Painted Women: A Study of Middle Class Culture in America, 1830–1870* (New Haven: Yale University Press, 1982).

95. *Eulalie and her Children v. Long and Mabry,* #3237, 9 La. Ann. 9 (1853), and #3479, 11 La. Ann. 463 (1853), testimony of Pierre Pouche, UNO; C. Vann Woodward, ed., *Mary Chesnut's Civil War* (New Haven: Yale University Press, 1981), 29 (March 18, 1861).

96. Harriet A. Jacobs, *Incidents in the Life of a Slave Girl, Written by Herself,* Jean Fagan Yellin, ed. (Cambridge, MA: Harvard University Press, 1987); Melton A. McLaurin, *Celia, a Slave* (Athens, GA: University of Georgia Press, 1991); *White v. Slatter,* #943, 5 La. Ann. 27 (1849), testimony of James F. Blakeny, UNO.

97. See Reid-Pharr, "Violent Ambiguity," in Blount and Cunningham, eds., *Representing Black Men,* 75–76.

4. Turning People into Products

1. *Alexander v. Hundley,* #5276, 13 La. Ann. 327 (1858), testimony of T. R. Davis, UNO.

2. *Dixon v. Chadwick,* #4388, 11 La. Ann. 215 (1856), plaintiff's brief, UNO.

3. On slavery, sale, life, and death see Orlando Patterson, *Slavery and Social Death: A Comparative Study* (Cambridge: Harvard University Press, 1982); Igor Kopytoff, "The Cultural Biography of Things: Commoditization as Process," in Arjun Appaudurai, ed., *The Social Life of Things: Commodities in Cultural Perspective* (Cambridge: Cambridge University Press, 1986), 64–91; and Akhil Gupta, "The Reincarnation of Souls and the Rebirth of Commodities: Representations of Time in 'East' and 'West,'" *Cultural Critique* (Fall, 1992), 187–211.

4. For the evolution of the market from a place to a power see Jean-Christophe Agnew, *Worlds Apart: The Market and the Theater in Anglo-American Thought, 1550–1750* (Cambridge: Cambridge University Press, 1986).

5. *Coulter v. Cresswell,* #2734, 7 La. Ann. 367 (1852), testimony of J. M. Wilson and David Wise, UNO; *Peyton v. Richards,* #3523, 11 La. Ann. 63 (1856), testimony of J. W. Boazman, UNO.

6. John Brown, *Slave Life in Georgia: A Narrative of the Life, Sufferings, and Escapes of John Brown, a Fugitive Slave Now in England,* L. A.. Chamerovzow, ed.

(London, 1855; Savannah, GA: The Beehive Press, 1991), 112; William Wells Brown, *Narrative of William Wells Brown, A Fugitive Slave, Written by Himself* (1847), in Gilbert Osofsky, ed., *Puttin' on Ole Massa* (New York, 1969), 193. For "blacking" see *Ledger of Accounts*, Tyre Glen Papers, RASP, and John White, *Day Book*, April 19, 1845, UMC; for tallow see White, *Day Book*, January 4, 1845, UMC.

7. For fattening diet see John White, *Day Book*, January 5, 29, April 12, 13, May 2, 1845, June 12, 1846, *passim*, UMC; for the quotation see A. J. McElveen to Ziba Oakes, September 8, 1856, reproduced in Edmund Drago, ed., *Broke by the War: Letters of a Slave Trader* (Columbia, S.C., 1991).

8. John Brown, *Slave Life in Georgia*, 95–96; William Wells Brown, *Narrative*, in Osofsky, ed., *Puttin' on Ole Massa*, 194; Moses Roper, *A Narrative of the Escape and Adventure of Moses Roper* (London, 1838), 62; Henry Bibb, *Narrative of the Life and Adventures of Henry Bibb, An American Slave, Written by Himself* (New York, 1845), in Osofsky, ed., *Puttin' on Ole Massa*, 115.

9. *Dohan v. Wilson*, #5368, 14 La. Ann. 353 (1859), testimony of Dr. J. H. Lewis, UNO; *Stilkwell v. Slatter*, unreported Louisiana Supreme Court case #4845 (1843), testimony of Dr. John J. Carr, UNO; *Murphy v. Mutual Benefit & Fire Insurance Company of Louisiana* #2244, 6 La. Ann. 518 (1851), testimony of Dr. John J. Carr, UNO. See also *Mulhollan v. Huie*, #3200, 12 La. 241 (1838), testimony of Abraham R. Jones, UNO; *Peterson v. Burn*, #912, 3 La. Ann. 655 (1848), testimony of William B. Williams, UNO; *Kock v. Slatter*, #1748, 5 La. Ann. 734 (1850), testimony of Dr. M. Mackie, UNO.

10. *Succession of Cresswell*, #2423, 8 La. Ann. 122 (1853), UNO; John White, *Day Book*, 1846, *passim*, UMC; *Perkins v. Shelton*, unreported Louisiana Supreme Court case #5654 (1859), testimony of E. F. Harrot, UNO; *Lynch and Wiesman v. McRae*, unreported Louisiana Supreme Court case #270 (1859), UNO; Solomon Northup, *Twelve Years a Slave*, Joseph Logsdon and Sue Eakin, eds. (Baton Rouge: Louisiana State University Press, 1968), 55; ordinance XLVII, articles 2 and 3 (passed June 8, 1841), in *Digest of the Ordinances and Resolutions of the General Council of the City of New Orleans* (New Orleans, 1845), 28.

11. John White, *Day Book*, February 3, 5, 14, 16, 19, 21, 1846, UMC.

12. N. C. Folger to John White, bill for clothing purchased in New Orleans, dated October 1, 1857 (and totaling $585.25), Chinn Collection, MHS; John White, *Day Book*, *passim*, UMC; Tyre Glen account with Bragg and Stewart, 1833, Tyre Glen Papers, RASP; Whitehead and Loftus Account Book, 1835–1837, Floyd Whitehead Papers, DU; *Succession of Cresswell*, unreported Louisiana Supreme Court case #3521 (1954), UNO. See also Charles Ball, *Fifty Years in Chains: Or the Life of an American Slave* (New York, 1859), 70–81; Roper, *Narrative*, 63; Bibb, *Narrative*, in Osofsky, ed., *Puttin' on Ole Massa*, 116, 136.

13. Eyre Crowe, "The Slave Market in New Orleans," *Harper's Weekly Magazine*, January 24, 1863, 197; Joseph Holt Ingraham, *The Southwest by a Yankee* (New York: Harper & Brothers, 1835), II, 193, 197; Robert Chambers "Journal," October 1853, in Frederick Law Olmsted, *The Cotton Kingdom: A Traveler's Observations on Cotton and Slavery in the American Slave States* (New York, 1862), II, 597.

14. Whitehead and Loftus Account Book, 1835–1837, Floyd Whitehead Papers, DU; N. C. Folger to John White, bill for clothing purchased in New Orleans, November 1, 1857, Chinn Collection, MHS; John White, *Day Book*, December 17, 1844, February 28, 1844, UMC; A and A. J. Walker, *Account Book*, 69 (March 14, 1852), Walker Papers, UNC.

15. John Brown, *Slave Life in Georgia*, 100; see also Northup, *Twelve Years a Slave*, 51.

16. John White, *Slave Record*, 1846, UMC; *Gourjon v. Cucullu*, #2324, 4 La. 115 (1852), list of Negroes on board brig *Seraphim*, Compte de Vente du 94 esclaves reçu par le brick *Seraphim*, and testimony of Charles Tremot, UNO.

17. *Code Noire*, sections 8 and 9, quoted in Judith Kelleher Schafer, *Slavery, the Civil Law, and the Supreme Court of Louisiana* (Baton Rouge: Louisiana State University Press, 1994), 165; *Laws of Louisiana, 1829, 1st Session, 9th Legislature* reproduced in Henry J. Levoy, ed., *The Laws and General Ordinances of New Orleans* (New Orleans, 1857), 269.

18. Michael Tadman, *Speculators and Slaves: Masters, Traders, and Slaves in the Old South* (Madison: University of Wisconsin Press, 1989), 153–154.

19. Brenda Stevenson, *Life in Black and White: Family and Community in the Slave South* (New York: Oxford University Press, 1996), 182–183, 224.

20. John White, *Slave Record*, 1846, UMC; *Coulter v. Cresswell*, #2734, 7 La. Ann. 367 (1852), testimony of J. W. Boazman and David Wise, UNO.

21. Robert Fogel and Stanley Engerman, eds., *The New Orleans Slave Sample, 1804–1862*, database available from the Inter-University Consortium for Political and Social Research.

22. Northup, *Twelve Years a Slave*, 51. See also John Brown, *Slave Life in Georgia*, 96–100.

23. For the traders' reputation see Tadman, *Speculators and Slaves*, 179–189.

24. Slave Sale Broadside, May 13, 1835, LSU; *Wright, Allen & Co. v. Railley*, #5731, 13 La. Ann. 536 (1858), testimony of Edward Sparrow, UNO. Washington, Jackson & Co. to Daniel Turnbull, October 13, 1859, Turnbull-Bowman Family Papers, LSU (thanks to Sally Proshek for this reference); *Smith v. Taylor*, #5755, 10 Rob. 133 (La. 1845), testimony of H. Cobbs; *Perkins v. Shelton*, unreported Louisiana Supreme Court case #5654 (1859), testimony of R. W. Levy, UNO.

25. "Sale of valuable Servants," 1838, mss 44 f. 86, HNO; *Hewes v. Baron*, #1641, 7 Mart. (N.S.) 134 (1828), testimony of Edward Durin, UNO.

26. Slave Sale Broadside, May 13, 1835, Lower Mississippi Valley Collection, Hill Memorial Library, LSU.

27. For the role of steamboats in shaping notions of "the good life" see Louis C. Hunter, *Steamboats on the Western Rivers: An Economic and Technical History* (Cambridge: Harvard University Press, 1949), 390–418.

28. *Fortier v. LaBranche*, #3289, 13 La. 355 (1839), testimony of L. Labarré, UNO.

29. *White v. Slatter*, #943, 5 La. Ann. 27 (1849), testimony of Francis H. Jump, UNO; *Coulter v. Cresswell*, #2734, 7 La. Ann. 367 (1852), testimony of David Wise, UNO.

30. For these insults see D. R. Hundley, *Social Relations in Our Southern States* (New York, 1860; reprinted Baton Rouge, 1960), 139–149; and Tadman, *Speculators and Slaves*, 179–192.

31. *Dixon v. Chadwick*, #4388, 11 La. Ann. 215 (1856), John W. Cole, UNO; *Hepp v. Parker*, #1788, 8 Mart. (N.S.) 473 (1830), testimony of L. A. Gaiennie, UNO; Douglas to William Hamilton, March 3, 1857, William Hamilton Papers, LSU; William D. Hennen, ed., *Digest of the Reported Decisions of the Superior Court of the Late Territory of Orleans; the Late Court of Errors and Appeals; and the Supreme Court of Louisiana* (Boston, 1852), 1409. *Hitchcock v. Hewes*, #1935, 1 La. 311 (1830), testimony of James Ervin, UNO; *Nixon v. Boazman and Busby*, #3485, 11 La. Ann. 750 (1856), testimony of A. Celoi and T. Reddington, UNO; *White v. Hill*, #3958, 10 La. Ann. 189 (1855), testimony of G. W. Munday, UNO; *Hewes v. Baron*, #1641, 7 Mart (N.S.) 134 (1828), plaintiff's petition and testimony of J. Dupin; *Lemos v. Daubert*, #4198, 8 Rob. 224 (La. 1844), testimony of Maurice Barnett, UNO.

32. James Redpath, *The Roving Editor; or Talks with Slaves in the Southern States* (New York, 1859), 252. On race and slavishness as imitation see Ariela Gross, "Pandora's Box: Slave Character on Trial in the Antebellum Deep South," *Yale Journal of Law and the Humanities*, 7 (1995), 283–288.

33. Anton Reiff, *Journal*, 42 (February 18, 1856), LSU.

34. *Eulalie, f.w.c. and her Children v. Long and Mabry*, #3237, 9 La. Ann. 9 (1854), testimony of Pierre Pouche, L. M. Foster, and the decision of the Supreme Court, UNO; *Euphemié, f.w.c. v. Juliet and Jourdan*, unreported Louisiana Supreme Court case #6740 (1865), plaintiff's petition, testimony of Juliette Maran, decision of the Supreme Court, UNO; see also *Eulalie, f.w.c. v. Long and Mabry*, #3979, 11 La. Ann. 463 (1856), and *Andrinette, f.w.c. and her Children v. Maran*, f.w.c., unreported Louisiana Supreme Court case #6741 (1865), UNO. The acronym "f.w.c." stands for "free woman of color" and indicates the presumption of freedom which was granted under Louisiana law to anyone who appeared to be "mulatto" and sued for their freedom. For "f.w.c." (and "f.m.c"), these cases, and those of others whose suits for freedom were heard by the Louisiana Supreme Court see Schafer, *Slavery, the Civil Law, and the Supreme Court of Louisiana*, 220–249.

35. *Merry, f.m.c. v. Chexnaider*, #1877, 8 Mart. (N.S.) 699 (1830), plaintiff's petition and decision of the Supreme Court, UNO; Northup, *Twelve Years a Slave*, 12–20; *Young, f.m.c. v. Egan*, #4075, 10 La. Ann. 415 (1855); John Wesley Dunn to Charles Dunn, January 3, 1845, John Wesley Dunn Letter, 81–73-L, HNO. See also Schafer, *Slavery, the Civil Law, and the Supreme Court of Louisiana*, 250–288.

36. Northup, *Twelve Years a Slave*, 25. See also John Brown, *Slave Life in Georgia*, 97–98; Bibb, *Narrative*, in Osofsky, ed., *Puttin' on Ole Massa*, 115; Frederika Bremer, *Homes of the New World: Impressions of America*, trans. Mary Howlitt (New York, 1853), II, 535.

37. Obediah Fields, memorandum, February 11, 1828, quoted in Tadman, *Speculators and Slaves*, 101; John White, *Day Book*, December 30, 31, 1844, January 8, 1845, *passim*, UMC; Northup, *Twelve Years a Slave*, 36; see also Bibb, *Narrative*, in Osofsky, ed., *Puttin' on Ole Massa*, 101.

38. Redpath, *The Roving Editor,* 248–249; Bremer, *Homes of the New World,* 373; Chambers, "Journal," in Olmsted, *Cotton Kingdom,* II, 378–379; John Brown, *Slave Life in Georgia,* 99–100; Juriah Harriss, "What Constitutes Unsoundness in the Negro?" *Savannah Journal of Medicine,* 1 (1858), 220–221; Samuel Cartwright, "Diseases and Peculiarities of the Negro Race," *DeBow's Review,* 11 (1851), 212.

39. L. M. Mills interview in John Blassingame, ed., *Slave Testimony: Two Centuries of Letters, Speeches, Interviews, and Autobiographies* (Baton Rouge: Louisiana State University Press, 1977), 503; William Wells Brown, *Narrative,* in Osofsky, ed., *Puttin' on Ole Massa,* 196; Bibb, *Narrative,* in Osofsky, ed., *Puttin' on Ole Massa,* 95, 139; John Brown, *Slave Life in Georgia,* 99–100; Northup, *Twelve Years a Slave,* 36.

40. For the general point about slave-importing states see Andrew Fede, "Legal Protection for Slave Buyers in the U.S. South: A Caveat Concerning *Caveat Emptor,*" *American Journal of Legal History,* 31 (1987), 322–358. For the specifics of Louisiana law see Judith Kelleher Schafer, "'Guaranteed against the Vices and Maladies Prescribed by Law': Consumer Protection, the Law of Slave Sales, and the Supreme Court in Antebellum Louisiana," *American Journal of Legal History,* 31 (1987), 306–321, and Schafer, *Slavery, the Civil Law, and the Supreme Court of Louisiana,* 127–179.

41. *Dohan v. Wilson,* #5368, 14 La. Ann. 353 (1859), decision of the Supreme Court, UNO.

42. Thomas Gibbes Morgan, ed., *Civil Code of the State of Louisiana* (New Orleans, 1853), articles, 2496–2508, 2512.

43. Fogel and Engerman, eds., *The New Orleans Slave Sample, 1804–1862,* database available from the Inter-University Consortium for Political and Social Research.

44. See, for example, *Rist v. Hagan,* #4503, 8 Rob. 106 (La. 1844); *Peterson v. Burn,* #912, 3 La. Ann. 655 (1848); *Slater v. Rutherford,* #1021, 4 La. Ann. 382 (1849); *Executors of Haggerty v. Powell,* #2215, 6 La. Ann. 533 (1851); *Coulter v. Cresswell,* #2734, 7 La. Ann. 367 (1852); *Person v. Rutherford,* #3585, 11 La. Ann. 527 (1856), UNO.

45. For forcing buyers to go to law see Bernard Kendig's statement that he "would do nothing unless compelled to do so by law," *Buie v. Kendig,* #6356, 15 La. Ann. 440 (1860), testimony of Isaac Doyle. For deductions see *Herries v. Botts,* #3635, 14 La. 432 (1840), testimony of Dr. E. H. Barton and *Matthews v. Pascal's Executors,* #3287, 13 La. 53 (1839), testimony of William Flower: "Pascal appeared to be satisfied that there were grounds for recision and proposed by a compromise to pay half the amount of the Negro Dempsey—alleging that he was a partner & had only half the sale." For exchanges and surcharges see *Nixon v. Boazman and Bushy,* #3485, 11 La. Ann. 750 (1856), testimony of Bernard Kendig; for traders putting buyers return requests off see *Blair v. Collins,* #6449, 15 La. Ann 683 (1860), plaintiff's petition, and *Executors of Haggerty v. Powell,* #2215, 6 La. Ann. 533 (1851), testimony of Hoyt. For dodging the day the prescription ran see *Smith v. Taylor,* #5755, 10 Rob. 133 (La. 1845), plaintiff's brief to the Supreme Court, UNO.

46. On "repeat players" see Gross, "Pandora's Box: Slavery, Character, and

Southern Culture in the Courtroom," unpublished Ph.D. dissertation, Stanford University, 1996, 245; John White, *Slave Record*, 1851, UMC; *Stewart v. Sowles*, #725, 3 La. Ann. 464 (1848), testimony of Theophilus Freeman, UNO.

47. *Kock v. Slatter*, #1748, 5 La. Ann. 734 (1850), testimony of James Blakeny, UNO.

48. For returned slaves resold see *Stewart v. Sowles*, #725, 3 La. Ann. 464 (1848); *Peterson v. Burn*, #912, 3 La. Ann. 655 (1848); *Kock v. Slatter*, #1748, 5 La. Ann. 734 (1850); *Romer v. Woods*, #1846, 6 La. Ann. 29 (1851); *Person v. Rutherford*, #3585, 11 La. Ann. 527 (1856); *Gatlin v. Kendig*, #6894, 18 La. Ann. 118 (1866). For higher prices and sale in different states see John White, *Slave Record*, 1851, *passim*, UMC. The other thing the traders did was return slaves themselves. Their legal rights were the same as any other slaveholders, and they could sue when they were dissatisfied or call previous owners "in warranty" when they were sued.

49. John White, Slave Record, *passim*.

50. John White, *Slave Record, 1846* (David Overton, Megan Wells, Esther Taylor, Runel Causey, Berry), 1851 (Mary Ellette and her five children), 1852 (Abram Godwin, Kate King, and her three children), UMC.

5. Reading Bodies and Marking Race

1. Joseph Holt Ingraham, *The Southwest by a Yankee* (New York: Harper & Brothers, 1835), I, 192–198. I have elided the following headings, the subjects of which are treated in other chapters, between "Demeanor of the Slaves" and "African Inferiority"; "Anxiety to be Sold" and "Buying a Wife." For racial "environmentalism" of the type Ingraham eventually espoused see George Fredrickson, *The Black Image in the White Mind: The Debate on Afro-American Character and Destiny, 1817–1914* (New York: Harper & Row, 1971), 12–16, 35–42, 126–129.

2. Ingraham, *The Southwest by a Yankee*, II, 194, 201, 239–240.

3. Winthrop D. Jordan, *White Over Black: American Attitudes to the Negro, 1550–1812* (Chapel Hill: University of North Carolina Press, 1968); Barbara Jeanne Fields, "Ideology and Race in American History," in J. Morgan Kousser and James M. McPherson, eds., *Region, Race, and Reconstruction: Essays in Honor of C. Vann Woodward* (New York: Oxford University Press, 1982), 143–177; Barbara Jeanne Fields, "Slavery, Race, and Ideology in the United States of America," *New Left Review*, 181 (1990), 95–118, quotation on 109; Thomas C. Holt, "Marking Race: Race-making, and the Writing of History," *American Historical Review*, 50 (1995), 1–20. My approach embarks from the premises outlined by Fields and Holt. I am also indebted to Henry Louis Gates, Jr., ed., *Race, Writing, and "Difference"* (Chicago: University of Chicago Press, 1986); David Theo Goldberg, ed., *Anatomy of Racism* (Minneapolis: University of Minnesota Press, 1990); Evelyn Brooks Higginbotham, "African-American Women's History and the Metalanguage of Race," *Signs*, 17 (1992), 251–274; Michael O'Malley, "Specie and Species: Race and the Money Question in the Nineteenth Century," Nell Irvin Painter, "Response to Michael O'Malley," *American Historical Review*, 99 (1994), 369–408; Colette Guil-

laumin, *Racism, Sexism, Power, and Ideology* (London: Routledge, 1995); and Mia Bay, *The White Image in the Black Mind: African-American Ideas about White People, 1835–1925* (New York: Oxford University Press, 1999).

4. For religion and science see William Stanton, *The Leopard's Spots: Scientific Attitudes to Race in America, 1815–1859* (Chicago: University of Chicago Press, 1960); Thomas Gossett, *Race: The History of an Idea in America* (Dallas: Southern Methodist University Press, 1963); Fredrickson, *The Black Image in the White Mind*; Stephen Jay Gould, *The Mismeasure of Man* (New York: W. W. Norton & Co., 1981); Reginald Horsman, *Josiah Nott of Mobile* (Baton Rouge: Louisiana State University Press, 1987). For law, see William Fisher III, "Ideology and Imagery in the Law of Slavery," *Chicago-Kent Law Review*, 68 (1993), 1051–1086; Ariela Gross, "Pandora's Box: Slave Character on Trial in the Antebellum Deep South," *Yale Journal of Law and Humanities*, 7 (1995), 267–316; Thomas Morris, *Southern Slavery and the Law, 1619–1860* (Chapel Hill: University of North Carolina Press, 1996); Martha Hodes, *White Women, Black Men: Illicit Sex in the Nineteenth-Century South* (New Haven: Yale University Press, 1997); Walter Johnson, "Slavery, Whiteness, and the Market: The Strange Story of Alexina Morrison," *Journal of American History* (forthcoming March 2000); for jokes, stereotypes, minstrel shows, and literary culture (mostly in the North) see Ronald T. Takaki, *Iron Cages: Race and Culture in Nineteenth-Century America* (Seattle: University of Washington Press, 1979); Alexander Saxton, *The Rise and Fall of the White Republic: Class, Politics, and Mass Culture in Nineteenth-Century America* (London: Verso, 1990); David Roediger, *The Wages of Whiteness: Race and the Making of the American Working Class* (London: Verso, 1991); Eric Lott, *Love and Theft: Blackface Minstrelsy and the American Working Class* (New York: Oxford, 1993); and Holt, "Race Marking." For brutality as the staging of racial difference see Kirsten Fischer, "Embodiments of Power: Slavery and Sexualized Violence in Colonial North Carolina," paper delivered at the Tenth Berkshire Conference of the History of Women, University of North Carolina, June 7, 1996.

5. *Winfield v. Little*, #170, 7 La. Ann. 536 (1852) (Alexandria), testimony of Frazier Miller, James Calvitt, and G. E. Barton, UNO. I have substituted "Winfield" where the trial record reads "plaintiff."

6. See, for example, *Hepp v. Parker*, #1788, 8 Mart (N.S.) 473 (1830), testimony of L. A. Gaiennie, UNO; *Lemos v. Daubert*, #4198, 8 Rob. 224 (La. 1844), testimony of Dr. Duprerris, UNO; *Slater v. Rutherford*, #1021, 4 La. Ann. 382 (1849), testimony of R. P. Wilmoth, UNO; *Bloodgood v. Wilson*, #3272, 10 La. Ann. 302 (1855), testimony of Capt. Rowley and Dr. B. H. Moss, UNO; *Blum v. Beebe*, #5921, 15 La. Ann. 65 (1860), testimony of Severin Klopman, UNO; *Girault v. Zuntz*, #6445, 15 La. Ann. 684 (1860), testimony of J. J. McCormack, UNO.

7. John Knight to William Beall, March 18, 1844, John Knight Papers, RASP. These inspections, it should be stated explicitly, were performed both in the cases of slaves sold at "private" sales in the traders' pens and those sold at public auction. Auction houses had the same sort of lay-out and made the same sort of provisions for buyers to inspect slaves as did traders. This meant that the same daily reproduction of

racial knowledge on the part of slaveholders and the same possibility for slippery misrepresentation on the part of the slaves (see Chapter 6) characterized auction sales as other sales even though the mechanism of sale—especially in its presentation of buying a slave as a competition between white men—was more exaggerated.

8. Laurence Kotlikoff, "The Structure of Slave Prices in New Orleans, 1804–1862," *Economic Inquiry*, 17 (1979), 496–517; Judith Kelleher Schafer, "New Orleans Slavery in 1850 as Seen in Advertisements," *Journal of Southern History*, 47 (1981), 33–56; Michael Tadman, *Speculators and Slaves: Masters, Traders, and Slaves, in the Old South* (Madison: University of Wisconsin Press, 1989), 25–31; Jonathan Pritchett and Herman Freudenberger, "A Peculiar Sample: The Selection of Slaves for the New Orleans Market," *Journal of Economic History*, 52 (1992) 109–128; Robert Fogel and Stanley Engerman, eds., *The New Orleans Slave Sample, 1804–1862*, database available from the Inter-University Consortium for Political and Social Research.

9. *Lyons v. Kenner and Taylor*, #4770, Z Rob. 50 (1842), testimony of S. Bennett, UNO; *White v. Slatter*, #943, 5 La. Ann. 27 (1849), testimony of S. F. Slatter, UNO; *Huntington v. Brown*, #15, 7 La. Ann. 48 (1865), testimony of D. Donvan, UNO.

10. *Landry v. Peterson & Stuart*, #1025, 4 La. Ann. 96 (1849), testimony of Pascal Lebesque and Dr. Joseph Ford, UNO; *Bloodgood v. Wilson*, #3272, 10 La. Ann. 302 (1855), testimony of Richard Lee Fern, UNO; *Frierson v. Irvin*, #1050, 4 La. Ann. 277 (1849), plaintiff's petition, UNO. "Griff" or "griffe" is a slave trade word. In the era of the Atlantic slave trade it designated the child of an African and a Creole slave, but by the nineteenth century it had come to mean the offspring of a "Negro" and a "mulatto." The history of the word mirrors in miniature the historical evolution of the categories of the slave business from those based on nation to those based on race. See Guillaumin, *Racism, Sexism, Power, and Ideology*, 29–152.

11. John Knight to William Beall, January 27, 1844, John Knight Papers, RASP; William Hamilton to Kitty Hamilton, November 27, 1856, William Hamilton Papers, LSU; William Connor to Lemuel Connor, October 23, 1849, Lemuel Connor Papers, LSU; *Folse v. Kittredge*, #6580, 15 La. Ann. 222 (1860), testimony of F. A. Williamson, UNO.

12. Samuel Cartwright, *Southern Medical Reports*, 2 (1850), 427; see also Samuel Cartwright, "Report on the Diseases and Physical Peculiarities of the Negro Race," *New Orleans Medical and Surgical Journal*, 7 (1851), 697; John Knight to William Beall, February 7, 1844, John Knight Papers, RASP.

13. *Roquest v. Boutin*, #5446, 12 La. Ann. 44 (1858), testimony of Maria Piaja, UNO; *Winfield v. Little*, #170 Alexandria, 7 La. Ann 536 (1852), testimony of G. E. Barton, UNO; Cartwright, "Diseases and Physical Peculiarities of the Negro," 697.

14. Joseph Queen to Alonzo Snyder, October 4, 1847, Alonzo Snyder Papers, LSU. *Girault v. Zuntz*, #6445, 15 La. Ann. 684 (1860), testimony of J. B. Poindexter, UNO.

15. William Chambers, "Journal," reproduced in Frederick Olmsted, *Cotton Kingdom: A Traveler's Observations on Cotton and Slavery in the American South* (New York, 1862), II, 374; price list on the back of Dickinson and Hill slave price circular, June 26, 1860, William A. J. Finney Papers, RASP; Tyre to Thomas Glen, January

9, 1836, Tyre Glen Papers, RASP; John Brown, *Slave Life in Georgia: A Narrative of the Life, Sufferings, and Escapes of John Brown, a Fugitive Slave Now in England*, L. A. Chamerovzow, ed. (London, 1855; Savannah, GA: The Beehive Press, 1991), 16; see also Phillip Thomas to William Finney, July 26, 1859, William A. J. Finney Papers, RASP. On height and slave traders' preferences see Pritchett and Freudenberger, "A Peculiar Sample," 109–128.

16. A. J. McElveen to Z. B. Oakes, August 25, 1853 in Edmund L. Drago, ed., *Broke by the War: Letters of a Slave Trader* (Columbia, SC: University of South Carolina Press, 1991), 53, *passim.* See also *Fox v. Walsh*, #4733, 5 Rob. 222 (1843), testimony of Dr. Warren Stone and Edgar Montegut, UNO.

17. Nathan Brown to M. H., January 13, 1838; Solomon Northup, *Twelve Years a Slave*, Joseph Logsdon and Sue Eakin, eds. (Baton Rouge: Louisiana State University Press, 1968), 52; Joseph Copes to Thomas J. Alsworth, March 16, 1859 and Joseph Copes to Jas. M. Grafton, April 2, 1859, Joseph Copes Papers, TU.

18. Charles Ball, *Fifty Years in Chains, or the Life of an American Slave* (1859; Detroit: Negro History Press, 1969), 68; *Stackhouse v. Kendall*, #1851, 7 La. Ann. 670 (1851), testimony of William S. Clark, A. Settle, and H. Stackhouse, UNO; *Banks v. Botts*, #2905, 10 La. 42 (1836), testimony of Oscar Kibbe and David B. Morgan, UNO.

19. *Marin v. Michel*, unreported Louisiana Supreme Court case #5298 (1858), testimony of Jacob Capan, Louis Caretta, and David Keane, UNO; Fredrika Bremer, *Homes of the New World*, 2 vols., Mary Howitt, trans. (New York: Harper Brothers, 1853), II, 203; Charles Richard Weld, *A Vacation Tour in the United States and Canada* (London: Longman, Brown, Green, and Longman, 1855), 300; James Redpath, *The Roving Editor, or Talks with Slaves in the Southern States* (New York: A. B. Burdick, 1859), 249–250; Henry Bibb, *Narrative of the Life and Adventures of Henry Bibb, An American Slave, Written by Himself* (1845), in Gilbert Osofsky, ed., *Puttin' on Ole Massa* (New York: Harper & Row, 1969), 114; Peter Randolph, *Sketches of Slave Life: Or Illustrations of the Peculiar Institution* (Boston: Published for the Author, 1855), 52; A. J. McElveen to Z. B. Oakes, July 10, 1853, July 29, 1852, May 10, 1854, in Drago, ed., *Broke by the War*, 43–51, 80; Cartwright, "Diseases and Physical Peculiarities of the Negro," 212.

20. Cartwright, *Southern Medical Reports*, 2 (1850), 427; John Knight to William Beall, February 7, 1844, John Knight Papers, RASP.

21. W. H. Yos to Owen Cox, May 7, 1849, Owen Cox Papers, LSU; John Knight to William Beall, January 27, 1844, John Knight Papers, RASP; Samuel Browning to Archibald Boyd, August 28, 1849, Archibald Boyd papers, RASP; Hector Davis price list, January 31, 1860, quoted in Tadman, *Speculators and Slaves*, 126.

22. Tadman, *Speculators and Slaves*, 29–31; Hector Davis price list, January 31, 1860, quoted in Tadman, *Speculators and Slaves*, 126. A. J. McElveen to Z. B. Oakes, January 6, 1852, in Drago, ed., *Broke by the War*, 43.

23. See White, 69–70, 95–103; Tadman, *Speculators and Slaves*, 121–132; Charles B. Dew, *Bond of Iron: Master and Slave at Buffalo Forge* (New York: W. W. Norton & Co., 1994), 24.

24. John Knight to William Beall, May 22, 1845, John Knight Papers, RASP. See Brenda Stevenson, *Life in Black and White: Family and Community in the Slave South* (New York: Oxford University Press, 1996), 161.

25. *Person v. Rutherford*, #3585, 11 La. Ann. 527 (1856), testimony of Alfred A. Robards; *Slater v. Rutherford*, #1021, 4 La, Ann. 382 (1849), testimony of R. P. Wimoth; *McDermott v. Cannon*, #5706, 14 La. Ann. 313 (1859), testimony of J. W. Boazman; *Lynch and Wiesman v. McRae*, unreported Louisiana Supreme Court Case #270 (1859), testimony of Calvin Rutherford, UNO.

26. Juriah Harriss, "What Constitutes Unsoundness in the Negro," *Savannah Journal of Medicine*, 2 (1858), 220; Weld, *A Vacation Tour*, 300–301; Redpath, *The Roving Editor*, 10; W. H. Yos to Owen Cox, May 7, 1847, Owen Cox Papers, LSU; Phillip Thomas to William Finney, December 24, 1859, William A. J. Finney papers, RASP; *Lemos v. Daubert*, #4198, 8 Rob. 224 (La. 1844), testimony of Dr. Allarsi, UNO; *Matthews v. Pascal's Executors*, #3287, 13 La. 53 (1839), testimony of Andrew Collins, UNO; *Roca v. Slawson*, #1781, 5 La. Ann. 708 (1850), testimony of Dr. John F. Hayes, UNO; Dew, *Bond of Iron*, 255; *Rist v. Hagan*, #4503, 8 Rob. 106 (La. 1844), testimony of Dr. R. H. Lewis and Johns Collins, UNO. One Louisiana doctor maintained that treatments like cupping and blistering left a more distinct impression on black bodies than on white ones: "I mean to say the boy had scars on his stomach which looked new as a Negro's skin will for ten days after a mustard plaster has been applied and has a much more distinct appearance on them than when applied to white persons." *Alexander v. Hundley*, #5276, 13 La. Ann. 327 (1858), testimony of Dr. James S. Sandige, UNO.

27. Northup, *Twelve Years a Slave*, 53; A. J. McElveen to Ziba Oakes July 10, 1853, August 4, 1853, July 10, 1856, in Drago, ed., *Broke by the War*, 43, 46, 123, *passim;* Weld, *A Vacation Tour*, 301; W. H. Yos to Owen Cox, May 7, 1841, Owen Cox Papers, LSU; *Lemos v. Daubert*, #4198, 8 Rob. 224 (La. 1844), testimony of Dr. Allarsi, UNO; *Rist v. Hagan*, #4503, 8 Rob. 106 (La. 1844), testimony of John Collins, UNO; *White v. Guyot*, #5086, 4 Rob. 108 (1843), testimony of Dr. Dancreau, UNO.

28. Herman Freudenberger and Jonathan Pritchett, "The Domestic United States Slave Trade: New Evidence," *Journal of Interdisciplinary History*, 21 (1991), 447–449; Judith Kelleher Schafer, "The Immediate Impact of Nat Turner's Insurrection on New Orleans," *Louisiana History*, 21 (1980), 361–376.

29. *Smith v. Taylor*, #5755, 10 Rob. 133 (La. 1845), testimony of Joseph Pulliam and John Bartel, UNO.

30. Judith Kelleher Schafer, *Slavery, the Civil Law, and the Supreme Court of Louisiana* (Baton Rouge: Louisiana State University Press, 1994), 130–131, 136–148; Gross, "Pandora's Box: Slave Character on Trial in the Antebellum Deep South," 283–295; Cartwright, "Diseases and Physical Peculiarities of the Negro," 707–715. Cartwright thought that "the hebetude of mind and obtuse sensibility of body . . . called by overseers 'Rascality'" could be detected in physiological signs: lesions on the skin; dry skin; spongy, dark, recessive gums.

31. William Pettigrew, document giving account of his reasons for selling Jim (in

New Orleans), written sometime after March 4, 1853, William Pettigrew Papers, UNC. Louisiana planter John Palfrey invoked an earlier (Calvinist) formulation of the same idea when he referred to the "natural depravity" of one of his slaves, John Palfrey to Palfrey and Taylor, January 5, 1820, John Palfrey Papers, LSU.

32. James D. Davidson to William Weaver, December 21, 1854, quoted in Dew, *Bond of Iron*, 105; John Knight to William Beall, July 7, 1844, John Knight Papers, RASP; John Bisland to D & H, n.d., John Bisland Papers, LSU; *Donnet v. Ramsay*, #1468, 6 Mart. (N.S.) 129 (1827), letter from Thomas Fleming to James Ramsay included in evidence, UNO. See also Kenneth S. Greenberg, *Honor and Slavery: Lies, Duels, Noses, Masks, Dressing as a Woman, Gifts, Strangers, Humanitarianism, Death, Slave Rebellions, The Proslavery Argument, Baseball, Hunting, and Gambling in the Old South* (Princeton: Princeton University Press, 1996), 24–50.

33. *Lemos v. Daubert*, #4198, 8 Rob. 224 (La. 1844), testimony of Maurice Barnett, UNO; *Peterson v. Burn*, #912, La. Ann. 655 (1848), testimony of Dr. Slade; Northup, *Twelve Years a Slave*, 52–53.

34. Weld, *A Vacation Tour*, 300.

35. *White v. Guyot*, #5086, 4 Rob. 108 (1843), testimony of Walter McEvers, UNO. *Herries v. Botts*, #3635, 14 La. Ann 432 (1840), decision of the Supreme Court, UNO.

36. *Lemos v. Daubert*, #4198, 8 Rob. 224 (La. 1844), testimony of Maurice Barnett and Dr. Allarsi, UNO. The fraud alleged in this case was on the part of the seller, Daubert, not the broker/auctioneer, Barnett; the law under which the suit was brought required that the malady sued for be one that was not readily apparent at the time of the sale. The same sensibility may be reflected in a Louisiana slaveholder's clearly bounded account of his search for the "dark marks on the back bone" which he believed proved African descent: "examined the girl down to the waist;" see *Morrison v. White*, #442, 16 La. Ann 100 (1861), testimony of G. H. Lyons, UNO.

37. *Person v. Rutherford*, #5383, 11 La. Ann. 527 (1856), testimony of Dr. James Clarke, UNO. For suits in which the plaintiff claimed to have missed existing syphilis when buying a slave see *Compton v. Woolfolk*, #2583, 6 La. 272 (1834); *Peterson v. Burn*, #912, La. Ann. 655 (1848); *Jourdan v. Virgil*, #1098, 5 La. Ann. 40 (1850); and *Roquest v. Boutin*, #5446, 14 La. Ann. 44 (1858). For a case in which a woman's syphilis was acknowledged at the time of her sale see *Virgil v. Dawson*, #854 (Monroe), 15 La. Ann. 532 (1860). For a case of a woman's varicose veins allegedly missed at the time of purchase see *Palms v. Kendig*, #6279, 15 La. Ann. 264 (1860). And for a case in which a man's undiscovered syphilis is mentioned, although not sued for, see *Matthews v. Pascal's Executors*, #3287, 13 La. 53 (1839), UNO.

38. Redpath, *The Roving Editor*, 246–252. None of this is to say that all of the shame in the slave market was of the heterosexual variety, or that the only reason that buyers did not strip slaves was the discomfort symbolized by the screens. Time and trouble may have kept some buyers from looking as closely as they would have liked, and there may have been a distinction attached to buying without looking too

closely. As slave dealer C. F. Hatcher put it about a slave he had sold without stripping: "I looked at the boy talked to him, he seemed perfectly sound & healthy. If the boy had been diseased at the time I should have perseved it." With a gaze as acute as his own, Hatcher thought he did not need to look any closer. *Lynch and Wiesman v McRae*, unreported Louisiana Supreme Court Case #270 (1859), testimony of C. F. Hatcher, UNO.

39. On race in the antebellum courts see Morris, *Southern Slavery and the Law*; Schafer, *Slavery, the Civil Law, and the Supreme Court of Louisiana*; Hodes, *White Women, Black Men*; Ariela J. Gross, "Litigating Whiteness: Trials of Racial Determination in the Nineteenth-Century South," *Yale Law Journal*, 108 (1998), 107–188; Walter Johnson, "Slavery, Whiteness, and the Market."

40. Schafer, "New Orleans Slavery in 1850," 53–54; Fogel and Engerman, eds., *The New Orleans Slave Sample, 1804–1862*, databaes available from the Inter-University Consortium for Social and Political Research.

41. Dew, *Bond of Iron*, 174, 193.

42. *George v. Greenwood*, #3687, 11 La. Ann. 299 (1856), testimony of John M. Crawford, UNO.

43. Kotlikoff, "The Structure of Slave Prices in New Orleans," 504.

44. Bibb, *Narrative*, in Osofsky, ed., *Puttin' on Ole Massa*, 114–117, 137; on the gendering of slaveholders' fears of slaves' resistance see Gross, "Pandora's Box: Slave Character on Trial in the Antebellum Deep South," 283–300. Kotlikoff, "The Structure of Slave Prices in New Orleans," 515. See also Stevenson, *Life in Black and White*, 181.

45. Fogel and Engerman, *New Orleans Slave Sample*; Schafer, "New Orleans Slavery in 1850," 53–54. See also Kotlikoff, "The Structure of Slave Prices in New Orleans," 502–506, and Stevenson, *Life in Black and White*, 196.

46. Phillip Thomas to William Finney, January 24, 1859, William A. J. Finney Papers, RASP.

47. *Morrison v. White*, #442, 16 La. Ann. 100 (1861), testimony of Moses Morrison, UNO. *Perkins v. Shelton*, unreported Louisiana Supreme Court Case #5654 (1859), testimony of Dr. Stephen T. Rushing, UNO; *White v. Slatter*, 943, 5 La. Ann. 27 (1849), testimony of Francis Jump, UNO; Northup, 58.

48. Fredrickson, *The Black Image in the White Mind*, 75–80; Joel Williamson, *New People: Miscegenation and Mulattoes in the United States* (New York: Free Press, 1980), 94–96; Stephen Jay Gould, *The Mismeasure of Man* (New York: W. W. Norton & Co., 1981), 39–52. [illegible] to Lemuel Connor, September 9, 1853, Lemuel Connor Papers, LSU.

49. Maria Donald to Ben, January 20, 1851, Campbell Papers, DU; *Coulter v. Cresswell*, #2734, 7 La. Ann. 367 (1852), testimony of David Wise, UNO.

50. Elizabeth Powell Conrad to Burr Powell, December 25, 1829 (?), quoted and analyzed in Stevenson, *Life in Black and White*, 197–198.

51. *Frierson v. Irvin*, #1050, 4 La. Ann. 277 (1849), Document B, UNO.

52. John Knight to William Beall, February 16, 1835, John Knight Papers, RASP; *Walker v. Haynes*, #6606 (Monroe), 15 La. Ann. 640 (1860), testimony of

J. D. Hair, UNO; *Cohn v. Costa*, 6252, 15 La. Ann. 612 (1860), testimony of Celeste DeRosemon, UNO; *White v. Slatter*, 943, 5 La. Ann. 27 (1849), testimony of Francis H. Jump and Hope H. Slatter, UNO; *Slater v. Rutherford*, #1021, 4 La. Ann. 382 (1849), testimony and re-examination of Hiram Goodrich, UNO. In *Life in Black and White*, 241, Brenda Stevenson has pointed out that light-skinned slaves may have been "socialized" from a very early age to hold the sensibilities that slaveholders attributed to their skin color.

53. John Knight to William Beall, February 16, 1835, John Knight Papers, RASP; Kitty Hamilton to William Hamilton, July 21, 1856, Hamilton Papers, LSU.

54. Phillip Thomas to William Finney, July 26, 1859, William A. J. Finney Papers, RASP; *Fisk V. Bergerot*, #6814, 21 La. Ann. 111 (1869), testimony of Charles Goddard, UNO; *White v. Slatter*, 943, 5 La. Ann. 27 (1849), testimony of James Blakeny, UNO.

55. *Hill v. White*, #4489, 11 La. Ann. 170 (1856), testimony of Lewis Bowers, UNO; *Williamson v. Norton (Western World)*, #2427, 8 La. Ann. 393 (1852), testimony of Rufus Blanchard on direct and cross examination, UNO; *Morrison v. White*, #442, 16 La. Ann. 100 (1861), testimony of W. J. Martin, Clawson, Cannon, and Kemper, UNO. For the whole Morrison story see Johnson, "Slavery, Whiteness, and the Market."

56. *Banks v. Botts*, #2905, 10 La. 42 (1836), testimony of Oscar Kibbe and David B. Morgan, UNO; *Coulter v. Cresswell*, #2734, 7 La. Ann. 367 (1852), testimony of David C. Ross and Mrs. Jacques Conrad, UNO; *Stackhouse v. Kendall*, #1851, 7 La. Ann. 670 (1851), testimony of James W. Field and William Clark, UNO; *Gottshalk v. DeLaRosa*, #2550, 6 La. 219 (1834), defendant's answer and testimony of John Hand, UNO; *Stewart v. Sowles and Hite*, #725, 3 La. Ann. 464 (1848), testimony of William Morgan and H. B. Kenner, UNO; *Slater v. Rutherford*, #1021, 4 La, Ann. 382 (1849), testimony of Hiram Goodrich and R. P. Wimoth, UNO.

57. *Foster v. Mish*, #6344, 15 La. Ann. 199 (1860), testimony of A. G. Collins, UNO; *Smith v. McDowell*, #4431, 3 Rob. 430 (1843), testimony of Richard Lands and John Hurkette, UNO; Bibb, *Narrative*, in Osofsky, ed., *Puttin' on Ole Massa*, 139.

58. Virginia Shelton to her brother, December 3, 1859, Campbell Papers, DU.

59. *Palmer v. Taylor*, #4755, 1 Rob. 412 (1842), testimony of William Dickson, UNO. See also *Freret v. Stackhouse*, unreported Louisiana Supreme Court case #5200 (1855), and W. H. Yos to Owen Cox, May 7, 1847, Owen Cox Papers, LSU.

60. Dew, *Bond of Iron*, 255; A. J. McElveen to Ziba Oakes, July 13, 1853, reproduced in Drago, ed., *Broke by the War*, 44; *Coulter v. Cresswell*, #2734, 7 La. Ann. 367 (1852), testimony of David Wise, UNO.

61. Weld, *A Vacation Tour*, 299.

62. Charles Ball, *Fifty Years a Slave, Or the Life of an American Slave* (New York, 1859), 35–36.

63. Ingraham, *The Southwest by a Yankee*, II, 135. See Lott, *Love and Theft*, and Eve Kosofsky Sedgwick, *Between Men: English Literature and Male Homosocial Desire* (New York: Columbia University Press, 1985).

6. Acts of Sale

1. *Daily Orleanian,* January 20, 1852, quoted in Robert C. Reinders, "Slavery in New Orleans in the Decade before the Civil War," *Mid-America,* 44 (1962), 213.

2. William Wells Brown, *Narrative of William Wells Brown: A Fugitive Slave, Written by Himself* [1847], in Gilbert Osofsky, ed., *Puttin' on Old Massa* (New York: Harper & Row, 1969), 194; J. D. Green, *Narrative of the Life of J. D. Green, a Runaway Slave from Kentucky, Containing an Account of His Three Escapes 1839, 1846, and 1848* (Huddersfield, U.K.: Henry Fielding, 1864), 29; John Brown, *Slave Life in Georgia: A Narrative of the Life, Sufferings, and Escapes of John Brown, a Fugitive Slave Now in England,* L. A. Chamerovzow, ed. (London, 1855; Savannah, GA: The Beehive Press, 1991), 21; Henry Bibb, *Narrative of the Life and Adventures of Henry Bibb, An American Slave Written by Himself* [1845] in Osofsky, ed., *Puttin' on Old Massa,* 115.

3. Charles Ball, *Fifty Years in Chains, or the Life of an American Slave* (1859; Detroit: Negro History Press, 1969), 45; John Parker, manuscript "Narrative," 30–31, Rankin-Parker Papers, DU; Bibb, *Narrative,* in Osofsky, ed., *Puttin' on Old Massa,* 139.

4. Josiah Henson, *An Autobiography of the Rev. Josiah Henson* (1881), in *Four Fugitive Slave Narratives* (Reading, MA: Addison-Wesley Publishing Company, 1969), 17; Solomon Northup, *Twelve Years a Slave* [1853], Joseph Logsdon and Sue Eakin, eds. (Baton Rouge: Louisiana State University Press, 1968), 56; Ball, *Fifty Years in Chains,* 70; William Wells Brown, *Clotel, or the President's Daughter: A Narrative of Slave Life in the United States* (1853; Upper Saddle River, NJ: Gregg Press, 1969), 208. For a general treatment of this theme, see Mia Bay, *The White Image in the Black Mind: African-American Ideas about White People, 1830–1925* (New York: Oxford University Press, 1999).

5. John Brown, *Slave Life in Georgia,* 90.

6. See "Slave Market," artist unknown, cover of Penguin edition of *Uncle Tom's Cabin* (New York, 1981); "The Auction," reproduced in John Blassingame, ed., *Slave Testimony: Two Centuries of Letters, Speeches, Interviews, and Autobiographies* (Baton Rouge: Louisiana State University Press, 1977), 500; Eyre Crowe, "A Slave Auction at Richmond, Virginia," *Illustrated London News,* September 27, 1856, and Eyre Crow, "A Slave Auction at the North of the Old Exchange, March 10, 1853," *Illustrated London News,* November 29, 1856, both of which are reproduced in Frederic Bancroft, *Slave Trading in the Old South* (Baltimore: J. H. Furst, 1931), frontispiece, 168.

7. William Chambers, "Journal," in Frederick Law Olmsted, *Cotton Kingdom, A Traveler's Observations on Cotton and Slavery in the American Slave States* (New York: Mason Brothers, 1862), II, 374; John Brown, *Slave Life in Georgia,* 106.

8. *Huntington v. Brown,* #15, 7 La. Ann. 48 (1865), testimony of Dennis Donovan, UNO.

9. Ball, *Fifty Years in Chains,* 70; Northup, *Twelve Years a Slave,* 53.

10. John Brown, *Slave Life in Georgia,* 106.

11. William Wells Brown, *Narrative*, in Osofsky, ed., *Puttin' on Ole Massa*, 203; *Hill v. White*, #4489, 11 La. Ann. 170 (1856), testimony of Thomas Frisby, UNO; Bibb, *Narrative*, in Osofsky, ed., *Puttin' on Ole Massa*, 110–111; John Brown, *Slave Life in Georgia*, 102–103, 105.

12. *Alexander v. Hundley*, #5276, 13 La. Ann. 327 (1858), testimony of John B. Womack, UNO; *Stewart v. Sowles*, #725, 3 La. Ann. 464 (1848), testimony of H. B. Kenner, D. W. Bowles, UNO.

13. *Succession of Cresswell*, unreported Louisiana Supreme Court Case #3521 (1853); *Lynch and Wiesman v. McRae*, unreported Louisiana Supreme Court Case #270 (1859), testimony of V. Hebert, O. B. Chapin, and C. M. Rutherford, UNO. On slavery in New Orleans and urban slavery generally, see Joseph Tregle, "Early New Orleans Society: A Reappraisal," *Journal of Southern History*, 18 (1952), 33; John W. Blassingame, *Black New Orleans, 1860–1880* (Chicago: University of Chicago Press, 1973), 8–10; Richard C. Wade, *Slavery in the Cities: The South, 1820–1860* (New York: Oxford University Press, 1964); Barbara Jeanne Fields, *Slavery and Freedom on the Middle Ground: Maryland during the Nineteenth Century* (New Haven: Yale University Press, 1985), 40–62.

14. *Hill v. White*, #4489, 11 La. Ann. 170 (1856), testimony of Thomas Frisby, UNO; Douglas Hamilton to William Hamilton, March 3, 1857, William Hamilton Papers, LSU.

15. John White, *Slave Record*, 1846, 1847, 1851, 1852, 1858, 1859, Chinn Collection, MHS.

16. *Buhler v. McHatton*, #3448, 9 La. Ann. 192 (1854), testimony of Henry Castle and A. Edgar, UNO.

17. *Eulalie and her Children v. Long and Mabry*, #3237, 9 La. Ann. 9 (1853), testimony of L. M. Foster, UNO.

18. John Brown, *Slave Life in Georgia*, 96; Northup, *Twelve Years a Slave*, 39; Bibb, *Narrative*, in Osofsky, ed., *Puttin' on Ole Massa*, 106, 112, [Aunt Sally], *Aunt Sally: Or the Cross the Way of Freedom* (Cincinnati: American Reform Tract & Book Society, 1859), 107.

19. Ball, *Fifty Years in Chains*, 71; Northup, *Twelve Years a Slave*, 53; John Brown, *Slave Life in Georgia*, 105; Bibb, *Narrative*, in Osofsky, ed., *Puttin' on Ole Massa*, 139–40; William Wells Brown, *Clotel*, 240.

20. Charles Weld, *A Vacation Tour in the United States and Canada* (London: Longman, Brown, Green, and Longman, 1855), 299–300.

21. Weld, *A Vacation Tour*, 300; Blassingame, ed., *Slave Testimony*, 388, 574, 580, 590, 635.

22. William Wells Brown, *Clotel*, 87–88; William Wells Brown, *My Southern Home* (Boston: A. G. Brown and Co., 1880), 111.

23. David Campbell to Mary Campbell, February 14, 1823, Campbell Papers, DU; Weld, *A Vacation Tour*, 301; Joseph Ingraham, *The Southwest by a Yankee* (New York: Harper Brothers, 1835), I, 195; unidentified woman quoted in B. A. Botkin, ed., *Lay My Burden Down: A Folk History of Slavery* (Chicago: University of Chicago Press, 1945), 157.

24. Louis Hughes, *Thirty Years a Slave: From Bondage to Freedom* (Milwaukee, 1897), 6; Ingraham, *The Southwest by a Yankee*, I, 192–198; James Redpath, *The Roving Editor, or Talks with Slaves in the Southern States* (New York, 1859), 253; C. S., Magoun, "Fatal Case of Puerperal Fever, Autopsy, &c.," *New Orleans Medical Journal*, 1 (1845), 434.

25. James Redpath, *The Roving Editor*, 253; W. H. Yos to Owen Cox, May 7, 1847, Owen Cox Papers, LSU.

26. Frederick Douglass, *Narrative of the Life of Frederick Douglass an American Slave, Written by Himself* [1845] (Garden City, NY: Dolphin Books, 1963), 91; Ball, *Fifty Years in Chains*, 67, 69–70; *Executors of Haggerty v. Powell*, #2215, 6 La. Ann. 533 (1851), testimony of Hoyt, UNO; *New Orleans Canal and Gas Company v. Botts*, #4545, 9 Rob. 305 (1844), testimony of D. S. Rogers, UNO. Ingraham, *The Southwest by a Yankee*, II, 195; Bibb, *Narrative*, in Osofsky, ed., *Puttin' on Ole Massa*, 114.

27. David Campbell to Mary Campbell, February 14, 1823, Campbell Papers, DU.

28. John Knight to William Beall, March 18, 1844, John Knight Papers, RASP.

29. Bibb, *Narrative*, in Osofsky, ed., *Puttin' on Ole Massa*, 114.

30. Northup, *Twelve Years a Slave*, 121.

31. Interview with L. M. Mills reproduced in Blassingame, ed., *Slave Testimony*, 503.

32. Bibb, *Narrative*, in Osofsky, ed., *Puttin' on Ole Massa*, 118. For other accounts of slaves being sent out to sell themselves, see William Wells Brown, *Narrative*, in Osofsky, ed., *Puttin' on Ole Massa*, 203; Blassingame, ed., *Slave Testimony*, 730; and *Executors of Haggerty v. Powell*, #2215, 6 La. Ann. 533 (1851), UNO.

33. Interview with Henry Thomas in Benjamin Drew, ed., *The Refugee: A Northside View of Slavery* (1846), in *Four Fugitive Slave Narratives* (Reading, MA: Addison-Wesley Publishing Company, 1969), 212; Alex Fitzhugh to R. H. Dickinson, February 24, 1846, quoted in Michael Tadman, *Speculators and Slaves: Masters, Traders, and Slaves in the Old South* (Madison: University of Wisconsin Press, 1989), 168. See Nell Irvin Painter, "Soul Murder and Slavery: Toward a Fully-Loaded Cost Accounting," in Linda Kerber, Alice Kessler-Harris, and Kathryn Kish Sklar, eds., *United States History as Women's History* (Chapel Hill: University of North Carolina Press, 1995), 125–146.

34. John Brown, *Slave Life in Georgia*, 98, 105.

35. Parker, "Narrative," 31.

36. Tadman, *Speculators and Slaves*, 185–186; Tyre Glen to Isaac Jarratt, January 12, 1835, Jarratt/Puryear Papers, RASP; A. J. McElveen to Ziba Oakes, February 7, 1854, quoted in Edmund Drago, ed., *Broke by the War: Letters of a Slave Trader* (Columbia, S.C.: University of South Carolina Press, 1991), 71.

37. James Redpath, *The Roving Editor*, 253; W. H. Yos to Owen Cox, May 7, 1847, Owen Cox Papers, LSU.

38. Phillip Thomas to William A. J. Finney, November 8, 1859, William A. J. Finney Papers, RASP; A. J. McElveen to Ziba Oakes, October 21, 1856, in Drago,

ed., *Broke by the War*, 133–135; J. E. Carson to William Weaver, March 12, 1859, quoted in Charles Dew, *Bond of Iron: Master and Slave at Buffalo Forge* (New York: W. W. Norton & Company, 1994), 254.

39. John Knight to William Beall, June 30, 1844, John Knight Papers, RASP.

40. Moses Roper, *A Narrative of the Adventures and Escape of Moses Roper from American Slavery* (1838; New York: Negro Universities Press, 1970), 71–72; *Perche v. L'Admirault*, #4613, 1 Rob, 365 (1842), testimony of Charles Poydras, UNO; *Whann v. Hufty*, #4982, 12 La. Ann. 280 (1857), decision of the Supreme Court, UNO; *Nixon v. Boazman*, #3485, 11 La. Ann. 750 (1856), testimony of Mrs. Maria Williams, UNO.

41. Ingraham, *The Southwest by a Yankee*, II, 197; Northup, *Twelve Years a Slave*, 57; Green, *Narrative*, 29.

42. *Hill v. White*, #4489, 11 La. Ann. 170 (1856), testimony of Thomas Frisby, UNO; *Roquest v. Boutin*, #5446, 14 La. Ann. 44 (1858), testimony of J. A. Bonneval, UNO; Thomas Butler to Ann Butler, April 30, 1830, Thomas Butler Papers, LSU; *Lemos v. Daubert*, 8 Rob. 224 #4190 (La. 1844), testimony of Dr. Allarsi, UNO. In general for trial see W. H. Yos to Owen Cox, May 7, 1847, Owen Cox Papers, LSU; *Matthews v. Pascal's Executors*, #3287, 13 La. 53 (1839), testimony of Andrew Collins, UNO; *Bloom v. Beebe*, #5921, 15 La. Ann. 65 (1860), defendant's answer, UNO; *Cornish, f.w.c. v. Shelton*, #4642, 12 La. Ann. 415 (1851), testimony of Mrs. Perine Weeks, f.w.c., UNO; *Cohn v. Costa*, #6252, 15 La. Ann. 612 (1860), defendant's answer, UNO; *Hepp v. Parker*, #1788, 8 Mart (N. S.) 473 (1830), testimony of L. A. Gaiennie, UNO; *White v. Slatter*, #943, 5 La. Ann. 27 (1849), testimony of James F. Blakeny, UNO.

43. Washington and Jackson & Co. to Daniel Turnbull, October 13, 24, 28, 31, 1859, Turnbull-Bowman Family Papers, LSU; *Executors of Haggerty v. Powell*, #2215, 6 La. Ann. 533 (1851), testimony of P. N. Brent, UNO.

44. Sarah Bradford, *Scenes in the Life of Harriet Tubman* (Auburn, NY, 1869), 13.

45. *Stoppenhagen v. Verdelet*, #3271, 10 La. Ann. 263 (1855), testimony of Sargent Pratt and Michael M. Miller, UNO; *Morrison v. White*, #442, 16 La. Ann. 100 (1861), testimony of Andre L. Hutt, UNO. On the Morrison case, see Walter Johnson, "Slavery, Whiteness, and the Market: The Strange Story of Alexina Morrison," *Journal of American History* (forthcoming March 2000).

46. On warranty law in general, see Andrew Fede, "Legal Protection for Slave Buyers in the U.S. South: A Caveat Concerning *Caveat Emptor*," *American Journal of Legal History*, 31 (1987), 322–358; Judith Kelleher Schafer, *Slavery, The Civil Law, and the Supreme Court of Louisiana* (Baton Rouge: Louisiana State University Press, 1994), 127–179; Thomas D. Morris, *Southern Slavery and the Law, 1619–1850* (Chapel Hill: University of North Carolina Press, 1996), 104–113.

47. *Banks v. Botts*, #2095, 10 La. 42 (1836), testimony of C. Rockwood, UNO; Robert S. Mills to James Henry, July 1, 1844, Robert S. Mills Letterbook, Robert S. Mills Papers, DU; *Matthews v. Pascal's Executors*, #3287, 13 La. 52 (1939), testimony of Andrew Collins, UNO.

48. A. J. McElveen to Ziba Oakes, October 27, 1853, May 13, 1854, in Drago,

ed., *Broke by the War*, 54, 80 (see also 82, 84, 87); *Roca v. Slawson*, #1781, 5 La. Ann. 708 (1850), testimony of L. E. Hooper, UNO; *Chretien v. Thread*, #612, 11 Mart. (O. S.) 11 (1822), decision of the lower court, UNO.

49. Tyre Glen to Isaac Jarratt, February 11, March 4, 1832, Jarratt/Puryear Papers, RASP; J. J. Toler to Ferguson, December 27, 1858, quoted in Tadman, *Speculators and Slaves*, 185.

50. *Caretta v. Lopez*, #6028, 15 La. Ann. 64 (1860), testimony of Manuel Lopez, UNO; *Nixon v. Boazman and Bushy*, #3485, 11 La. Ann. 750 (1856), testimony of Joseph Beard, UNO; *Brabo v. Martin*, #2458, 5 La. 275 (1833), testimony of J. J. Simon, UNO. For law made out of the imagined intentions of slaves see Walter Johnson, "Inconsistency, Contradiction, and Complete Confusion: The Everyday Life of the Law of Slavery," *Law and Social Inquiry*, 22 (1997), 423–425; Ariela Gross, "Pandora's Box: Slave Character on Trial in the Antebellum Deep South," *Yale Journal of Law and the Humanities*, 7 (1995), 308–309. Gross argues that the courts of Louisiana were alone among southern courts in admitting evidence about slaves' intentions.

51. *Fox v. Walsh*, #4733, 5 Rob. 222 (1843), testimony of John Lyall, UNO; John Brown, *Slave Life in Georgia*, 104; Bibb, *Narrative*, in Osofsky, ed., *Puttin' on Ole Massa*, 118.

52. An argument most cogently put in Eugene D. Genovese, *Roll, Jordan, Roll: The World the Slaves Made* (New York: Vintage, 1974), esp. 597–598.

53. The list, which includes the most challenging and exciting work done in the humanities in the last two decades, begins with Edward Said's *Orientalism* (New York: Vintage, 1978).

7. Life in the Shadow of the Slave Market

1. See, for instance, St. Louis *Missouri Democrat*, February 1, 1855; Memphis *Eagle and Enquirer*, April 20, 1857; Montgomery *Confederation*, December 8, 1859; New Orleans *Picayune*, supplement, January 4, 1860; *Lexington Kentucky Statesman*, January 13, 1860, all reproduced in Frederic Bancroft, *Slave-Trading in the Old South* (Baltimore: J. H. Furst & Co., 1931).

2. John Knight to William Beall, August 12, 1844, John Knight Papers, RASP; *Palmer v. Taylor*, #4755, 1 Rob. 412 (La. 1842), testimony of Dr. Skipwith, UNO.

3. Charles Ball, *Fifty Years in Chains; or, The Life of an American Slave* (New York: Dayton, 1859), 105. Solomon Northup, *Twelve Years a Slave*, Sue Eakin and Joseph Logsdon, eds. (Baton Rouge: Louisiana State University Press, 1968), 62–68.

4. Henry Bibb, *Narrative of the Life and Adventures of Henry Bibb, an American Slave, Written by Himself* (1845), in Gilbert Osofsky, ed., *Puttin' on Ole Massa* (New York: Harper & Row, 1969), 119; Ball, *Fifty Years in Chains*, 105, 111–118. See also John Brown, *Slave Life in Georgia: A Narrative of the Life, Sufferings, and Escape of John Brown, a Fugitive Slave*, L. A. Chamerovzow, ed. (London, 1855; Savannah, GA: The Beehive Press, 1991), 20.

5. On the unfamiliarity of the work that upper-South slaves had to do in the

lower South, see Steven F. Miller, "Plantation Labor Organization and Slave Life on the Cotton Frontier: The Alabama-Mississippi Black Belt, 1815–1840," in Ira Berlin and Philip Morgan, eds., *Cultivation and Culture: Labor and the Shaping of Slave Life in the Americas* (Charlottesville: University Press of Virginia, 1993), 155–169.

6. Louis Hughes, *Thirty Years a Slave: From Bondage to Freedom* (Milwaukee: Southside Printing Co., 1899), 17–19, 36–37; Moses Grandy, *Narrative of the Life of Moses Grandy, Late a Slave in the United States of America* (Boston, 1847), 7.

7. See, for example, Ball, *Fifty Years in Chains*, 147; T. H. Breen, *Tobacco Culture: The Mentality of the Great Tidewater Planters on the Eve of Revolution* (Princeton, NJ: Princeton University Press, 1985), 46–58; *Pilié v. Ferriere*, #1724, 7 Mart. (N.S.) 648, testimony of L. G. Heligsberg and Madame Bertier, UNO.

8. Northup, *Twelve Years a Slave*, 134–135.

9. See Elaine Scarry, *The Body in Pain: The Making and Unmaking of the World* (New York: Oxford University Press, 1985).

10. *Hewes v. Baron*, #1641, 7 Mart. (N.S.) 134 (1828), testimony of Mrs. Ann Hewes, UNO; *Roquest v. Boutin*, #5446, La. Ann. 44 (1858), testimony of Mrs. William Duffy, Anna Ratta, and Catherine Paul, UNO; *Palmer v. Taylor*, #4755, 1 Rob. 412 (La. 1842), testimony of Dr. Skipwith, UNO; *White v. Guyot*, #5086, 4 Rob. 108 (1843), testimony of Dr. Dancreau, UNO; *Executors of Haggerty v. Powell*, #2215, 6 La. Ann. 533 (1851), testimony of James Todd, UNO.

11. For the frequency of runaway advertisements noting the slaves' out-of-state origin as an indicator of the extent of the domestic slave trade see Steven Deyle, "The Domestic Slave Trade in America," unpublished Ph.D. dissertation, Columbia University, 1995, 64.

12. *Dunbar v. Skillman*, #1575, 6 Mart. (N.S.) 539 (La. 1828), testimony of Robert Nelson, UNO; *Pilié v. Ferriere*, #1724, 7 Mart. (N.S.) 648, testimony of Mary Ann Poyfarre and Celeste, UNO; *Walker v. Cucullu*, #326, 18 La. Ann. 246 (1866), plaintiff's petition, testimony of J. Ernest Cucullu, UNO; *Peyroux v. Chayat (widow)*, #3432, 13 La. 459 (1839), testimony of Jacques Matthieu, UNO. See also *Zanico v. Habine*, #228 5 Mart (O.S.) 372 (1818), UNO.

13. *Ogden v. Michel*, #5127, 4 Rob. 154 (1839), testimony of Absolem Timms, UNO; *Fortier v. LaBranche*, #3289, 13 La. 355 (1839), testimony of Bertrand Barre, UNO; *Winn v. Twogood*, #2920, 9 La. 422 (1836), testimony of Robert A. Wright, UNO; Bibb, *Narrative*, in Osofsky, ed., *Puttin' on Ole Massa*; Ball, *Fifty Years in Chains;* John Brown, *Slave Life in Georgia; Walker v. Haynes*, #6606, 15 La. Ann. 640, Monroe (1860), testimony of J. D. Hair and H. L. Wilcox, UNO; *Fazende v. Hagan*, 9 Rob. 306 #4824 (La. 1844), testimony of B. A. Fortier, UNO.

14. *Chretien v. Thread*, #612, 11 Mart. (O.S.) 11 (1822), testimony of Robert Fox, UNO; *Cohn v. Costa*, #6252, 15 La. Ann. 612 (1860), testimony of Celeste DeRosemon, UNO.

15. See, especially, Norrece T. Jones, Jr., *Born a Child of Freedom, Yet a Slave: Mechanisms of Control and Strategies of Resistance in Antebellum South Carolina* (Hanover, N.H.: University Press of New England, 1990), and Deborah Gray White,

Ar'n't I a Woman? Female Slaves in the Plantation South (New York: W. W. Norton & Co., 1985). On time as a dimension of the contest between master and slave, see Mark H. Smith, "Old South Time in Comparative Perspective," *American Historical Review*, 101 (1996), 1432–1469, and Walter Johnson, "Writing the History of the Atlantic Slave Trade in the Age of Global Capital: Some Speculations on Time, Temporality, and Atlantic Slavery," in *Amerikastudien/American Studies* (forthcoming).

16. Ann Patton Malone, *Sweet Chariot: Slave Family and Household Structure in Nineteenth-Century Louisiana* (Chapel Hill: University of North Carolina Press, 1992), 13–35, 36–40; Brenda E. Stevenson, *Life in Black and White: Family and Community in the Slave South* (New York: Oxford University Press, 1996), 206–257.

17. John Knight to William Beall, July 7, 1844, John Knight Papers, RASP. See also *Stewart v. Sowles*, #725, 3 La. Ann. 464 (1848), testimony of Thomas Boylan, UNO: "her husband had a boy named Isaac but the boys called him Scott."

18. Northup, *Twelve Years a Slave*, 140–143.

19. *Calvitt v. Haynes*, #108, 8 Mart. (O.S.) 712 (1820), testimony of Mrs. Calvitt, UNO.

20. *Zimmer v. Thompson*, #3238, 13 La. 22 (1834), testimony of Estell Medard, UNO.

21. Ball, *Fifty Years in Chains*, 131–134, 147.

22. See Paul Gilroy, *The Black Atlantic: Modernity and Double Consciousness* (Cambridge, MA: Harvard University Press, 1992).

23. Samuel A. Cartwright, "Directions for Treatment of Negroes," copy dated June 22, 1844, and transcribed by John Knight on June 27, 1844, John Knight Papers, RASP.

24. Northup, *Twelve Years a Slave*, 135; *Dunbar v. Skillman*, #1575, 6 Mart. (N.S.) 539 (La. 1828), testimony of George Long, UNO.

25. *Alexander v. Hundley*, #5276, 13 La. Ann. 327 (1858), testimony of Franklin Matthews, George Branton, and James Sandige, UNO. See also *Fox v. Walsh*, #4733, 5 Rob. 222 (1843), testimony of George Allen, UNO and *Virgin v. Dawson*, #854 (Monroe), 15 La. Ann. 532 (1860), testimony of William Hampton, UNO. For the frequency of discussion of slave prices in antebellum newspapers, see Deyle, "The Domestic Slave Trade in America," 72–73.

26. For relations between white men constructed over the bodies of sexual and racial others see Eve Kosofsky Sedgwick, *Between Men: English Literature and Homosocial Desire* (New York: Columbia University Press, 1985); Eric Lott, *Love and Theft: Blackface Minstrelsy and the American Working Class* (New York: Oxford University Press, 1995).

27. Northup, *Twelve Years a Slave*, 66.

28. Hughes, *Thirty Years a Slave*, 13.

29. For the legal liability of slaveholders for crimes committed by their slaves see Thomas D. Morris, *Southern Slavery and the Law, 1619–1860* (Chapel Hill: University of North Carolina Press, 1996), 249–261.

30. *Bloom v. Beebe*, #5921, 15 La. Ann. 65 (1860), testimony of Henry Beebe,

UNO; *Fox v. Walsh*, #4733, 5 Rob. 222 (1843), testimony of George Allen, UNO; Ball, *Fifty Years in Chains*, 108.

31. *Marin v. Michel*, unreported Louisiana Supreme Court case #5298 (1858), testimony of Charles Bienvenu and Louis Caretta, UNO; Ogden v. Michel, #5127, 4 Rob. 154 (1839), testimony of Absolem Timms, UNO; *Stillwell v. Slatter*, unreported Louisiana Supreme Court case #4845 (1843), testimony of Alexander English, UNO; *Bruce v. Stone and Taylor*, #2389, 5 La. 1 (1832), testimony of Robert Montgomery, UNO; *Alexander v. Hundley*, #5276, 13 La. Ann. 327 (1858), testimony of T. R. Davis, UNO. I have regularized the quotation from Montgomery.

32. *Fellowes et al. v. Young et al.*, #3951, 10 La. Ann. 267 (1855), testimony of Dr. A. G. Trask, UNO; *Dixon v. Chadwick*, #4388, 11 La. Ann. 215 (1856), testimony of Edward Lennox, UNO; *Palmer v. Taylor*, #4755, 1 Rob. 412 (La. 1842), testimony of Dr. Skipwith, UNO.

33. John Knight to William Beall, June 24, 30, and July 7, 1844, John Knight Papers, RASP.

34. John Knight to William Beall, August 12, 1844, November 10, 1844, May 7, 1845, May 22, 1845, John Knight Papers, RASP; Act of Sale of Beverly Plantation and sixty-six slaves to John N. Helen, [1845], John Knight Papers, RASP.

35. J. F. Smith to James Tutt, April 29, 1845, James Tutt Papers, DU; *Chretien v. Thread*, #612, 11 Mart. (O.S.) 11 (1822), testimony of Samuel Springs and judgment of the lower court, UNO; *Ogden v. Michel*, #5127, 4 Rob. 154 (1839), testimony of Amos Adams, UNO; *Buhler v. McHatton*, #3448, 9 La. Ann. 192 (1854), testimony of Dr. David Devall, UNO; *Stillwell v. Slatter*, unreported Louisiana Supreme Court case #4845 (1843), testimony of L. B. Wright, UNO; *Coulter v. Cresswell*, #2734, 7 La. Ann. 367 (1852), testimony of S. B. Funnel, UNO; *Stewart v. Sowles*, #725, 3 La. Ann. 464 (1848), testimony of Theophilus Freeman, UNO.

36. See Margaret Jane Radin, "Property and Personhood," *Stanford Law Review*, 34 (1982), 957–1015.

37. On slaves stealing themselves see Judith Kelleher Schafer, *Slavery, the Civil Law, and the Supreme Court of Louisiana* (Baton Rouge: Louisiana State University Press, 1994), 90–126, and *Winn v. Twogood*, #2920, 9 La. 422 (1836), testimony of Robert A. Wright, UNO.

38. *Winfield v. Little*, #170 (Alexandria), 7 La. Ann. 536 (1853), testimony of J. A. Wise, UNO; *Cohn v. Costa*, #6252, 15 La. Ann. 612 (1860), testimony of Celeste DeRosemon, UNO; *Bertholi v. Deverge*, #4521, 4 Rob. 431 (1843), testimony of Catherin Bayou, UNO; *White v. Hill*, #3958, 10 La. Ann. 189 (1855), testimony of T. R. Harvey, UNO; *Kock v. Slatter*, #1748, 5 La. Ann. 734 (1850), testimony of F. W. Pike, UNO; *Shaffer v. Green and White*, unreported Louisiana Supreme Court case #601 (1848), testimony of Chauncey Lewis, UNO.

39. *Kock v. Slatter*, #1748, 5 La. Ann 734 (1850), questions to F. W. Pike, UNO; *Slater v. Rutherford*, #1021, 4 La. Ann. 382 (1849), testimony of S. S. Rice, UNO; *McDermott v. Cannon*, #5706, 14 La. Ann. 313 (1859), testimony of F. B. Withers, UNO; *Bloom v. Beebe*, #5921, 15 La. Ann. 65 (1860), testimony of Catherine and L. Klopman, UNO.

40. Lewis Clarke, speech published in the *National Anti-Slavery Standard*, October 27, 1842, and reproduced in John Blassingame, ed., *Slave Testimony: Two Centuries of Letters, Speeches, Interviews, and Autobiographies* (Baton Rouge: Louisiana State University Press, 1977), 163.

41. See Eugene D. Genovese, *Roll Jordan, Roll: The World the Slaves Made* (New York: Vintage Books, 1974).

42. *Donnet v. Ramsay*, #1468, 6 Mart. (N.S.) 129 (1827), UNO; *Slatter v. Rutherford*, #1021, 4 La. Ann. 382 (1849), testimony of Robert R. Robinson, UNO; *Walker v. Haynes*, #6606, 15 La. Ann 640 (1860), testimony of H. L. Wilcox, UNO.

43. William D. Henning, ed., *A Digest of the Reported Decisions of the Superior Court of the Late Territory of Orleans, the Late Court of Errors and Appeals, and the Supreme Court of the State of Louisiana* (Boston, 1852), 1411; for the best treatment of the history of redhibition law, see Schafer, *Slavery, the Civil Law, and the Supreme Court of Louisiana*, 90–179; for warranty law generally, see Ariela Gross, "Pandora's Box: Slave Character on Trial in the Antebellum Deep South," *Yale Journal of Law and the Humanities*, 7 (1995), 267–316, and Morris, *Southern Slavery and the Law*, 102–131.

44. *White v. Guyot*, #5086, 4 Rob. 108 (1843), defendant's response, UNO; *Walker v. Cucullu*, #326, 18 La. Ann. 246 (1866), defendent's response, UNO; *Bruce v. Stowe and Taylor*, #2389, 5 La. 1 (1832), plaintiff's questions, UNO; *White v. Hill*, #3958, 10 La. Ann. 189 (1855), testimony of Edward DeLong, UNO; *Calvitt v. Haynes*, #108, 8 Mart. (O.S.) 712 (1820), testimony of Lett, UNO; *Bocod v. Jacobs*, #2101, 2 La. 408 (1831), testimony of Adams, UNO.

45. Kenneth Greenberg, *Honor and Slavery: Lies, Duels, Noses, Masks, Dressing as a Woman, Gifts, Strangers, Humanitarianism, Death, Slave Rebellions, The Proslavery Argument, Baseball, Hunting, and Gambling in the Old South* (Princeton: Princeton University Press, 1996), 3–23.

46. *Lemos v. Daubert*, #4198, 8 Rob. 224 (La. 1844), testimony of Dr. Allarsi, UNO; *White v. Guyot*, #5086, 4 Rob. 108 (1843), testimony of Dr. Dancreau, UNO; *Pilié v. Ferriere*, #1724, 7 Mart. (N.S.) 648 (La. 1829), testimony of Mary Ann Poyfarre and Celeste, UNO; *Walker v. Cucullu*, #326, 18 La. Ann. 246 (1866), testimony of Jean Landier, UNO. On all of this see Gross, "Pandora's Box," 267–316; Walter Johnson, "Inconsistency, Contradiction, and Complete Confusion: The Everyday Life of the Law of Slavery," *Law and Social Inquiry*, 22 (1997), 423–425.

47. *Pilié v. Ferriere*, #1724, 7 Mart. (N.S.) 648 (La. 1829), testimony of Mary Ann Poyfarre and Celeste, UNO; *Walker v. Cucullu*, #326, 18 La. Ann. 246 (1866), testimony of Marc Saupy, UNO; *Slater v. Rutherford*, #1021, 4 La. Ann. 382 (1849), testimony of S. S. Rice, UNO.

48. See, for example, *Hooper v. Owens*, #2405, 7 La. Ann. 206 (1852), testimony of George Dolinger, UNO; *Pilié v. Ferriere*, #1724, 7 Mart. (N.S.) 648 (La. 1829), testimony of Alfred Passement, UNO; *Shaffer v. Green and White*, unreported Louisiana Supreme Court case #601 (1848), testimony of John Wood, UNO; *Slater v. Rutherford*, #1021, 4 La. Ann. 382 (1849), testimony of Dr. William Mills, UNO;

Kock v. Slatter, #1748, 5 La. Ann. 734 (1850), testimony of William Dickson, Dr. Sabin Martin, and Dr. P. W. Johnson, UNO.

49. My forthcoming article, "Southern Medical Science and Slavery," will treat physicians' role as "the ultimate slave buyer" in these cases.

50. *Hewes v. Baron,* #1641, 7 Mart (N.S.) 134 (1828), testimony of Dr. Perlee, UNO; see also *Zimmer v. Thompson,* #3238, 13 La. 22 (1839), testimony of Dr. Abuzzy, UNO. For all that follows see Gross, "Pandora's Box," and Johnson, "Inconsistency, Contradiction, and Complete Confusion," 423–425.

51. John Knight to William Beall, June 30, 1844, RASP; *Palmer v. Taylor,* #4755, 1 Rob. 412 (La. 1842), testimony of Dr. Skipwith, UNO.

52. *George v. Greenwood,* #3687, 11 La. Ann. 299 (1856), testimony of John M. Crawford, UNO. See Gross, "Pandora's Box," 310–314, where it is argued that such testimony was often contested on the grounds of its origin, but was generally admitted.

53. *Nixon v. Boazman and Bushy,* #3485, 11 La. Ann. 750 (1856), testimony of Joseph Beard, UNO; *Fortier v. LaBranche,* #3289, 13 La. 355 (1839), testimony of Michael Perry, UNO. According to Gross ("Pandora's Box," 303), testimony about slaves' intentions was generally barred in all southern states except for Lousiana.

54. *Kock v. Slatter,* #1748, 5 La. Ann. 734 (1850), testimony of Francis Jump and questions (reconstructed through the answers) to F. W. Pike, UNO; *Walker v. Cucullu,* #326, 18 La. 246 (1866), testimony of J. Ernest Cucullu, UNO.

55. *Dunbar v. Skillman,* #1575, 6 Mart. (N.S.) 539 (La. 1828), testimony of Stephen Jones, UNO.

Epilogue: Southern History and the Slave Trade

1. Frederic Bancroft, *Slave Trading in the Old South* (Baltimore: J. H. Furst and Company, 1931); Allan Kulikoff, *The Agrarian Origins of American Capitalism* (Charlottesville: University Press of Virginia, 1992), 226–269; Michael Tadman, *Speculators and Slaves: Masters, Traders, and Slaves in the Old South* (Madison: University of Wisconsin Press, 1989); Stephen A. Deyle, "The Domestic Slave Trade in America," unpublished Ph.D. dissertation, Columbia University, 1995.

2. Herbert G. Gutman, *The Black Family in Slavery and Freedom, 1750–1925* (New York: Vintage, 1976); Anne Patton Malone, *Sweet Chariot: Slave Family and Household Structure in Nineteenth-Century Louisiana* (Chapel Hill: University of North Carolina Press, 1992); Brenda E. Stevenson, *Life in Black and White: Family and Community in the Slave South* (New York: Oxford University Press, 1996).

3. William H. Freehling, *The Road to Disunion: Secessionists at Bay, 1776–1854* (New York: Oxford University Press, 1990); Robert W. Fogel, *Without Consent or Contract: The Rise and Fall of American Slavery* (New York: W. W. Norton & Co., 1989); Stephen Deyle, "The Domestic Slave Trade in America," 80–98.

4. James Oakes, *The Ruling Race: A History of American Slaveholders* (New York: Vintage Books, 1982); James Oakes, *Slavery and Freedom: An Interpretation of the Old South* (New York: Alfred A. Knopf, 1990); John Ashworth, *Slavery, Capitalism, and*

Politics in the Antebellum Republic, I: Commerce and Compromise, 1820–1850 (Cambridge: Cambridge University Press, 1995), 262–279, quotation on 268–269.

5. The idea that the slaveholding regime was defined by an internal dynamic which pushed it westward is shared by historians as different as Eugene D. Genovese in *The Political Economy of Slavery: Studies in the Economy and Society of the Slave South* (New York: Vintage, 1967) and James Oakes in *The Ruling Race*. For the importance of "the West" in defining the conflict between "the North" and "the South" see Barrington Moore, "The Last Capitalist Revolution," in his *The Social Origins of Dictatorship and Democracy: Lord and Peasant in the Making of the Modern World* (Boston: Beacon Press, 1966), 111–155; Eric Foner, *Free Soil, Free Labor, Free Men: The Ideology of the Republican Party before the Civil War* (New York: Oxford, 1970); and James M. McPherson, *Battle Cry of Freedom: The Civil War Era* (New York: Oxford University Press, 1988), esp. 47–169.

6. Theodore Dwight Weld, *American Slavery as It Is: Testimony of a Thousand Witnesses* (New York: American Anti-Slavery Society, 1839). For this strain of antislavery thinking, see Elizabeth B. Clark, "'The Sacred Rights of the Weak': Pain, Sympathy, and the Culture of Individual Rights in Antebellum America," *Journal of American History*, 82 (1995), 463–493; for the abolitionist investment in slaves' mortified bodies, see Saidiya V. Hartman, *Scenes of Subjection: Terror, Slavery, and Self-Making in the Nineteenth-Century America* (New York: Oxford University Press, 1997).

7. James W. C. Pennington, *The Fugitive Blacksmith; or, Events in the History of James W. C. Pennington* (1849; Westport, CT: Negro Universities Press, 1971), iv–vii.

8. Charles Ball, *Slavery in the United States: A Narrative of the Life and Adventures of Charles Ball, a Black Man who Lived Forty Years in Maryland, South Carolina, and Georgia, as a Slave* (New York: J. S Taylor, 1837); William Wells Brown, *Narrative of William Wells Brown: A Fugitive Slave, Written by Himself* (1847), in Gilbert Osofsky, ed., *Puttin' on Ole Massa* (New York: Harper & Row, 1969); Solomon Northup, *Twelve Years a Slave*, Joseph Logsdon and Sue Eakin, eds. (Baton Rouge: Louisiana State University Press, 1968); John Brown, *Slave Life in Georgia: A Narrative of the Life of John Brown*, L. A. Chamerovzow, ed. (London, 1855; Savannah, GA: The Beehive Press, 1991); Louis Hughes, *Thirty Years a Slave: From Bondage to Freedom* (Milwaukee: Southside Printing Company, 1897); Henry Bibb, *Narrative of the Life and Adventures of Henry Bibb, An American Slave, Written by Himself* [1845], in Osofsky, ed., *Puttin' on Ole Massa*, 171.

9. *The Liberator*; Fredrika Bremer, *The Homes of the New World*, 2 vols., Mary Howitt, trans. (New York: Harper Brothers, 1853); Charles Richard Weld, *A Vacation Tour in the United States and Canada* (London: Longman, Brown, Green, and Longman, 1855); Frederick Law Olmsted, *Cotton Kingdom: A Traveler's Observations on Cotton and Slavery in the American Slave States*, 2 vols. (New York: Mason Brothers, 1862); Harriet Beecher Stowe, *Uncle Tom's Cabin, or, Life Among the Lowly* (London: Ingram, Cooke, 1852).

10. Genovese, *Roll, Jordan, Roll*, 97–112; James L. *Roark, Masters Without Slaves:*

The Southern Planters in the Civil War and Reconstruction (New York: W. W. Norton & Co., 1977); Nell Irvin Painter, Exodusters: Black Migration to Kansas after Reconstruction (New York: Alfred A. Knopf, 1977); Leon Litwack, Been in the Storm So Long: The Aftermath of Slavery (New York: Alfred A. Knopf, 1979); Jacqueline Jones, Labor of Love, Labor of Sorrow: Black Women, Work, and the Family from Slavery to the Present (New York: Basic Books, 1985); Julie Saville, The Work of Reconstruction: From Slave to Wage Laborer in South Carolina (Cambridge: Cambridge University Press, 1994), Leslie A. Schwalm, A Hard Fight for We: Women's Transition from Slavery to Freedom in South Carolina (Urbana: University of Illinois Press, 1997); Tera W. Hunter, To 'Joy my Freedom: Southern Black Women's Lives and Labors after the Civil War (Cambridge: Harvard University Press, 1997); Steven Kantrowitz, Ben Tillman and the Reconstruction of White Supremacy (Chapel Hill: University of North Carolina Press, forthcoming).

ACKNOWLEDGMENTS

A teacher of mine once told me that she always begins new books by reading the acknowledgments. That way, she said, you can get a read on authors, find out where they're coming from, who helped them out, who their friends are. If that's right, then I'm in good shape because I've been very lucky in the help I've had along the way.

Jan Dizard, Margaret Hunt, Kevin Sweeney, Henry Steele Commager, and especially Robert Gross all helped me get a start in scholarship. John Murrin, Sean Wilentz, James McPherson, Peter Lake, and especially Dirk Hartog and Dan Rodgers asked me the questions I am still trying to answer. My greatest intellectual debt is to Nell Painter; she is a great teacher, a wise advisor, and a lasting friend.

Friends in Louisiana kept me company when the archives were closed. Special thanks to Bo Conn, Richard Kilbourne, Jr., Reid Mitchell, Paul Paskoff, and Joseph Tregle. John and Catherine Malinin-Dunn, Suzanne Marchand and Victor Stater, and, incomparably, John Hazlett and Morrey McElroy opened their houses to me and provided examples of what friendship can be. Jonathan Pritchett and especially Judith Schafer were generous with their own research and ideas as I began exploring a topic that they had been working on for years. And archivists and assistants at the New Orleans Public Library, the Orleans Parish Notarial Archives, The Historic New Orleans Collection, the Supreme Court of Louisiana Collection at the University of New Orleans, the Howard-Tilton Memorial Library at Tulane, the Lower Mississippi Valley Collection at LSU, the Western Historical Collection at the University of Missouri, the Missouri Historical Society in St. Louis, the Southern Historical Collection at UNC, and the Perkins Library at Duke were unfailingly knowledgeable and helpful. Special thanks to Sally Reeves, Irene Wainwright, Greg

Osborne, Wayne Everard, and above all Marie Windell, who made every day I spent at UNO a joy.

I am grateful to the Association of Princeton Graduate Alumni, the Woodrow Wilson Foundation, the Mellon Foundation, and the Dean's office at NYU for the support I've needed to finish the book. Thanks also to participants in the Faculty Resource Network's seminars at NYU (particularly Larry Watson and David Organ) and to the folks at the Center for the Humanities at Wesleyan University (especially Betsy Traube, Henry Abelove, Claire Potter, Christina Crosby, Cameron McFarlane, and the incandescent Janet Jakobsen) for friendship and intellectual companionship.

Many people have read parts of the manuscript or provided other material support. I am grateful to Kathy Baima, Jane Baun, Alastair Bellany, Karin Burrell, Vernon Burton, Joyce Chaplin, Marcus Daniel, Vince DiGirolamo, Lisa Duggan, Jon Earle, Antonio Feros, Debbie Hall, Devin Hall, John Giggie, Sally Gordon, Brad Gregory, Ariela Gross, Cheryl Hicks, Yanni Kotsonis, Barbara Krauthamer, Karen Kupperman, Eric Love, Ben Maddox, Jonathan Martin, April Masten, Michael Millender, Molly Mitchell, Philip Morgan, Daniel Olson, Molly Nolan, Michael O'Malley, Gunther Peck, Darryl Peterkin, Geoff Plank, Carl Prince, David Reimers, Peggy Reilly, David Roediger, Tricia Rose, William Seward, Nikhil Singh, Jack Tchen, Peter Thompson, Sinclair Thomson, Johanna Waley-Cohen, Danny Walkowitz, Kenneth Warren, Ben Weiss, John Wertheimer, Deborah Gray White, Louise Young, and Marilyn Young. A few stalwarts—Steve Aron, Mia Bay, Tom Bender, Sharon Block, Stanley Engerman, Ada Ferrer, Gary Hewitt, Martha Hodes, Robin Kelley, Darline Levy, Hal Morris, Chris Rasmussen, Jeffrey Sammons, Jerry Seigel, and Henry Yu — have read the whole thing, and I am grateful to them, along with my editors at Harvard University Press, Joyce Seltzer and Susan Wallace Boehmer, for their engagement, their criticism, and their support. Steve Kantrowitz has read the manuscript many times and provided most of the commas and many of the ideas that gave it final shape. Robert Zimmerman was always there when I needed him most.

My academic friend of longest standing is Markku Peltonen; intellectually and personally he remains my example (thanks also to Soili Paananen). Grace and Larry Spruch, many members of my family, and my friends and relatives in Italy have all buoyed my mood during time away from the book. Willoughby Johnson and Christy Miller have provided sustaining friendship over the years. My parents, Walter and Mary-Angela Johnson, were my first teachers and last proofreaders; it's nice to be able to say thank you for everything in between. Grazia Lolla has read these chapters many, many times. My one believed in me when others did not and laughed when others did; the dedication of this book seems so small in comparison to all she has given me. And finally, thanks to Giulia Owen Johnson for showing up just in time to be shoehorned into the last version of proofs.

INDEX